Eighth Edition

RECREATION PROGRAMMING

Designing, Staging, and Managing the Delivery of Leisure Experiences

J. Robert Rossman

Barbara Elwood Schlatter

Publishers: Joseph J. Bannon/Peter Bannon
Sales and Marketing Manager: Misti Gilles
Marketing Assistant: Kimberly Vecchio
Director of Development and Production: Susan M. Davis
Graphic Designer: Marissa Willison
Production Coordinator: Amy S. Dagit
Technology Manager: Mark Atkinson
Cover Illustration by Lori Walls

ISBN print edition: 978-1-57167-946-8
ISBN ebook: 978-1-57167-947-5
ISBN etext: 978-1-57167-948-2
Library of Congress Control Number: 2019937508

Printed in the United States.

SAGAMORE ◆◆ VENTURE

1807 N. Federal Dr.
Urbana, IL 61801
www.sagamorepublishing.com

Dedication

The eighth edition of Recreation Programming: Designing, Staging, and Managing the Delivery of Leisure Experiences *is dedicated to John R. (Jack) Kelly, a pioneer in investigating sociological dimensions of leisure. When Jack accepted appointment at the University of Illinois in 1975, he was one of the first sociologists to do so in a department of leisure studies. He was closely watched by fellow sociologists. His work led them into studying the many social dimensions of leisure as a legitimate and important social science endeavor. He was a lecturer on leisure sociology for Barb and Bob's major professor. His work in symbolic interaction and his referring Bob to symbolic interactionist Norman Denzin for additional study provided the academic foundation for this book.*

Jack has authored many books on the sociology of leisure. He is an international authority on the sociology of leisure, and his works are read and cited by sociologists around the world. After many years of retirement, he still contributes as a Sagamore–Venture author.

Contents

Preface vii

Acknowledgments ix

About the Authors xi

Introduction xiii

Part I: Foundations for Programming

1 Basic Programming Concepts 3

2 How Individuals Experience Leisure...21

3 Six Key Elements of a Situated Activity System 37

4 Developing Leisure Products in the Experience Economy 57

5 Collaborating in Developing an Organization's Strategy.............73

Part II: Determining Agency Culture

6 Developing the Agency's Programming Mission.........................93

7 Developing Strategic Directions...125

Part III: Targeted Program Development

8 Obtaining Participant Input 141

9 Writing Program Design and Outcome Statements 173

10 Program Design 185

11 From BBP to Intentionally Designed Leisure Experiences 209

12 Creative Programming..219

Part IV: Operational Strategies

13 Preparing the Program Plan..241

14 Techniques for Program Promotion 267

15 Registration Procedures 285

16 Staffing and Supervising Program Operations 309

17 Developing a Program Pricing Philosophy.................................335

18 Determining Program Costs...349

19 Pricing Program Services..361

Part V: Follow-Up Analysis

20 Program Evaluation Techniques 379

21 Developing a Comprehensive Evaluation System.....................411

22 Making Decisions About Program Services 449

Index 465

Preface

The first edition of this book was published almost three decades ago. When it was first released, it included many innovative concepts, and a few risk takers adopted it. Since then, the book has been adopted for use at over 100 universities in the United States, Canada, Australia, New Zealand, Thailand, Taiwan, and other countries.

The profession and its knowledge base have continued advancing. We have incorporated into this eighth edition the implications of the latest research in leisure behavior, as well as the latest professional practices. It is gratifying that much of the research completed during the past three decades has continued confirming the theoretical base of this book. Leisure is a phased, sequential experience resulting from interaction. How an experience is produced determines the quality of an an individual's leisure experience. Staging leisure experiences through designed programs is a complex undertaking. There is a continuing need for well-educated programmers who can design, stage, and evaluate excellent leisure experiences and services.

Leisure remains a desired human experience. There is no doubt in our minds that people will continue to demand leisure experiences and services. Who supplies them will shift to suppliers who are able to deliver the types and formats of experiences and services desired. Thus, programming will continue to be an important, primary function in all leisure service agencies.

Acknowledgments

We are grateful to the many colleagues and students who have shared their thoughts about how to improve the book and programming. We welcome their contributions and any you may add. We want to thank the following colleagues who have given us feedback useful in developing the eighth edition of this book:

Larry Allen, *Clemson University*
Mat Duerden, *Brigham Young University*
Brent Beggs, *Illinois State University*
James Busser, *University of Nevada–Las Vegas*
Gary Ellis, *Texas A&M University*
Amy Hurd, *Illinois State University*
Jean Keller, *University of North Texas*
Deb Kerstetter, *Penn State University*
Marta Moorman, *University of Nebraska at Kearney*
Michael A. Mulvaney, *Illinois State University*
Rob Stiefvater, Jr., *North Carolina Central University*

Students from the University of North Texas, Southern Illinois University, Virginia Commonwealth University, the University of Florida, Indiana University, the University of Nevada–Las Vegas, Texas A&M University, and Illinois State University have provided valuable feedback about the book as it has developed over the past 30 years. Practitioners and agency directors from around the country were generous in providing us with photographs of excellent programs. We received more photographs than we could use. The agencies providing photographs and, in most cases, the photographers, are cited with each photograph.

We also want to acknowledge the help provided by the staff at Sagamore-Venture. Joe Bannon, Sr., publisher at Sagamore-Venture, has provided ongoing support for the book for over three decades and was instrumental in encouraging development of the original volume. Peter Bannon, Susan Davis, Marissa Willison, and Amy Dagit at Sagamore-Venture have made significant contributions to producing this edition. We are grateful to all of them for their dedicated, professional work on this book.

About the Authors

J. Robert Rossman, PhD, has been designing and staging leisure experiences for over 50 years as a practitioner, scholar, and consultant. His early career responsibilities included many of the typical part-time jobs in this field including serving as an arts and crafts instructor, life guard, swimming instructor, camp counselor, and pool manager. Upon graduation with a BS in public park and recreation administration "with distinction" from Indiana University in 1968, he accepted appointment as a National Recreation and Park Association intern in Oak Park, Illinois. From this position he was appointed as the assistant director of Recreation for the Village of Oak Park, Illinois, where he was responsible for the operation of seven recreation centers and numerous community special events.

His formal education was completed with an MS in park and recreation administration (1975) and PhD (1981) in leisure studies from the University of Illinois. Throughout his career, he has pursued studying programming. His work has provided new techniques and methods for programming. His academic mentors included Ted Deppe, Janet MacLean, Joe Bannon, Allen Sapora, and Jack Kelly. Professional mentors included Sandy Little, Bob Toalson, and Jim Talley. His more recent colleagues and coauthors have included Gary Ellis, Barbara Elwood Schlatter, and Mat Duerden.

This text is the eighth edition of *Recreation Programming: Designing and Staging Leisure Experiences,* which has been in publication for over 30 years. It is estimated that over 80,000 recreation and park professionals have read the text while completing university curricula. Additionally, many use it as a desk reference for their day-to-day work. It has become a classic book in the field.

Dr. Rossman has spoken and made presentations around the world about the unique programming ideas presented in this book. During his academic career, he taught undergraduate and graduate classes at five universities including the University of Illinois; the University of North Texas; the University of Nevada, Las Vegas; Illinois State University; and Texas A & M University. He also taught short courses at Srinakharinwirot University in Bangkok, Thailand, and at Beijing Sport University in Beijing, China. At Illinois State University, he holds the titles of professor and dean emeritus.

He remains active as an author, scholar, and consultant about designing and staging leisure experiences and managing experience-producing organizations. The two universities he attended have recognized his accomplishments. The Department of Leisure Studies at the University of Illinois has presented him the Charles K. Brightbill Award. Indiana University has given him the Legend Award and the W. W. Patty Distinguished Alumni Award. During graduate school, he earned membership into Phi Kappa Phi National Honor Society. He was elected a Fellow in the American Academy for Park and Recreation Administration, which has designated him a Legend for outstanding contributions to the field. His peers elected him a Fellow in the Academy of Leisure Sciences and have designated him a Distinguished Colleague. He lives in Phoenix, Arizona, where he enjoys swimming, golf, singing in his church choir, travel, and his grandchildren.

Barbara Elwood Schlatter, PhD, began her career designing outdoor recreation experiences for adolescents with learning disabilities in rural Vermont. As a Peace Corps Volunteer, she facilitated after-school sport programs and organized community events in Jalapa, Guatemala.

Barb earned her bachelor's, master's, and doctorate degrees from SUNY Cortland, Springfield College, and the University of Illinois, respectively. Her career in higher education spanning 30 years includes academic appointments at SUNY Cortland, Chicago State University, and Illinois State University, where she is professor and assistant director in the School of Kinesiology and Recreation. Her teaching specializations include advanced experience facilitation, recreation programming, special events and tourism, and outdoor recreation. Her scholarly work is published in the *Journal of Park and Recreation Administration*; *Research Quarterly for Exercise and Sport*; *Journal of Physical Education, Recreation, and Dance*; and *LARNet: The Cyber Journal of Applied Leisure and Recreation Research*.

She was the keynote speaker at the third ASEAN Conference on Physical Education, Health, and Sport in Nakhonpathom, Thailand, and has delivered conference presentations in Guatemala, South Korea, China, Brazil, Sweden, Netherlands, Costa Rica, Poland, and Argentina on topics of recreation program planning practices. Barb was a visiting professor at Srinakharinwirot University in Bangkok, Thailand, in 2009 and 2016, teaching classes in leisure management and outdoor leadership.

Barb served as president of the Academy of Leisure Sciences and holds memberships in the World Leisure Organization and the National Recreation and Park Association. She is an elected Fellow in the American Academy for Park and Recreation Administration.

Barb enjoys traveling, bicycling, playing the banjo and guitar, and spending time with family and friends.

Introduction

An urban music festival planner reviews a comprehensive security program for an upcoming public park concert venue as one of many staging tasks. A visitor center worker in Wisconsin manages the Explorium where travelers see a 7,000-pound replica of a woolly mammoth being hunted by a Paleo hunter. A park ranger runs a sense tour as part of a plant education program for memory care patients and persons with partial sight. Visitor experiences focus on plant fragrances and other sensory inputs.

A recreation specialist plans paddleboarding and archery lessons to injured service members and veterans at the San Diego Park and Recreation Department. At the Playa Hermosa Ecolodge in Nicaragua, guests see and learn about the endangered olive ridley turtles that inhabit the area. Ecotourism businesses in the Dominican Republic deliver canopy tours, cave tubing trips, and much more to cruise ship travelers. University recreation management students organize an adventure bike race in which co-ed teams of four encounter mystery challenges along the Katy Trail in Missouri, the longest rail trail in the United States.

A park guide facilitates a First Day Hike in a Georgia state park to families ringing in the New Year by taking a hike in the middle of winter. A special event planner works with college alumni to organize an elaborate reunion weekend that includes a fundraiser golf tournament, a luncheon boat cruise, and a bike adventure along a local greenway.

A therapeutic recreation specialist runs a Wounded Warrior program for service members who served in Middle Eastern conflicts and are severely disabled. The specialist creates individual program plans that allow the clients to resume their favorite pastimes such as skiing, tennis, or bicycling with modifications.

Recreation professionals design, stage, implement, and evaluate myriad recreation programs at commercial, public, and quasi-public agencies across the country. At a Sandals retirement community, a lifestyle director hires local health and wellness experts to provide Tai Chi classes and administer wellness assessments to residents. A children's discovery museum worker plans hands-on attractions featuring life-size, roaring dinosaur skeletons and simulated fossil digs. Program directors at a residential camp in Vermont design challenging and adventurous programs for the campers.

Designing, staging, and evaluating recreation and leisure services is programming. Programming is a major responsibility in all leisure service organizations. The National Recreation and Park Association in their *2017 NRPA Agency Performance Review* documents that programming is the number two responsibility reported by public park and recreation agencies, closely following operating and maintaining park sites, their number one responsibility. They stated, "Programming is the key outreach method that drives usage of park and recreation facilities and, when associated with registration fees, also happens to be the largest non-tax revenue source for most agencies" (NRPA, 2017, p. 7). Furthermore, many commercial recreation operations and not-for-profit organizations exist solely to provide specific recreation programs, a golf course, for example. Programming is a central concern of managers in all leisure service agencies and is usually an identified part of the mission of a leisure service agency.

Programming: The Focus of the Profession

Designing and staging recreation and leisure services is the major function of the leisure service profession. Leisure experiences are the basic units of service that the leisure service profession provides. Although there is great interest in providing experiences across the economy these days, producing leisure experiences is one of the most difficult for agencies to deliver because leisure is a complex interactional form. Engaged leisure experience is the conduit through which other desirable outcomes can be accomplished. It is not beyond fun and games in the sense of bypassing them, but through the contexts and interactions of fun and games. The context of leisure interaction facilitates access to leisure experiences, and this unique experience facilitates the accomplishment of additional desirable outcomes.

Professional practice is based on the recreation and leisure discipline, which seeks to understand the antecedents to leisure, the phenomenology of experiencing leisure, and the results of participating in leisure. Nagel (2018) reported, "Nothing increases park use and physical activity as much as programming—providing supervised activities to help people make active use of available space" (p. 62). Programming is the reason the profession and leisure service organizations exist. Programmers, better than any other professional group, should understand the phenomena of leisure, how humans engage in and experience leisure, the results of this experience, and how to facilitate an individual's experience of leisure. Our professional responsibility is to manipulate environments to facilitate leisure experiences for patrons. Tillman (1973) characterized the centrality of programming to the profession when he declared, "Crown program. Long live the king!" (p. ix).

Over the past 30 years, programmers' responsibilities have expanded greatly. They include operating special events, many of which today are called experiential marketing; contracting for services with external vendors; developing program services from a marketing approach; organizing leagues and tournaments; developing socially purposeful programs; and others. Additional developments include the infusion of computer technology into the management of program services, the need to provide inclusive services that address social justice concerns, and the need to manage program operations to reduce risk. Today, programmers use an increasingly complex set of delivery formats and techniques.

Numerous techniques are available for developing successful programs, including strategic planning, brainstorming, needs analysis, community surveys, evaluation, systems analysis, and marketing. All of these techniques can certainly be used in developing successful programs. But none address leisure program development directly, comprehensively, and uniquely. They are all only piecemeal techniques that fail to provide the comprehensive insights into programming for developing successful programs.

One of the difficulties in writing a programming book is drawing the boundaries around the various functions needed in managing leisure services and leisure service agencies. The delivery of good leisure services requires that all management functions be performed properly, including leadership, supervision, programming, and management of services, agencies, and facilities. In preparing this text, we have tried to restrict its content to the essential elements of programming and the usual responsibilities of a programmer, although there is indeed some unavoidable overlap into other functions.

To program, programmers must understand programming concepts, the theory of how recreation and leisure program services are developed, and how leisure is experienced. More explicit, theory-based information about programming has begun to appear in journals. The programmer's knowledge base must enable him or her to operate on two levels. First, the programmer is a manager and must be able to design, stage, and evaluate leisure services within a specific agency context. Second, the programmer must do this in a manner that facilitates the occurrence of leisure experiences at the behavioral level—that is, for individuals within interactions in social occasions.

This text includes information and techniques based on current knowledge about experiencing leisure and the current professional techniques and practices you need to learn and master to design, manage, stage, and evaluate leisure experiences in any organization including government, commercial, and not-for-profit agencies. *Recreation Programming: Designing and Staging Leisure Experiences*, eighth edition, teaches the programmer to design and stage program services by learning the theory and techniques of recreation programming including (1) basic leisure theory that explains how leisure is experienced; (2) the generic structure of situated activity systems in which social interaction produces leisure experiences; (3) how programs are designed; and (4) procedures and techniques that programmers use to manage, stage, and evaluate recreation programs in a variety of agencies. Providing meaningful leisure experiences is important to individuals, society, and our profession. We hope this book will provide you the ability to deliver excellent services to your participants and give you a sufficient educational background to continue being an accomplished programmer throughout your career.

References

National Recreation and Park Association. (2017). *2017 NRPA agency performance review*. Ashburn, VA: Author.

Tillman, A. (1973). *The program book for recreation professionals*. Palo Alto, CA: Mayfield.

Bibliography of Books on Programming

Carpenter, G. M., & Howe, C. Z. (1985). *Programming leisure experiences: A cyclical approach*. Englewood Cliffs, NJ: Prentice-Hall.

Edginton, C. R., Dieser, R. B., Lankford, S. V., & Kowalski, C. L. (2018). *Recreation and leisure programming: A 21st century approach*. Urbana, IL: Sagamore-Venture.

Farrell, P., & Lundegren, H. M. (1991). *The process of recreation programming: Theory and technique* (3rd ed.). State College, PA: Venture.

Gelb, M. J. (1998). *How to think like Leonardo da Vinci: Seven steps to genius every day*. New York, NY: Delacorte Press.

Jordan, D. J., DeGraaf, D. G., & DeGraaf, K. H. (2010). *Programming for parks, recreation, and leisure services: A servant leadership approach* (3rd ed.). Urbana, IL: Sagamore-Venture.

Kraus, R. (1997). *Recreation programming: A benefits-driven approach*. Boston, MA: Allyn and Bacon.

Murphy, J. F., Williams, J. G., Niepoth, W. E., & Brown, P. D. (1973). *Leisure service delivery systems: A modern perspective*. Philadelphia, PA: Lea and Febiger.

Nagel, C. (2018, December). ACTIVE Parks, Healthy Cities; Recommendations from the national study of neighborhood parks. *Parks & Recreation, 53*, 60–64.

Patterson, F. C. (1991). *A systems approach to recreation programming*. Prospect Heights, IL: Waveland Press.

Russell, R. V. (1982). *Planning programs in recreation*. St. Louis, MO: Mosby.

Russell, R. V., & Jamieson, L. M. (2008). *Leisure program planning and delivery*. Champaign, IL: Human Kinetics.

Tillman, A. (1973). *The program book for recreation professionals*. Palo Alto, CA: Mayfield.

PART I

Foundations for Programming

Recreation programming, designing and staging experiences that people enjoy and that provide them a good life, is personally and professionally rewarding. The pursuit of happiness afforded from participating in leisure is not a trivial matter; it is of such importance that it is mentioned as one of three human rights in the U.S. Declaration of Independence—life, liberty, and the pursuit of happiness. In his book *Authentic Happiness*, Positive Psychologist Martin E. P. Seligman discusses the power of participating in experiences that create positive emotions and allow us to use our positive traits to pursue accomplishments that ultimately provide the happiness of meaning and purpose. In this pursuit, some individuals adopt shortcuts to positive feelings. But to experience the happiness of true gratification and have lasting, sustainable memories, we need to believe that we are entitled to our positive feelings because they resulted from our own accomplishments. Designing and staging leisure experiences that provide these outcomes is recreation programming.

This book is predicated on the notion that individuals desire to participate in leisure and that there is a body of knowledge and practice that programmers can learn that enables them to facilitate leisure experiences. In designing and staging interactional encounters, the programmer directs and facilitates participants' engagements so they result in a leisure experience. Additionally, staging leisure experiences requires a unique production paradigm wherein the programmer must engage the participant in co-creating the experience. Programmers also need to understand how experience-producing organizations manage the development and delivery of experiences and services.

Part I develops a foundation for successful programming. Chapter 1 explains basic concepts of programming and operational definitions of leisure behaviors. Chapter 2 discusses social science theory that explains leisure behavior. This is one of the more difficult chapters in the book, but understanding its content is necessary as it will guide the professional programmer's development and management actions throughout the Program Development Cycle. The material in Chapter 3 flows from the discussion in Chapter 2. Chapter 3 explains the generic structure of situated activity systems, in which leisure experiences occur, and how the programmer manipulates them. Chapter 4 discusses leisure service products and how they may be packaged for distribution and sale. Chapter 5 explains a method for collaboratively developing the organization's strategic programming mission. At the end of this section, there is a two-page diagram of the Program Development Cycle. Margin notes next to the diagram briefly explain the cycle. A more complete explanation can be found at https://www.sagamorepub.com/products/recreation-programming-8th-ed; however, each of the remaining chapters in the book explains and elaborates on the steps in the cycle and provides technical information about how to accomplish them.

Chapter 1: Basic Programming Concepts

Chapter 2: How Individuals Experience Leisure

Chapter 3: Six Key Elements of a Situated Activity System

Chapter 4: Developing Leisure Products in the Experience Economy

Chapter 5: Collaborating in Developing an Organization's Strategy

Exotic Animals Community Event
Photo courtesy of Elmhurst Park District. Photo by Kassandra Collins.

1 *Basic Programming Concepts*

KEY TERMS

Program, Programming, Program Development, Leisure, Recreation, Games, Play, Sport, Tourism, Event

The ultimate goal of programming is to stage leisure experiences for program participants. Accomplishing this requires that the programmer learn the concepts that tie together leisure experiences, program definitions, the act of programming, and the management activities that an agency must implement to stage successful programs.

Programming Concepts Defined

Program

A program is a designed opportunity for leisure experience to occur. Program is an elastic concept that describes a variety of operations, including activities, events, or services conducted by leisure service organizations. The term *program* can refer to a single activity, such as a bike ride, or a class meeting over several weeks. It can refer to a collection of activities, such as the cultural arts classes operated by an organization. It can refer to a single event, such as a softball skill workshop or a weeklong festival. It can refer to the services an agency offers, such as a drop-in auto hobby shop or a desk selling discount tickets to area events. It can also refer to the total set of operations an agency offers, including all of its activities, events, and services. Any of these may be called a program.

> The ultimate goal of programming is to stage leisure experiences for program participants.

This definition is broad and is intended to include more than typical programs organized with a face-to-face leader. The key point is the notion of intentional design in which the programmer conceptualizes a leisure experience and intervenes in some way to stage it for the participants. In some instances, this intervention may be minimal, but in others, it may be near total. The intervention may be through face-to-face leadership, a designed physical environment, or the regulation of leisure behavior through the development and enforcement of policies. Design always involves intentional intervention, regardless of its type or magnitude.

Two assumptions in this definition need further explanation. First, the notion of design assumes that we know how leisure is construed and experienced by individuals (Mannell & Kleiber, 1997) and that we can stage experiences to facilitate its occurrence. Second, it assumes that we know the attributes of the leisure experience. What outcomes must result for individuals to label some experiences as leisure but not others? The ability to program requires a thorough knowledge of the process of experiencing leisure, how to design and stage these experiences, and the outcomes that define the experience. This knowledge will be introduced in the appropriate sections throughout the book.

> Leisure is construed by how a participant processes his or her experiences of a program and interprets what has occurred.

Leisure is not a set of identifiable activities, events, or services. If that were the case, we could simply give you the list below and move on to how to organize each of them.

The attributes that make them leisure experiences are not inherent in the activities, events, or services that are usually called leisure. Rather, leisure is construed by how a participant processes his or her experiences of a program and interprets what has occurred (Csikszentmihalyi, 1991; Kelly, 1987; Patterson, Watson, Williams, & Roggenbuck, 1998). Modern programming is more than simply searching for the most popular activity that can be offered. Programmers must understand that leisure is a state of mind most likely experienced when participants enter freely chosen programs that enable them to achieve realistic personal goals by consciously directing interaction in a social occasion. Samdahl (1988) said, "Leisure can be viewed as a distinctive pattern of perceiving and relating to ongoing interaction. That is to say, leisure is a particular definition of a situation" (p. 29).

Discussing delivering the leisure experience, Kelly (2013) observed, "Delivery of the possibility of a leisure experience is a process, not a product" (p. 109). He continues discussing the process, saying, "The focus, however, is on the receivers who also are active in the process. The leisure experience is never just receptive, passive. It is an involving process in which the players are all acting in one way or another" (p. 109). Thus, a program provides an opportunity for leisure to occur but cannot ensure that it does, since this ultimately depends on how a participant interprets his or her experience of participating and directs his or her own interactions in the encounter.

Programming

Programming is designing, staging, and delivering leisure opportunities by intervening in social interaction, that is, by manipulating and creating environments in a manner that maximizes the probability that those who enter them will have the leisure experiences they seek. Individuals achieve satisfaction from a leisure experience depending on how they guide and interpret their participation in the leisure occasion. Because the programmer understands what patrons must experience to construe an experience as leisure and understands how this experience is produced through social interaction, a program that facilitates (i.e., increases) the probability of a leisure experience occurring can be designed and staged. These are key notions. The practice of all professions, including leisure service provision, is predicated on information developed through the scientific method and then applied to practical problems.

Designing social interactions that will facilitate the leisure experience must be based on knowledge about experiencing leisure and how it is produced in social occasions. Kelly (1999) suggested that all definitions of leisure presuppose that it occurs in an action context: "Something happens in directing attention, processing information, defining meaning, and producing the experience" (p. 136). He added, "The distinctive element of leisure action is that it is focused on the experience rather than external outcomes. It is engaged in primarily for the experience of the action" (p. 136). The programmer is responsible for designing programs with participation processes that will facilitate participants' opportunities to engage in actions that will result in a leisure experience. Thus, how a program is staged is more important for facilitating a leisure experience than the specific activity itself.

Furthermore, programmers must understand that leisure is a multiphase experience (Stewart, 1999) and begin by planning to engage the participant through the three phases of human experience—anticipation, participation, and reflection (Busser, 1993; Little, 1993). New standards for experiential engagement, introduced with the emergence of *The Experience Economy* (Pine & Gilmore, 1999), suggest that programs should be staged—a theatrical metaphor indicating the comprehensiveness of the details and sensibilities that the programmer must deal with if the participant is to achieve the intended experience. Good programming, then, is designed intervention that is staged based on knowledge about social interaction and the social psychology of experiencing leisure. The Framed Experience Model of programming, discussed in Chapter 10, provides the reader with a technique for designing programs based on these theories and concepts.

> Leisure is a multiphase experience.

Program Development

Program development is the overall management process in which the programmer designs, stages, manages, and delivers program services within the context of a specific agency. It includes understanding and developing an agency's mission, assessing needs, developing a strategy for their delivery, designing programs, staffing them, staging them, delivering them, and evaluating them so that the programmer can document the benefits that have been provided, as well as determine their future. All programs are delivered by some type of organization. Therefore, the programmer must learn to manage program services successfully within an organizational context. Successful program development results in programs that meet the needs of the agency, patrons, and community. Programming is one key function in program development. The overall process of program development is diagrammed in the Program Development Cycle (at the end of Chapter 5). Now complete Exercise 1.1.

Definitions of Related Concepts

Concepts we use influence how we act. The linguistic labels attached to various forms of human behavior shape our attitudes and actions. The lack of precise definitions in the recreation and leisure field is often a cause of concern to new students. This book offers concepts necessary for understanding and accomplishing programming: *leisure, play, recreation, games, sport, tourism,* and *events*. Each concept refers to a different type of leisure experience; therefore, each must be programmed somewhat differently. This section discusses the concepts in relationship to each other to help clarify their meanings.

Kelly (1983) contended that leisure is central to today's society. He stated that leisure is "crucial life space for the expression and development of selfhood, for the working out of identities that are important to the individual. [It is] . . . central to the maintenance of the society itself as a social space for the development of intimacy" (p. 23). Driver, Brown, and Peterson (1991) took the position that multiple behaviors or experiences (Stewart, 1999) are included under the concept of leisure. Leisure, then, is the broadest concept (Neulinger, 1981), encompassing play, recreation, games, sport, tourism, and events, each of which can be viewed as a form of leisure that can be distinguished by more specific defining characteristics.

Leisure

Leisure has been defined in several ways. Murphy (1974) identified six types: classical leisure, leisure as discretionary time, leisure as a function of social class, leisure as form of activity, anti-utilitarian leisure, and a holistic concept of leisure. Neulinger (1974) suggested that all definitions of leisure are either quantitative or qualitative and concluded that leisure is a state of mind characterized primarily by perceived freedom and intrinsic motivation. Often, the discipline training of the individual defining leisure will influence the definition. Thus, definitions have been provided by economists, sociologists, psychologists, and social psychologists.

The perspective used throughout this book is that leisure is a social experience constructed through interaction in social occasions (Iso-Ahola, 1999; Samdahl, 1988). Iso-Ahola (1980) emphasized this point by stating that "leisure studies is a human service field in which social interaction is the main ingredient" (p. 7). Samdahl (1992) found that over 50% of the occasions labeled as leisure by those involved included some type of social interaction. Hamilton-Smith (1991) also assumed leisure is best understood as a social construct that can be defined in a variety of ways, including leisure as time, leisure as action, leisure as action within time and space, and leisure as experience.

> Leisure is a social experience constructed through interaction in social occasions.

Leisure is an experience most likely to occur during freely chosen interactions characterized by a high degree of personal engagement that is motivated by the intrinsic satisfaction that is expected to result. After a first reading, this definition may seem relatively simple, but it incorporates three complex concepts: freedom, intrinsic satisfaction, and engagement.

Freedom. Freedom has been a central defining element of leisure since man first contemplated the meaning of leisure. Modern research has confirmed the primacy of freedom (Iso-Ahola, 1999). Freedom from something and freedom to have or do something have been primary themes of leisure definitions (Sylvester, 1987). In our society, the social obligations of work, family, friends, civic duties, and so forth can obscure the meaning of "freely chosen" or "free choice," or at least make it more difficult to sort them out. Some leisure occasions are determined by the degree to which they free individuals from social role constraints (Samdahl, 1988). In discussing decisions to purchase leisure experiences, Kelly (2013) reminded us repeatedly, "No one has to do it" (p. 3 and elsewhere). The "freedom from" notion, then, occurs in situations in which an individual is freed from social role constraints to explore and accomplish something.

The other operant condition is freedom to have "a sense of opportunity and possibility" (Kleiber, 1999, p. 3). The notion of freely choosing something can only be determined from the perspective of the individual making the choice. Thus, the notion of freedom is a matter of individual perception (Neulinger, 1981). The evidence suggests that individuals must believe they could have chosen not to do an activity, before it meets the test of being freely chosen (Kelly, 1982). As Patterson et al. (1998) explained, "Situated freedom is the idea that there is a structure in the environment that sets boundaries on what can be perceived or experienced, but that within those boundaries recreationists are free to experience the world in highly individual, unique, and variable ways" (pp. 425–426).

Programmers should remember that leisure must be freely chosen from the perspective of the individual making the choice. Additionally, individuals must perceive that they have options and choices in a program in order to explore, move forward in their personal stream of experience, and "become something new" by participating in a novel experience, that is, one that is experienced in this way for the first time. Freedom experienced in this manner creates a unique condition for an optimal self-actualizing experience to occur (Csikszentmihalyi & Kleiber, 1991).

> Leisure must be freely chosen from the perspective of the individual making the choice.

Thus, freedom plays a functional role in construing the leisure experience. Although optimal experiences may occur in other spheres of life, they are more likely to do so when the conditions of freedom just explained occur. Overprogramming, by providing too much structure to an occasion, will leave the participant few or no choices. This may destroy the very experience that the programmer is trying to facilitate. Entertaining, rather than engaging participants, is a good example of overprogramming to the point that participants have no choice. It is an error frequently made by individuals who stage events but have no understanding of leisure behavior. Although it keeps the programmer in control of the event, it does not allow participants the freedom needed to experience leisure.

Intrinsic satisfaction. Intrinsic satisfaction is the second major dimension of leisure. Psychologists have used several terms to describe participating in this experience, including *autotelic activities*, *arousal-seeking behavior*, and *optimal experience*. "The key element of an optimal experience is that it is an end in itself," wrote Csikszentmihalyi (1991, p. 67); it is intrinsically satisfying. The behavior associated with pursuing intrinsically satisfying activities has also been called "arousal-seeking behavior," based on the need of maintaining optimal arousal. Ellis (1973) proposed this theory, and it assumes that people are not normally quiescent; rather, they seek and act to increase stimulation.

Intrinsically satisfying activities provide satisfaction through the interactive engagement, and that satisfaction provides sufficient motivation for the individual to continue participating. Thus, no external reward is necessary. The feedback received from such participation indicates that what is occurring is congruent with an individual's goals, thereby strengthening and validating the self (Csikszentmihalyi, 1991). This affords a freedom from concern with oneself that frees an individual to focus psychic energy more intensely on the demands of the current interactive engagement. These engagements demand and consume an individual's complete focused attention. The motivation to participate in interaction to seek this experience is powerful and real (Neulinger, 1981).

Programmers should understand how this occurs. Unfortunately, intrinsic satisfaction is not wholly contained within activities. In fact, people similarly describe their optimal experiences in different activities, and their descriptions are consistent across sociological and cultural variables (Csikszentmihalyi, 1991; Iso-Ahola, 1999). Thus, it is not a matter of prescribing a list of intrinsically satisfying activities and expecting individuals to find intrinsic satisfaction in them.

Intrinsic satisfaction is a personally interpreted perception of a situation. This perception is construed through interaction in a social occasion (Csikszentmihalyi, 1991; Samdahl, 1988; Shaw, 1985; Unger, 1984). Individuals' past experiences and current expectations help them determine whether an engagement is intrinsically satisfying. What arouses an individual today is part of a stream of interactions between the individual's natural abilities and previous experiences. Participants will conclude that they were intrinsically motivated when programs provide opportunities for developing competence, self-expression, self-development, or self-realization (Mannell, 1999). Different individuals find different activities intrinsically satisfying because of factors such as their own skill levels in an activity, their level of socialization into it, and the previous opportunities and experiences they have had with it. Although these factors initially influence their likelihood of participating, their interpretation of the interactions in an activity on a given day will determine whether it is a leisure experience for them.

> Intrinsic satisfaction is a personally interpreted perception of a specific situation. This perception is construed through interaction in a social occasion.

Thus, how an activity is staged and how an individual interprets his or her participation in it are more important than the activity type (e.g., softball, oil painting, gardening) in determining whether an individual will have a leisure experience. Programmers need to devote more attention to how activities are staged rather than continually searching for the perfect activity that will provide a leisure experience.

Engagement. Finally, experiencing an event requires, at a minimum, that an individual engage in and interpret it. Leisure occurs in an action context. As Kelly

(1999) wrote, "Something happens in directing attention, processing information, defining meaning, and producing results" (p. 136). Experiencing is more than a passive state of mind; it denotes processing and ordering information in one's consciousness (Csikszentmihalyi, 1991; Kelly, 1990). That is, an individual must engage in it. Kahneman (2011) discussed System 1 and System 2 thinking. The first he termed slow thinking and the second fast thinking. Engagement as discussed here relates to System 2 thinking, when an individual "allocates attention to the effortful mental activities that demand it . . . (Kahneman, 2011, p. 21). People choose leisure experiences because they demand their attention and engagement in a challenging and pleasurable way.

Many who are entering the experience economy and producing events and other kinds of programs repeatedly confuse entertainment with engagement (Pine & Gilmore, 1999). They design events to entertain rather than engage. Leisure is more likely to occur when individuals play an active role in organizing and self-directing outcome; that is, they have the opportunity for positive affect (Kleiber, Caldwell, & Shaw, 1992; Kleiber, Larson, & Csikszentmihalyi, 1986). Ajzen and Driver (1992) reported that "perceived behavioral control" improved their ability to predict leisure behavior, again verifying the importance of having control over outcomes of the leisure experience.

People experience leisure by active engagement in and interaction with various combinations of elements in an environment; they thereby have the perception that they are directing the outcome of the event and are thus the cause of an act. This engagement can be as simple as reading a book and interpreting its meaning. In this case, the reader self-directs the interpretation. It can also include participating in a lively social discussion with friends or family. Participating in rule-bounded games and sports also provides a significant number of opportunities for self-directed social interaction and self-directed outcomes. When these types of engagement result in experiences that are enjoyable, fun, or pleasurable, the event is more likely to be construed as leisure (Mannell & Kleiber, 1997). Thus, leisure experiences are self-directed and interpreted in a specific way.

Overall, then, to experience leisure, an individual must freely choose to engage an environment and perceive that this engagement provides intrinsic satisfaction that rewards and sustains the engagement. Intrinsic satisfaction partly results from experiences that provide opportunities for positive affect, that is, *effortful mental activity* (Kahneman, 2011, p. 21) that results in self-directing the outcome of the engagement. Experiencing leisure is something that individuals do, not something programmers do to individuals. Neulinger (1981) insisted that leisure is not a noun, but a verb that implies action, process, and experience. Leisure is something to be consciously processed and experienced, not something that is acquired and possessed. It occurs in a social context with form and structure; that is, it is situated action (Kelly, 1999). In designing and staging a program, the programmer provides selected elements of a situation and thereby specifies form and structure for the leisure occasion. The programmer is responsible for staging the proper form and structure to situate an activity system that facilitates a leisure experience. The notions of a situated activity system and a participant's co-production of experience will be developed further in subsequent chapters.

Games

Games are leisure experiences with formal rules that define the interactional content, attempt to equalize the players, and define the role that skill and chance will play in determining the outcome. Formal rules create an unknown or problematic outcome, the resolution of which can only be achieved through playing the game. This applies to table games, athletic contests, and other gaming situations.

Games are rule bounded, and the rules delineate the arena of focused reality that will be addressed during the gaming occasion (Goffman, 1961). Games are popular leisure experiences because the rules of a well-constructed game create an area of focus with a high probability for a leisure experience. To create this focus, rules must clearly define the gaming encounter and the role that skill and chance will play in determining the outcome.

Game rules must define the focus of the contest and what is being contested. A game winner should have exhibited more of the particular skill being contested in the game than other participants have. In some games, the rules minimize the role of chance and maximize the effect of skill on the gaming outcome.

On the other hand, chance is solely responsible for the outcome of some games. For example, the winner of Chutes and Ladders, a popular children's game, is determined entirely by chance. Thus, parents often play the game with young children who are not able to play a game of strategy or skill. In a game whose outcome is determined entirely by chance, the players are immediately made equal—each is equally dependent on chance to win the gaming encounter.

Some games require a mixture of skill and chance. This mixture is characteristic of many table games that must sustain interest among players with unequal levels of skill. Trivial Pursuit is a good example. No matter how many questions are answered, a lucky roll of the die is still necessary for a player to land in the final winning position. A more highly skilled player can answer many more questions than other players and still lose the game because of unlucky rolls of the die.

The element of chance in a game is usually settled with the toss of a coin, the roll of the die, or the use of some type of manual or electronic spinning device. More complex contests may begin with a coin toss or some other mechanism for determining the order of play or an initial position. In football, for example, the winner of a coin toss may choose which end of the field to defend, or to receive or kick the ball to start the game. Depending on weather conditions, this choice can affect the outcome of the game. Nonetheless, it is a matter of chance, unrelated to any of the skills that football is supposed to test. Chance, then, as a major determinant of the gaming outcome is often used in making unequal players equal or determining initial advantage totally unrelated to any game skill.

Game rules define the skills that will be contested and the role that skill and chance will play in determining the outcome. Leisure service professionals must understand the function of rules in games, because much game programming involves modifying rules or facilities so that those with insufficient skills or fewer skills can participate on a more equal basis.

Recreation

Recreation is leisure engaged in for the attainment of personal and social benefits. Recreation has always been characterized as socially purposeful and moral; that is, it incorporates a rightness and a wrongness. Hutchison (1951) stated, "Recreation is a worthwhile, socially accepted leisure experience that provides immediate and inherent satisfaction to the individual who voluntarily participates ..." (p. 2). Jensen (1979) commented on the inherent morality of recreation, stating, "In order to qualify as recreation, an activity must do something desirable to a participant" (p. 8). Recreation is considered to have a specific moral purpose in society.

> Recreation is leisure that is engaged in for the attainment of personal and social benefits.

Recreation has always been viewed as restoration from the toil of work. De Grazia (1964) assumed this view, writing, "Recreation is activity that rests men from work, often by giving them a change (distraction, diversion), and restores (re-creates) them for work" (p. 233). Thus, he credited recreation with having social significance by functionally relating it to work. With this view, recreation is instrumental to work because it enables individuals to recuperate and restore themselves to accomplish more work. These concepts were introduced at a time when work involved hard labor as humans forged materials into useful products with economic value. Most work today requires much less fatiguing labor and thus our need for recreation as recuperation from work is less apparent.

But recreation is good not only for individuals—it is also good for society. Recreation has been used as a diversion from government repression, war, economic depression, congested urban conditions, and so forth. It is beneficial to society when people are engaged in socially purposeful activities in their free time as opposed to drinking, gambling, taking drugs, and other personally and socially degenerative engagements. Recreation always has morality associated with it, and there are good and bad forms of recreation. For example, drug use is considered morally degenerative. Therefore, to a recreation professional, the notion of "recreational drug use" is not possible.

Moreover, organizations that provide recreation services are viewed as social institutions that espouse the positive aspects inherent in the recreation activities they offer. Specific moral ends or purposes are usually attributed to providers such as municipal recreation agencies, churches, the Girl Scouts and Boy Scouts, the armed services, and other similar organizations. More recently, recreation programs that combat exposure to adverse social conditions and the general lack of positive opportunities have been developed for at-risk youth. And the notion that recreation has a role to play in achieving social justice through ensuring the equitable distribution of opportunities for recreation and leisure has become an important moral end for the profession to accomplish.

Thus, recreation is a specific form of leisure behavior that is characterized as having a pervasive morality. It is an institutionalized form of leisure that the programmer can manipulate to accomplish socially desirable goals and objectives that are often defined by the sponsoring agency. It is the form of leisure behavior that programmers most often try to facilitate. In developing recreation programs, the programmer is often expected to go beyond providing a leisure experience and to intervene to accomplish a socially purposeful goal. In these instances, recreation is a conduit to socially purposeful outcomes beyond a leisure experience. Recreation's usefulness as a unique conduit to socially purposeful ends, compared to education, religion, and other conduits, should not be overlooked or undersold. Chapter 11 presents specific techniques for accomplishing socially purposeful intentional design.

Play

Play is leisure with the childlike characteristics of spontaneity, self-expression, and the creation of a nonserious realm of meaning. As a specific form of leisure, play has these further defining characteristics.

Play incorporates a dualism that distinguishes it from the real world. Play involves a lack of seriousness in which interaction is free flowing, as it progresses from place to place and takes on new forms as focus, needs, and demands shift (Denzin, 1975). It is an expansive interactional form that is not guided by conventional rules of interaction; thus, it is not a game. Hunnicutt (1986) suggested, "Play may well be one of those things that we do to understand other things and to create a truth" (p. 10).

Play is the most spontaneous form of leisure behavior, and its occurrence depends on the consent and conscious participation of the players. Lynch (1980) showed that players recognize and signal each other when interactions shift into a play mode, thereby suspending the normal rules of interaction. The inconsequential nature of play establishes a sense of self and reality that the player cannot otherwise attain in daily life. To "play with" an object, person, or an idea is to experience the meaning of the object, person, or idea in a fundamentally new way. Because of this, play is one of the most difficult forms of leisure to program.

Sport

Sport is leisure that involves institutionalized competitive physical activity. It can be thought of as a game whose rules require physical competition. Many programmers are employed in organizing sport competitions and managing sport venues.

In defining sport, one is faced with the question of professional athletes, that is, is their participation leisure? Although they are highly visible and well known to the wider population, few individuals are employed as athletes. Not completely resolving this issue does not influence a large number of individuals. Nevertheless, most sport scholars include professional athletes in the rubric of sport participation. For our purposes, we will assume that whether someone is paid or unpaid, it is the experience the athlete has while participating that determines whether an event, including participation in sport, is leisure.

Three key concepts define sport: physical exertion, rules, and competition of physical skills. Most academics who have studied sport agree that it includes only activities that require physical exertion. They do not include activities such as card playing, playing chess, and other similar activities under the rubric of sport. In our sedentary world, the need to expend physical energy is a unique attribute that separates sport from everyday life.

> Three key concepts define sport: physical exertion, rules, and competition of physical skills.

Rules are a second attribute that define the sporting event and regulate participation: "The essence of sport lies in its patterned and regulated form. Through the social process of institutionalization—the formalizing and standardizing of activities—sport is regulated" (Leonard, 1998, p. 13). In addition to the rules for competitions, sport as an institution is also regulated by league rules. The modification and enforcement of rules often becomes the focus of sport, attracting as much attention from the sport media and fans as the competitions do. Owners of professional teams spend many hours contemplating rule changes. Consider the use of instant replay in professional sports in recent years, which has expanded as technology has advanced. Football, baseball, basketball, hockey, and soccer use instant replay to varying degrees.

Most sports are games with rules that function like the game rules previously discussed, except that all sport games involve physical exertion and are contests of physical skills. Rules affect the character of a game, including the strategies participants use to compete and the skills they may need to participate. Rules often differ for collegiate versus professional competitions or national versus international competitions. Programming sporting competitions inevitably involves the programmer in rule discussions, as teams will try to manipulate rules to assure themselves of a competitive advantage on the playing field.

The final attribute of sport is that it involves a competition of physical skills. The rules of each sport require participants to possess and showcase specific physical skills (e.g., eye–hand coordination [table tennis], flexibility [gymnastics], strength [weight lifting], endurance [marathon running]). The most popular sports, such as basketball, football, baseball, and hockey, require athletes to possess multiple physical skills in various combinations to succeed. Often, programmers will help develop rule modifications to accommodate participation in sport of individuals who possess less physical skill than needed to compete successfully in open competitions.

A significant amount of association with sport in the United States involves individuals watching others participate in sport (i.e., being a sports fan, now called the *fan experience*). This type of involvement does not, of course, provide the benefits or challenges of participating in sport. In general, it is not part of a programmer's daily tasks, except for contending with sport fans who attend sporting events organized by the programmer and planning occasional trips to sporting events.

Additionally, a recreation programmer may spend much of his or her time organizing participation in youth sports. In many cases, the programmer will be working with adult groups who organize and operate youth sports. Currently, the focus of programmers in operating youth sports has been on improving the skills of adults coaching youth and dealing with the behavior of parents who attend youth sport games. The National Alliance for Youth Sport's sole purpose is to improve youth sport experiences for children (https://www.nays.org). They currently have over 3,000 participating organizations. To this end, they offer assistance for dealing with bullying in youth sports, background checks of adult organizers and coaches, concussions, and other current issues in operating youth sports.

Tourism

Touring is a rapidly expanding form of leisure in which individuals travel for opportunities to experience leisure. Additional defining dimensions that characterize touring are restoration, change of pace, and individual purposes. Touring for leisure is distinguished from travel for business or commercial purposes. A tourist is defined as someone who travels at least 50 miles from home and stays at least 1 night for the purpose of recreation or leisure. Touring is ripe with opportunities for leisure, as leisure experiences can result from the travel itself and from engagements during travel.

An enduring feature of tourism is its use as an escape from and renewal for work. Many people still pursue the annual vacation to restore themselves for work. A 2-week annual vacation is often the norm for beginning employees. In North America, the number of days of annual vacation often increases with job seniority, sometimes reaching 4 or 5 weeks per year for employees with longevity in a position. In other countries, annual vacation days from work frequently exceed those provided in North America. In many cases, these days are used as an opportunity to travel and get away from home and work. Leisure experiences that will refresh and restore one for work are pursued.

But tourism encompasses more than simply restoring individuals for work. Retirees who no longer work are a growing segment of the tourism industry. For them, touring provides a change of pace from the routine of their lives: a chance to visit new and exotic places. Thus, travel to places, with schedules and activities that are different from a routine pattern of work or routine imposed by continual interaction with the same individuals, places, and events, is pursued through traveling and becoming a tourist. Since becoming a tourist requires an individual to be away from home, touring will likely result in a change of the individual's daily pace. With a change of pace as a benchmark for defining a touring experience, touring can provide this change through a variety of engagements including rest, relaxation, culture, sport, escape, adventure, and many others.

> An enduring feature of tourism is its use as an escape from and renewal for work.

A final dimension of uniqueness in tourism is the diversity of individual purposes for touring. This diversity has resulted in emerging niche tours that include sport tourism, ecotourism, gambling tours, medical tourism, and many other specialized touring groups and tours. Some purposes include specialized destinations such as golf courses, gardens, or wineries. Some utilize specialized forms of transportation such as cruises, bus tours, trekking, or a new possibility, space touring. Unique associations are the basis for some tour cohorts. For example, tours organized for university alumni, members of specific religious denominations, or members of a civic organization. Many other market segments form the basis for organizing touring groups or themed organized tours.

Programmers work in the tourism industry as tour organizers for the hotel industry, transportation businesses, attraction venues, or tour companies that package tours. Ironically, the attractions that are the reason for travel are often the least expensive part of a trip. The majority of tourism dollars are spent on transportation, housing, and food—not admission to the recreation attractions that are the primary reason for traveling to a specific locale. Because the total cost of travel, lodging, and food are likely to far exceed the total cost of admissions to recreation amenities or venues, the price of admission to a recreation amenity or venue is relatively inelastic and is one of the lower costs incurred during trips.

Events

Events, along with tourism, have become specialized programming categories with increasing demand. Some recreation professionals, including wedding planners, event managers, corporate event managers, and others, are dedicated to designing and operating events. In many leisure service organizations, events are one of several types of program formats operated during the year.

One difficulty in defining events for this book is that they cross boundaries. That is, not all events are leisure. There are religious events, commercial events, education events, and so on. Berridge (2007) pointed out that practitioners and academics continue to struggle, without complete success, to develop a suitable definition of *events* that all will accept. However, some unique characteristics that most agree on will enable us to provide a working definition that separates events from other programming forms.

Events are infrequently experienced by participants. While many other types of programming discussed occur routinely and regularly, events by definition are made special partly because they occur seldom and are thus not experienced repeatedly in the short term. Although the timing of some events is regular (e.g., Christmas, New Year's, Veterans Day), they still occur infrequently and provide diversion from habitual routine. Similarly, a trip to an amusement park is done infrequently by participants, but operating the amusement park is a daily routine for employees. Thus, attending the amusement park is an event for participants.

Events often require an agency to shift from its normal program delivery format to create an unusual event for itself and its participants. Additionally, the staging of events usually requires significant agency resources. Agencies and participants often look forward to an event because it provides a different programming format. For example, a sports management organization that normally operates competitions including leagues and tournaments may need to design and stage an annual awards banquet. This is an unusual programming format for the organization, one that is outside of its normal programming practices. Additionally, this is not the usual program format experienced by the organization's regular participants.

> Agencies and participants often look forward to an event because it provides a different programming format.

Similarly, arts organizations often have a gala opening night for an opera, symphony, or other performance series. Opening night celebrates the beginning of the season, and opening night occurs only once a year. Staging a pre- or post-event celebration with hors d'oeuvres, drinks, and other amenities creates a different programming format for opening night compared to other performance nights.

Finally, events often provide experiences beyond a participant's normal range of choices and beyond the routine of ordinary life, by providing opportunities for ritual, celebration, or festivity. Although some forms of leisure are experienced alone, these leisure forms are almost always a shared experience. The bonding with others and the shared values that result from these experiences are important parts of participant interaction and the memories that result. Often, events provide opportunities for symbolic behavior that reveals the values and mores of a given culture or group. For example, an awards banquet is usually a celebration of excellence wherein specific individuals are given awards for superior performance. The event symbolically recognizes the values of the group. Although individuals are lauded for their accomplishments, these individuals also symbolize the notion that excellence is venerated by the group who has gathered to celebrate excellence. For an interesting account of the contributions of rituals, celebrations, and festivals, see deLisle (2014).

Events are a unique form of leisure participation defined by their infrequent occurrence, their different format of participation, and the change of pace they provide from routine activities.

Programming Implications

Leisure is considered the most general and encompassing concept, while recreation, play, games, sport, tourism, and events are viewed as specific forms of leisure. Figure 1.1 (page 18) illustrates the central defining concepts of each leisure form and its relationship to others. The boundaries of each form overlap, illustrating the nebulous character of each form of leisure. For example, game rules are often structured to allow players to play in a spontaneous, free-flowing, and creative manner. Nonetheless, when game players serendipitously discover a new move or game strategy that gives them an advantage, the programmer can modify rules to quash it or accommodate it within the rule structure of the game.

When recreation activities are programmed, they are often made to appear as much like leisure as possible; perceptions of free choice and intrinsically rewarding activities are included in the program. However, the programmatic goals of the agency sponsoring and operating a program may foster an activity structure that does not permit ongoing freedom of choice in the activity. The use of prescriptive programming methods such as intentionally designed outcome-based programming can lead to highly structured programs that impose the agency's desired outcome on participants. Programmers need to realize the central concepts of each of these forms of leisure and should design and operate programs that are least obstructive to a participant's desired experiences. Programmers often face a situation in which the best programmatic manipulation is simply to "stay out of the way" (Kelly, 2013, p. 109) to avoid destroying the experience desired. In this case, the programmer must understand the experience and make sure that the design or operation of a program does not have built-in blocks to the leisure experience desired by the participant or intended by the agency. Now complete Exercise 1.2.

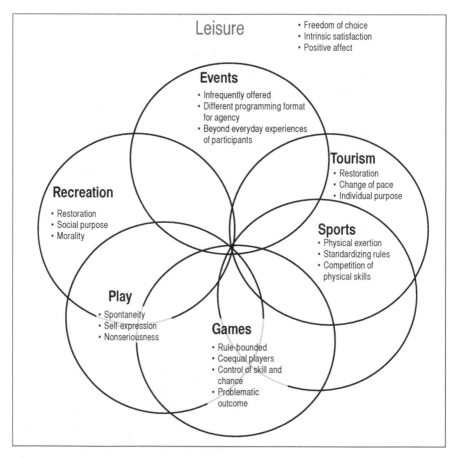

Figure 1.1. Relationships Among Central Definitions of Leisure, Recreation, Play, Games, Sport, Tourism, and Events

Conclusion

Programming is the central focus of the leisure service profession and a primary mission of leisure service organizations. Programmers stage opportunities for leisure to occur. Leisure is a primary social space in modern society for exercising free choice and the development of self. Leisure occurs through interactions in social occasions that are characterized by perceived freedom, intrinsic satisfaction, and opportunities for exercising positive affect. Recreation, games, play, sport, tourism, and events are specific forms of leisure with additional defining concepts.

References

Ajzen, I., & Driver, B. (1992). Planned behavior and leisure choice. *Journal of Leisure Research, 24*, 207–224.

Berridge, G. (2007). *Events design and experience.* San Francisco, CA: Elsevier.

Busser, J. A. (1993). Leisure programming: The state of the art (introduction). *Journal of Physical Education, Recreation, and Dance, 64*(8), 25, 33.

Csikszentmihalyi, M. (1991). *Flow: The psychology of optimal experience.* New York, NY: Harper Perennial.

Csikszentmihalyi, M., & Kleiber, D. A. (1991). Leisure and self-actualization. In B. L. Driver, P. J. Brown, & G. L. Peterson (Eds.), *Benefits of leisure* (pp. 91–102). State College, PA: Venture.

De Grazia, S. (1964). *Of time, work, and leisure.* Garden City, NJ: Doubleday-Anchor.

deLisle, L. (2014). *Creating special events* (2nd ed.). Urbana, IL: Sagamore.

Denzin, N. K. (1975). Play, games, and interaction: The contexts of childhood socialization. *Sociological Quarterly, 16*, 458–478.

Driver, B. L., Brown, P. J., & Peterson, G. L. (1991). *Benefits of leisure.* State College, PA: Venture.

Ellis, M. J. (1973). *Why people play.* Englewood Cliffs, NJ: Prentice-Hall.

Goffman, E. (1961). *Encounters.* Indianapolis, IN: Bobbs-Merrill.

Hamilton-Smith, E. (1991). The construction of leisure. In B. L. Driver, P. J. Brown, & G. L. Peterson (Eds.), *Benefits of leisure.* State College, PA: Venture.

Hunnicutt, B. K. (1986). Problems raised by the empirical study of play and some humanistic alternatives. In *Abstracts from the 1986 Symposium on Leisure Research* (pp. 8–10). Arlington, VA: National Recreation and Park Association.

Hutchison, J. (1951). *Principles of recreation.* New York, NY: Roland.

Iso-Ahola, S. E. (1980). *The social psychology of leisure and recreation*. Dubuque, IA: Wm. C. Brown.

Iso-Ahola, S. E. (1999). Motivational foundations of leisure. In E. L. Jackson & T. L. Burton (Eds.), *Leisure studies: Prospects for the twenty-first century* (pp. 35–51). State College, PA: Venture.

Jensen, C. R. (1979). *Outdoor recreation in America*. Minneapolis, MN: Burgess.

Kahneman, D. (2011). *Thinking fast and slow*. New York, NY: Farrar, Straus, and Giroux.

Kelly, J. R. (1982). *Leisure*. Englewood Cliffs, NJ: Prentice-Hall.

Kelly, J. R. (1983). *Leisure identities and interactions*. Boston, MA: Allen and Unwin.

Kelly, J. R. (1987). *Freedom to be: A new sociology of leisure*. New York, NY: Macmillan.

Kelly, J. R. (1990). *Leisure* (2nd ed.). Englewood Cliffs, NJ: Prentice-Hall.

Kelly, J. R. (1999). Leisure behaviors and styles: Social, economic, and cultural factors. In E. L. Jackson & T. L. Burton (Eds.), *Leisure studies: Prospects for the twenty-first century* (pp. 135–150). State College, PA: Venture.

Kelly, J. R. (2013). *Leisure business strategies: What they don't teach you in business school*. Urbana, IL: Sagamore.

Kleiber, D. (1999). *Leisure experience and human development: A dialectical interpretation*. New York, NY: Basic Books.

Kleiber, D., Caldwell, L., & Shaw, S. (1992, October). *Leisure meaning in adolescence*. Paper presented at the 1992 Symposium on Leisure Research, Cincinnati, OH.

Kleiber, D., Larson, R., & Csikszentmihalyi, M. (1986). The experience of leisure in adolescence. *Journal of Leisure Research, 18*, 169–176.

Leonard, W. M., III. (1998). *A sociological perspective of sport* (5th ed.). Needham Heights, MA: Allyn and Bacon.

Little, S. L. (1993). Leisure program design and evaluation. *Journal of Physical Education, Recreation, and Dance, 64*(8), 26–29, 33.

Lynch, R. L. (1980). Social play: An interactional analysis of play in face-to-face social interaction. *Dissertation Abstracts International, 41*, 804A.

Mannell, R. C. (1999). Leisure experience and satisfaction. In E. L. Jackson & T. L. Burton (Eds.), *Leisure studies: Prospects for the twenty-first century* (pp. 235–251). State College, PA: Venture.

Mannell, R. C., & Kleiber, D. A. (1997). *A social psychology of leisure*. State College, PA: Venture.

Murphy, J. F. (1974). *Concepts of leisure: Philosophical implications*. Englewood Cliffs, NJ: Prentice-Hall.

Neulinger, J. (1974). *The psychology of leisure*. Springfield, IL: Charles C. Thomas.

Neulinger, J. (1981). *To leisure: An introduction*. Boston, MA: Allyn and Bacon.

Patterson, M. E., Watson, A. E., Williams, D. R., & Roggenbuck, J. R. (1998). An hermeneutic approach to studying the nature of wilderness experiences. *Journal of Leisure Research, 30*, 423–435.

Pine, B. J., II, & Gilmore, J. H. (1999). *The experience economy: Work is theatre and every business a stage*. Boston, MA: Harvard Business School Press.

Samdahl, D. M. (1988). A symbolic interactionist model of leisure: Theory and empirical support. *Leisure Sciences, 1*, 27–39.

Samdahl, D. (1992). Leisure in our lives: Exploring the common leisure occasion. *Journal of Leisure Research, 24*, 19–32.

Shaw, S. M. (1985). The meaning of leisure in everyday life. *Leisure Sciences, 7*, 1–24.

Stewart, W. P. (1999). Leisure as multiphase experiences: Challenging tradition. *Journal of Leisure Research, 30*, 391–400.

Sylvester, C. D. (1987, January). The politics of leisure, freedom, and poverty. *Parks and Recreation, 1987*, 59–62.

Unger, L. S. (1984). The effect of situational variables on the subjective leisure experience. *Leisure Sciences, 6*, 291–312.

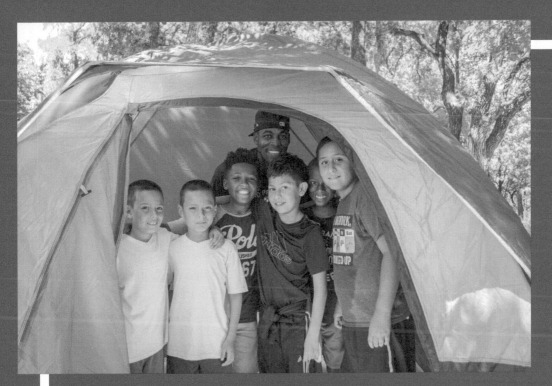

"Outdoor Camp" Participants Learning How to Make Camp at Loyd Park on Joe Pool Lake
Photo courtesy of City of Grand Prairie Parks, Arts and Recreation Department.

2 *How Individuals Experience Leisure*

KEY TERMS

Experience, Symbolic Interactionism, Phases of the Leisure Experience, Leisure Objects, Interaction, Interaction Ritual, Meaning, Self-Reflexive, Phenomenology of Experience

It seems everyone wants to provide experiences these days including businesses, tourism agencies, event planners, sport managers, leisure providers, marketers, arts managers, museum curators, and the list goes on. These seemingly diverse organizations share a common goal—an intention to provide memorable experiences. The word *experience* is often used as a modifier that supposedly adds worth to an endeavor, giving us experience design, experience marketing, a customer experience, a purchasing experience, a dining experience, a tourist experience, and many others the reader has likely seen. The ubiquitous use of the word could cause one to assume its meaning is well defined and known. But the literature includes many conceptions of experience.

Part of the confusion about providing experience lies in understanding what constitutes an experience and, furthermore, what constitutes a leisure experience. Understanding the meaning of experience is an important first step for developing a technique for designing memorable leisure experiences. There is a divide between those who assume an experience is doing something that stimulates and engages an individual's consciousness, as in entertainment, and those who assume an experience involves individuals interacting in the production of an encounter and co-creating it through a series of conscious decisions that allow them to make choices that affect the outcome of the experience, as is accomplished in a leisure experience. This difference influences the entire conceptualization of experience, the roles we assume that the stager and participant will undertake, and how outcomes and memories will be produced.

Shedroff (2001) began his book *Experience Design 1* by suggesting that everything is "technically" an experience. At a minimum, experience requires absorption of information, that is, conscious attention to what is transpiring. Absent this, an individual is unaware that something is occurring and thus is not in an experience. So we would add that everything we are consciously aware of is technically an experience. Shedroff elaborated, "The elements that contribute to superior experiences are knowable and reproducible, which make them designable" (p. 2). This suggests that there is a continuum of experiences from inferior to superior. The question is, what variables account for differences across this continuum? What makes an experience "inferior" or "superior"?

Pine and Gilmore (1999) in the book that launched widespread interest in experience, *The Experience Economy*, suggested that experience "occurs whenever a company intentionally uses services as the stage and goods as props to engage an individual" (p. 11). Throughout the book, they continued to develop the degree of engagement as a critical variable in determining the quality of an experience and caution readers to not make the mistake of "equating experiences with entertainment" (p. 29). They continued, "Remember that staging experiences is not about entertaining customers, it's about *engaging* them" (p. 30). We deduce that the depth of an experience directly depends on the degree of engagement demanded in episodes of interaction designed and staged by the program designer. Thus, some of the differences noted deal with experiences other than leisure experiences. All leisure is an experience, but not all experiences are leisure.

To design and stage program services that deliver engaging leisure experiences, programmers must understand how leisure is experienced and produced in occasions of social interaction. This requires an understanding of symbolic interactionism (the social science that provides the theoretical base for programming), how interaction in social occasions provides opportunities for co-production by participants, and the implications of these for program design and staging. These unique bodies of information provide the knowledge base that enables programmers to develop successful recreation programs that facilitate leisure experiences.

A Social Science Theory of Programming

The theory of leisure programming presented in this book is based on a social science theory that views leisure as an interactional episode, consistent with the symbolic interactionist perspective of H. Blumer and N. K. Denzin. Sociological theory has three major approaches: structure-functionalist, conflict, and symbolic interactionist. Each is useful in different ways for investigating the nature of human social order. The structure-functionalist approach examines the basic structure of society, the roles and functions of its institutions, and how roles and institutions affect individual and collective action in society. Conflict sociology examines the role of conflict in a society and how power struggles affect the order of a society. Symbolic interactionism examines the "different dimensions of the construction of social reality through the seemingly autonomous activities of individuals," according to Eisenstadt and Curelaru (1977, p. 46). They continued,

> [Symbolic interactionists'] . . . major contribution was in the exploration of different levels and types of "informal" and "subterranean" situations of human interaction which cut across formal arrangements and institutional settings, of the less fully organized dimension of everyday life: their phenomenology and nature; the structure and rules of interaction that take place within them, as distinct from the formal institutional definition of goals; the mechanisms of interaction through which such situations are constructed and their perception by the participants in them; their impact on different levels of formal social organization. (Eisenstadt & Curelaru, 1977, pp. 46–47)

Symbolic interactionism is well established as an approach for understanding leisure behavior (Kelly, 1987; Kuentzel, 1990; B. Lee & Shafer, 2002; Y. Lee, 1990; Samdahl, 1992). B. Lee and Shafer (2002) pointed out, "Leisure experiences are believed to be dynamic and to emerge through the interaction process" (p. 290). It is a relevant approach because it examines the social process of human behavior in the face-to-face interactions that constitute the bulk of leisure, play, recreation, game, tourism, event, and sport participation. The sole joy of leisure may be in participating in its construction (Kuentzel, 1990; Podilchak, 1991). For programmers, an interactionist approach is important for explaining how individuals structure their participation in leisure occasions and how they experience these occasions (Samdahl, 1988, 1992). Thus, it will be used as the theoretical base of recreation programming presented in this book.

> An interactionist approach is important for explaining how individuals structure their participation in leisure occasions and how they experience these occasions.

Symbolic Interaction Theory

Symbolic interactionism rests on three premises (Blumer, 1969; Denzin, 1978). Denzin (1978) provides a capsule explanation of the symbolic interactionists' theoretical perspective:

> Symbolic interactionism rests on three basic assumptions. First, social reality as it is sensed, known, and understood is a social production. Interacting individuals produce and define their own definitions of situations. Second, humans are assumed to be capable of engaging in "minded," self-reflexive behavior. They are capable of shaping and guiding their own behavior and that of others. Third, in the course of taking their own standpoint and fitting that standpoint to the behaviors of others, humans interact with one another. Interaction is seen as an emergent, negotiated, often unpredictable concern. Interaction is symbolic because it involves the manipulation of symbols, words, meanings, and languages.
>
> Integral to this perspective is the view that the social world of human beings is not made up of objects that have intrinsic meaning. The meaning of objects lies in the actions that human beings take toward them. Human experience is such that the process of defining objects is ever-changing, subject to redefinitions, relocations, and realignments. The interactionist assumes that humans learn their basic symbols, their conceptions of self, and the definitions they attach to social objects through interactions with others. Each person simultaneously carries on conversations with himself or herself and with significant others. Behavior is observable at the symbolic and the behavioral levels. (p. 7)

Blumer (1969) distinguished three slightly different assumptions of symbolic interactionism. When considered together with Denzin's assumptions, they present a comprehensive picture of symbolic interactionism:

> Symbolic interactionism rests in the last analysis on three simple premises. The first premise is that human beings act toward things on the basis of the meanings that the things have for them. Such things include everything that the human being may note in the world—physical objects, such as trees or chairs; other human beings, such as friends or enemies; institutions, such as a school or a government; guiding ideals, such as individual independence or honesty; activities of others, such as their commands or requests;

and such situations as an individual encounters in his [or her] daily life. The second premise is that the meaning of such things is derived from, or arises out of, the social interaction that one has with one's fellows. The third premise is that these meanings are handled in, and modified through, an interpretive process used by the person in dealing with the things he [or she] encounters. (p. 2)

Implications of Symbolic Interaction for Leisure Programming

A theory that provides a basis for recreation programming should focus the programmer's attention and effort on the factors relevant for facilitating a leisure experience and thus provide direction to the programmer's programming efforts. The symbolic interactionist perspective suggests that leisure is a unique meaning attributed to specific social occasions that are created by the individuals involved through interaction with objects in the occasions (Csikszentmihalyi, 1991; Kuentzel, 1990; B. Lee & Shafer, 2002; Samdahl, 1988, 1992; Shaw, 1985; Unger, 1984). Five points need to be developed for a full explanation and understanding of the implications of the theory for recreation programming: the phases of the leisure experience, the nature of objects acted on during interaction, how meaning is derived through interaction, how interaction is produced, and the phenomenology of experiencing leisure.

Phases of the Leisure Experience

There is growing evidence that leisure is a multiphase experience (Madrigal, 2003; B. Lee & Shafer, 2002; Stewart, 1998b). At a minimum, it is experienced in three phases: anticipation, participation, and reflection. These are derived from Mead's (1934) concept of the "specious present"—the moment of participation. It is preceded by mental images of anticipation and succeeded by imaged reflections. Clawson and Knetsch (1966) applied this concept to outdoor recreation, expanding it to five phases: anticipation, travel to, on-site, travel back, and recollection.

Often, programmers only plan interventions for the participation phase and thus do not consider the total experience. This may cause the programmer to miss important opportunities for intervention and facilitation of the outcomes desired. Since satisfaction with a program is a function of fulfilling a participant's expectations, during the anticipation phase programmers must either discover participants' expectations or try to manipulate them. For example, Skipper (1992) demonstrated that the wording of advertising flyers can influence the number of participants who register and attend an event. McCarville (1993) found that patrons' expectations are influenced by how they are dealt with during phone inquiries about a program, registration procedures, and so on. Raymore (2002) outlined three types of facilitators to leisure (intrapersonal, interpersonal, and structural) that can "enable or promote

> There is growing evidence that leisure is a multiphase experience.

the formation of leisure preferences" and "encourage or enhance participation" (p. 39). All of these can be known in the anticipation phase and planned for in the design of a program.

Post-program interventions influence reflection on a program. The distribution and solicitation of evaluation information is an important customer satisfaction activity and a source of information that can be used for documenting program outcomes and improving future operations of the program (Howe, 1993; Little, 1993). Patterson, Watson, Williams, and Roggenbuck (1998) found that participants spent the time immediately following an intense outdoor recreation experience sorting through and analyzing the meaning of what occurred. Kiewa (2001) found evidence that climbers reflect on their climbing experiences to reconcile how the experience affects their narration of self. Post-program debriefing, publishing photographs, staging reunions, and selling souvenirs are interventions designed to influence the recollection phase of a leisure experience.

Symbolic interaction theory suggests that the programmer's responsibility for intervention needs to be expanded from dealing exclusively with the participation phase of an experience to including the anticipation and reflection phases.

The Nature of Leisure Objects

Objects are anything that can be indicated, pointed out, or referred to (Blumer, 1969). Objects receive our focused attention and are consciously dealt with during interaction. Human beings act toward objects on the basis of the meanings that they have for the objects, and the meaning of the objects is derived through interaction.

The three categories of objects include physical, social, and symbolic. Physical objects such as balls, bats, and craft supplies may be used in the leisure occasion. Social objects include other people, including leaders, friends, mothers, and other participants in a program. Most leisure occasions are participated in with family or friends (Cheek, Field, & Burdge, 1976). People are the ultimate interactive objects, because another person offers more social interaction possibilities than any other type of object. Symbolic objects are ideas, philosophies, doctrines, and they too present possibilities for interaction. That is, individuals can form a line of behavior based on them. Notions about moral or immoral recreation influence the leisure behavior of many individuals. Concepts about cooperation and competition also influence interactions in leisure occasions. Programmers often program to reify abstract concepts, such as those associated with Valentine's Day, for example, love, Cupid, hearts, and other symbolic objects.

> Objects receive our focused attention and are consciously dealt with during interaction.

These three types encompass all possible objects that can be indicated, pointed out, or referred to in social occasions. They are the objects of all interaction. Programmers need to learn which objects make essential contributions to the leisure experience intended and which are superfluous so that decisions can be made about which must be included in a given program. Chapter 3 focuses further on the objects included in leisure occasions.

How Interaction Is Produced in Social Occasions

Goffman (1959) defined face-to-face interaction as "the reciprocal influence of individuals upon one another's actions when in one another's immediate physical presence" (p. 15). B. Lee and Shafer (2002) found empirical proof of this process in a study of trail users. Goffman (1967) also described how individuals organize their behavior in social occasions that arise from "the comingling of persons and the temporary interactional enterprises that can arise there from" and characterized the comingling of individuals as "a shifting entity necessarily evanescent, created by arrivals and killed by departures" (p. 2).

Social gatherings are constructed by the interactions of minded, self-reflexive individuals who align their actions based on their interpretations of the meaning they attribute to the actions of others in the occasion. Note that symbolic interactionism has as one of its root assumptions the notion that human beings are capable of minded, self-reflexive behavior (Denzin, 1978). That is, they are capable of guiding their own behavior and developing a joint line of behavior with others through interaction with them. This notion is crucial for defining the engaging dimension of leisure experiences. Individuals must be actively engaged in the joint construction of the occasion and this occurrence is a necessary condition for perceptions of competence and consequent intrinsic satisfaction with participation.

> Social gatherings are constructed by the interactions of minded, self-reflexive individuals who align their actions based on their interpretations of the meaning they attribute to the actions of others in the occasion.

The Interaction Ritual

Experiencing a program occurs through interaction across a continuum of engagements as represented by the three phases of an interaction ritual, as illustrated in Figure 2.1 (page 28). The increasing complexity of transitioning from simple conscious awareness of transpiring events to truly interacting in an experience and co-creating them is the variable that alters the degree of engagement in an experience. The three phases of the interaction ritual account for this variation by moving through conscious attention to enacting behaviors that contribute to and sustain the engagement.

Interaction begins with Phase 1, intake; an individual is consciously aware of what is occurring. This is the minimum for an experience to occur, but often an experience does not progress from this level of engagement. These experiences are typical of the entertainment discussed by Pine and Gilmore; individuals passively absorb information and sensations, but the experience is often fleeting.

Phase 2 of interaction involves thinking—interpreting, processing, and sometimes planning a course of action that responds to the information received in Phase 1. Experience in this phase is characterized by individuals engaging in a minded, self-reflexive internal discourse wherein their concepts or thoughts may be modified and/or they develop and evaluate possible lines of behavior to enact in

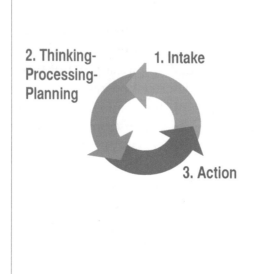

1. **Intake**—Consciously aware of each other's presence, co-present individuals take account of all objects in the occasion and each other's actions.

2. **Thinking-Processing-Planning**—Individuals interpret the meaning of all objects in the occasion through a minded, self-reflexive, internalized conversation and may alter current concepts or views or form candidate plans of action.

3. **Action**—Individuals enact a response (i.e., a line of behavior) based on this interpretation and affect the course of interaction, thereby co-creating the experience.

Figure 2.1. Interaction Ritual[1]

---

[1] The concept of an Interaction Ritual is inspired by the symbolic interaction theory and the many works of Erving Goffman cited in the chapter. Goffman authored a book with the title *Interaction Ritual* (1967), resulting in the term being widely used to label various types of interaction.

Phase 3. That is, they develop candidate plans they may act out. Continuing with our example of entertainment, Phase 2 often involves high culture forms of entertainment. An excellent theatrical production, for example, frequently presents a dilemma that challenges our previously held notions, forcing us to reconstruct our concepts or thinking about an issue. Participating in this mind game is personally rewarding and is a more serious and engaged involvement than the involvement that occurs in the first phase. This type of experience provides a higher probability of providing a memorable experience. However, in Phase 2 the participant is not involved in directing or sustaining the interaction of the experience. Phase 2 is lower in affordance (i.e., the number of interactive possibilities presented by an occasion of interaction) than Phase 3, where the level of engagement requires that participants explore different possible contributions to sustaining ongoing interaction.

In Phase 3, individuals choose and enact a line of behavior responding to their interpretation of what has occurred in the previous two phases; in doing so, they contribute a response that sustains interaction and affects outcome, thereby co-creating the experience. Sustained participation and co-production involves repeating this same basic three-phase ritual. Interacting at this level, engaged in co-creating an experience, provides maximal engagement and the highest probability of providing a memorable experience. We believe this is what Seligman (2002) is championing when he discusses sustainable happiness and moving away from shortcuts to happiness. "Authentic happiness comes from identifying and cultivating your most fundamental strengths and using them every day in work, love, play, and parenting" (Seligman, 2002, p. xiii).

Experiences wherein stimulations are provided for and to people, although engaging for the moment, do not provide this sustainable engagement or longer term happiness. Often, as much of the event literature suggests, the programmer uses wow or novelty to enhance participation. But these techniques cannot compete in creating meaning or sustaining continuing participation interest with programs wherein participants are involved in co-creation. Diller, Shedroff, and Rhea (2008) concluded, "Our own work in the field has led us to the conviction that for companies to achieve enduring competitive advantage through experience design, their innovations cannot be based simply on novelty" (p. 3). They continued by discussing the importance of evoking meaning; "Increasingly, companies must address their customers' essential human need for meaning" (Diller et al., 2008, p. 3).

In discussing experiences desired by the Creative Class, Florida (2002) commented that they "prefer more active, authentic, and participatory experiences, which they can have a hand in structuring" (p. 167). The interactive social engagement provided in Phase 3 creates perpetual novelty (Schmitt, 1999) that is a continuing source of self-generated wow and novelty. Having this opportunity to co-create is the source of engagement and fun in a leisure experience for participants. The emergent nature of this interaction and the engagement required in Phase 3 of the Interaction Ritual is a source of sustainable happiness that is not provided when interaction does not include engaging co-creation opportunities for participants.

Evidence of this engaged interaction and negotiation of meaning has emerged in the research literature (Stewart, 1998a; B. Lee & Shafer, 2002). Based on an investigation of rock climbers, Kiewa (2001) concluded that the notion of positive affect or control of participation in an activity cannot occur unless the participant deliberately and willingly embraces participation in an activity. She observed that a program determined and structured by another cannot provide the experience desired. The point cannot be made too often that the implication of this process for programming is the need for creating opportunities for participants to engage in action. Thus, the programmer must be concerned with the process of participating, that is, the occurrence and order of interactions in a leisure event. Chapter 10 also deals with this topic. Now complete Exercise 2.1 (page 30).

> The notion of positive affect or control of participation in an activity cannot occur unless the participant deliberately and willingly embraces participation in an activity.

Deriving Meaning From Interaction in Leisure Occasions

The meaning of objects arises out of the interaction an individual has with them. Meaning is not inherent in an object: "Creating meaning involves bringing order to the contents of the mind by integrating one's actions into a unified flow experience" (Csikszentmihalyi, 1991, p. 216). Thus, meaning is derived through interaction with social objects. Blumer (1969) stated,

> [Symbolic interactionism] sees meaning as arising in the process of interaction between people. The meaning of a thing for a person grows out of the ways in which other persons act toward the person with regard to the thing. Their actions operate to define the thing for the person. Thus, symbolic interactionism sees meanings as social products, as creations that are formed in and through the defining activities of people as they interact. (pp. 4–5)

Meaning is produced socially through interaction with physical, social, and symbolic objects. Therefore, meaning is situationally specific, and the meaning of an object can change from occasion to occasion. For example, Mann (1973) pointed out that queues for leisure events have a different meaning than queues for other functions. Hunnicutt (1986) suggested that to "play" with an object is to experience it in a totally different way than through any other modes of interaction.

Furthermore, meaning is negotiated within the context of interaction. Y. Lee (1990) documented that individuals situationally interpret leisure based on the social context in which they have the experience. Often, participants, especially individuals who are new to an activity, do not have well-defined expectations about what they will derive from participating in an activity (Patterson et al., 1998). Meaning and expectations are negotiated and developed through participation. Hultsman (1998) found that over a multiday event, satisfied participants were capable of coping with an event by modifying their behavior or their expectations. Construing the meaning of a leisure experience, then, seems to occur while an activity is being experienced (Kelly, 1999), as well as immediately after the event (Kiewa, 2001; Patterson et al., 1998).

Meaning arises out of the interaction an individual has with objects in an occasion. Interaction in leisure occasions results in a different meaning than interaction in other occasions because of the perceived freedom of participants, the intrinsic satisfaction of participating, and finally because of the satisfaction of being the cause of an act, that is, being an active participant in creating and sustaining the interactions. Meaning occurs within and as a result of interaction (Goffman, 1983; Kelly, 1999), and the leisure experience emerges from this interaction (Stewart, 1998b). Thus, programmers must be concerned with the interactions in a program and ensure the occurrence of key, meaning-deriving interactions that will result in participants construing that they had a leisure experience. More in Chapter 10. Now complete Exercise 2.2.

Exercise 2.2.
Symbolic Interaction Theory and You

1. Write down the name of an object in your life that is meaningful to you (e.g., new CD, hockey stick, backpack, swimsuit).
2. Write down three ways that you "act toward that object." In other words, what do you do with it?
3. What the object means to you is related to social interactions that you have had with the object. Write down two completely different social interactions that resulted in you feeling completely different about the object.
4. Wait a second! Do you suppose the "objects" we've been discussing always have to be tangible objects? Why or why not?

Experiencing Leisure

How, then, do individuals experience leisure? "Experience is going through an episode or event as well as processing the perceptions of that time period," according to Kelly (1987, p. 20). More recent research has confirmed that during participation, "people's situational identities are, in essence, constantly being tested as interactions occur" (B. Lee & Shafer, 2002, p. 306). Furthermore, "recreation activities are be-havioral constructions that people build" (More & Averill, 2003, p. 372). Interaction in an episode includes sensing one's self, the selves presented by others, and other elements in the environment. It occurs through the conscious direction and inter-pretation of an individual's behavior in response to actions of others encountered in the environment whether or not they are present. An example of this last point is the influence a coach may have on the choices a player may make in a game situation. The coach is not a present interactant in the game, but his or her influence still par-tially determines outcome. We evaluate the interaction during and after an episode by determining how our own self has been confirmed or altered by the experience. We achieve order and satisfaction within an episode of interaction when we have made decisions that enable us to reach our personal goals, which may be to confirm or change our personal narrative of our self-concept. Four implications from this theory directly affect the programmer's efforts.

Occasions of Interaction Are Emergent Productions

Interaction is constructed in real time in which self-reflexive individuals choose the line of behavior they will follow. Despite staff efforts to plan and predict how behavior will play out in a given program, individuals who enter activities may in-terpret the meaning of the objects differently, and thus their respondent actions may differ accordingly. Programmers must understand how humans shape meaning and how that meaning shapes action. Each occasion of interaction is constructed anew each time it is experienced, and a past success does not guarantee that the same combination of circumstances will again lead to the same outcome—because in a program there are often different individuals who will respond differently and even the same individuals may respond differently.

Occasions of Interaction Are Fragile

Providing the experience desired in an occasion is sometimes difficult because of the fragility of social occasions. More and Averill (2003) indicated that all recreation activities are made up of two subsystems—"prototypic subsystems (those present in virtually all instances of the activity) and design subsystems (optional subsystems that adapt the activity to serve multiple goals)" (p. 372). Prototypic subsystems are the structural elements of a given activity that must be present for the activity to be true to its form, for example, the rules of a game or sport event that make it baseball versus basketball for instance. Design subsystems are more flexible and thus may be manipulated so that they meet the intended outcomes of a specific operation of a program or participant outcome expectations. Programmers should avoid impos-ing structures that are so rigid that they will interfere with an individual's perceived freedom to enact behaviors that will enable them to experience intrinsic satisfac-tion. Programmers can destroy the experience they are trying to facilitate by forcing programmatic controls and manipulations on the operation of a program.

People Always Play a Role in Constructing Leisure Occasions

According to symbolic interaction theory, individuals always play a part in shaping the direction of an interactional episode and the meaning of that interaction. Csikszentmihalyi (1991) emphasized this point: "It [happiness] does not depend on outside events, but rather on how we interpret them" (p. 2). Thus, optimal experience is something individuals make happen through the conscious interpretation and volitional direction of interaction (i.e., co-creation). The autonomy of the individual must be respected in program development. If the programmer provides too much direction, the patron may not have a sufficient opportunity for involvement and the engagement needed to perceive they are the cause of an act.

> Optimal experience is something individuals make happen through the conscious interpretation and volitional direction of interaction.

The Programmer Must Help Situate the Event by Providing Some Form and Structure to the Occasion

It is crucial that programmers understand this concept and how it enables those present in an occasion to be set free so leisure may be experienced. Patterson et al. (1998) described this phenomenon as "situated freedom," and Kelly (1999) called it "situated action." Goffman (1983) explained that occasions of interaction are directed by a series of enabling conventions, in other words, rules of interaction that may range from formal through tacitly agreed-to conventions. Participating in interaction, then, requires participants to pay the small price of agreeing to abide by the conventions so that they may obtain the large benefit of participating in the interaction facilitated by the conventions without having to renegotiate the rules continually.

The conventions that situate a leisure event come from three sources: the relational history of participants, the structures provided by societal mores, and the rules required by the activity (i.e., rules of the game) or directions provided by the programmer. Many leisure experiences occur during informal interactions with family and friends where an individual's true self is already a known and accepted entity. Thus, the individual does not need to continually renegotiate who one is (Samdahl, 1992), and the true self can interact with a degree of freedom not possible in interactions where the self must be continually renegotiated and redefined. In a similar manner, the rules of interaction create or define a social order and the acceptable roles a person can assume in this defined occasion of interaction. For example, in an occasion with formalized rules, such as a game of racquetball, two players previously unknown to each other may play and know the roles and expectations each will perform to sustain the occasion of interaction. This is possible because they both know and accept the rules of interaction in racquetball and are thus freed to attend to the defined requirements of the game. In this way, conventions of interaction create the freedom to present a known self and to interact freely. This uniqueness is one defining characteristic of leisure occasions.

Knowledge about the phenomenology of experiencing leisure, then, gives the following direction to programmers: To facilitate leisure experiences, the programmer must design an encounter (i.e., a situated activity system). This requires situating an occasion of leisure by providing social order (form and structure) through normative structures that provide interactive social space. This space must reach Phase 3 of interaction to afford participants engaging opportunities to co-create experiences that result in recollections and memories of perceived freedom and intrinsic satisfaction for them, plus provide fun, enjoyment, and/or relaxation. Now complete Exercise 2.3.

Exercise 2.3.
Programming as Symbolic Interaction

Discuss the different roles a programmer would take if he or she were to design a program intended to provide a leisure experience, as opposed to a program intended simply to be an opportunity for the leisure experience to occur.

- What is the role of the programmer if one assumes that when individuals interact they play a major role in defining the leisure experience?
- What are the three essential perceptual results needed if individuals are to define programs as leisure? How can programmers ensure that they occur?

Conclusion

Professional programmers rely on leisure theory and social behavioral theory to guide the development of programs. Symbolic interaction theory attempts to understand behavior at the level of face-to-face interaction; it assumes that individuals participate in co-creating occasions of interaction and thereby construing meaning from them. The theory suggests that programmers must focus attention on how they design and stage programs and how participants experience programs. Understanding how to intervene in a manner that facilitates leisure is a crucial programming concept that includes understanding how interaction occurs, how meaning is produced through interaction, and what meanings must result for an occasion to be construed as leisure.

References

Blumer, H. (1969). *Symbolic interactionism.* Englewood Cliffs, NJ: Prentice-Hall.

Cheek, N. H., Field, D. R., & Burdge, R. J. (1976). *Leisure and recreation places.* Ann Arbor, MI: Ann Arbor Science.

Clawson, M., & Knetsch, J. L. (1966). *Economics of outdoor recreation*. Baltimore, MD: Johns Hopkins Press.

Csikszentmihalyi, M. (1991). *Flow: The psychology of optimal experience*. New York, NY: Harper Perennial.

Denzin, N. K. (1978). *The research act* (2nd ed.). New York, NY: McGraw-Hill.

Diller, S., Shedroff, N., & Rhea, D. (2008). *Making meaning: How successful businesses deliver meaningful customer experiences*. Berkeley, CA: New Riders.

Eisenstadt, S. N., & Curelaru, M. (1977). Macrosociology theory, analysis, and comparative studies. *Current Sociology, 25*(2), 44–47.

Florida, R. (2002). *The rise of the creative class*. New York, NY: Basic Books.

Goffman, E. (1959). *The presentation of self in everyday life*. Garden City, NY: Doubleday.

Goffman, E. (1967). *Interaction ritual*. Garden City, NY: Anchor Books.

Goffman, E. (1983). The interaction order. *American Sociological Review, 458*(2), 1–17.

Howe, C. Z. (1993). The evaluation of leisure programs. *Journal of Physical Education, Recreation, and Dance, 64*(8), 43–46.

Hultsman, W. (1998). The multi-day, competitive leisure event: Examining satisfaction over time. *Journal of Leisure Research, 30*, 472–497.

Hunnicutt, B. K. (1986). Problems raised by the empirical study of play and some humanistic alternatives. In *Abstracts from the 1986 Symposium on Leisure Research* (pp. 8–10). Arlington, VA: National Recreation and Park Association.

Kelly, J. R. (1987). *Freedom to be: A new sociology of leisure*. New York, NY: Macmillan.

Kelly, J. R. (1999). Leisure behaviors and styles: Social, economic, and cultural factors. In E. L. Jackson & T. L. Burton (Eds.), *Leisure studies: Prospects for the twenty-first century* (pp. 135–150). State College, PA: Venture.

Kiewa, J. (2001). Control over self and space in rock climbing. *Journal of Leisure Research, 33*, 363–382.

Kuentzel, W. F. (1990, October). *Motive uniformity across recreational activities and settings: A synthesis of research*. Paper presented at the National Recreation and Parks Association Research Symposium, Phoenix, AZ.

Lee, B., & Shafer, C. S. (2002). The dynamic nature of leisure experience: An application of affect control theory. *Journal of Leisure Research, 34*, 290–310.

Lee, Y. (1990, October). *Immediate leisure experiences: A phenomenological approach*. Paper presented at the 1990 National Recreation and Park Association Leisure Research Symposium, Phoenix, AZ.

Little, S. L. (1993). Leisure program design and evaluation. *Journal of Physical Education, Recreation, and Dance, 64*(8), 26–29, 33.

Madrigal, R. (2003). Investigating an evolving leisure experience: Antecedents and consequences of spectator affect during a live sporting event. *Journal of Leisure Research, 35*, 23–48.

Mann, L. (1973). Learning to live with lines. In J. Helmer & N. A. Eddington (Eds.), *Urbanman: The psychology of urban survival* (pp. 42–61). New York, NY: Macmillan.

McCarville, R. E. (1993). Keys to quality programming. *Journal of Physical Education, Recreation, and Dance, 64*(8), 34–36, 46, 47.

Mead, G. H. (1934). *Mind, self, and society*. Chicago, IL: University of Chicago Press.

More, T. A., & Averill, J. R. (2003). The structure of recreation behavior. *Journal of Leisure Research, 35*, 372–395.

Patterson, M. E., Watson, A. E., Williams, D. R., & Roggenbuck, J. R. (1998). An hermeneutic approach to studying the nature of wilderness experiences. *Journal of Leisure Research, 30*, 423–435.

Pine, B. J., II, & Gilmore, J. H. (1999). *The experience economy: Work is theatre and every business a stage*. Boston, MA: Harvard Business School Press.

Podilchak, W. (1991). Distinctions of fun, enjoyment, and leisure. *Leisure Studies, 10*, 133–148.

Raymore, L. A. (2002). Facilitators to leisure. *Journal of Leisure Research, 34*, 37–51.

Samdahl, D. M. (1988). A symbolic interactionist model of leisure: Theory and empirical support. *Leisure Sciences, 1*, 27–39.

Samdahl, D. M. (1992). The common leisure occasion. *Journal of Leisure Research, 24*, 19–32.

Schmitt, B. H. (1999). *Experiential marketing: How to get customers to sense, feel, think, act, relate to your company and brands.* New York, NY: The Free Press.

Seligman, M. E. P. (2002). *Authentic happiness.* New York, NY: The Free Press.

Shaw, S. M. (1985). The meaning of leisure in everyday life. *Leisure Sciences, 7*, 1–24.

Shedroff, N. (2001). *Experience design 1.* Indianapolis, IN: New Riders.

Skipper, B. A. (1992). The relationship between desired results and the marketing tools used in recreation programming. *Dissertation Abstracts International, 53*, 3364A.

Stewart, W. P. (Ed.). (1998a). Leisure as multiphase experience [Special issue]. *Journal of Leisure Research, 30*(4).

Stewart, W. P. (1998b). Leisure as multiphase experiences: Challenging tradition. *Journal of Leisure Research, 30*, 391–400.

Unger, L. S. (1984). The effect of situational variables on the subjective leisure experience. *Leisure Sciences, 6*, 291–312.

Fun on the Water Slide
City of Aurora Department of Parks, Recreation, and Open Space. Photo by Sherri-Jo Stowell.

3 *Six Key Elements of a Situated Activity System*

KEY TERMS

Situated Activity System, Six Elements of a Situated Activity System, Social Interaction, Interacting People, Physical Setting, Leisure Objects, Structure , Relationships, Animation, Service Continuum

This chapter discusses the elements that situate an instance of interaction. All instances of leisure involve the interactions of one or more persons who are orienting their behavior toward themselves and other physical, social, or symbolic objects (Denzin, 1975). This co-orientation of selves occurs in a situated social system; that is, it occurs in a social occasion that has an identifiable set of elements that give it structure.

> All instances of leisure involve the interactions of one or more persons who are orienting their behavior toward themselves and other physical, social, or symbolic objects.

Erving Goffman dedicated his career to investigating and identifying the dynamics of face-to-face interaction in social occasions in an effort to identify the generic set of elements that are present in these occasions. From Goffman's work, Denzin (1975) identified six generic elements that structure social occasions:

differentially self-reflexive actors; place or setting itself (e.g., the physical territory); social objects which fill the setting and are acted on by the actors in question; a set of rules of a civil–legal, polite–ceremonial, and relationally specific nature which explicitly or tacitly guide and shape interaction; a set of relationships which bind interactants to one another; and a shifting set of definitions reflective of each actor's co-orientation to self and others during the interaction sequence. (p. 462)

These six elements situate instances of social interaction and form their structure. To develop leisure services, the programmer must consider or manage these six key elements to provide opportunities for participants to actively engage their environment. Their effect on a program is fundamentally important—a change in any one element changes the situation of the program. Collectively, they constitute a structured social system for instances of interaction to occur. We call these instances the use of a situated activity system or an encounter, and we use these terms interchangeably in the remainder of the text.

Murphy, Williams, Niepoth, and Brown (1973) stated, "The basic method used by agencies to structure opportunities which encourage different kinds of recreation behaviors is the creation and/or manipulation of physical and human environments" (p. 77). The literature on leisure programming has never elaborated on the generic elements to be created and manipulated. An assumption of this text is that a leisure program is a series of encounters, each of which is a unique configuration of these six elements. These six are the key elements of program production because they are all that a programmer can manipulate, or needs to manipulate, in developing a leisure program.

Interaction occurs as a linear sequence of encounters, with only one encounter given focused attention at any given moment by the individuals in the social occasion. Any one element can be the most important element in any encounter. The importance of any element can shift with the transition from one encounter to another. Interaction is made up of interaction within an encounter and the shifting attention demanded from changing the structure (i.e., the configuration of the six elements) of each succeeding encounter. Within an individual program, each element assumes a shifting role of importance as the interactions of the program progress.

> Interaction occurs as a linear sequence of encounters.

The task of the leisure programmer is to identify the unique configuration of these six elements that situate each encounter and to anticipate how the series of encounters that make up the program will be animated to move participants through the program. The programmer anticipates and plans how the action sequences in each encounter will unfold and then puts in place the mechanisms needed to guide the occurrence of the intended interactions. The programmer initially accomplishes this by vicariously experiencing the program before it occurs. In this process, the programmer tries to anticipate and predict the outcomes of interactions within a program and the order in which events during the interaction will unfold. The process is analogous to writing the script of a play, except that in the most desirable programmed leisure experiences, the interactants are not bound by the script, but play a role in shaping the event or co-producing it. Chapter 10 explains the program design process in greater detail.

This viewpoint makes clear the problematic nature of program design, planning, and staging. Interacting individuals is one of the six elements that situate an instance of interaction. But after entering an occasion, the individuals are not bound to follow the action scenarios designed by the programmer. The overall outcome of a program depends on the interactions of individuals with the other five elements, the interactions of individuals with each other, and the interaction of all six elements with each other. Pfeffer and Salancik (1978) make clear the problematic nature of interdependent events: "Interdependence is the reason why nothing comes out quite the way one wants it to. Any event that depends on more than a single causal agent is an outcome based on interdependent agents" (p. 40). This is the case for designing and staging leisure programs.

A familiarity with social interaction theory will help programmers understand how humans experience and construct their participation in leisure programs. Research on social interaction has led to the development of a generic structure of a social occasion, namely, the six elements that situate instances of interaction and provide a social system for it to occur. Programmers can create and manipulate these elements to program leisure experiences. Because of the emergent and negotiated nature of interaction (Stewart, 1998), any program plan is best viewed as a probability estimate of what the programmer believes will happen during a planned interaction. Any program plan must have a "loose–tight" notion to it. There must be a tight enough structure to move participants toward the desired goals of the program, but it must be loose enough to accommodate participants interacting and negotiating their way through the engagements of the program.

Although the elements that situate a program can be reduced to six generic categories, a programmer would be deceived by believing that only six variables need to be manipulated. The number of possibilities within each element is large.

Furthermore, the number of possible combinations of elements is even larger. The six elements, however, provide a compact conceptual framework from which programmers can organize their efforts. Programmers create this situated production by understanding the existence of these elements and controlling or manipulating them. Some elements may be unalterable in some programs and therefore not subject to manipulation. For example, the programmer's agency may own a specific venue that must be programmed. In this instance, the venue is an unalterable element. In developing a program design, the programmer must anticipate the implications that an unalterable element has on the remaining elements that can be manipulated.

Six Key Elements

We have renamed the six elements identified by Goffman and Denzin, to clarify conceptually their role in program design. The new names are interacting people, physical setting, leisure objects, structure, relationships, and animation. This section presents an explanation of the role and effect that each element has in a program.

Interacting People

Leisure is a human experience created by differentially self-reflexive individuals interacting in social occasions. As discussed, social occasions are constructed by interacting individuals who build a line of behavior after taking account of their own behavior and that of others in the occasion. Effective programming requires the programmer either to anticipate who the specific individuals will be and design the program for them, or to design the program for a specific type of individual and then recruit this type of individual into the program, for example, a program for 9-year-old boys.

> When a different cohort of individuals come into a program, it changes.

When a different cohort of individuals come into a program, it changes. A perfect illustration of this point is the operation of programs for youth. Often, the same program can be operated successfully year after year. The configuration of the other five elements does not change—only the individuals in the program change. For example, in a typical program for youth, there may be a different cohort of 6-year-old children who participate in the same program each year. Even though the basic program has not changed, it continues to be successful. What has changed are the individuals in the program. Since one of the program elements has changed, the program has in fact changed.

Many programmers have had similar experiences. Having operated a program that originally failed, they offer the same program a second time with no change other than the individuals; with this one change, the program succeeds. One possible reason for program failure, then, is the recruitment of individuals into a program that is inappropriate for them. If a different group of individuals is recruited, the program may succeed with no other changes.

Because people are one of the major elements of program design, programmers must take great care in investigating or anticipating who these individuals are and what benefits they seek from participation. A solid understanding of lifespan development will aid programmers in understanding the benefits that participants seek from participation in leisure. To do so, it is necessary that programmers understand the physical, social, and psychological development of individuals; their gender, age, and skill level; and other pertinent information about them. For example, from birth to late adulthood humans develop socially, physically, and psychologically. The preschool years are characterized by child-centered play, careful supervision, gross motor development, short attention spans, and the need for immediate gratification. The childhood years are marked by increased social skills, awareness of others, fine motor skill development, creativity, and competency (Patterson, 1991).

Adolescent characteristics include puberty, social awkwardness, and peer acceptance. A desire for autonomy often spurs conflict between adolescents and their parents. During young adulthood, finding meaningful relationships and finding meaningful work are central concerns. Taking risks asserts one's independence and demonstrates skill competency (WGBH Educational Foundation, 2001).

In adulthood, wisdom and expertise develop concomitantly with learning and knowledge. The need for belonging is often filled by marriage or a relationship with a significant other. The physical body gradually changes in appearance as one grows older. Social commitments may involve children, work, and civic responsibilities. In this time, "leisure can represent activity, status, diversion, and autonomy" (Patterson, 1991, p. 32).

Older adulthood is marked by age-related physical and biological change. An individual's experience in retirement is influenced by factors of socioeconomic status. Life satisfaction will often depend on staying involved with family and friends, with leisure serving as the catalyst.

These are a few examples of how social, physiological, and psychological characteristics intermingle, change, and influence leisure participation throughout the lifespan. This is an important matter that is too large of a discussion to cover thoroughly in this text. For more information for these and other human characteristics that matter in designing a program, consult the human development literature.

Marketing literature has pointed out the need for designing programs for specific individuals through market segmentation (Howard & Crompton, 1980, p. 338) and developing services for a well-defined target market. Although agency goal statements often suggest that programs are for all people regardless of race, age, gender, ethnic origin, and so forth, we know that every program, to be successful, must be targeted for a specific group of individuals we can define with some precision.

> Every program, to be successful, must be targeted for a specific group of individuals we can define with some precision.

The programmer deals with this issue in one of two ways—either through macro or micro market segmentation (Crompton, 1983, pp. 10–19).

Macro segmentation involves developing services for a cohort of individuals who are seeking similar benefits from participation in recreation programs. The notion of a benefit package comes from the personal meaning of leisure that was discussed in Chapter 1. Crompton (1983) pointed out that the desires of each potential client are likely to be unique, but agencies cannot afford the resources to develop services for each client. Because of resource limitations, the programmer is then forced to compromise and group together individuals who desire similar benefits from participating in specific leisure occasions. These benefits may include any number of psychological outcomes, such as achievement, autonomy, socialization, or risk. Driver and Brown (1975) identified a number of possible psychological outcomes of leisure participation. In macro segmentation, the programmer develops a service to satisfy a projected benefit package that has been identified and then recruits into the program individuals who want this projected benefit package.

But programmers have no assurance that such a group indeed exists for the service identified. For example, through market research the programmer could produce evidence that a group of individuals desires physical fitness and social interaction. This is a benefit package that is sought. Further investigation identifies a group of mothers, 23 to 30 years of age with preschool children, who would like an aerobics fitness program in their neighborhood between 9:30 and 11:30 in the morning, with nursery service provided. The programmer then develops this service for and the benefit package sought by the individuals identified. Sometimes, however, it is impossible for programmers to identify further the specific cohort of individuals who desire this service, so they develop it solely based on data suggesting that a group of unidentified individuals seek this benefit package. In these cases, programs are developed slowly through trial and error until the individuals who desire the benefits of the program are recruited into the program.

When using micro segmentation, programmers identify cohorts of specific individuals by using traditional segmentation variables from one of three categories: geographic location descriptors (neighborhood, city, distance from program location), sociodemographic descriptors (age, income, gender, education), or behavioral descriptors (usage rates, level of specialization, psychological benefits sought; Crompton, 1983, p. 14). After identifying target groups, the programmer develops specific services to fill the benefit package desired by people in the targeted group.

The difference between these two techniques is in the timing, or the point at which the programmer begins dealing with individuals. In macro segmentation, the programmer first identifies a benefit or a package of benefits and then tries to identify the characteristics of the individuals who want the benefits. Sometimes, though, it is impossible for the programmer to identify individuals initially. In this case, the programmer has only a projected benefit package that is desired by a group of individuals whose identity is unknown. In micro segmentation, the programmer first identifies the individuals and then the benefits they seek.

The individuals who participate are thus a key element in program design. All programs are either consciously or inadvertently designed to meet the needs of a specific cohort of individuals. Effective programming involves matching the right group of individuals with the correct service so that the benefits they seek can be obtained. A principle of program design implied by this element can be stated as follows: *When the individuals in a program change, the program changes. Changing the individuals in a program may be the only change needed for making an unsuccessful program successful. Further, it is essential for the programmer to plan programs for the identified needs of specific individuals or the projected needs of a group believed to exist in the service community. The more information a programmer can obtain about the individuals who will be in a program, the better chance the programmer has of designing, operating, and staging a program that will meet the needs of the participants.*

The Physical Setting

The physical setting for a program is the second element to be discussed. The physical setting includes the venue where a program will occur and one or more of the following sensory components: sight, smell, hearing, taste, and touch. Each sensory component may affect a program if it is consciously or unconsciously included in or if it is inadvertently omitted from the program design. The physical setting is an expansive concept, so not all possible permutations can be discussed here. However, it is important for the programmer to recognize that the physical setting is one of the key elements that situate a program; if the setting changes, the program will change. Three considerations about the physical setting for a program are especially important.

First, programmers must understand the uniqueness of a venue and its setting. Too often, they try to duplicate a program that was successful elsewhere, only to fail because they do not understand that a unique setting was the key element contributing to the success of the program. For example, one military installation started a successful program in which the patrons would bring their lunch every Friday and listen to a small music combo while eating. Several other installations tried unsuccessfully to duplicate the program. They served the same type of food, had the same type of music, and used the same promotional materials and strategy. Eventually, the success of the original program was attributed to its unique setting—the venue where it occurred was an oceanside area where the combos played on a hill with beautiful ocean waves breaking in the background creating unique sights, sounds, and tactile effects. This unique venue and its sensory amenities simply could not be duplicated at other installations.

> The physical setting is one of the key elements that situate a program.

> Programmers must be able to analyze what elements contribute to the success of their programs.

Programmers must be able to analyze what elements contribute to the success of their programs for several reasons. First, knowing if a unique physical setting is the major element contributing to a program's success and whether the setting can be duplicated is critical information the programmer needs before attempting to duplicate a program that was successful elsewhere. Sometimes, if the setting cannot be duplicated, the program cannot be successfully duplicated.

Second, programmers must understand the limits of a setting. Too often, the setting is not adequate for a program. For example, one of the authors was once asked to operate a program with active games for elementary school children in a neighborhood recreation center that had not been designed for active play. In fact, to create an open setting, the architect had put glass walls on almost two full sides of the room to be used for active games. After replacing several panes of glass, the administration suspended playing active games "because the building was not designed for active play"! Some settings are simply not suitable for certain programs. An inappropriate setting may even detract from an event.

Third, the appearance and atmosphere of settings can be manipulated with decorations, lighting, and other physical alterations. Programmers should therefore realize when a unique physical setting is necessary for the success of a program. After determining that a unique setting is needed, the programmer can begin to find or create such a setting for the program. If programmers do not understand how a unique setting contributes to the success of a program, they cannot hope to duplicate the program elsewhere.

Usually, the more a physical environment is altered, the more expensive the alteration becomes. For example, an artificial ice rink can be kept frozen during the summer, although the high energy consumption that is needed to keep it frozen is expensive. Making an inadequate setting adequate is almost always possible if enough resources are available. But the cost of doing so may far exceed potential benefit. It is therefore important for the programmer to understand how essential a unique physical setting is to the success of a program before beginning expensive alterations of the physical environment.

> It is important for the programmer to ascertain whether the program to be staged requires a unique setting for success.

The physical setting is the second program element a programmer must evaluate. Although there is much to consider, it is important for the programmer to ascertain whether the program to be staged requires a unique setting for success. Knowing the limits of a setting and the many ways to alter it to make it adequate is also important information for the programmer.

Leisure Objects

As Chapter 2 discussed, the three types of objects are physical, social, and symbolic. In programming, the programmer must be able to identify the key objects that fill a leisure setting and are acted on when people interact during a program. Not every object needs to be identified, only the key objects that must be present for a program to occur and be successful. The question to answer that brings focus to this inquiry is, what objects are needed to support the interactions intended for the program?

For example, at the Park District of Oak Park, Illinois, one author, along with other staff, was attempting to develop a different program design for the annual children's Egg Hunt. Several objects were identified that were considered critical for such an event. The list included enough eggs for all children to have a good probability of finding at least one egg; a beautiful park with grass, trees, and bushes for hiding the eggs; and a costumed Bunny for children to visit in a surrealistic forest created with painted panels. The park was obviously the concern of the previous section on physical setting. However, the eggs and the Bunny were important objects that would contribute to this event. They were assumed to be so critical that they could not be excluded; if these objects were not available, the event would not occur.

Too often, programmers are willing to continue with an event even though they do not have enough objects or do not have the objects that are essential to operate a program successfully. Appropriate objects, whether physical, social, or symbolic, are sometimes the critical program elements. Programmers need to be able to determine which objects are essential, which are optional, and which detract from the event being planned and should be excluded. For the Egg Hunt to be successful, the programmer assumed it was essential that each child find an egg. If there were not enough eggs to make this possible, the event could not occur. Eggs are an essential object for an egg hunt—there is no substitute for them. Special prize eggs were also provided that, if found, entitled the bearer to a large chocolate rabbit. These prizes were considered optional and were to be included as long as the budget allowed for their purchase. In previous years, the beginning of the hunt was signaled with a track starting pistol that shot blanks. During the redesign of this program, the gun was considered detrimental to the atmosphere intended for the event, so the hunt began with an air horn.

> *What objects are needed to support the interactions intended for the program?*

Programmers must identify the key objects that are essential to supporting the interactions intended in a program. Objects can be essential to the success of a program, optional to its success, or detrimental to it.

Structure

All programs are provided organizational structure by a set of rules and program formats that guide interactions. The structure provided by the programmer determines how interactions unfold. Rules make certain interactions possible while restricting others. Here the term *rules* is used in a generic sense to include civil–legal, polite–ceremonial, and relational rules. With this conceptualization, programmers need to consider all of the rules—including laws, administrative regulations imposed by the agency, the codified rules of a game, the ceremonial rules of a game, and the relational rules of everyday discourse. Programmers must anticipate and and plan into the program design how each or all of these rules will affect the interactions in a program. At the same time, they need to ensure there are enough rules to direct interactions in a manner desired, but not so many rules that the freedom needed for a leisure experience to occur fails to emerge from the interactional episode being planned.

The regulating effects that rules impose on a program cannot be underestimated. It is known that the leisure experience is in large part determined by the perceived freedom a participant achieves as a result of interactions in a program. Because of this, too many rules or inappropriate ones can destroy the experience the programmer is trying to facilitate. A Ziggy cartoon that appeared many years ago illustrated this point well. In the cartoon, Ziggy is shown entering a park, where he is confronted with a series of signs that read, "Keep off the grass," "No picnicking is in this area," "No swimming," "No bicycle riding," and so forth. The last sign reads, "This is your park, enjoy it! Your Park Commission." It is not being suggested that leisure settings should have no regulations. However, programmers need to understand how regulations impinge on perceived freedom, and they must ensure that programs are not overregulated to the point that participants do not perceive freedom.

Well-written rules can foster perceived freedom. Rules that guide interactions create a known arena for interaction that fosters a perception of freedom for participants. For perceived freedom to emerge, structure for interaction must be present. Game rules, for example, create a known interactive structure in which some interactions are permitted and others are banned. Within the permitted range of interactions, game players have total freedom to act. With some actions banned by game rules, players have total freedom to engage in the other actions permitted.

> Rules that guide interactions create a known arena for interaction that fosters a perception of freedom for participants.

When rule structures are unclear or constantly changing, anxiety is introduced and perceived freedom is quashed. This point was made clear in an article one author was asked to referee. The author of the article had been a participant observer in a river float trip operated by a commercial outfitter. There were several rafts in the group, and each raft was skippered by an employee of the outfitter. Group members were required to change rafts daily; consequently, they also changed skippers each day. Each skipper had his own rules about how passengers were to sit in the raft when it was going over rapids, where passengers were to sit, how trash was to be disposed of, and so on. The net effect of this constant change was that the skippers, who were supposed to be providing patrons with a pleasant experience, were constantly at odds with them and badgering them about the proper way of doing things on "their" boat. The pleasure that would have been possible on the trip never fully emerged because of the constant badgering of patrons by the staff. In this case, requiring patrons to deal with rule changes daily interfered with their enjoyment of the event. The stable rule structure necessary for perceived freedom to emerge was never allowed to develop.

The structure format used to organize and operate a program is also one of its regulatory mechanisms. The programmer can use any one of several different structures to operate a program. For example, softball can be offered as an instructional workshop, a league, a tournament, or a special event. Farrell and Lundegren (1978) termed these organizing structures *program formats* and state that program format is the "basic structure through which an activity is presented" (p. 82). They identified five formats: (1) clinics, workshops, and classes; (2) tournaments; (3) clubs; (4) special events; and (5) open facilities (Farrell & Lundegren, 1978). In their second edition (Farrell & Lundegren, 1983), they renamed these five formats (1) education, (2) competition, (3) activity club, (4) performance or special event, and (5) open facility (p. 82). The U.S. Navy identified five similar formats: (1) open house, (2) special events, (3) skill development, (4) competition, and (5) clubs and groups. They also added to this list a sixth format: self-directed noncompetitive, which includes many of their rental and check-out services, through which the Navy Recreational Services unit simply provides equipment of various types to sailors.

Program formats are organizational rules that structure program services. When selecting a format, programmers are determining to some degree the satisfaction of a program patron while limiting the probability that other satisfactions will be realized (Rossman, 1984). When a format is selected, then, it influences to some degree the experience the patron has in the program. Program format is one of many rules that structures the social system of a program and influences the satisfaction of the patron.

Structure situates a social system in which interaction can occur. Programmers must provide enough structure so that a program takes the form intended and the desired interactions that make up the content of the program can occur. However, overregulating or unclear rules will impinge on the perceived freedom necessary for a true leisure experience to occur and will interfere with the experience desired by the patrons or intended by the program designer.

Relationships

Participants in a program may have a preexisting relationship that binds them to each other. People most frequently participate in leisure with family and friends. To design a program properly, the programmer needs to determine whether the participants have a relational history with each other. If indeed they do, the programmer needs to determine the nature of this history and assess its potential effect on the program being designed. If the interactants do not have a relational history, the programmer must determine whether it is necessary to develop a relationship between participants during the program. Mechanisms for accomplishing this include icebreakers, first-comer activities, and other social recreation activities that can be planned into the program design.

> Program format is one of many rules that will structure the social system of a program and influence the satisfaction the patron may experience.

However, the programmer may not need to create a relational history. Not all events require that those who attend know each other. Recreation personnel tend to force friendliness even when it is unnecessary. Forcing this issue often adds nothing to an event and may even detract from it. Individuals unknown to each other can co-experience many events without knowing the rest of the individuals who are participating. Bus trips to 1-day events are such an example. Often, preexisting small groups of two to five people will attend such an event, but it is not necessary for the programmer to implement a program mechanism that forces all 30 participants to get to know each other. In fact, doing so may keep individuals from having valued interaction time with their own small group and may lead to dissatisfaction with the event.

It is also important that the programmer does not design events in a way that could destroy relational histories that might otherwise contribute to a participant's satisfaction with an event. For example, at one university, demand for tickets to basketball games increased dramatically because of the team's excellent record. To promote open access to games, athletic department officials decreed that henceforth no one would be permitted to purchase more than 10 tickets at any one time. An unexpected outcry of protest arose against this policy. The athletic department had inadvertently destroyed the opportunity for friendship groups to attend ball games together. Many preexisting groups from fraternities, sororities, and dorms were larger than 10 individuals. Although in this instance the demand for tickets was so great that the policy could stand, the athletic department clearly did not consider the interactants' relational history, which contributed to their satisfaction with the event, when creating the operational policies. This decision worked to the overall detriment of participant satisfaction with the event.

Understanding the role that relationships play in interactions within a program and anticipating how they may contribute to or benefit from participant satisfaction is an important element of a situated activity system. Programmers cannot simply assume that the best course of action is always to foster or create relationships between individuals who attend an event.

Animation

Animation deals with how a program is set into motion and how the action is sustained throughout the program. To animate a program, the programmer must design its structure in such a way that spontaneous, natural movement is achieved. This can be accomplished in a number of ways. Obviously, providing a leader is one solution and a possible source of action that can move a program through time. How to plan and anticipate the scenario of action that will occur in a program is covered in more detail in Chapters 10 and 13. The process is analogous to action planning in other fields.

> Animation deals with how a program is set into motion and how the action is sustained throughout the program.

In theater, planning animation is known as "blocking." A director blocks a play by describing during rehearsals where each actor will be situated at each moment, how the actors are to move through each scene, and how and where they should focus their attention at each moment. In dance, determining the content and sequence of each movement is known as "choreographing." In sport, it is known as developing a "play."

In a similar way, to animate a program, the designer needs to anticipate how individuals will move through a program and how they will learn about the process and the timing of their movement. Additionally, programmers need to predict how the sequence of interactions that make up a program will unfold. The program designer must then provide sufficient structure and direction to animate the program so that participants will have the intended experience.

Providing a recreation leader who personally leads, and thereby animates, a program is one method for implementing animation. It is important for programmers to understand the role that a unique leader can play in a program. They will be unable to duplicate a program whose success depends on a uniquely skilled leader if they do not have another leader with similar skills. One of the authors observed this phenomenon in the production of a variety show. One agency sponsored an annual variety show modeled after the popular television program *The Gong Show*. The variety show was tremendously successful, but other agencies could not duplicate it because its success depended on a talented amateur comedian who was the emcee each year. The skills for emceeing the show accounted for a good deal of the success of the show. Other programmers failed to understand that unless they could duplicate this animation element of the program, they could not successfully duplicate the program, despite successfully duplicating the other five elements. The success of the variety show was primarily because of the unique manner in which a single individual animated the program.

> The designer needs to anticipate how individuals will move through a program and how they will learn about the process and the timing of their movement.

Understanding this notion of being an animator can clarify the role of individuals in drop-in operations. Too often, people employed to operate a facility see their role as simply opening the facility, regulating its use, and closing it at the appropriate time. They never understand that they are one of the six critical elements that will determine the success or failure of a leisure locale. The demeanor they use to greet, inform, and close each participant's experience will matter greatly to each participant.

Programs can often be animated without a leader. For example, for most Disneyland attractions, the program is animated with mechanical and electrical devices. The program moves forward through time whether the patron is ready or not! Self-guided tours are also animated without a leader through signs with instructions and arrows, recorded messages, and similar devices.

The amount of direction that programmers should provide in animating a program is somewhat problematic. Providing too much direction can interfere with an individual's perception of freedom and of being the cause of an act that is essential to intrinsic satisfaction. However, a lack of direction can be anxiety provoking and thereby produce dissatisfaction.

Animation not only involves the use of a leader, but is also a higher level concept that deals with moving the participant through a program. Providing a face-to-face leader is one way, but not the only way, of accomplishing this movement. The program designer must anticipate how to move the participant through a program and must put in place the devices necessary to implement this movement and ensure participants understand them.

The act of programming involves developing opportunities for leisure by designing (i.e., manipulating or creating) one or more of the six situating elements that structure a program. In developing programs, programmers must control these elements by creating them, manipulating them, or being aware of the circumstances created by any element they cannot control. They must then consider the circumstances of the uncontrolled element in their manipulations of the remaining elements. These six elements are the basic organizing framework around which programmers can develop all program services. All programs are simply variations of these elements. Now complete Exercise 3.1.

The Service Continuum

The amount of a service that is arranged and provided can vary from program to program. Many participants want to provide some of the elements of a program themselves. It is theoretically possible for the programmer to provide a program completely so that the participants do not need to do anything except attend the activity, event, or service. At Disneyland, for example, participants simply pay their admission fee and get on a ride. The provider does everything else. It is also possible that individuals do not need the programmer at all and can use a service without assistance from a programmer. We know that the majority of leisure occurs at home in self-organized activities. Although the theoretical extremes of this continuum involve unlikely circumstances (see the Addendum at the end of this chapter for an explanation of this point), the middle part of the continuum has some practical implications for program development. Specifically, how much of a program must a programmer provide, and how much may one reasonably expect the participant to provide?

Figure 3.1 (page 52) illustrates the service continuum. On the left end of the continuum are services that are totally provided by individuals in a program. When offering services in this mode, the agency is said to be operating in a *facilitator* role. On the right end of the continuum are program services that are totally provided by the agency. When offering services in this mode, the agency is said to be operating in a *direct provider* role. Where an individual program is located on the service continuum is a function of the ratio of agency-provided to participant-provided program elements.

The left column of the table below lists the six elements that situate a program. Assume you are to identify these elements for two Fourth of July special events. One is to operate on an Air Force base and the other at a nursing home. Complete the following tasks:

- Identify the key components for each element. What are the most defining characteristics for each element that will be present and that will need to be dealt with, or that should be present and thus will need to be created?
- Compare the two programs. What element(s) distinguish the difference(s) between the two programs?
- Discuss how the elements for either of the programs form a system for the program. If this is not apparent, consider the implications of operating either of the programs with the population for the other.

Six Elements	Air Force Base	Nursing Home
Interacting People		
Physical Setting		
Objects		
Structure (Rules and Program Format)		
Relationships		
Animation		

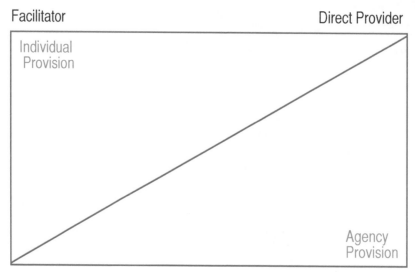

Facilitator   Direct Provider

Individual
Provision

Agency
Provision

Figure 3.1. The Service Continuum

Two major issues affect whether an agency will operate in a facilitator or direct provider role. One is cost. It is assumed that as one moves from being a facilitator to a direct provider, costs increase. Although this is not true in every case, it is generally true. Being a direct provider of all leisure services in a community would be prohibitively expensive. Allowing the participants to provide part or all of the elements of program service is less expensive for the agency.

The second major issue is the relative importance to the participant that they play a role in developing and providing the leisure service. Some individuals want a completely packaged service, while others want to perform a major role in designing, planning, and operating a leisure experience. For example, outdoor recreation outfitters successfully market two kinds of services: trips complete with a guide plus an itinerary or simply outfitting groups with equipment for a specified time. In the latter case, the participants design and stage the entire program except for the equipment.

Between the extremes, many organizational formats require varying degrees of effort from the individual and the agency. The six organizational formats discussed are placed on the service continuum in Figure 3.2. This figure illustrates that any activity may be operated in a variety of program formats that require varying degrees of agency and individual input into the program. From left to right on the continuum, the agency assumes an increasing role in developing and operating the program, while the individual assumes a lesser role.

Which type of service an agency will develop depends on the type of agency one is in and the philosophy, role, and mission of the agency. Some agencies offer only one type of service. Most comprehensive agencies offer multiple types of program formats to give patrons flexibility. Now complete Exercise 3.2.

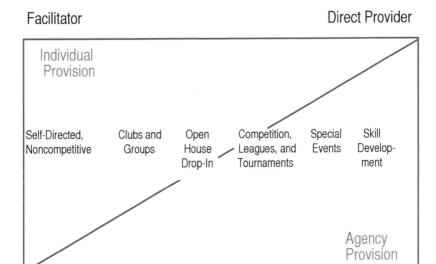

Figure 3.2. The Service Continuum With Programming Formats

Directions: Select three activities, such as yoga, guitar playing, or chess, and provide examples of how each activity could be operated in six formats, using each of the formats included in the table below. Note the creative writing activity as an example.

Programming Formats:

Activity	Clubs & Groups	Open Facility	Competition, Leagues, & Tournaments	Special Events	Skill Development
Creative Writing	Writing Club	Use of Computer Lab	Poetry Slam	Short Story Contest	Humorous Writing Class

Conclusion

Leisure occurs in a situated activity system that is made up of six interrelated elements. The act of programming involves anticipating the configuration of each of the six elements within each encounter of a program, accommodating or manipulating the elements of these configurations, anticipating the sequence of encounters that will make up the program, and anticipating the shifting importance that each element will assume as the program moves through time. Because these six elements situate a program and constitute its structure, they are all that the programmer needs to control, or can control, when designing a program. These elements are of such fundamental importance that if one of them is changed, the program also changes. Programmers need to be able to analyze their programs using these elements and to determine which element or combination of elements is central to the success of an individual program. To create, manipulate, or duplicate a program requires this level of understanding. Programmers can develop program services that require varying degrees of design input and operational effort from the agency and the individual participant.

References

Crompton, J. (1983). Selecting target markets—A key to effective marketing. *Journal of Park and Recreation Administration, 1*(1), 7–26.

Denzin, N. K. (1975). Play, games, and interaction: The contexts of childhood socialization. *Sociological Quarterly, 16*, 458–478.

Driver, B. L., & Brown, P. J. (1975). A socio-psychological definition of recreation demand, with implications for recreation resource planning. In Committee on Assessment of Demand for Outdoor Recreation Resources, Assembly of Behavioral and Social Sciences, National Research Council, National Academy of Sciences, *Assessing demand for outdoor recreation* (pp. 64–88). Washington, DC: U.S. Government Printing Office.

Farrell, P., & Lundegren, H. M. (1978). *The process of recreation programming.* State College, PA: Venture.

Farrell, P., & Lundegren, H. M. (1983). *The process of recreation programming: Theory and technique* (2nd ed.). New York, NY: Wiley.

Howard, D. R., & Crompton, J. L. (1980). *Financing, managing, and marketing recreation and park resources.* Dubuque, IA: Wm. C. Brown.

Murphy, J. F., Williams, J. G., Niepoth, W. E., & Brown, P. D. (1973). *Leisure service delivery systems: A modern perspective.* Philadelphia, PA: Lea and Febiger.

Patterson, F. C. (1991). *A systems approach to recreation programming.* Prospect Heights, IL: Waveland Press.

Pfeffer, J., & Salancik, G. R. (1978). *The external control of organizations: A resource dependence perspective.* New York, NY: Harper and Row.

Rossman, J. R. (1984). Influence of program format choice on participant satisfaction. *Journal of Park and Recreation Administration, 2*(1), 39–51.

Stewart, W. P. (1998). Leisure as multi-phase experiences: Challenging tradition. *Journal of Leisure Research, 30*, 391–400.

WGBH Educational Foundation. (2001). Life span development [Activity for video series *Discovering Psychology*]. Retrieved from http://www.learner.org/series/discoveringpsychology/development/dev_nonflash.html

Addendum

The two extremes of the service continuum are theoretical points. On the left side, where individuals provide the entire program for themselves, there is no need for the programmer at all. This point is on the continuum only as a point of reference to illustrate program formats that require the participant to be involved in the design and delivery of the program.

The right end of the continuum, which illustrates programs in which the participant has no role, is also a theoretical point. As discussed, the leisure experience always requires the participant to be active in the construction of the experience. At a minimum, the participant must take in and interpret the meaning of the sensory stimuli provided. Leisure is not something that is done to individuals, but rather something that they play a role in constructing. What the right end of the service continuum illustrates, then, are those programs designed and operated wholly by a programmer.

Family Fun Fest (Special Family Event at Chickahominy Riverfront Park)
Courtesy James City County Parks and Recreation. Scott Brown Photography.

4 Developing Leisure Products in the Experience Economy

KEY TERMS

Experience Economy, Experience, Commodities, Entrepreneurial, Revenue Stream, Product, Goods, Services, Activity Classifications, Activities, Events, Personal Service, Supplies, Equipment, Venue

The introduction of *The Experience Economy* (Pine & Gilmore, 1999) has created great interest in programming and staging experiences throughout many sectors of the economy beyond leisure-experience-producing organizations. Conventional wisdom among leisure providers was that we were in the service sector of the economy. Although we will continue to provide services, staging experience is the next stage in the progress of economic value (Schmitt, 1999). This development demands that we reexamine what business we are in. This chapter details what this has to do with recreation programming and developing leisure products.

Today, economists classify economic value into four sectors, as outlined in Table 4.1. Each economic value sector provides a specific economic activity, which is also included in the table. These activities follow the historical development of economic activity, but each continues today. The portion of overall economic activity each represents has shifted over time. For example, humans' first economic endeavor was extracting, principally mining and agriculture (i.e., harvesting activities). A great shift of human endeavor occurred when people became so proficient at farming that fewer individuals were needed to produce sufficient food. In about 1850, the Industrial Revolution occurred and there was a great migration of population from rural to urban areas. This was accompanied by a shift in how individuals participated in the economy—people now worked in factories and produced manufactured goods. Another shift occurred in about 1980, when delivering services became 50% or more of the gross national product. This shift to a service economy created great economic upheaval, with many service jobs paying less than established manufacturing jobs. Nevertheless, as manufacturing became more efficient, fewer people were needed to work in this sector of the economy, and many workers were relocated into providing services. At the beginning of the 21st century, many became convinced that we are moving into the experience economy (Pine & Gilmore, 1999) wherein commodities, goods, and services are most successfully sold when they are marketed as contributing to experiences. In the title to their book, Pine and Gilmore (1999) claim *Work Is Theatre and Every Business a Stage*.

Table 4.1

Evolution of Economic Value and Activity

Principal Economic Activity	Economic Value Created
Extracting	Commodities
Manufacturing	Goods
Delivering	Services
Staging	Experiences

Note. Adapted from Pine and Gilmore (1999).

Although commodities were traditionally thought of as mining and agricultural products, today the term *commoditized* is applied as a pejorative term—a state of affairs to be avoided. Companies do not want their products to be considered commodities, because commodities compete solely on price, not on other product features. According to Shaw and Ivens (2005), "For the first time in centuries, differentiation on price, quality, and delivery is an unsustainable business strategy" (p. xix). Commodities (e.g., iron ore) have always had this characteristic. For the most part, iron ore is iron ore. It shows little product differentiation and therefore competes solely on price. However, as manufacturing processes improve, many manufactured goods are similar and of high quality, with less product differentiation on product features alone. In a similar way, the service economy has struggled to differentiate its products. Until using these products, customers may not understand differences between services. Thus, not only are commodities commoditized, but also many products and services. Competition for customers has shifted to the customer's experience with a product or service. Shaw and Ivens asserted, "The customer experience is the next competitive battleground" (p. xix).

These experiences have several implications for programming. First, many other providers will now be developing experiences; we will have additional competition for our patron's attention. Second, new concepts about how to think about and develop programs are being introduced. For example, Pine and Gilmore (1999) use the theatrical metaphor of "staging" programs, and we have incorporated this concept in this text as appropriate. Third, the attributes of the leisure experience that we put forth describe the ultimate experience to be developed. Leisure is a "gold standard" experience, and we know how to stage it. Fourth, consumers prefer to spend their resources on services and experiences rather than on commodities and goods. Services and experiences are higher-valued economic ends. The success of mass retailers such as Walmart, where goods can be purchased at a very low cost, suggest that people prefer to acquire goods at the least cost possible to free up personal assets to spend on services and experiences. Fifth, and perhaps most important, the programs we have produced for years—leisure experiences—are now a category of economic activity. Since the entire economy is shifting to providing experiences as an important economic end, surely we will not need to continually spend time justifying providing experiences!

Some have argued that experience is not a separate sector of the economy but a variant of the service sector. We believe that it is fundamentally different. A service is a set of intangible activities carried out on the customer's behalf (Pine & Gilmore, 1999). For example, when we organize a trip for individuals, they are freed from the burden of doing it themselves. Experiences, however, are a set of events staged to engage the customer in a memorable way (Pine & Gilmore, 1999). They are created through interaction and result in pleasant memories to be recalled in the future. This notion of engagement and participation by the participant in creating the experience separates a service from an experience, a concept we have termed *co-production*. Engagement is a well-known phenomenon to recreation and leisure programmers, as we have been focusing on operationalizing engagement for the past 30 years.

Providing leisure experiences places us primarily in the experience sector of the economy, although we also provide services, and in some cases, we market goods. Today, employment opportunities go beyond public parks and recreation or youth-serving agencies for students who complete programs in which they learn to design, stage, and evaluate experiences. Leisure experiences are one of the most difficult experiences to stage because of their emergent, co-produced nature. But, for those who can stage them, their competencies should enable them to deliver other types of experiences as well. There is a brief mention of experience marketing in Chapter 2. Do not sell yourself or your knowledge, skills, and abilities short.

One difference is that programmers in hospitality, event management, tourism, and commercial recreation are expected to be entrepreneurial employees in these emerging experience industries. Additionally, employees in traditional leisure provision organizations are also expected to be more entrepreneurial. They meet this responsibility by developing a variety of products that Kelly (1985) defined as "something that is designed, made, developed, and distributed" (p. 342). Programmers are responsible for developing marketable leisure experience products that will attract a participant base and provide adequate revenue streams. *A revenue stream is the income generated by a product that can be brought to the marketplace and sold. Ultimately, the financial objectives of the organization must be met or it will cease to exist.*

> Programmers in hospitality, event management, tourism, and commercial recreation are expected to be entrepreneurial employees.

Leisure Products

As the previous section discussed, all products can be classified as commodities, goods, services, or experiences. *Product is the inclusive term that identifies commodities, goods, services, and experiences that may be brought to the marketplace and sold for use in leisure.*

Commodities are not offered as recreation and leisure products. However, the other three are offered. A *good* is tangible; an individual has something in his or her possession after its purchase. For example, tennis racquets, suntan oil, and jet skis are goods sold in the leisure market. A *service* is intangible. It involves an activity being carried out on the customer's behalf, but the customer does not possess a physical item as a result of the purchase. A typical leisure service would be regripping golf clubs. *Experiences* involve engaging participants in a series of staged encounters that result in reflective, pleasant memories. A memorable vacation to an exotic island, participation in a leisure education program, or participation in a peak experience can be part of an individual's consciousness for many years.

Goods

Goods are physical entities marketed for use in leisure. The two types of goods are supplies and equipment. They can range in cost from a $1.00 table tennis ball to expensive ski equipment and are provided by a wide range of manufacturers and retailers. Table 4.2 presents examples of each type of goods for two activities.

Table 4.2

Types of Products

Product Type	Activity	
	Tennis	**Shooting**
Goods		
Supplies	Balls, rosin	Gun powder, bullets, targets
Equipment	Racquets, clothes, and shoes	Guns, ear protectors, eye guards
Services	Stringing racquets	Loading shells
	Scheduling and renting court time	Selling time on a shooting range
Experiences	Tournaments	Instructions on gun safety and shooting
	Fantasy camp	Hunting trip

Supplies. *Supplies are consumable products used by participants while participating in leisure occasions.* Because they are consumed and thus need to be continually replenished by participants, sales for supplies represent an ongoing source of income for the agency.

Selling supplies at or near the point of use is usually a lucrative source of revenue for leisure service agencies. In most cases, supplies offered at these locations are sold at a premium price because the demand for them at these locations is inelastic. This means that within a range of prices, the supplies will be purchased regardless of price and that demand is not reduced by price. For example, after a difficult hike to the rim of the Grand Canyon, a hiker is not likely to run the risk of dehydration and will buy bottled water on-site that costs $3.50 instead of $0.99 at Walmart. This is price inelasticity.

Many supplies for participating in leisure can be provided on-site at premium prices. In addition to the supplies for participating in the activity, a considerable market exists in associated merchandise such as food, beverages, and souvenirs. Today, entrepreneurial programmers use the general principle of providing the supplies that facilitate participation in a leisure activity at a point close to use, and they use these sales as an additional revenue stream to support the agency.

Equipment. *Equipment is a nonconsumable product for participating in leisure.* The sale of equipment is a potential source of revenue for a leisure service agency, but the equipment inventory will not turn over as frequently as the supply inventory. Examples of equipment include fishing rods and reels, ballet shoes, scuba equipment, and golf clubs. Leisure service agencies sell equipment in a variety of settings. Commercial operations almost always have a pro shop or other retail outlet to sell equipment associated with the activity offered in the facility.

Sport and leisure equipment retailing is undergoing a polarization. Large sport equipment megastores sit at one end of the retailing spectrum, along with e-sales. They offer primarily a low price and use few or no knowledgeable clerks to assist customers. The other end of the retailing spectrum includes small specialty shops with higher prices and knowledgeable sales staff. Any agency deciding to retail sport and leisure equipment will need to consider the local market and how it will position its retail operation relative to existing outlets. Regardless of the retailing strategy, equipment sales can also be an important revenue stream for an agency.

Services

Two types of services may be developed for leisure markets: personal services, and equipment and venue rentals. All can be offered at multiple sites in many formats.

Personal services. *A personal service is a helpful function related to leisure participation for which a fee is charged.* Often, customers could complete these functions, but for some reason, such as the lack of time, skill, or specialized equipment, they cannot or prefer not to perform them. Instead, they choose to hire someone to perform them. For example, stringing a tennis racquet requires a special machine and some skill at using it. The cost of the machine and the time put into developing the skill make it impractical and uneconomical for most to string their own racquets. In contrast to this, many fly fishermen would not consider using a fly they had not tied themselves, even though pretied ties are readily available in the marketplace. Scraping and varnishing a boat is a difficult but manageable job that does not take specialized skill, just hard work. Some hire individuals to perform this service, whereas others perform it themselves. A person can hunt game without a guide, but a guide will usually have intimate knowledge of an area and know the recent migration patterns of the game being hunted. Thus, they offer for sale unique access to the experience sought. This last example illustrates how indiscrete these categories can be. A good guide can turn a service into a memorable experience if their work is well organized and they engage the participant in an appropriate manner that allows them to participate in the evolving action of the event.

Myriad services associated with leisure participation can be organized and offered for sale. Recognizing and developing these services into revenue streams is an important skill for programmers. These additional examples of personal services supporting leisure participation could be sold:

- sale of tickets with point-of-sale convenience provided for a surcharge;
- rental of on-site storage lockers;
- sale of guide services;
- retail sales at point-of-need or -participation—for example, the sale of bottled water at the Grand Canyon;
- repair service—ski repair offered at the base of a ski slope;
- maintenance services—racquet stringing, skate sharpening, and so on;
- Activity service amenities—fish-cleaning services offered at a boat dock, or golf caddies; and
- personal amenities—a masseuse in a fitness club or a locker room attendant who provides toiletry articles and warm towels.

THE SERVICE ENCOUNTER

Regardless of the type of service being offered, how it is offered matters. The service encounter refers to the sum of face-to-face interactions between the patron and provider in the delivery of a service and the emotional feelings generated by these interactions. The outcomes of these interactions endure through the recalled memories of the encounters, and these memories are the enduring product of the service encounter.

Training employees to deliver good service encounters is a major part of a programmer's job. The programmer prepares employees to deliver good service in three steps:

- Lead by example and deliver the good service you expect of your employees.

- Train new employees to deliver good service by outlining expectations, role-playing service encounter episodes, and providing on-the-job supervision and tutoring to further develop employees' skills.

- Reinforce training and establish good service by providing ongoing, supportive supervision and rewarding good service delivery.

What is a good service encounter? What should employees strive for in delivering good service? As our economy has moved from a production to a service economy, these are major questions perplexing all organizations. Because of its importance, much research and writing has occurred on this topic. Distilled from this research, here are our recommendations about the most desired features of a good service encounter:

- Speedy, Prompt Service. After presenting themselves to be served, people expect to receive service promptly. How long is too long varies by individual and the service situation. But we all have a sense of how long is too long to wait for recognition by a server in a sit-down restaurant, and similarly, we have a notion of an appropriate wait time in a variety of service situations. Waiting too long for service or having a service encounter take too long results in unsatisfied patrons.

- Efficient, Effective Service. That staff are prepared to get it right the first time matters greatly. Not having answers to reasonable questions and not having or completing the correct forms are seen as product defects in a service encounter. Patrons expect to have their business completed when they leave the service encounter.

- Friendly, Authentic Service. For some individuals, friendliness is the benchmark of good service; for others, it is promptness and effectiveness. The best encounters have a feel of authentic interaction and caring that result from the demeanor of service staff toward the patron. As part of this general concept, patrons expect to be treated with civility, with courtesy, and in a friendly manner. Expressing genuine caring and empathy for patrons' needs is also important.

There are cultural differences in how patrons view a service encounter. Some age groups and cultures expect to be treated with appropriate role distance, formality, and deference. For example, it is unlikely that a senior citizen will find it friendly for a teenage employee to refer to them by their nickname. Thus, one-size-fits-all training may not work well in a heterogeneous, diverse community.

In other situations, friendliness of the staff is an essential part of the service. For example, the atmosphere created by staff in a health club is an essential, signature feature of health clubs and other membership operations.

Thus, programmers need to understand the role and function of the service encounters that they are preparing staff to deliver, and they need to ensure that staff have appropriate training and authority to meet the expectations of patrons.

When these services are examined in this manner, it becomes apparent that the programmer has many opportunities to develop a variety of complementary services that can expand current product lines. These activities will help make their units a revenue contributor to the leisure service enterprise employing them.

Equipment and venue rentals. *An important service that is often provided is the rental of recreation and leisure equipment and venue space.* Customers may desire to rent equipment for many reasons. If they are beginners, they may be simply exploring the activity and will not want to invest in equipment until they are certain of their future participation. Some will rent different types of equipment to try it out. Others will rent equipment on-site because it is too bulky to bring to the recreation area. For example, scuba divers almost always rent air tanks and weights, although they may bring the rest of their gear to a dive site. Renting equipment at an initial low cost of investment is a significant way that leisure service agencies help individuals experiment with and learn about recreation and leisure activities. Equipment rentals can be an important revenue stream for many recreation and leisure facilities.

> Venues are locales used to stage leisure experiences.

Venues are locales used to stage leisure experiences. They include buildings, special facilities, and park areas. Some activities require a specific, dedicated facility, whereas others can use a more general facility. The provision of venues for leisure is a major role for leisure service agencies. Some venues are owned by individuals (e.g., a swimming pool), which makes them a good. Most often, because of high cost and relatively infrequent use, specialized leisure venues offer access through paid admission. Individuals essentially rent time in a venue, and providing these venues is an important service of leisure services agencies. The revenue from renting leisure venues is an important revenue stream to many agencies.

Leisure service agencies can charge fees for the use of leisure venues in many ways. How these sales contribute to an agency's revenue varies by the type of agency. No single agency offers every type of venue. The same venue may have many financial arrangements. For example, water play facilities are operated under every conceivable financial arrangement, including public and private beaches at salt and freshwater locations, free public pools, member-only private pool clubs, commercial water parks, and privately owned home pools.

The provision of recreation facilities is undertaken by all four types of leisure service agencies. The public leisure system offers many recreation venues on a no-cost basis, although it is not uncommon for these systems to charge for expensive, newly constructed, specialized facilities. In general, the public system limits its facilities to those that are relatively inexpensive to build and that serve a large number of people. They typically provide baseball, football, hockey, softball, and soccer fields; tennis, volleyball, and basketball courts; swimming pools, beaches, and marinas; and golf courses. The public system has the primary responsibility for providing a community's open space, which positions it as the major provider of recreation and leisure play space. Leisure service agencies in larger cities also provide cultural and educational amenities, such as zoos, museums, and aquariums, plus regional facilities, such as arboretums and spectator sport stadiums.

Rental of specialized leisure facilities is often the major source of earned income for many commercial leisure service agencies. For example, an indoor tennis facility obtains a significant amount of its income from the rental of court space, that is, the sale of access to leisure space. Crossley (1990) outlined how providers of commercial facilities and retailers of supplies and equipment can use multitier programs to expand their revenue streams. Additionally, complementary revenue streams in such a facility could include the sale of instructions, pro shop sales, nursery services, and an annual membership fee.

Commercial, not-for-profit, and private leisure service agencies operate a variety of leisure facilities. Occasionally, their facilities will duplicate those provided by the public system, in which case they market additional value-added features not included in public facilities, such as easier access and nicer amenities. In other cases, they build specialized or expensive facilities that could not be justified with public expenditures. Not-for-profit agencies, such as YMCAs, also sell access to recreation facilities and space as a major source of revenue. Private associations are frequently formed to build a specific facility for members, for example, a private country club offering golf, swimming, and a club house with dining and a cocktail lounge.

Experiences

Experiences are a series of staged events that engage a participant and result in pleasant, recallable memories. Kelly (2013) explained nine phenomena that make leisure businesses different from others; *that no one has to do it* and that *leisure is an experience* are two of the nine (pp. 1–9). Leisure experiences occur through engaged interaction in a situated activity system, as has been explained in Chapters 2 and 3. They are the principal unique product of leisure service provision, and knowledge about staging experiences to facilitate leisure is the unique professional expertise of the programmer. Two major types of leisure experiences offered are activities and events.

Activities. An activity is focused participation in a specific occasion of interaction, for example, baseball with specific objects of interaction, rules, and physical spaces. Activities are the basic unit of participation in leisure and recreation; therefore, they are the primary unit that may be packaged for sale. Individuals usually participate in activities with family or friends. Thus, the programmer often markets activities to networks of peers rather than to individuals unknown to each other.

A wide variety of activities are considered leisure. Some are enduring and have continued to attract a significant number of participants for many years (e.g., swimming, walking, softball, and other sports). Yet other activities, such as snowmobiling and oil painting, attract a smaller number of intensely interested individuals. Skateboarding and paintball battles are examples of activities with growing participation.

> An activity is focused participation in a specific occasion of interaction.

The leisure service manager is left with the problem of determining which activities to offer initially and then which to develop further. Unfortunately, some activities require expensive facilities, and one is always left with the dilemma that

Table 4.3

Activity Classifications

Arts:
• Performing; music, dance, drama
• Visual; crafts
• New arts (technology-based arts such as computer graphics)
Cognitive and literary activities
Self-improvement/education
Sports, games, and athletics
Aquatics
Environmental activities; outdoor recreation, risk recreation
Wellness and fitness
Hobbies, social recreation
Volunteer services
Travel and tourism

interest may wane before the investment capital for building a specialized facility is recovered. Table 4.3 presents a typology of activity classes, developed from classifications published by Edginton, Hanson, and Edginton (1992), Farrell and Lundegren (1991), and DeGraaf, Jordan, and DeGraaf (1999), which may help the reader understand the breadth of possible activities.

It is generally considered good practice for municipal leisure service agencies to offer a comprehensive inventory of activity classes to afford the largest number of citizens opportunities to participate. However, many leisure service organizations offer only one class or type of activity, for example, a tennis club or a country club. Now complete Exercise 4.1.

To provide comprehensive services that are in demand, programmers must keep abreast of popular interest in a breadth of activities. Additionally, they must understand how activities can be delivered as a product that can attract participants. Programmers can use these six methods of selling activities to create revenue streams:

1. **Selling instruction in the activity.** Sales can be segmented by level of ability, including beginner, novice, advanced, refresher courses, and improvement workshops. Sales can be further segmented by how the instructional program is organized. For example, an agency could offer the same activity as a 6-week class, a weekend clinic, or a 1-day workshop.

2. **Renting equipment needed to participate in the activity.** (This is discussed in more detail in the Goods section.)

3. **Charging admission to unique space needed to participate in the activity.** For example, fees for rounds of golf, rental of tennis courts, and the signing of hunting leases, all of these involve charging for access to unique and sometimes expensive leisure space.

4. **Selling equipment needed to participate in an activity.** Pro shops at a golf course, for example, sell recreation and sport equipment needed for participation.

5. **Charging for organizing and arranging participation in an activity,** for example, trips and tours, or providing unique access, for example, an organized boat tour to scuba dive specific sites.

6. **Selling needed ancillary supplies** such as food, water, and lodging, while participating in an activity. For example, a major portion of travel and tourism dollars is spent on food, lodging, and transportation, not on the amenities that motivate individuals to take the trip in the first place.

The programmer must take a strategic approach to marketing and matching activities to specific networks of interested individuals. Often, programmers spend too many resources trying to attract new participants to an activity, when their best marketing strategy would be to increase the usage of infrequent users. For example, Warnick and Howard (1996) documented that golf and tennis appeal to small cohorts of the population: "Eighty-eight percent of the adult population reported never playing even one round of golf during 1999, while tennis had an even narrower appeal, with 93% indicating never playing the sport at any time during the same period" (p. 74). They further explained that about 2% of the population accounts for approximately 75% of play in each sport.

Thus, the wise programmer spends more effort on retaining current customers and trying to move those with infrequent and moderate rates of play to more frequent participation. Expanding product lines to encourage more play is one good strategy. For example, although an agency already offers participants the opportunity to play in softball leagues, it may increase sales of this product by expanding the ways it

> The wise programmer spends more effort on retaining current customers and trying to move those with infrequent and moderate rates of play to more frequent participation.

is packaged for sale. Consider the ideas included in Table 4.4 for expanding the softball product line.

Table 4.4
Expanding the Softball Product Line

Idea	Description
Softball tournaments	Weekend or weeklong.
Softball weekend getaway	A tournament is offered at a camp and all players stay in the camp's dorms, eat meals together, have skills improvement clinics, and so on.
Softball fantasy camp	A weekend or weeklong camp of softball with instruction, play, video-taping of each player, and so on.
Softball equipment pro shop	Sell a range of softball equipment at a variety of price points.
Softball skills improvement clinic	With professional players as a lead draw.
Softball diamond rental	Rent your softball diamonds for practice.

In a similar fashion, the programmer needs to continually scan other activities that are offered, for ways to expand these product lines by increasing or expanding participation and thereby increasing revenues. Now complete Exercise 4.2.

Events. Events are a collection of activities usually organized around a theme or purpose. They may become a special event if there is something unique to them. Leisure service managers are responsible for conceptualizing, organizing, and staging desirable leisure activities and events so they may be sold to create a revenue base. Their duration can vary, but five typical formats are presented in Table 4.5. Events are financed in different ways.

> Events are a collection of activities usually organized around a theme or purpose.

For example, a parade may be operated with no charge to spectators. In this case, organizations that have entries in the parade will finance the event and perhaps pay an entry fee. The parade organizers may also receive in-kind services from the city government for police to maintain crowds and control traffic. Another possible arrangement involves paying for these services with profits from entry fees or other activities offered in an accompanying festival or other event.

Exercise 4.2.
Creating Revenue Streams

A new commercial recreation business, Fly Fishers Unlimited, desires to create revenue streams for the sport of fly-fishing. The venue for Fly Fishers Unlimited is along a wild and scenic river, 2 hours from a major metropolitan center.

Use the six methods of selling to brainstorm possible revenue streams for this business. It is not necessary for the reader to be an expert fly fisher to do this exercise. Rather, it is more important that the reader begin to develop the ability to consider the potential revenue streams in a variety of activity areas.

Table 4.5

Formats of Events

Format	Example
Less than 1 day	A parade
1 day	A health fair, clinic, or workshop
Weekend	A weekend softball tournament
1 week	County fair
1 month	A community's centennial celebration

The organization and operation of events can be specialized. For example, Table 4.6 includes 10 events that could be operated for motorcycle enthusiasts by managers of large park areas or private landowners. This list is presented as an example of the wide variety and specialization of events that can be organized and sold.

Table 4.6

Off-Road Vehicle Events

Event	Description
Enduro	An endurance event.
Grand Prix	An event operated to see who can complete the course in the shortest time.
Hare and Hound	Operated on a marked course over natural terrain with a mass, dead-engine start.
Hare Scrambles	Similar to Hare and Hound but operated over a closed course, usually as a multilapped race.
Scrambles	Held on a relatively short prepared course with left and right turns, hills, and usually a few jumps.
Hill Climb	A short race to see who can make it to the top of a very steep hill first.
Ice	Operated on ice-covered courses up to a half-mile long, with classes for studded and nonstudded tires.
Motocross	Usually operated on a relatively small course, entirely visible from one location by a group of paying spectators. Raced on a dirt track with various combinations of tight turns, jumps, and a few other obstacles, such as a water jump. Individual heats usually last 20–45 minutes and have 20–30 riders.
Observed Trails	This event challenges a motorcycle rider's balance and finesse and involves negotiating a prescribed course of significant obstacles.
Trail Rides	Strictly fun rides with no timekeeping or racing.

Note. From Motorcycle Industry Council (1992–1993).

Off-road vehicle events have many possible revenue streams, including entrance fees for contestants, spectator admission fees, pit/garage fees, concession sales, souvenir sales, and parking fees. It is especially important for the programmer to plan many free activities during large events; these draw a crowd and thereby create a critical mass of customers. However, the programmer must provide enough revenue-producing activities to support the non-revenue-producing activities.

Most large special events operated today must have additional financial support from corporate sponsors (Schmader & Jackson, 1997). To obtain this support, the leisure service manager will need to offer benefits to the sponsor. Schmader and Jackson (1997) identified 10 factors that corporations look for in an event (Table 4.7).

Table 4.7
Top 10 Factors Corporate Sponsors Look for in an Event

1.	Total audience
2.	Sponsor service/follow-through
3.	Sponsorship fee
4.	Other sponsors
5.	Name in the event title
6.	Event history/success
7.	Right of first refusal
8.	Signage
9.	Media coverage
10.	Category exclusivity

Note. From Schmader and Jackson (1997).

Experience marketing is another form of events being currently offered, as discussed in Chapter 2. Participation in these events is often free, as the costs are being paid by the company whose products are being introduced, touted, or used. The use of a company's brands and products in a leisure experience is often the main engagement of these events.

Frequently, leisure service managers in not-for-profit, governmental, and private agencies will also organize and operate fund-raising events that are not leisure programs but whose purpose is to finance leisure programs that cannot be operated on a complete cost recovery basis (Busser, 1990). For example, all-community garage sales, bake sales, and car washes may be offered.

Conclusion

Programmers in all agencies are expected to be entrepreneurial. To accomplish this, they need to understand the business we are in, the breadth of leisure products that may be developed, and their market value. This chapter discussed many ideas for packaging these products and bringing them to the marketplace for sale. The successful entrepreneurial programmer will provide a comprehensive set of leisure products that fully serve the agency's target population and earn sufficient revenues to meet the financial goals of the agency.

References

Busser, J. A. (1990). *Programming: For employee services and recreation.* Champaign, IL: Sagamore.

Crossley, J. (1990, March). Multi-tier programming in commercial recreation. *Parks and Recreation, 1990,* 68–72.

DeGraaf, D., Jordan, D. J., & DeGraaf, K. H. (1999). *Programming for park, recreation, and leisure services: A servant leadership approach.* College Station, PA: Venture.

Edginton, C. R., Hanson, C. J., & Edginton, S. R. (1992). *Leisure programming: Concepts, trends, and professional practice.* Dubuque, IA: WCB Brown and Benchmark.

Farrell, P., & Lundegren, H. M. (1991). *The process of recreation programming: Theory and technique* (3rd ed.). State College, PA: Venture.

Kelly, J. R. (1985). *Recreation business.* New York, NY: John Wiley and Sons.

Kelly, J. R. (2013). *Leisure business strategies: What they don't teach you in business schools.* Urbana, IL: Sagamore.

Motorcycle Industry Council. (1992–1993, Winter). Types of OHV events. In *The OHV planner* (pp. 1, 4). Irvine, CA: Author.

Pine, B. J., II, & Gilmore, J. H. (1999). *The experience economy: Work is theatre and every business a stage*. Boston, MA: Harvard Business School Press.

Schmader, S. W., & Jackson, R. (1997). *Special events: Inside and out* (2nd ed.). Urbana, IL: Sagamore.

Schmitt, B. H. (1999). *Experiential marketing*. New York, NY: Free Press.

Shaw, C., & Ivens, J. (2005). *Building great customer experiences*. New York, NY: Palgrave Macmillan.

Warnick, R. B., & Howard, D. R. (1996). Market share analysis of selected sport and recreation activities: An update—1972 to 1992. *Journal of Park and Recreation Administration, 14*(2), 53–79.

Mountain Biking
Photo courtesy of Boise Parks and Recreation.

5 *Collaborating in Developing an Organization's Strategy*

KEY TERMS

Strategic Directions, Forward-Thinking, Rationality, Metrics, MBO, SMART, Hierarchical Arrangement, Staff Collaboration

Programmers design and stage programs in an organization, and the mission of that organization will, in part, determine the programs operated. To allocate the organization's resources efficiently and effectively, programmers expend great effort when developing an organizational strategy for implementing programs.

In some organizations, the products or services partially provide a strategy for the organization. For example, Ford Motor Company produces automobiles and pick-up trucks. Although there is a great range of automobiles and trucks that can be produced, Ford is given some organizational focus and strategy because they are producing automobiles and pick-up trucks. The general product line of leisure services, by comparison, is much broader. No organization can offer the entire spectrum of leisure programs available. From this wide assortment of programs, the organization will need to narrow its offerings. The process of narrowing the range of programs to be offered and developing a strategy for their delivery involves determining the strategic programming direction of the organization.

Developing an organization's strategic direction should have the attention of all levels of the organization from the policy-making board through first-line program managers and leaders. Collaboratively developing a strategic direction across all levels of an organization helps ensure coordination throughout, thereby ensuring unity of purpose in the organization and that all efforts are accomplishing the mission of the organization. Good practice in developing the strategic direction of the organization requires integrating strategic planning with operations management.

Strategic direction is developed at four integrated but distinct organizational levels, illustrated in Figure 5.1 (page 75). Managers at each level of the organization have specific roles to fulfill to execute this process, and several types of statements must be developed for the development of a fully integrated strategy for the organization. This chapter comments on each of these, and future chapters discuss them more fully. Now complete Exercise 5.1.

Four Management Levels

The first task is to develop the mission of the organization. The organization's governing board and top-level managers develop the mission. Although these individuals write and approve the mission, they are well advised to seek input from the organization's constituency or market and other staff members when formulating it.

From the mission, statements of strategic direction, 3- to 5-year planning statements, are developed. These are statements of intended future accomplishments for implementing the mission. Top- and mid-level staff, with consultation of other staff, usually develop these statements and present them to a policy-making board for approval.

Staff document and assume accomplishment of each strategic direction when management by objectives (MBO) statements developed for them have been implemented and accomplished. Mid-level managers usually develop these, and these statements usually accompany budget development. MBO statements are written in measurable language, as are all other statements used in further defining the strategy

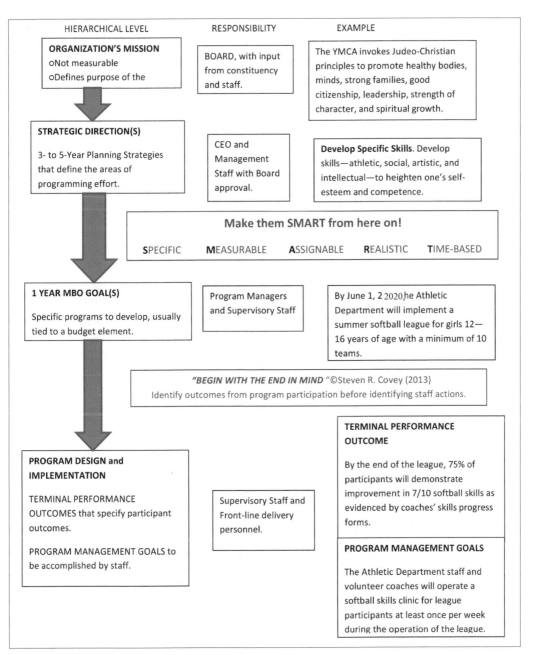

HIERARCHICAL LEVEL	RESPONSIBILITY	EXAMPLE
ORGANIZATION'S MISSION ○Not measurable ○Defines purpose of the	BOARD, with input from constituency and staff.	The YMCA invokes Judeo-Christian principles to promote healthy bodies, minds, strong families, good citizenship, leadership, strength of character, and spiritual growth.
STRATEGIC DIRECTION(S) 3- to 5-Year Planning Strategies that define the areas of programming effort.	CEO and Management Staff with Board approval.	**Develop Specific Skills**. Develop skills—athletic, social, artistic, and intellectual—to heighten one's self-esteem and competence.

Make them SMART from here on!

SPECIFIC   MEASURABLE   ASSIGNABLE   REALISTIC   TIME-BASED

1 YEAR MBO GOAL(S) Specific programs to develop, usually tied to a budget element.	Program Managers and Supervisory Staff	By June 1, 2 2020 he Athletic Department will implement a summer softball league for girls 12—16 years of age with a minimum of 10 teams.

"BEGIN WITH THE END IN MIND "©Steven R. Covey (2013)
Identify outcomes from program participation before identifying staff actions.

PROGRAM DESIGN and IMPLEMENTATION TERMINAL PERFORMANCE OUTCOMES that specify participant outcomes. PROGRAM MANAGEMENT GOALS to be accomplished by staff.	Supervisory Staff and Front-line delivery personnel.	**TERMINAL PERFORMANCE OUTCOME** By the end of the league, 75% of participants will demonstrate improvement in 7/10 softball skills as evidenced by coaches' skills progress forms. **PROGRAM MANAGEMENT GOALS** The Athletic Department staff and volunteer coaches will operate a softball skills clinic for league participants at least once per week during the operation of the league.

Figure 5.1. Collaborating in Building the Strategy of an Agency

Exercise 5.1.
Coordinating and Collaborating Strategy

Examine Figure 5.1 and discuss in class how the four levels of management's work activities are coordinated through staff collaboration in developing the strategy of an organization. What must managers at each level do to facilitate this collaboration? How does this collaboration benefit the organization?

of the agency. Today, MBO and other succeeding statements should be written to be SMART—Specific, Measurable, Assignable, Realistic, and Time-based. The next section further explains SMART.

Finally, staff write terminal performance outcomes that define participant outcomes to be realized from participation in a program and program management goals that identify specific actions that staff must undertake to implement and stage the program as designed. These are also written in the SMART format. First-line managers and employees who stage programs usually write these statements.

The remainder of this chapter and Chapters 6, 7, and 9 discuss how these statements are developed and a process for achieving collaboration during their development. Collectively, these provide the process for developing the strategic programming direction of an organization.

Positive Outcomes of a Good Strategic Direction

Why develop an organizational strategy? By developing and publishing a strategy, the organization publicly announces its purpose and intended outcomes to its constituency and staff. This makes clear to the public the outcomes they should expect from the organization and helps staff coordinate their efforts to use the resources of the organization efficiently and effectively to achieve the outcomes intended and announced in the strategy. Strategy formation is a collaborative planning process that requires coordination across all levels of the organization and results in a strategic plan. Formulating and implementing the strategy as written ensures consistency in organizational behavior and positions the agency in its market.

> By developing and publishing a strategy, the organization publicly announces its purpose and intended outcomes to both its constituency and staff.

A strategy will be planned in the present and implemented in the future. Our inability to forecast the future accurately is a problem in all planning. We may be tempted to devise strategies that assume the future will simply be a continuation of the present. But chances are good that the future will not simply be a continuation of current circumstances. (See Kelly, 2013, Chapter 3 for a good discussion of how change affects leisure services.) Good strategy planning forces the organization to analyze and consider changes that will occur over time and plan its role for that future. A good organizational strategic development process implements forced forward-thinking.

The process of planning a strategy should require the organization to exercise rationality about its future. A rational organization considers alternate futures and hopefully selects the optimal one to pursue (i.e., a strategy that they have or can acquire the resources to implement and that has the effect desired on its constituency). Considering alternate futures and alternative strategies for accomplishing those futures should be a part of the process.

Finally, if written properly, the strategic plan provides benchmarking metrics (i.e., criteria for measuring and documenting accomplishments of the organization). Frequent review of progress in meeting intended outcomes provides feedback to managers about the progress of the organization in implementing the strategic plan. Timely review allows managers sufficient opportunity to make adjustments as warranted to ensure the plan is executed and implements managerial control of the process.

Framing the Mission Statement

"A mission statement is a statement of the organization's purpose—what it wants to accomplish in the larger environment," according to Kotler and Armstrong (2018, p. 65). It directs the efforts of independent work groups toward the accomplishment of the organization's reason for existing. A mission statement should define what the agency will not accomplish, as well as what it will accomplish. Figure 5.2 illustrates this notion. For example, mission statements include the provision of recreation services and facilities. Concomitantly, they exclude other possible tasks that the agency could undertake but chooses not to for a variety of reasons.

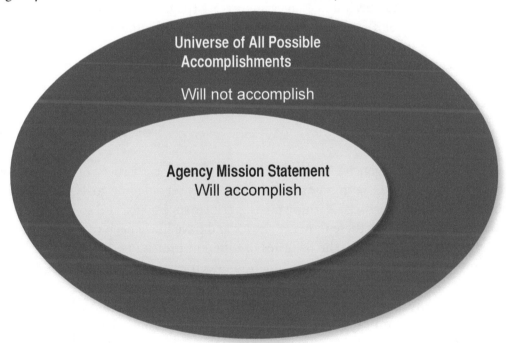

Figure 5.2. Limits Defined by the Mission Statement

Mission statements are somewhat elastic in what they include. They are purposely nebulous to provide maximum flexibility for the agency in the future. Mission statements are considered long-term commitments of the agency and are not usually altered in the short run. A narrow, specific mission statement would commit the agency to providing a narrow range of services to its clients. A nebulous statement gives the agency maximum leeway to respond to changing demands and needs without continuously rewriting the mission statement. Developing a mission statement, then, requires the agency to define some area(s) for accomplishment without being so restrictive that it has no flexibility for accomplishing the mission. Chapter 6 provides additional details about writing a mission statement.

Strategic Directions

Although the mission is not written in measurable language, the agency can assume it has been accomplished when staff have accomplished a sufficient number of strategic directions articulated in the 3- to 5-year strategic planning directions. Strategic directions are usually not written in measurable language either. This may introduce a great deal of confusion into the process. Often these are called strategic goals or objectives, and we are taught that goals and objectives are to be written in measurable language. This presents a conundrum. We have called them directions instead, but this is more than just a word game. Strategic directions are written in more general language because they are likely to be pursued for 3 to 5 years or longer and should be sufficiently nonspecific to provide a general direction for effort over this 3- to 5-year period or longer. Figure 5.1 (page 75) includes, for example, "Develop Specific Skills" as a strategic direction. It is accepted that doing this will implement the stated mission, and a lot of different skills could be developed under the general planning statement of "Develop Specific Skills." Moreover, this strategic planning direction indicates that for many years, this organization will continue to offer programs that develop specific skills.

Goals and Objectives

Leisure service agencies use goals and objectives for a variety of purposes in addition to developing a programming strategy. They set outcome goals, profit goals, budget goals, income goals, learning goals, performance goals, and so on. Students are required to develop these in many classes and have likely been required to use a variety of methods that are the favorites of different professors. Most agencies will use only one of these processes. To function effectively in an organization, leisure services professionals must be proficient in this process.

The relationship between the mission statement and subsequent goals and objectives of an agency is hierarchical. Simply put, staff succinctly write down what they intend to do, along with criteria for determining its accomplishment. The process is given coherence through the development of a series of linguistic statements that are arranged hierarchically beginning with broad statements and moving successively through to more narrow and specific statements.

> The relationship between the mission statement and subsequent goals and objectives of an agency is hierarchical.

Beginning with MBO statements, all succeeding statements are written in the SMART format. These statements will be accomplished in a specific time, usually within the year, and thus action on them will occur relatively soon. Using the SMART format to write these statements ensures accomplishing several important management issues during their implementation. The SMART format is an acronym, and this section explains each of the letters of the acronym.

Specific

The statement should be specific enough so an observer can determine whether it has been accomplished. How specific is specific enough? We suggest a practical approach to this called achieving operational clarity. If the individuals responsible for supervising, implementing, and receiving the actions intended in the statement agree and understand the wording and meaning of the statement, it is operationally clear and will meet the intended needs of using goals and objectives in the operation of the organization. Additionally, the position of a statement in the hierarchy will also determine how specific it needs to be. Statements higher in the hierarchy are less specific than those lower in the hierarchy.

Measurable

Is the outcome or action intended measurable? What evidence can be readily collected or observed that will verify accomplishment of the statement? Measuring accomplishments can be difficult when statements include accomplishments that are too nebulous or undefined. For example, a program statement that is certainly a laudable outcome but difficult to measure is "to increase personal responsibility in youth." Requiring that a measurement device be included in a statement forces development of statements that indeed can be measured!

Assignable

People who take action accomplish goals and objectives. The statement should specify who is responsible for accomplishing the goal or objective. Is it the participants, program leaders, program supervisors, or someone else? Thus, the statement assigns responsibility for accomplishing the goal to someone, and this individual or work group will be held accountable for accomplishing it.

Realistic

Can the organization accomplish what is intended? Often, organizations identify accomplishments that are well intended and lofty but not realistic. Available resources are usually a limiting factor. Does the organization have the financial wherewithal, the facilities, the appropriate staffing, and so forth, to accomplish what is being proposed?

Timely

A date deadline is one of the most frequently used measures of accomplishment. Was the intended action accomplished by a definite deadline? Use of this mechanism ensures that actions are accomplished in a timely manner and that staff take the initiative to accomplish their responsibilities on time.

The SMART acronym, of course, spells the word *smart*. If all of the parts of the SMART acronym are implemented, the strategic plan of the organization should be well articulated and understood by constituents, board, and employees.

Goals and objectives achieve meaning when they are a part of a series of statements that have been logically and sequentially developed. Examining a single goal or objective out of context cannot convey meaning any more than a sentence taken out of context from a novel can convey the meaning of a novel. Writing goals and objectives and writing novels both require a considerable degree of writing skill and an ability to express one's thoughts clearly with written language in a well-developed, clear, and logical fashion. This skill can be learned.

How to Write Goals and Objectives

The linguistic structure of goals and objectives can be simple or complicated. Neophytes often err by trying to write a statement that is too complicated. For beginners, we recommend that each linguistic statement—that is, each goal or objective—be written in the form provided in this section.

Subject

Each statement must have a subject. Sometimes, this indicates who will perform the action that accomplishes the task. In other cases, it specifically conveys what is to be accomplished. Each statement should have only one subject. Do not use conjunctions to add multiple subjects in the same statement.

Verb

Each statement should include a verb indicating the action to be taken. It is best if each statement includes only one verb, as measuring accomplishment is easier if there is only one action that needs to be measured. For an excellent list of verbs useful for writing goals and objectives, see the work of Gronlund (1970).

Measurement Device

Each statement should make clear what devices will be used for measuring and documenting the accomplishment of the goal or objective. Additionally, it should include a specific time frame for accomplishing the action.

Consider the following agency program-planning goal: "The athletic supervisor will operate a women's softball league during the summer of 2020 with a minimum of eight teams." This goal begins by identifying who is responsible for accomplishing it. This is the subject of the statement. The action to be implemented is *operate*, which indicates an intention of the agency to accomplish it by designing, organizing, publicizing, and staging the event. The verb *operate* is a summative, final outcome that includes all of the other actions necessary for the agency to complete the operation of the event. It is sufficiently specific for its position in the hierarchy. In this example, what will be accomplished is the object of the verb *will operate*—a women's softball league. The timing device is "during the summer of 2020." In stating this, the agency has said that it will consider the goal accomplished if the league operates during the summer of 2020 with at least eight teams. It is assumed that this is a realistic possibility for the agency to accomplish this goal (i.e., it has sufficient human, fiscal, and physical resources). As written then, it is SMART and the agency will be able to determine if it has been accomplished.

What is unclear in this goal? It does not specify where the league will be held, specific dates and times of operation, and other details of operation. However, these details are unnecessary at this level of goal development. The details of league operation will be presented later in an additional series of program design goals and objectives. For this goal, it is important that the agency has committed its resources to a specific program with a targeted completion date and has identified someone responsible for implementing it.

In writing goal and objective statements, keep the thought conveyed simple. Never use a conjunction in a goal or objective statement. A conjunction adds to the statement a second thought (a second verb, subject, or measurement device) that will unnecessarily complicate the goal or objective. If there are two goals or objectives, then write two statements—do not try to join them together into one statement. It is also important to be parsimonious in writing goals and objectives. Try to write a simple, clear, concise statement that conveys what you intend to accomplish.

Hierarchical Arrangement

The relationship between the mission statement and subsequent goals and objectives of an agency is hierarchical. The mission statement delimits, in a general way, what the agency is trying to accomplish. The mission statement is not measurable. Its accomplishment is measured through the development of a succeeding series of strategic directions, goals, and objectives that progressively become more narrow and specific. Many succeeding levels of goals and objectives can exist between the mission statement and the final, measurable objectives. The number of statement levels depends on the complexity of the organization and the complexity of the content area for which goals and objectives are being written.

Figure 5.1 (page 75) shows this organizational hierarchy with examples. The mission statement defines the purpose of the agency and provides direction about what the agency will accomplish in the larger community, but it is not necessarily measurable. Generally, the agency director, in consultation with the board, is responsible for this portion of the hierarchy. The short-range planning directions are not measurable either, but they outline an area of program development and begin to define what the agency will accomplish. Usually, the agency director, in consultation with the unit directors, prepares these strategic planning statements and a board approves them. At the next level, MBO statements are prepared. These usually accompany budget preparation and allow program managers to further define services that will be developed. Finally, program managers (and sometimes leaders) develop program design goals at two levels. One level, the final strata, focuses on participant outcomes, what participants will be able to do or have experienced as a result of participating in the program (e.g., skill attainment, attitude changes, fellowship building). Later chapters refer to these as Y statements. The other level of statements specifies the planned interventions the programmer will implement to facilitate the Y outcomes. These are later referred to as X statements and include the implementation details and animation strategies programmers complete to stage the program. Chapters 6, 7, and 9 provide additional examples and discussions of all of these.

Goals and Objectives: How Are They Different?

There is a great deal of confusion about the difference between goals and objectives. In this book, we take a pragmatic approach to this problem and assume there is no practical difference between a goal and an objective. It can thus be deduced that the relationship between goals and objectives is determined by the position each statement occupies in a hierarchy of goal and objective statements. Furthermore, objectives for some levels in an organization become goals for employees occupying the next lower level in the organization.

However, the relationship between the goals and objectives is important. First, the relationship between the mission statement and subsequent goals and objectives is hierarchical. Therefore, if all of the objectives identified for a goal are accomplished, the goal is considered accomplished. Second, one must consider the location in the organizational structure for which the goal or objective is being developed. Often, objectives for one level become the goals to be accomplished in the next descending level of the organization. In this way, goals and objectives network the activities of the organization and allow work activity to be coordinated and unified from the highest statement in the organization (mission statement) through the activities of a part-time recreation leader, wherein an objective states what the leader intends for participants to accomplish in a program.

> If all of the objectives identified for a goal are accomplished, the goal is considered accomplished.

Two assumptions govern goal and objective theory and the development of goal and objective statements:

1. The accomplishment of the strategic directions that support the mission statement or a set of objectives that support an individual goal will be accepted as proof of mission or goal accomplishment.
2. Any list of goals or objectives that the organization uses to document accomplishment is only a partial list of the many goals and objectives that could have been developed. Selection of any goal or objective is normative; any goal or objective selected is a sample from a larger list of possible goals or objectives that could have been selected. Figure 5.3 illustrates this latter point and the next section discusses it further.

Figure 5.3. Limits Defined by Goals and Objectives

Representative Nature of the Goals and Objectives Selected

Figure 5.3 is a further elaboration of Figure 5.2 (page 77). Figure 5.3 shows three types of ovals: A, B, and C. Oval A illustrates the entire universe of all possible accomplishments that the agency could undertake. Oval B illustrates the space from the entire universe of possible accomplishments that the agency has delimited with its mission statement and thereby indicated its intent to accomplish. Oval C represents the space occupied by any goal the agency has indicated it intends to accomplish.

Figure 5.3 illustrates that any goal or objective is only a representative sample from the entire universe of goals and objectives that could be drawn from the universe defined by the mission statement.

The space outside Oval B but within Oval A represents possible accomplishments that have been excluded from the mission statement. The space within Ovals C_1 and C_2 illustrates the accomplishments that could be achieved within the space of possible accomplishments defined by these two goals. The space outside Ovals C_1 and C_2 but within Oval B includes all other possible goals that could be accomplished within the parameters defined by the mission statement. Any set of goals, then, represents only a small portion of all possible goals that could be selected. The Xs within Ovals C_1 and C_2 represent objectives for accomplishing each goal. Again, each oval has room for many more Xs. This illustrates that any list of objectives identified for a goal is only a partial list of all possible objectives that could be developed for documenting goal accomplishment.

The selection of goals and objectives should be implemented with careful consideration. Usually, only three to five statements are written. As Figure 5.2 (page 77) illustrates, the use of goals and objectives to demonstrate agency accomplishments allows the agency to be evaluated on only a small portion of the activities that could be used. Additionally, a limited amount of resources can be applied to any project, and more statements reduce the amount of resources that can be applied to each. For example, if there is only one objective, 100% of the resources available can be applied to it. If there are two objectives, now only 50% of the resources can be applied to each, and so on with additional objectives. Thus, it is important that the few goals and objectives selected represent the total mission and typical undertakings of the agency.

Staff Collaboration in Developing Goals and Objectives

How goals and objectives are developed in an organization is important to their successful use in the organization. Where should goals and objectives originate in the organization? Should they originate at the top and be passed down through succeeding organizational levels to the bottom-most employees? Or should goals and objectives originate at the bottom and be passed through each hierarchical stratum until they accumulate at the top?

In the former case, employees often have very little commitment to goals imposed from above. In the latter case, employees find it difficult to develop goals when uninformed by any type of organizational direction. This latter method often results in a collection of widely diversified goals, with little of the focus needed for an effective, unified organizational strategy.

The most reasonable procedure involves originating the goals from the top of the organization and passing them through each managerial level to the employees below. Through a process of iterative negotiation, each group of employees will need to develop a set of objectives they intend to achieve, to accomplish the goals. For example, the director of recreation may indicate to the sport supervisor that one of the director's objectives for 2020 is "To operate two new sport leagues for teenage girls during 2020 with at least six teams in each." The director informs the sport supervisor that one of her goals for 2020 will be "The sport supervisor will operate two new sport leagues for teenage girls during 2020 with at least six teams in each." The director asks the sport supervisor to develop objectives within the week for implementing this goal. The sport supervisor responds in 3 days with the following objectives:

- The sport supervisor will operate a field hockey league for girls 14–16 years old for 6 weeks during April and May 2020 with at least six teams enrolled.
- The sport supervisor will operate a soccer league for girls 16–18 years old for 8 weeks during June to August 2020 with at least six teams enrolled.

Although several iterations may be required before completion of a final list of objectives acceptable to the director and the sport supervisor, this process encourages collaborative employee action and input and results in employee efforts that implement the mission of the organization. Furthermore, once the two objectives for implementing the director of recreation's goal are agreed to, they become two of the annual goals the sport supervisor will implement. The sport supervisor will then need to develop additional objectives for implementing each goal. In this way, the activities of employees are effectively networked and coordinated with the use of goals and objectives. Chapter 7 provides additional examples that illustrate this process.

Conclusion

An agency develops its strategic programming direction by preparing a series of hierarchically arranged linguistic statements including mission, strategic directions, MBO, and a series of goals and objectives. Through a publicly visible strategy, an agency defines what it will accomplish from the large number of possible activities it could undertake. Consultation, collaboration, and coordination with constituents, board members, and staff are essential for obtaining commitment for implementation. In this way, the collective resources of the agency focus on accomplishing tasks that demonstrate fulfillment of the mission. It is important that the agency selects goals and objectives that are comprehensive yet diverse enough to represent its breadth of service responsibilities. Chapters 6, 7, and 9 include additional information for using these concepts in programming, as well as examples.

References

Gronlund, N. D. (1970). *Stating behavioral objectives for classroom instruction.* New York, NY: Macmillan.

Kelly, J. R. (2013). *Leisure business strategies: What they don't teach you in business schools.* Urbana, IL: Sagamore.

Kotler, P., & Armstrong, G. (2018). *Principles of marketing* (17th ed., Global ed.). Harlo, United Kingdom: Pearson Education.

The Program Development Cycle

Information included thus far has provided background information needed to develop successful programs. Programs should be developed in a methodical and cyclical manner. The Program Development Cycle (PDC), a process diagram of the steps for developing programs, is presented on the next two pages. The cycle includes four major stages and nine specific steps. For a detailed explanation about the role and function of each stage and step, visit https://www.sagamorepub.com/products/recreation-programming-8th-ed.

In practice, programs are not developed in the linear, sequential process illustrated, but rather in an iterative, interactive process requiring continued recycling of these steps until completion of an operational program plan. The process diagram gives the illusion that each step takes a similar amount of the programmer's time. Recent research has indicated that this is not the case. The amount of time programmers report spending on each step is discussed below.

Once thoroughly planned, a program can be operated. Successful programs are the result of several trial-and-error developmental operations. Organizations acquire an inventory of quality programs by carefully planning them with the steps of the PDC, operating them, evaluating them, and reworking them to be operated again based on their observations. Progressive program organizations have a number of new programs under development at all times. Successful programs are nurtured and developed further. Unsuccessful programs are dropped. Having to rework a program through several trial-and-error operations is the normal course for successful program development, not an indication of failure.

How much time do programmers spend on each step of the PDC? This was one question asked in research on programming practices conducted by Schlatter and Chang (2018). The PDC flow chart that follows on page 88 was drawn so the size of the boxes for each step on the diagram reflect the percentage of time programmers indicated they spent on each step. The single most time-consuming activity is Step 7, Implementation. Three steps including Program Design, Planning, and Implementation consume more than 50% of a programmer's time. However, this does not mean they are the most important steps to successful programs, only the most time consuming.

As succeeding chapters develop, the reader will see that implementation is a broad activity, and thus we have devoted more chapters to it than any other step. Even though some steps take more time and some are more important than others, it is necessary for programmers to complete each of the steps thoroughly to develop excellent program services.

The remaining chapters explain each step of the PDC. The PDC is illustrated at the beginning of each chapter, and the step being discussed in the chapter is highlighted. When there are multiple methods for accomplishing a step, each is explained, thereby giving the programmer multiple options for action and eventual success.

The Program Development Cycle

© 2000 J. Robert Rossman and Barbara Elwood Schlatter

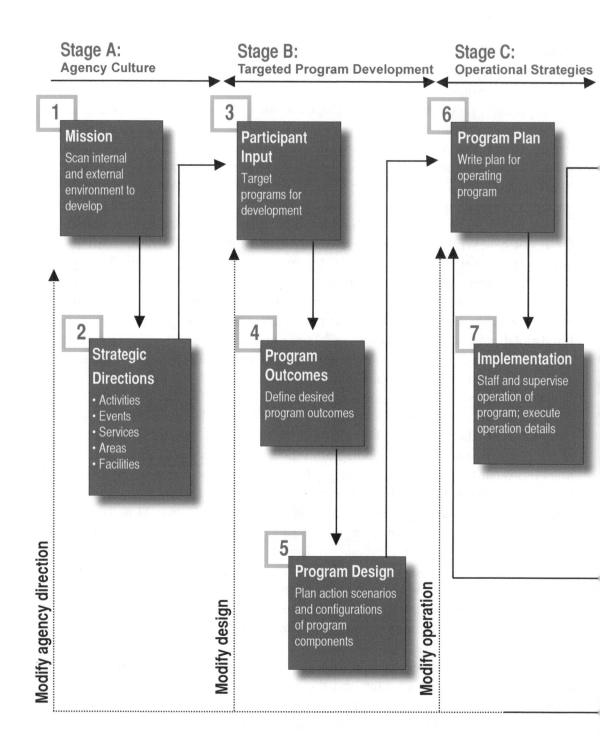

Stage D:
Follow-Up Analysis

8
Evaluation
Judge program
worth and
document
benefits provided

9
**Disposition
Decision**

Drop
Modify
Continue

Terminate

STAGE A:
AGENCY CULTURE

In this stage, the programmer develops an understanding of the programming philosophy and overall programmatic goals of the agency. This stage is relatively static because of the stability of the mission and strategic direction of the agency. Programmers usually do not write agency missions but must understand them so the program services developed help fulfill the mission.

STAGE B:
TARGETED PROGRAM DEVELOPMENT

In this stage, the unique program needs and desires of specific population groups are identified, program outcome goals that are consistent with the mission of the agency are specified, and a program that can meet these goals is designed. Programs developed should be desired by participants, should be within the resource capabilities of the agency, and should fulfill its mission.

STAGE C:
OPERATIONAL STRATEGIES

In this stage, an implementation plan is developed and the program is delivered to clients. The programmer oversees and manages the details for operating the program. Managing the implementation of program services includes many functions and is the most time-consuming stage of programming.

STAGE D:
FOLLOW-UP ANALYSIS

In this stage, the programmer oversees the evaluation of the program. With this evaluation data, a disposition decision is made about the future of the program. It may be continued, dropped, or modified. Deciding to modify a program may require reworking its implementation method or its conceptualization and design, or rethinking the overall mission or goals of an agency.

Overall, although the model suggests that programs are developed in a methodical and systematic way, in reality it is an iterative, interactive process requiring continued recycling of the steps until an operational program is developed. Most often, successful programs are the result of ongoing, incremental expansion and improvement over time.

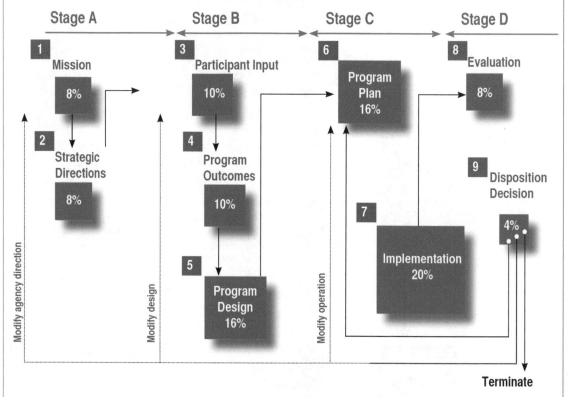

ALLOCATING TIME TO PROGRAM DEVELOPMENT

Stage A   Stage B   Stage C   Stage D

1 Mission — 8%

2 Strategic Directions — 8%

3 Participant Input — 10%

4 Program Outcomes — 10%

5 Program Design — 16%

6 Program Plan — 16%

7 Implementation — 20%

8 Evaluation — 8%

9 Disposition Decision — 4%

Modify agency direction

Modify design

Modify operation

Terminate

Note. From Schlatter, B. E., & Chang, Y. (2018). Survey of program and event planning practices. Illinois Park and Recreation Association.

PART II

Determining Agency Culture

Part II discusses Stage A of the Program Development Cycle. This stage involves assessing the culture in which the programming organization operates, developing a mission statement, and developing strategic directions for the organization. The leisure service programs discussed in this book are always designed and delivered by programmers operating in an organization. In addition to designing, staging, and evaluating leisure experiences, the programmer is a supervisory-level manager in most agencies and therefore must understand the environment in which the organization operates and how this environment influences the services that it can develop and operate.

This section includes two chapters. Chapter 6 explains how to develop the mission statement of the organization through assessing the threats and opportunities in its environment and its own internal strengths and weaknesses. Chapter 7 discusses developing strategic program directions the agency will pursue and provides examples that illustrate this process.

Chapter 6: Developing the Agency's Programming Mission

Chapter 7: Developing Strategic Directions

Stage A: Determining Agency Culture

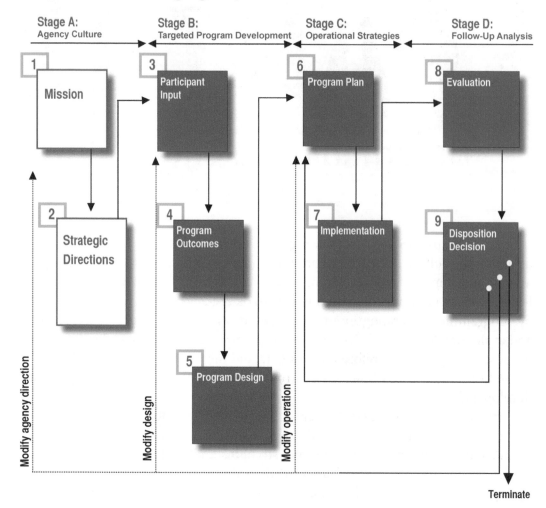

Daddy Daughter Dance
Photo courtesy of Elmhurst Park District. Photo by Kassandra Collins.

6 *Developing the Agency's Programming Mission*

KEY TERMS

Mission, Individual Needs, Macro Environment, Resource Dependency, Organizational Needs, Community, Public Interest, Community Needs

Step 1: Mission

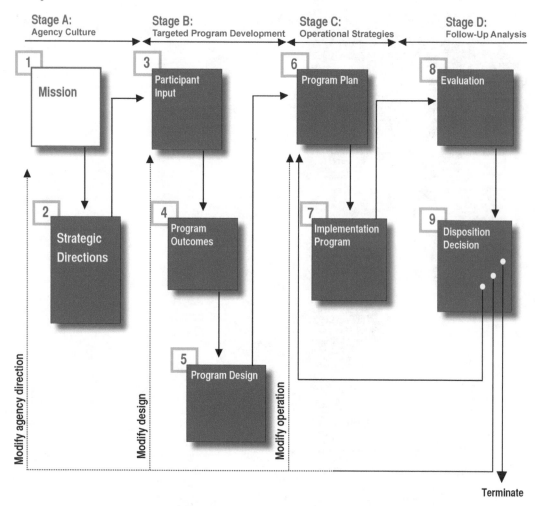

In Kofi Darbi's (2012) literature review, he stated, "Several works (Campbell, 1997; Mullane, 2002; Rigby, 1994; Matejka et al., 1993; Campbell & Yeung, 1991) have delineated how mission and vision statements can be used to build a common and shared sense of purpose and also serve as conduit through which employees' focus are shaped." As stated in Chapter 5, a mission statement defines the purpose of an agency and outlines what it intends to accomplish in the larger environment. Knowles (1970) described this environment as a "pool of needs," which includes individual, organizational, and community needs. Developing successful services requires that programmers meet the identified needs of individuals and communities, and contribute to the organizational need to fulfill a purpose and role in the community. The recent efforts by community recreation and park agencies to develop services that could positively affect youth at risk and to develop health and wellness programs and opportunities for adult populations are examples of community purposes and roles that might be fulfilled.

Implementing Intentionally Designed Experiences

Incorporating intentionally designed leisure experiences into agency mission statements requires agency personnel to reposition themselves as providers of essential services with serious and important outcomes for those who participate. The Arlington County Department of Parks and Recreation mission statement found in Exhibit 6.5 makes clear its responsibility in fostering vibrant program offerings that encourage good health and well-being

To succeed, programmers must understand how the conflicts and demands created by the issues surrounding these three—individual, organizational, and community needs—influence program development. Collectively, this analysis leads to the development of a mission that will provide direction to day-to-day operations, as well as confirm the need to develop some programs and restrict others. Kotler and Armstrong (2018) asserted, "A clear mission statement acts as an 'invisible hand' that guides people in the organization" (p. 65). Although a mission statement is not developed every year, it influences every program in operation. Thus, the programmer must understand the mission and its implications.

This chapter deals with the issues that should be analyzed in the development of a mission statement. The discussion is roughly organized around the three types of issues that must be analyzed: individual, organizational, and community. These divisions are somewhat arbitrary and overlap in some cases. Furthermore, individual needs are not completely investigated at this point. The more detailed analysis that permits the development of specific, custom-tailored program services is covered later in the Program Development Cycle and will be discussed in Chapter 8.

> Although a mission statement is not developed every year, it influences every program in operation.

Generally, the analysis conducted in the development of a mission statement answers the following questions:

Individual: Who are our patrons? What kinds of services do they want? What types of services can we provide them; that is, what business should we be in?

Organizational: What are the strengths and weaknesses of our organization? What are the activities, events, services, areas, and facilities we can develop a unique ability to offer?

Community: What are the threats and opportunities in our environment? Where can we make a difference that matters?

Table 6.1 lists what is included in each of these (page 96).

Table 6.1

Issues That Must Be Analyzed to Develop a Mission

Need	Includes
Individual	Macro trends Effects on local community
Organizational	Resources Organizing authority Organizational strengths and weaknesses
Community	Resources Community needs Public interest Assessing current opportunities Relationships among providers

Assessing Individual Needs

Every organization must determine who it intends to serve, and articulate this intention in the mission statement. Government agencies are required to serve all who are within their jurisdiction, so their mission statements are usually egalitarian and inclusive. However, a commercial agency, for instance, a tennis club, may want to serve individuals who have higher than average incomes, in one activity. Thus, its mission statement would narrowly define its service population. Many not-for-profit organizations also have mission statements that reflect a more restricted target population they intend to serve.

If the agency plans to restrict the type of service it intends to provide, or put in place similar restrictions, the mission statement should reflect this. For example, Little League organizations have a restricted age group they serve and a single activity they provide.

Scanning and Monitoring the Environment

The needs of any population are influenced by social forces that create opportunities and pose challenges for an agency. These forces can be local, regional, or national in origin. Programmers can gather information about them and their potential effects, either positive or negative, on the leisure service agency by scanning and interpreting information about the environment at the agency on an ongoing basis. Potential sources of information for this analysis include local, regional, and national print and broadcast media; government-issued technical reports; planning reports; political activity; and developments in the entertainment industry.

> The needs of any population are influenced by social forces that create opportunities and pose challenges for an agency.

Given the variety of reports, information, and so forth that programmers should consider, they need to remain aware of possible threats to program continuation and seize special opportunities for program development. For example, the large percentage of working women today threatens mother–tot programs unless they are scheduled around the workday. Unless programmers alter the scheduling of these types of programs, they are likely to fail because no client group will be available to attend them.

Programmers must also remain aware of national trends and media happenings to seize on ideas and develop timely programs. There is a timeliness to programming that programmers can only achieve by scanning the external environment of the organization for emerging trends. In each case, the programmer must answer the question, *what are the specific operational implications of this, if any, for my agency?*

Programmers should prepare themselves to track systematically what is happening in five areas: demographic, social, technological, economic, and political. Developments in each area are certain to have discernible effects on programming. The first three of these will have the greatest effect on individual leisure needs. The latter two could affect any of the three—individual, organizational, or community needs. Each trend should be analyzed from a local, regional, and national perspective. It is important for programmers to ascertain whether national or regional developments will affect the local community. This section gives a brief review of each key indicator.

> It is important for programmers to ascertain whether national or regional developments will affect the local community.

Demographic and Social Trends

Russell (2014) identified several striking changes in American consumers by looking at trends in U.S. census data, providing insight for program and event planners. First, urban populations grew 2.1% between 2010 and 2012, placing greater needs on local governments for housing, public transportation, and parks. Another trend is the growth of minority populations (Asians, Blacks, and Hispanics), who make up more than one third of the nation's population and have the ability to affect the economy and politics. By meeting the needs of a diverse population, businesses position themselves to be the first choice for consumers.

The prevalence of obesity continues to be a serious health concern in the United States, with 39.8% among adults and 18.5% among youth (Centers for Disease Control and Prevention, 2016). Many communities have responded to these concerns by partnering with after-school programs that promote physical activity. The Centers for Disease Control and Prevention has also taken a lead in helping after-school programs learn to prevent childhood obesity, by encouraging fruits and vegetables for snacks, replacing sugar-sweetened drinks with water, adding 30 minutes of physical activity at least 3 days a week, eliminating TV and movies, and limiting computer use to educational purposes.

The leisure of millennials, those born between 1981 and 1996, can be seen in several trends (Weinswig, 2016). Compared to other age groups, millennials spend less on their leisure, probably because they do not make as much money as other groups. They like to spend money on dining experiences. They also exhibit interest in fitness and health, including yoga. Millennials prefer experiences over possessions and enjoy sharing them on social media, also known as the "Instagram effect."

Being socially consciousness, especially about the environment, is important to millennials.

The senior population continues to grow and is estimated to make up 21% of the population by 2040 (Crompton, 2013). Madren (2014) noted the response by park and recreation agencies to the changing needs of seniors in sport programming. Adapting traditional sports with less equipment, smaller playing fields, and shorter seasons makes it easier for the programmer to pull teams together. Dodgeball, kickball, and Wiffle Ball are seeing a comeback in adult sport programming (Madren, 2014). Races such as Tough Mudder and Run Amuck, where participants confront courses full of obstacles, continue to grow in popularity alongside more traditional 10K, half marathons, and marathons. Neon fun runs, where people wear neon-colored shirts and carry glow sticks, appeal to new participants who may have otherwise avoided traditional sports because of the level of competition and commitment required. See the Trends in Parks and Recreation (Dolesh, 2018) box for additional innovations in municipal park spaces.

Trends in Parks and Recreation (Dolesh, 2018)

- Innovative park locations such as tops of buildings and vacant underground spaces
- Parks as supervised opioid injection sites
- Use of drones for search and rescue, and surveillance
- Park and recreation facilities used for evidence-based health delivery
- Monetary gifts to parks by wealthy citizens

Technology

Emerging technologies continue to change how people plan for and experience leisure. Survey findings revealed that American youth between the ages of 8 and 18 are spending more than 8 hours a day using entertainment media (Common Sense Media, 2016; Henry J. Kaiser Family Foundation, 2010). Moreover, parents of tweens and teens spend more than 9 hours a day with screen media. As people spend more time plugged into their computers, smartphones, and gaming devices, they will spend less face-to-face time with other people. An additional concern is that overuse of technology leads sedentary lifestyles and social isolation.

Others see technological advances, especially with mobile apps, as a new frontier for helping people get healthy and fit. Apps can count calories, measure speed and distance, calculate calories burned, and much more (Eddy, 2014). Parents extol the educational benefits that technology brings to their children (Common Sense Media, 2016). Many leisure service providers embrace these technologies in their facilities to help participants achieve fitness and health goals. Questions remain, however, in terms of which technologies should be used and their effects. Video games, for example, are standard activity options on military installations, especially in conflict areas where personnel wish to escape during periods of rest. It seems a fitting provision for soldiers who have grown up on video gaming. Other agencies embrace *Wii Fit* for dance and sport competitions. Technology will continue to transform leisure in negative and positive ways.

Economics

In 2018, ten years after the Great Recession began, the economy appears to be recovering (Abruzzese, 2017). There are still challenges ahead for middle and lower income families to achieve upward mobility. In both strong and weak economic times, it is necessary for programmers to ask questions regarding the local economy in terms of its diversification and stability. How much annual income do the majority of customers have? How much discretionary income is available to target audiences? How many individuals have low incomes and are in need of subsidized services? What percentage of leisure service market share does the business currently have? Is this likely to increase, resulting in an increased income? Are there additional competitors who are likely to cut into the agency's market share and, if so, what financial implications will there be to the agency? What is the current tax base and tax rate, and are either of these likely to increase or decrease? If so, what will be the implications for program and event planners?

Politics

Understanding the political climate of the community is essential for program and event planners, especially those in municipal recreation. They need to learn the political orientation of their local elected officials. Do these officials support public recreation? The National Recreation and Park Association (NRPA, 2017) indicated that local government officials view recreation as sixth in importance among 10 service offerings of local governments. How political is the administration of the agency? Are there positions in the agency that are patronage jobs (meaning a political party, after winning an election, gives government jobs to its supporters as a reward)? Also, how receptive are local elected officials to using the powers of government to encourage privately developed recreation enterprises? What is the political climate in the state? What is the political climate in the nation? Is it conservative or liberal, and what are these attitudes likely to do to funding and program operations?

Assessing Organizational Needs

Organizations are dynamic entities whose needs must be met to keep operating. One of the most important needs of an organization is to continue its existence. This is most assured if it fulfills an identifiable role in the larger society that controls its resources. Because no agency can offer everything, it is important that the agency identifies its strengths and weaknesses to discover a distinctive competence that provides it a competitive advantage on some aspect important to the market (Zikmund & d'Amico, 2002, p. 36).

Resource Dependency

All organizations, including programming organizations, are resource dependent: Their survival depends on successfully acquiring the resources needed for delivering services to their client groups. The level of resources available determines, to some degree, the mission of the organization. Adequate or unique resources create the differential advantage for the agency to provide unique opportunities, but a lack thereof will be a limitation and thereby restrict what the agency can accomplish. Thus, resources are an issue at organizational and community levels. Pfeffer and Salancik (1978) took the following position:

> Our position is that organizations survive to the extent that they are effective. Their effectiveness derives from the management of demands, particularly the demands of interest groups upon which the organizations depend for resources and support. (p. 2)

The mission of the organization must focus organizational efforts toward meeting the needs of its relevant clients and publics. Resource dependency is complicated by the fact that no organization is completely self-contained, and organizations compete with and depend on other organizations for resources. Pfeffer and Salancik (1978) commented on this dilemma:

> Organizations are embedded in an environment comprised of other organizations. They depend on those other organizations for the many resources they themselves require. (p. 2)

The accomplishments of the organization may partly depend on what other organizations allow it or want it to accomplish. Organizational success, then, is partly determined by the external environment of the organization.

Organizing Rationale

Often, leisure service organizations are created to offer specific types of recreation programming and to achieve specific purposes. Kraus (1985) identified eight types of organizations that offer recreation service: public recreation and park agencies; voluntary, nonprofit organizations, including sectarian and nonsectarian; commercial recreation enterprises; private-membership organizations; armed forces recreation; campus recreation; corporate recreation; and therapeutic recreation.

These organizations have specific social ends that they attempt to provide through participation in recreation activities. An overriding need of such organizations is the accomplishment of the social ends identified as part of the rationale for creating the organization. As Tillman (1973) observed, "Agencies use [a] recreation program as a tool for obtaining their objectives" (p. 19). Different agencies offer different leisure services because of the social ends they are organized to promote. For example, the Boy Scouts of America offers different programming than YMCAs.

Although they both serve youth, their program services differ because their articulated social missions differ.

Marketing literature suggests that individual needs should be the central driving force in organizations. This is a desirable goal for all leisure service organizations to strive for. However, the social ends of the organization narrow the range of programs that will be provided and thereby have an overriding influence on the mission of the organization in the short run. For example, the organizational mission of campus recreation organizations limits their concern to students, faculty, and alumni from a specific university. After accepting this parameter, the organization focuses its concern on the wants of its targeted client groups, and the marketing concepts and ideas for determining individual wants become useful. Similarly, armed forces recreation providers primarily concern themselves with active-duty military personnel, their dependents, civilian employees, and retirees. They direct programming efforts in the armed services toward helping one of these groups. Thus, the mission of the organization influences the program services it delivers. Now complete Exercise 6.1.

Exercise 6.1.
How the Mission of an Organization Influences Event Development

Identify and discuss how the same event, such as a Fourth of July Special Event, would differ if organized by each of the agencies or companies paired below. How does the mission of the organization influence the way this event would be developed?

Chicago Park District........................U.S. Army MWR (Morale, Welfare, and Recreation)
YMCA.. Private Country Club
Retirement Village .... Nursing Home
A Disney Cruise .... Harbor Beach Resort, Ft. Lauderdale

Assessing the Organization

An organization can determine how well it is doing by assessing its strengths and limitations. The checklist approach for self-evaluation of public leisure service organizations (van der Smissen, 1972) has been revised and updated by the Commission for Accreditation of Park and Recreation Agencies (CAPRA). One hundred forty-four standards have been established for park and recreation professionals and citizen advisory or policy boards to evaluate their agencies. Of the 144 standards, 37 have been designated as essential for accreditation purposes.

Of the 10 major categories of standards, one is Programs and Services Management. Each standard has an accompanying written description and supporting performance measures that determine the degree of compliance exhibited in an agency. The Program and Services Management category is outlined in Exhibit 6.1. Three of these standards have been designated as essential for accreditation purposes.

Although the CAPRA standards are designed for public recreation organizations, many of the standards in it are also important for commercial and not-for-profit leisure service organizations. The standards can also be adapted and used in these two types of organizations for conducting an organizational self-assessment.

Exhibit 6.1. CAPRA Assessment Criteria

6.0 Programs and Services Management

    6.1 Recreation Programming Plan

        6.1.1 Program and Service Determinants

        6.1.2 Participant Involvement

        6.1.3 Self-Directed Programs and Services

        6.1.4 Leader-Directed Programs and Services

        6.1.5 Facilitated Programs and Services

        6.1.6 Cooperative Programming

    6.2 Program Objectives

    6.3 Scope of Program Opportunities

        6.3.1 Outreach to Diverse Underserved Populations

    6.4 Community Education for Leisure Process

        6.4.1 Community Health and Wellness Education and Promotion

    6.5 Participant and Spectator Code of Conduct

Note. From Commission for Accreditation of Park and Recreation Agencies (2014).

A Marketing Approach to Organizational Assessment

To obtain a comprehensive view of the position of the organization in a community or market, programmers need to obtain the key public's image of the organization. An image is "the sum of beliefs, ideas, and impressions that a person holds of an object" (Kotler, 1982, p. 57). The use of a SWOT analysis is often recommended (Zikmund & d'Amico, 2002, p. 42). SWOT is an acronym for the process of examining the internal strengths and weaknesses of an organization, as well as its external opportunities and threats.

The organization must make the important decision of which key publics to investigate. Some publics will be more influential in determining the future success of the organization than others. In the public sector, the organization surveys the entire population of the jurisdiction. For a YWCA or other similar not-for-profit organization, it would examine thoroughly the views of its members and also sample nonmembers to investigate whether they hold views substantially different from members. Similarly, in a commercial agency, the organization would examine a sample of the total market, that is, all actual and potential buyers.

> To obtain a comprehensive view of the position of the organization in a community or market, programmers need to obtain the key public's image of the organization.

Exhibit 6.2 (page 104) illustrates an instrument for assessing internal strengths and weaknesses. The items included are thought to be organizational assets that may result in a competitive advantage. In many cases, they may need to be rewritten to fit the specific circumstances of the agency, but the topics are relevant. Respondents can classify them as "strengths" or "weaknesses" and further indicate if they believe they are major or minor. Responses to this instrument provide the agency with the public's image of them.

From these data, a picture of the strengths and weaknesses of the organization will emerge. This influences the mission of the organization in a variety of ways, depending on the results of the investigation. For example, in a large suburb of a major Midwestern city, it was discovered that a unique strength of the recreation operation was its lakefront parks. Programs operated in these parks were almost sure to succeed and further enhanced residents' image of living in a unique community.

In a medium-sized southern city, a major limitation for the recreation organization was the image of its staff, facilities, and programs. In this instance, the organization needed a major overhaul to successfully operate programs that would attract the target market in sufficient numbers. There were too many serious limitations in essential areas of operation. It was therefore recommended that new personnel policies be implemented, the structure of the financial base and practices of the agency be reorganized, the organizational structure be changed, and the powers and duties of the board be changed. In this case, the organization needed radical change to begin meeting the leisure needs of the community and its individuals.

No organization has enough resources to operate from a position of strength in all areas, that is, to operate all programs for which need could be demonstrated. The idea of assessment is to document organizational strengths and weaknesses so the agency can develop a mission that will direct organizational effort toward its strengths, and to avoid operation in areas where it has weaknesses. The notion of strategic planning and marketing is to match clients' expressed desires with organizational strengths and resources so that targeted markets are well served. To be significant contributors to overall organizational effort, programmers need to understand the role and process of organizational assessment and how it relates to the development of the mission of the organization.

Exhibit 6.2. Organizational Assessment Criteria

Criteria	Strengths			Weaknesses	
	Major	Minor	Neutral	Minor	Major
Board					
Legal authority?	☐	☐	☐	☐	☐
Political leadership?	☐	☐	☐	☐	☐
Responsiveness?	☐	☐	☐	☐	☐
Management					
Accountable?	☐	☐	☐	☐	☐
Visionary leadership?	☐	☐	☐	☐	☐
Flexible?	☐	☐	☐	☐	☐
Staff					
Adequate number?	☐	☐	☐	☐	☐
Skilled?	☐	☐	☐	☐	☐
Enthusiastic?	☐	☐	☐	☐	☐
Service-minded?	☐	☐	☐	☐	☐
Finance					
Adequate resources?	☐	☐	☐	☐	☐
Equitable resource allocations?	☐	☐	☐	☐	☐
Reasonable program prices?	☐	☐	☐	☐	☐
Facilities	☐	☐	☐	☐	☐
Adequate (size, number, and quality)?	☐	☐	☐	☐	☐
Attractiveness?	☐	☐	☐	☐	☐
Good distribution?	☐	☐	☐	☐	☐
Accessibility?	☐	☐	☐	☐	☐
Marketing					
Service reputation?	☐	☐	☐	☐	☐
Partnering in the community?	☐	☐	☐	☐	☐
Promotion effectiveness?	☐	☐	☐	☐	☐

Note. Adapted from Kotler (1991, p. 51).

Once a mission is written, programmers are expected to develop program services that contribute to the mission, thereby helping further build the strengths and weaknesses of the organization. Successful programming is measured, in part, by how well the services contribute to the identified mission and are operated within the resource limitations of the agency. Recreation in the Streets (Rossman, 1973) is an example of a program whose success was partly attributable to its contribution to the agency mission and identified community needs. An analysis of the program is included as Case Study 6.1 (page 123). The Warrior Games, developed by the U.S. Navy, is another example of a program that meets individual, organizational, and community needs. It is presented in Case Study 6.2 (page 124). Both case studies are located at the end of this chapter.

Additional parts of SWOT include scanning the community for unique opportunities the organization may provide and for threats to the organization. Some of this data will result from the scanning activities discussed earlier. But it is critical when completing these scans that programmers know to look for unique opportunities or threats. For example, the public recreation system in every community has the unique asset of an inventory of parkland that often provides the community opportunities no other organization can provide. Contrastingly, the public recreation system sometimes suffers because it cannot move into new markets quickly enough. So learning during an environmental scan that a group of private investors intends to build a new, modern, well-appointed skateboard park could be a threat to the unique position of the agency of owning the only skateboard park in town. The future financial viability of the skateboard park could be threatened. Once an agency no longer has a monopoly position, it will likely need to develop new operational strategies to ensure its operation has a unique value proposition for consumers.

> No organization has enough resources to operate from a position of strength in all areas.

Assessing Community Needs

A notion of *community* implies a set of common ideas or shared beliefs that serve as a binding force for a group of people. Obviously, many ideas and beliefs compete for attention and resources in any larger community. In commercial operations, the notion of community is analogous to the total market, and in a not-for-profit organization, it is analogous to the target or service population.

Community Needs

A marketing approach for assessing community needs is usually executed through social marketing. Kotler and Armstrong (2018) defined social marketing as "the use of traditional business marketing concepts and tools to encourage behaviors that will create individual and societal well being" (p. 249). The organization uses the usual marketing techniques and processes to market social ideas and provide outcomes that are socially purposeful. In the case of public recreation, this means designing and delivering meaningful leisure services that lead to outcomes desirable for the community and build a sense of community.

Kraus (1985) expressed concern about the use of marketing concepts as a major philosophical orientation for the delivery of leisure services:

At the same time, unquestioning acceptance of the marketing point of view raises a number of important issues in terms of the role that recreation and park agencies have traditionally had. When recreation is viewed primarily as a product to be sold, the issue of social value or achieving positive personal outcomes through leisure involvement becomes secondary. (pp. 70–71)

Since this was written, the social marketing concept was developed as a way of addressing these concerns. Zikmund and d'Amico (2002) asserted that social marketing can be in perfect harmony with marketing concepts and stated that it "requires that marketers consider the collective needs of society as well as individual consumers' desires and the organization's need for profits" (p. 21). The community-need orientation of community recreation has been part of the movement since its origins at the beginning of the 20th century and was part of the social-welfare, social-reform movement of the period. The traditional viewpoint assumes that recreation meets a greater community need, as the following section explains, as well as individual needs.

Recreation and the Public Interest: The Social Idea to Be Marketed

The notion of public interest implies a certain relationship of people to society. Friedmann (1973) described the public interest:

The public interest is a republican idea whose origins reach back to the golden age of Greece. It has not always gone by its present designation. At other times, it has been called the commonwealth, the general welfare, or the public good. All these terms express the notion of something shared or held in common. To the extent that something is held in common, that which is shared binds men to one another: The good that is shared creates a moral community whose members agree to be jointly responsible for that which is precious to them. The idea of a public good therefore implies the existence of such a community and the commitment of its members to it. (p. 2)

For many years, recreation was considered one of several public services (e.g., education, libraries, police protection, and fire protection) to be provided in the public interest. The whole notion of Social Justice emanates from this pact of citizens being bound to each other and therefore responsible for the welfare of all included in the commonwealth. Peterson and Schroth (n.d.) presented a rationale for its provision by government:

Leisure, used in a constructive manner, is basic to the self-fulfillment and life enrichment of the individual and therefore helps to strengthen the stability of the family, the community, and the nation.

How people use their leisure time is an important social question. By providing recreation resources, a community is contributing to the physical, mental, and social health of its residents.

Leisure and recreation are recognized as effective ways to enhance life in a community by developing leadership potential and stimulating popular participation for community betterment.

It is only through public recreation services that a large portion of the population will have access to many recreational facilities, such as pools, tennis courts, picnic areas, and golf courses.

Recreation and leisure services consume space. Local government is best suited to acquire, develop, and maintain that space in the best interest of the entire community.

Government sponsorship of recreation services assumes equal participation by all ages, races, and creeds, all seasons of the year; it is democratic and inclusive.

By providing a park and recreation agency, citizen participation on park and recreation boards can be assembled, and the community can focus its attention on protecting public lands and developing facilities and programs. Concentration on long-range plans will help assure proper growth of the system as the community expands.

It is only through government that equitable, fair-share financing is available for the acquisition, development, and maintenance of park facilities and programs.

A park and recreation board can, through cooperative agreements with school boards, library boards, and other governmental agencies, energize and maximize the leisure and recreation potential of a community. (pp. 2–3)

Recreation remains a service to be provided by government in the public interest. What the public interest is in a specific community and what is to be included in a local government's provision of recreation services vary widely from community to community, depending on the identified needs and resources of each community.

The notion of community needs also extends beyond the public interest notion of community recreation. Other organizations that sponsor recreation programs do so to serve a larger sense of community and community need. They have a parallel notion of community need that should be met. Today, the YMCA's corporate slogan is, "At the Y, strengthening community is our cause" (YMCA, n.d. "Our Cause," para. 1). In armed forces recreation operations, the Morale, Welfare, and Recreation unit accomplishes the notion of community needs by meeting the need to prepare troops for *combat readiness* through wellness and fitness programs. The unit meets the need to build the *esprit de corps* of troops by offering programs that provide team-building skills. Similarly, in a corporate recreation operation, the recreation unit meets the need for healthy workers by offering a wellness program, thereby helping meet an important need of the organization. Thus, community recreation providers, as well as recreation operations in all organizations, must ensure the notion meets the needs of its community.

Assessing Leisure Opportunities

Assessing the needs of a community requires an assessment of the range of leisure options available in a community, an understanding of the leisure service system, the role of each provider in the community, and an understanding of the macro environment of the community. Remember, the notion of community need is not simply the aggregation of identified individual needs, but the needs created by a sense of community. Its genesis is the moral contract between individuals who are part of the community and therefore held jointly responsible for the overall good of the community.

Each community has a leisure delivery system made up of public, private, voluntary or quasi-public, and commercial subsystems (Sessoms, 1980). A comprehensive assessment of community needs begins with an inventory of existing service options offered by the complete leisure service delivery system. It is important for the agency to determine the scope and depth of service already available in the community (Bannon, 1976) and the individuals served and not served by the current system.

The public recreation organization has the responsibility in every community to ensure that the leisure needs of the total population are met. This does not mean that they must provide all leisure services. It means that they are ultimately responsible for assessing community recreation needs, maintaining an inventory of the complete community recreation system, conducting individual needs assessments, interpreting needs assessment data, being the catalyst for implementing needed services, and thereby in effect coordinating what is available from the entire system. To accomplish this, the public system may encourage the establishment of a commercial recreation enterprise to meet an identified need or encourage the development of a YMCA. The public recreation organization is the provider of last resort. One of their unique functions is that they are ultimately responsible for meeting the overall leisure needs of the community. To do this, they must comprehend the entire leisure delivery system. As Sessoms (1980) indicated,

> Efforts are made sometimes to coordinate each subsystem without much concern for overall integration. More and more municipal leisure service agencies are beginning attempts to bring the resources of the public, voluntary, private, and commercial interests into play, but in the past these efforts were the exception, not the rule. (p. 126)

The public recreation organization, then, has the unique role of assessing and coordinating the development of the community leisure service system, including its subsystems. A community assessment includes the items displayed in Exhibit 6.3.

> Each community has a leisure delivery system made up of public, private, voluntary or quasi-public, and commercial subsystems.

Once gathered, these data must be analyzed so that the information can be placed into a meaningful pattern and can permit insights into met and unmet needs. Analysis of the comprehensiveness of the leisure service delivery system of the community may be enhanced through use of the Programmer's Evaluation Cube (Exhibit 6.4, page 110). The evaluation cube is a three-dimensional matrix, with life stages on one axis, program activity types on a second axis, and programming formats on a third axis. In conducting this analysis, the programmer examines current services to determine if they are comprehensive and complete on a number of dimensions. Gaps in service become apparent in this analysis. The programmer can expand the basic idea of using a cube for this type of analysis by changing the variables on the cube to analyze further the comprehensiveness of services. For example, program distribution by gender, geographic neighborhoods, and family income would be a legitimate set of variables for analysis. It is axiomatic that the overall leisure service delivery system should provide comprehensive services that include

> The public recreation organization, then, has the unique role of assessing and coordinating the development of the community leisure service system.

1. a wide variety of activity types, including sports, individual activities, fitness activities, hobbies, art, drama, music, and social recreation in the community;
2. a variety of programming formats;
3. service opportunities for all age groups; and
4. service, through some provider in the system, to residents in the community regardless of age, gender, religion, socioeconomic class, geographic location, or other factors.

Exhibit 6.3. Community Needs Assessment Agenda

Open Space Inventory

- Total amount of public park acreage in the community
- Total amount of acreage devoted to recreational use owned by other providers and an estimate of the percentage of population served by the provider
- A map indicating the location of all recreation spaces
- Knowledge about the size of each recreation space

Facility Inventory

- A list of all public recreation facilities, including type, location, and who is serviced by the facility
- A list of all other recreation facilities, including type, location, and who is serviced

Program Services

- A list of all program services offered by public, private, commercial, and quasi-public recreation agencies in the community, including the types of services offered and who is serviced by the programs

Exhibit 6.4. The Programmer's Evaluation Cube

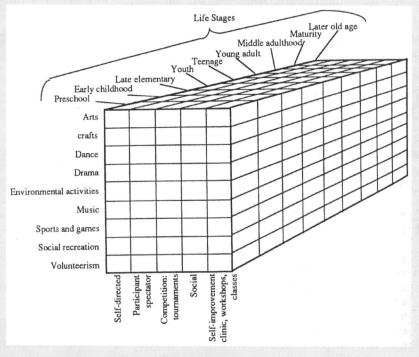

Note. From Farrell and Lundegren (1991). Reprinted with permission.

In examining these data to determine community need, the programmer searches for gaps in services. These gaps may be due to resource limitations or a lack of interest and resources, or may be inadvertent because the gap was previously unknown. In any case, the programmer analyzes existing gaps to determine whether they need to be filled with additional services.

Community Partnerships

Programmers should also assess the adequacy of cooperation and coordination among providers in a community. They can accomplish this by examining agreements establishing partnerships between agencies. Indicators of a coordinated community leisure service system include the number of joint ventures between leisure service providers; the number of joint programs; evidence of sharing resources, facilities, and staff; evidence of coordinated scheduling; and other similar types of evidence.

In a 2012 white paper jointly sponsored by NRPA and the American Academy for Park and Recreation Administration (AAPRA), Rossman (2012) found that over 65% of the agencies participating in the study reported that their agencies developed new operational strategies during the past year (2011) to respond to changes in the environment of their organization (p. 19). Additionally, he found that partnering was a major strategy that agencies used to respond to economic downturn that enabled them to sustain or expand services.

Focusing on the Individual

It is interesting to consider which of these entities—individual, organizational, or community needs—is the driving force that determines agency direction and consequently the content and focus of program services. This dilemma has been conceptualized and discussed elsewhere as a problem of determining whether the organization will have a selling or marketing orientation (Howard & Crompton, 1980; Crompton & Lamb, 1986). A sales orientation places community or organizational needs first and assumes that the organization will convince patrons to consume what they have produced. In contrast, a marketing orientation places consumer needs and wants first. In this case, the organization first discovers what patrons want, then focuses on producing it.

Kotler's (1991) societal marketing concept further explains the relationship of these three need packages to each other:

> The societal marketing concept holds that the organization's task is to determine the needs, wants, and interests of target markets and to deliver the desired satisfactions more effectively and efficiently than competitors in a way that preserves or enhances the consumer's and society's well-being. (p. 26)

With this concept, the driving force is the identified wants and needs of target markets, that is, groups of individuals the agency intends to serve. In this case, the program manager *restructures the organization as needed* to respond to identified client wants and needs. However, program services are still limited by community needs or desires because anything offered must "preserve or enhance" the "consumer's and society's well-being" (Kotler, 1991, p. 26). Because of this latter requirement, developing a philosophy and mission for a not-for-profit organization is somewhat more problematic than developing a philosophy and mission for a commercial recreation operation.

The rise of interest among other sectors of the economy in providing experiences further focuses product development on the individual. Whether an organization is developing a service, a product, or an experience, the focus of product development and marketing has become use by an individual and how its use enhances an individual's experience.

Relationship of the Three Entities to Mission

Figure 6.1 (page 112) illustrates the relationship of each entity to the other. The outermost ring in a series of concentric rings represents the agency mission. As this figure illustrates, the agency mission must encompass individual needs, community needs, and organizational strengths and limitations. However, because no agency has unlimited resources, the agency cannot meet all identified needs, so it must establish priorities for distributing scarce resources. Individual needs are the centermost priority. They influence community needs, organizational needs, and agency mission. The identified needs of individuals are tempered and influenced by community needs and organizational strengths and limitations before they become part of the mission of the agency.

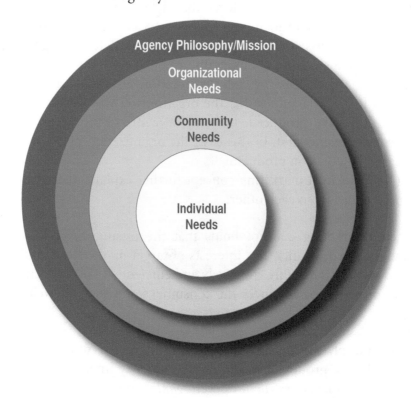

Figure 6.1. Relationship of Mission to Individual, Community, and Organizational Needs

The mission of an agency should be feasible within the limitations imposed on the agency by its own resource limits, by community needs, and by individual wants. Staff should not be asked to accomplish results that they lack the skills or resources to achieve. The mission should motivate staff by giving them clear direction about what they are to accomplish. The mission should communicate how the organization creates value for participants (Kotler & Armstrong, 2018). Finally, the mission should be unique enough to distinguish the organization from other organizations providing similar services.

To be successful, organizations must meet organizational needs and the communal needs of the environment in which they operate. Determining organizational and communal needs is antecedent to developing an agency philosophy or mission statement. One may eventually try to change organization or community perceptions of its needs to better accommodate individual needs once identified. But one must first take inventory of the current state of affairs to have a starting point.

Writing the Mission Statement

Kofi Darbi (2012) observed, "Mission statements are widely believed to be antecedents to any strategy formulation effort (Thompson & Strickland, 1992; Wheelen & Hunger, 1998; Lyles et al., 1993)" (p. 96). Chapter 5 provided an overview of the role of the mission statement of an agency. Thus far, this chapter has reviewed the issues that need to be analyzed so that the mission statement can be written. The analysis portion of this task is complex but necessary because the mission statement must be as clear and simple as possible. There are no step-by-step guidelines to direct its preparation. The reader is reminded that its purpose is to announce to external parties the unique role and function of the agency in the community and to provide direction to employees within the agency to ensure that their activities are coordinated and contribute to accomplishing the mission of the agency. Exhibit 6.5 (page 114) presents examples of mission statements from different agencies. Read and compare the mission statements in Exhibit 6.5 and then proceed with the text that follows.

Each of these mission statements is different but consistent with the current trend of writing short mission statements. Each uses linguistic statements to define or "frame" an area of reality that the agency will attempt to accomplish. None of these statements is clear, specific, or measurable. However, they initiate the process of specifying what the agency will accomplish. From the entire realm of possibilities that the agency could do, the mission statement begins by limiting what the agency will actually do.

> The mission statement begins by limiting what the agency will actually do.

The Arlington County Department of Parks and Recreation mission statement says a lot in a few words without getting too specific. Central to Arlington's mission is the promotion of wellness and vitality through programs and spaces. The concise statement is easy to remember and clearly communicates what the department does. Arlington focuses on meeting the needs of its residents through attractive public spaces and dynamic programs.

Brinker International, a restaurant management firm that operates several restaurant brands, is unique in the way it encourages its customers to take control of their dining experience in terms of pace and convenience. Rather than the wait and kitchen staff controlling the pace of dining, customers co-create their dining experience.

Managing the minutia and meeting client needs are the cruxes of the Woods Event Management mission. No matter the size or scope of the event, Woods promises to create memorable events in a professional manner. Unlike Brinker International, Woods Event Management does not mention event attendees playing a role in creating the memorable experience.

Where the mission of Cayuga Nature Center (a quasi-public agency) encourages the responsible use and appreciation of the natural world, the Adirondack Extreme Adventure Course (a commercial agency) mission makes no such claim. Their mission of fun for everyone suggests that participants will be experience enjoyable challenges in the natural world.

Exhibit 6.5. Mission Statements

ARLINGTON COUNTY DEPARTMENT OF PARKS AND RECREATION

Mission

The Department of Parks and Recreation promotes wellness and vitality through dynamic programs and attractive public spaces.

Discussion

Arlington's mission statement is short and concise, which means that it can be easily remembered by staff, participants, and stakeholders. The statement makes clear its responsibility in fostering vibrant program offerings that encourage good health and well-being. Also key to the mission is the provision of public spaces.

While the mission appears limited to opportunities for dynamic program offerings and public spaces, in actual operation the mission includes all of the resources needed including facilities, land acquisition, land development, adequate financing, and other resources for producing recreation and leisure opportunities, for the department to make these opportunities available.

We weave the Arlington mission and strategic goals throughout Chapter 8 to illustrate examples of strategic directions, networking goals and objectives, as well as their codification.

Note. From Arlington County Department of Parks and Recreation (2016).

BRINKER INTERNATIONAL, INC., DALLAS, TEXAS

Mission

Serving the world a great taste of life through the Power of Welcome.

To implement this mission, they identify five strategic priorities:

1. hospitality,
2. restaurant atmosphere,
3. food and beverage excellence,
4. international expansion, and
5. pace and convenience.

Discussion

Brinker International, Inc., a restaurant management firm that operates well-known restaurant brands Chili's, Maggiano's Little Italy, and On the Border, provides an excellent example of mission and strategic directions in their 2008 annual report. From their 2008 annual report, we have pulled quotes that expand conventional restaurant concern with food, hospitality, and atmosphere to also include the experience of dining in their restaurants. This example illustrates the importance of experience, as well as how improving experience can be part of the strategic direction of the organization.

Not surprising, Brinker concentrates on serving excellent food and beverages in a novel, appropriate atmosphere. But its goals for hospitality and pace and convenience depend heavily on the interactions of their staff with guests. To implement hospitality, Brinker identifies the following strategic direction:

Exhibit 6.5. (continued)

Our top priority remains creating a culture of hospitality that establishes emotional connections with our guests and engages our Team Members. We believe that providing a consistently warm, welcoming, and engaging dining experience will continue to differentiate Brinker brands from all others in the industry. Hospitality also builds guest loyalty, as evidenced by the feedback we gather in our guest satisfaction surveys. And as we deliver an outstanding guest experience, we also engage and retain the loyal Team Members who enable us to deliver on our hospitality promise. At Brinker, we call hospitality the "Power of Welcome."

- Get Real – by making a human connection with every guest, every Team Member, at every opportunity, every day.
- Make it Right – with the freedom to serve. We'll do whatever it takes to make sure our guests feel special and leave happier than when they came in. (pp. 01–02)

Clearly, their corporate strategy is for their employees to engage customers in implementing hospitality. This takes more than making announcements to guests. It requires interactive conversation.

To further the interactive nature of the dining experience, Brinker implements a strategy to put the customer in control of the pace and convenience of the dining experience. Their strategy for pace and convenience follows:

Perhaps our most exciting area of focus is transforming the casual dining experience in terms of pace and convenience for the guest. From what our guests tell us in satisfaction surveys, pace and convenience are all about guest choice—putting them in control of the dining experience. Whether the guest is in a hurry or wants to relax over a leisurely meal, Brinker brands deliver an experience like no other in the industry. (p. 05)

Normally in a restaurant, the wait and kitchen staff control the pace of dining. Brinker is attempting to implement a strategy that will put the guest in charge of pace. Some customers are in a hurry, while others want a leisurely pace. Brinker believes empowering customers to set the pace is unique in the industry and will distinguish its brands over others.

Both of these strategic directions illustrate the importance of building customer experiences into an organization's ongoing operations, as well as the importance of facilitating opportunities for customers to be participants in the experiences delivered and to co-create them.

Note. From Brinker International (2009).

WOODS EVENT MANAGEMENT, INC.

Mission

Details! Details! Details! Let us take care of yours!

Woods Event Management, Inc., will be the leader in managing business events, focusing on the needs of our clients. The primary objectives of the corporation are:

- To provide the necessary expertise in managing the client's program from initial concept to completion of the event.
- To exceed our client's expectations.
- To provide an event that will be remembered as a "unique experience."
- To maintain a consistent, high level of service.
- To be fair, honest and ethical in all dealings with our employees, clients, and suppliers.

Exhibit 6.5. (continued)

Discussion

The mission for Woods Event Management assures clients that their programmed event or experience will be memorable and executed professionally. Two essential components to their mission (or any mission) are meeting customer needs and taking care of event details. Woods delivers a wide range of events from large to small, weddings to conferences, and golf outings to family reunions.

Note. From Woods Event Management (n.d.).

SAN DIEGO PARK AND RECREATION DEPARTMENT, SAN DIEGO, CALIFORNIA

Our Mission

To provide healthy, sustainable, and enriching environments for all.

Our Vision

To connect all to the City's diverse world class park system.

Discussion

San Diego Park and Recreation's mission is brief, broad, and far reaching to include the city's diverse population that are supported through park spaces that are ecologically balanced.

Note. From City of San Diego Park and Recreation Department (n.d.).

CARNIVAL CRUISE LINE

Mission: Choose Fun

Carnival Cruise Lines prides itself on delivering fun, memorable vacations to our guests by offering a wide array of quality cruises which present outstanding value for the money.

Discussion

Carnival's mission centers on fun for its customers. The ship's crew is ready to deliver an enjoyable experience for its customers whether it is in the dining room, in the casino, in a youth program, poolside, or on an excursion.

Note. From Carnival Cruise Lines. (n.d.).

NAVY MORALE, WELFARE, AND RECREATION

Our Mission

Navy MWR's mission is to deliver high-quality, customer-focused programs and services that contribute to resiliency, retention, readiness, and quality of life.

Our Goals

Navy MWR conducts activities and events, and delivers high-quality, innovative recreation programs in state-of-the-art facilities worldwide.

Exhibit 6.5. (continued)

Why Choose Us

Navy MWR provides excellent customer service, convenient program availability, modern facilities and amenities, a safe program environment, and low or competitive pricing. The money you spend using MWR programs and services is reinvested into the overall program.

Discussion

To meet their mission, the Navy focuses on the meeting the needs of their customers in order to one's overall improve quality of life. This is accomplished through the facilitation of creative events and programs in advanced venues.

Note. From Navy Morale, Welfare, and Recreation (n.d.).

MERAGE JEWISH COMMUNITY CENTER OF ORANGE COUNTY, IRVINE, CALIFORNIA

Our Mission

To build a welcoming Jewish community by inspiring and enriching Jewish identity.

Our Values

Excellence: Exceeding expectations in leadership, staffing, operations programming and service.

Jewish Culture: Fostering meaningful connections to the land and people of Israel and the Jewish community worldwide and celebrating ourJewish identity, history, roots and culture l'dor v'dor (generation to generation).

Community: Always providing a warm, supportive environment, welcoming all no matter where or whether our community worships, whatever their age or lifestyle.

Family-oriented: Fitness, education and enrichments, Israel and Jewish connections, we have programs for all, from young to not-so-young. Programs for families and for individuals. We are a place for your whole family.

Discussion

An interesting aspect of this mission statement is the desire to celebrate and enrich Jewish life while inviting involvement of all community persons regardless of their age or religious background.

Note. From Merage Jewish Community (n.d.).

CAYUGA NATURE CENTER, ITHACA, NEW YORK

The Cayuga Nature Center is a community resource that cultivates awareness, appreciation and responsibility for the natural world through outdoor and environmental education.

Discussion

Cayuga Nature Center overlooks the Cayuga Finger Lake in upstate New York. The mission gently advocates for personal responsibility in the natural world. Its programs and services celebrate the mission through activities that promote discovery, challenge, exposure, and innovation.

Note. From Cayuga Nature Center (n.d.).

Exhibit 6.5. (continued)

ADIRONDACK EXTREME ADVENTURE COURSE

Fun for Everyone

Our Aerial Tree Top Adventure course is an elevated obstacle course set in the beautiful Adirondack Mountains and securely suspended between the trees at 10 to 60 feet off the ground.

Some of the features of course include giant Tyrolean Zip lines, suspended bridges, swinging surprises, Tarzan swings, nets and much, much more.

Come on your own or bring your group, party or an event. Take a journey and explore the outdoors like you never have before.

Discussion

The mission suggests that participants will conquer and persevere through human-made challenges in the natural environment. The adventure obstacle course has similar programmatic elements to those offered at the Cayuga Nature Center; however, the notion of appreciating and caring for nature is missing. It is replaced with phrasing that suggests the company wants to make money by encouraging as many customers as possible, regardless of the impact on the natural environment.

Note. From Adirondack Extreme (n.d.).

ARTS COUNCIL OF NEW ORLEANS

Mission Statement

We believe the arts are essential to the life of the community. It is the mission of the Arts Council of New Orleans to support and to expand the opportunities for diverse artistic expression and to bring the community together in celebration of our rich multi-cultural heritage.

Discussion

This private nonprofit organization strives to meet the arts and cultural needs of the New Orleans area through partnering with the City, governmental agencies, community groups, and other non-profits. The council administers grants, honors deserving organizations and individuals with awards, advocates for policies and funding priorities that benefit the arts, and serves as a resource for the arts community. The council centers its operation on advocacy, awards, grants, and partnerships as opposed to the provision of organized programs and services.

Note. From Arts Council of New Orleans (n.d.).

TULANE UNIVERSITY CAMPUS RECREATION

Mission Statement

The Department of Campus Recreation encourages personal growth by providing recreational and wellness opportunities to the Tulane community. We are committed to creating an environment which fosters the physical and social development of students, lifelong learning, respect, and cultural diversity.

Discussion

Campus recreation is often the focal point for student activity on university campuses. Not only does campus recreation offer a wide variety of programming, but it often features state-of-the-art facilities similar to Tulane, which include tennis courts, a synthetic turf field, quad spaces, and a

Exhibit 6.5. (continued)

pool. An interesting aspect of campus recreation for those studying recreation is that these facilities often employ professional staff with backgrounds in recreation and numerous part-time student staff who are interested in the recreation field. In fact, campus recreation units are often the largest student employer on campus.

Note. From Tulane University Campus Recreation (n.d.).

THE FIELD MUSEUM

Public Learning: Offering Greater Understanding About Environments And People

Unlike schooling, learning in a museum is self-motivated, self-directed, and can be lifelong. Unlike print and electronic media, information is communicated primarily through real, tangible objects. Museum learning usually takes place during leisure time and without the direction of a teacher. The exhibit is the principal avenue of learning. Exhibits are augmented by people-mediated programs and a visitor-oriented museum-wide staff who reach out to assist all visitors. Services to schools and communities extend the museum experience to people beyond our walls. To stimulate a public sense of inquiry, curiosity and delight, our exhibits and programs are not only informative, but also entertaining and inspiring. We focus on critical environmental and cultural issues which are engaging and relevant to the public's daily lives and civic responsibilities. We must be a vital educational and recreational destination for both our local and world-wide communities.

Discussion

Gone are the days of static, one-dimensional museum exhibits! The Field Museum's Public Learning mission is to spark the visitor's curiosity through interactive, educational, and entertaining programs and exhibits. Staying current on environmental and cultural issues is essential for the museum to be significant to the citizenry. Finally, the museum extends its reach to communities by offering opportunities beyond the museum campus.

Note. From The Field Museum. (n.d.).

The mission of the Merage Jewish Community Center of Orange County describes a commitment to serving the Jewish community, as well as the entire Orange County community. This differs somewhat to the Navy Morale, Welfare, and Recreation (MWR) mission, as the MWR primarily serves active-duty, reserve, and retired Navy personnel and their families, but does not serve civilian employees who work at U.S. Navy facilities.

It is important for the reader to recognize that all mission statements have an underlying philosophy that provides a foundation for action in the agency. Often this philosophy is not explicit; it is made apparent only through ongoing actions taken by the organization. Whether explicit or implicit, an underlying philosophy guides the actions an agency takes. Now complete Exercise 6.2 (page 120).

Break into four small groups and select one of the following types of recreation and leisure service agencies: (1) municipal recreation and park department, (2) commercial recreation business, (3) community-based therapeutic recreation agency, or (4) campus intramural recreation department. Using Figure 6.1 (page 112) and Exhibit 6.2 (page 104) as guides, write a brief mission statement for your selection.

Discussion questions:

- Did the mission statements vary as a function of the agency type?
- What are the difficulties of writing a mission statement?
- What were the underlying philosophies of each?
- To what extent were the mission statements flexible?

Conclusion

The mission statement of the agency emerges from an analysis of individual, organizational, and community needs. This chapter discussed issues related to and methods for analyzing them, and it provided sample mission statements from 12 agencies. The mission statement states the purpose of the agency, identifies the population it will serve, makes clear the value it will create for participants, and finally, specifies what business the organization is in. It should be based on an analysis of the strengths and weaknesses of the organization and an analysis of the threats and opportunities facing the agency in the larger community environment. For programmers to achieve ongoing success requires that their programs meet individual, organizational, and community needs. Case studies of two such programs are provided following the References section.

References

Abruzzese, L. (2017). Good-ish times for the global economy. In *The World in 2018* (p. 22). London, England: The Economist.

Adirondack Extreme. (n.d.). About us. Retrieved October 25, 2018, from https://adirondackextreme.com/about-us/

Arlington County Department of Parks and Recreation. (2016). *Strategic plan 2016–2020*. Retrieved from http://arlingtonparks.us/docs/mobile/index.html#p=1

Arts Council of New Orleans. (n.d.). Mission statement. Retrieved October 25, 2018, from http://www.artscouncilofneworleans.org/article.php?story=about.whoweare

Bannon, J. J. (1976). *Leisure resources: Its comprehensive planning*. Englewood Cliffs, NJ: Prentice-Hall.

Brinker International. (2009). *2008 Brinker International, Inc. annual report*. Retrieved from http://www.brinker.com/company/Brinker2008/AnnualReport2008.pdf

Carnival Cruise Lines. (n.d.). About us. Retrieved October 25, 2018, from http://www.carnival.com/cms/fun/about_us.aspx?icid=CC_Footer_103

Cayuga Nature Center. (n.d.). About us. Retrieved October 25, 2018, from https://www.priweb.org/index.php/about-us

Centers for Disease Control and Prevention. (2016). Prevalence of obesity among adults and youth. Retrieved from https://www.cdc.gov/nchs/products/databriefs/db288.htm

City of San Diego Park and Recreation Department. (n.d.). Mission statement and vision. Retrieved from http://www.sannet.gov/park-and-recreation/general-info/mission.html

Common Sense Media. (2016). The Common Sense: Plugged-in parents of tweens and teens. Retrieved from https://www.commonsensemedia.org/research/the-common-sense-census-plugged-in-parents-of-tweens-and-teens-2016

Crompton, J. L. (2013, December). Are your seniors moving to center stage? *Parks and Recreation, 48*(12), 37–41.

Crompton, J. L., & Lamb, C. W., Jr. (1986). *Marketing government and social services.* New York, NY: Wiley.

Dolesh, R. (2018, February). Top trends in parks and recreation for 2018. *Parks and Recreation, 53*(2), 39–41.

Eddy, N. (2014, January 17). iPhone apps to help track your health and fitness. Retrieved from http://www.eweek.com/mobile/iphone-apps-to-help-track-your-health-and-fitness

Farrell, P., & Lundegren, H. M. (1991). *The process of recreation programming: Theory and technique* (3rd ed.). State College, PA: Venture.

The Field Museum. (n.d.). Mission statement. Retrieved October 24, 2018, from https://archive.li/3IXok

Friedmann, J. (1973). The public interest and community participation: Toward a reconstruction of public philosophy. *Journal of American Institute of Planners, 39*(1), 2–12.

Henry J. Kaiser Family Foundation. (2010, January 20). Generation M2: Media in the lives of 8- to 18-year-olds. Retrieved from from http://www.kff.org/entmedia/mh012010pkg.cfm

Howard, D. R., & Crompton, J. L. (1980). *Financing, managing, and marketing recreation and park programs.* Dubuque, IA: Wm. C. Brown.

Jacobs, J. (1961). *The death and life of great American cities.* New York, NY: Vintage Books.

Knowles, M. S. (1970). *The modern practice of adult education: Andragogy versus pedagogy.* New York, NY: Association Press.

Kofi Darbi, W. P. (2012). Of mission and vision statement and their potential impact on employee behaviour and attitudes: The case of a public but profit-oriented tertiary institution. *International Journal of Business and Social Science, 3*(4), 95–109.

Kotler, P. (1982). *Marketing for nonprofit organizations* (2nd ed.). Englewood Cliffs, NJ: Prentice-Hall.

Kotler, P. (1991). *Marketing management: Analysis, planning, implementation, and control* (7th ed.). Englewood Cliffs, NJ: Prentice-Hall.

Kotler, P., & Armstrong, G. (2018). *Principles of marketing* (17th ed.). New York, NY: Pearson.

Kraus, R. G. (1985). *Recreation program planning today.* Glenview, IL: Scott Foresman.

Madren, C. (2014). A sporting shift: New trends in adult sports require dynamic planning by park and recreation agencies. *Parks and Recreation, 49*(2), 49–53.

Merage Jewish Community. (n.d.). About. Retrieved from https://www.jccoc.org/main/about/

National Recreation and Park Association. (2017). *Local government officials' perceptions of parks and recreation.* Retrieved from https://www.nrpa.org/publications-research/research-papers/local-government-officials-perceptions-of-parks-and-recreation/

Navy Morale, Welfare, and Recreation. (n.d.). Mission statement. Retrieved October 25, 2018, from http://www.mwr.navy.mil/

Peterson, J. A., & Schroth, R. J. (n.d.). *Guidelines for evaluating public parks and recreation*. West Lafayette, IN: Cooperative Extension Service, Purdue University.

Pfeffer, J., & Salancik, G. R. (1978). *The external control of organizations: A resource dependence perspective*. New York, NY: Harper and Row.

Rossman, J. R. (1973, March–April). Recreation in the streets. *Illinois Parks and Recreation, 4*, 4–5.

Rossman, J. R. (2012). *White paper: The agile organization: Transforming your agency to survive and thrive in any economy*. Arlington, VA: National Recreation and Park Association.

Russell, C. (2014). The top 10 demographic trends. *American Consumers Newsletter*. Retrieved from http://www.newstrategist.com/the-top-10-demographic-trends/

Sessoms, D. H. (1980). Community development and social planning. In S. G. Lutzin (Ed.), *Managing municipal leisure services* (pp. 120–139). Washington, DC: International City Management Association.

Tillman, A. (1973). *The program book for recreation professionals*. Palo Alto, CA: Mayfield.

Tulane University Campus Recreation. (n.d.). About. Retrieved October 25, 2018, from http://www.reilycenter.com/?page_id=5

van der Smissen, B. (1972). *Evaluation and self-study of public recreation and park agencies: A guide with standards and evaluative criteria*. Arlington, VA: National Recreation and Park Association.

Weinswig, D. (2016). Deep dive: Millennials and leisure. Retrieved from Fung Global Retail and Technology website: https://www.fungglobalretailtech.com/wp-content/uploads/2016/11/Millennials-and-Leisure-November-18-2016.pdf

Woods Event Management. (n.d.). About. Retrieved October 25, 2018, from http://www.woodseventmgmt.com/about.htm

YMCA. (n.d.). About us. Retrieved October 24, 2018, from http://www.ymca.net/about-us

Zikmund, W. G., & d'Amico, M. (2002). *Effective marketing: Creating and keeping customers in an e-commerce world* (3rd ed.). Cincinnati, OH: South-Western.

Case Study 6.1. Recreation in the Streets

Recreation in the Streets was developed in 1973 in Oak Park, Illinois. The community is the first suburb west of Chicago's corporate boundary. During the late 1960s and early 1970s, the population in the Chicago neighborhoods east of Oak Park had changed from all White to all Black. The typical pattern of racial turnover in segregated White Chicago neighborhoods was one of increasing distrust of new neighbors (Black or White) and increasing isolation of existing residents in their own homes. This isolation intensified until each resident, at his or her own breaking point, moved, and the neighborhood once again became totally segregated, this time with all Black residents. Oak Park developed a community goal of establishing and maintaining racially integrated neighborhoods. To accomplish this, the City needed to find White and Black buyers for homes offered for sale and to create open neighborhoods where residents know and trust each other.

All city departments were asked to foster and facilitate an open dialogue among residents. The goal was to encourage them to interact with each other and in doing so create a safe, stable neighborhood (Jacobs, 1961). To contribute to this policy, the Oak Park Recreation Department developed the Recreation in the Streets program with the following goals:

1. to place leaders from local neighborhood playgrounds into neighborhoods one day per week in order to create visibility for the leaders and their program, and to foster trust in the leadership provided at the neighborhood recreation centers;
2. to create interaction among neighbors on city blocks and to create a visible program service that would enable residents to come out of their homes and meet each other; and
3. to temporarily create additional play space in an urban environment by making the street into a playground.

The program consisted of having three leaders from a neighborhood recreation center visit a residential block one morning per week from 9:00 a.m. until noon. Traffic was blocked off from the street, and a trailer filled with recreation equipment was delivered to the block at about 8:30 a.m. When leaders arrived, they set up a volleyball net, a puppet stage, and other equipment in the street. The leaders then conducted an organized program consisting of events such as parachute games, bicycle and tricycle races, street hockey, volleyball games, chalk drawing on the street, and craft projects. The morning concluded with a luncheon cookout, and the street was reopened at noon. Each of the seven neighborhood recreation centers visited a different block each week for the 7 weeks of the summer program.

In addition to facilitating interaction during the event, Recreation in the Streets was designed to require the interaction of neighbors in requesting and operating the event. To be selected for a visit, a block resident had to obtain the signatures of at least 50% of the block residents on a petition for service to be provided by the Recreation Department. Blocks to be visited were selected on the basis of their existing service (blocks farthest from existing services received highest priority) and their previous history of receiving visits. Once a block was selected for a visit, the individual who initiated the petition was responsible for designating a home on the block where the trailer could be parked, for circulating notices that the street would be closed the next day for the event, and for obtaining a charcoal grill for the cookout.

Residents clearly had to interact before the event; otherwise, it could not occur. Recreation in the Streets is an example of a program that was designed to build on an existing strength of the Oak Park Recreation Department, that is, its well-distributed neighborhood recreation centers. In addition, it met an identified community need of fostering interaction among residents. In this program, individual, community, and organizational needs, as well as organizational mission, were met within the resource limits of the agency.

Case Study 6.2. Warrior Games

In 1985, a ship commander requested that Navy recreation personnel create a program for sailors who were given 24-hour duty leave from extended training missions operating out of Guantánamo Bay, Cuba. Ships operating out of the bay are sent on training missions that simulate combat situations for 14 to 21 days at a time. They return infrequently to base for a 24-hour leave. It was important that some type of recreation be available to provide release from the continual strain of simulated combat conditions. It was equally important that the training mission of creating esprit de corps, teamwork, and leadership not be broken during these short leaves. The recreation program, then, needed to provide opportunities for fun, teamwork, and leadership.

A series of Warrior Games was developed and was operated as competitions among units. These games presented the sailors with a problem that needed to be solved. The solution did not require superior strength or skill. To successfully solve the problem and win the competition, someone in the unit had to exercise leadership and get the unit to operate as a team. For example, in one game a unit had to submerge a large inflated ball in a swimming pool by organizing unit members to lock hands and legs to form a "human cargo net" to drape over the ball. This could be done only with the organized cooperation of the entire unit. Similarly, in each Warrior Game, a different problem had to be solved quickly through the cooperation of the entire unit.

In this program, organizational needs (the Morale, Welfare, and Recreation unit's need to contribute to combat readiness), community needs (command needs to continue the themes of the training mission), and individual needs (for a playful diversion) were met with a single program operating within the resource limits of the organization. Excellence in organized recreation programming requires that the needs of all three entities be met simultaneously.

Learning Archery During the Recreation Centers' Outdoor Camp
Photo courtesy of City of Grand Prairie Parks, Arts, and Recreation Department.

7 Developing Strategic Directions

KEY TERMS

3–5-Year Strategic Directions, Management by Objective (MBO),
Networking Goals and Objectives, Operational Clarity, Systems Approach

Step 2: Strategic Directions

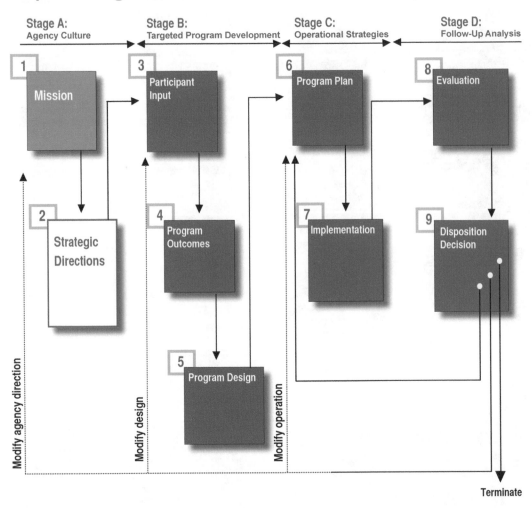

Agencies give additional direction and focus to their mission by developing a series of specific strategic directions and a series of supporting goals and objectives. As Chapter 5 indicated, a mission statement is not measurable. The sample mission statements included in Chapter 6 are not measurable. Therefore, agencies must develop a series of linguistic statements to provide a means for operationalizing and measuring their mission statement. This is accomplished in Step 2 of the Program Development Cycle. The next level of strategy development is a series of 3- to 5-year strategic directions that are often followed with 1-year management by objective (MBO) statements that specify programs the agency will implement.

> The next level of strategy development is a series of 3- to 5-year strategic directions.

3- to 5-Year Strategic Directions

For an example of statements of 3- to 5-year short-range planning goals, see Arlington County Department of Parks and Recreation (2016; presented as

Figure 9.1 on page 175). The department further develops its mission statement, to promote "wellness and vitality through dynamic programs and attractive public spaces" (presented in Chapter 6), through five short-range planning goals:

1. Provide excellent programs, services, places, and spaces.
2. Steward natural and historical resources.
3. Build community, promote wellness, and ensure equal access for all.
4. Manage access efficiently and effectively.
5. Cultivate an effective, dynamic workforce.

These five strategic directions are examples of statements that do not include measurement devices (i.e., they are not SMART). Some agencies refer to these as strategic goals, but the confusion created with this language has been discussed previously. These are strategies the organization will pursue to implement its mission over the next 3 to 5 years.

Implementing Intentionally Designed Experiences

Recreation and park agencies that adopt an intentionally designed experience derive from their mission statement 3- to 5-year planning directions. These planning directions should be based on the fundamental premise that the agency envisions itself to be a key element for improving and enhancing community life. The resultant program management goals should exude these qualities.

As this chapter will describe, intentionally designed planning goals, like any planning directions, will be networked fully into the agency from the administrative level to the programming level. The further those planning goals are networked into the agency, the more directive and specific they become for programmers.

Identification and articulation of strategies published in a plan announces to the public and employees the outcomes an organization will pursue and how it will pursue them. Strategy formation is a collaborative planning process that results in a plan that ensures consistency in organizational behavior while the organization pursues its strategies. Much could be done to implement Arlington County's mission, but the board and CEO have agreed that these are the initiatives the organization needs to address over the next 3–5 years to implement its mission. The strategies should also position the organization in its market. An examination of the strategic directions presented reveals that they are comprehensive and address initiatives including program development, revenue production, interagency cooperation, marketing, and others.

Management by Objectives

In the next level of development, the organization writes MBO statements to implement strategic directions. MBO statements must be SMART. For example, the first strategic direction for Arlington County, "to provide excellent programs, services, places, and spaces," could be implemented in fiscal year (FY) 2020 with the following possible MBO statements:

1. The Superintendent of Parks and Recreation will hire a Fitness and Wellness Supervisor within the first two months of FY 2020.
2. The Superintendent of Parks and Recreation will budget $75,000 for fitness and wellness programs during FY 2020.
3. The Superintendent of Parks and Recreation will operate 20 fitness and wellness programs during FY 2020.

These examples illustrate statements typical of an MBO system. They are SMART. That is, they are specific, measurable, assignable, realistic, and time-based. Again, this is usually where organizations integrate strategic planning activities with budgeting. The development of a specific program service has become a budget element with resources committed to its implementation—thus the need for them to be in the SMART format so the organization can assess and document their implementation.

As is the case in the use of goals and objectives, it is assumed that the CEO and the superintendent of parks and recreation jointly agree that the successful accomplishment of these MBO statements will be accepted as proof that the strategic direction, "to provide excellent programs, services, places, and spaces," has been accomplished. This is the implicit assumption of the process. We accept this, knowing

> This is usually where organizations integrate strategic planning activities with budgeting.

that the MBO statements identified are just a partial list of all that could be done to accomplish the stated strategic direction. Here are possible MBO statements that might be added to the fitness and wellness programming list already prepared:

(Continuing the previous list)

4. During FY 2020 the Superintendent of Parks and Recreation will establish a facility reservation system that is operable by May 1, 2020.
5. During FY 2020 the Superintendent of Parks and Recreation will establish five new fitness-based programs for teens (age 13–17) that will have total enrollments of 150 individuals or more.

So the superintendent of parks and recreation has at least five MBO statements to accomplish for 2020. Most likely, the superintendent will have additional MBO statements. Since strategic directions are not SMART and thus not measurable, the process continues with the development of additional MBO support statements that are SMART and measurable for each strategic direction. The additional statements provide metrics for the organization to assess and document its outcomes.

Also, this list shows examples of different ways of writing MBO statements. Different phrasing can be used, as well as different types of measurement devices for achieving more flexibility in possible ways of implementing and measuring success. Although we provide just a few examples, the best way for the reader to learn how to implement this process is through tutored practice. Students should expect that their instructor will require in-class or homework assignments to provide practice in writing these and other types of goals and objectives.

Networking Goals and Objectives
Further in the Organization

Continuing with the Arlington example, we illustrate further how goals and objectives are networked throughout the organization and how their use provides additional direction and focus to program management. After hiring the fitness and wellness supervisor and budgeting the funds for the year, the superintendent gives the objective of "to operate 20 fitness and wellness programs during FY 2020" to the new fitness and wellness supervisor as one of his or her goals for FY 2020. The superintendent asks for a list of objectives outlining how the fitness and wellness supervisor intends to accomplish this goal. The fitness and wellness supervisor could then develop the following list of objectives:

1. To operate lunch and learn fitness and wellness presentations for seniors during the spring of 2020.
2. To offer basic bicycle maintenance, repair classes, and workshops for teens and adults during the summer of 2020.
3. To operate an introduction to martial arts series for teens during September 2020.
4. To operate a weekly family fitness instructional class during the fall of 2020.

These statements could be made more specific still with additional measurement devices. For example, the second objective could be rewritten as "during the summer of 2020 the fitness and wellness supervisor will operate basic bicycle maintenance, repair classes, and workshops for teens and adults with an attendance of 60 participants or more." The addition of these measurement devices further defines how success in accomplishing this objective will be measured. How detailed an objective must be is a matter of professional practice in a specific organization. Remember, using goal and objectives is a means to the end of developing useful programs and services and of measuring and documenting the accomplishments of the organization. Goals and objectives should be developed to the point that they provide operational clarity; that is, those responsible for implementation understand their meaning, and the whole process therefore helps the organization achieve and document its accomplishments.

It is certainly possible and often the practice for agencies to further develop goals and objectives if there are additional levels of employees or the outcomes stated are still broad and need further refinement. For example, the fitness and wellness supervisor may hand the objective of "during the summer of 2020 the fitness and wellness supervisor will operate basic bicycle maintenance and repair classes and workshops for teens and adults with an enrollment of 60 participants or more" to a program supervisor. This statement is now an annual performance goal for the program supervisor, who will need to develop a series of SMART objectives to accomplish the goal. Again, an objective for the fitness and wellness supervisor becomes a goal for the program supervisor, as it is passed to a different level of the organization. This is how goals and objectives are networked through an organization.

The following objectives that document accomplishment of the goal can then be prepared:

1. The program supervisor will offer a 4-week class for teens on basic bicycle maintenance and repair during the summer of 2020 with an enrollment of 15 or more.
2. The program supervisor will offer a 4-week class for adults on basic bicycle maintenance and repair during the summer of 2020 with an enrollment of 15 or more.
3. The program supervisor will offer a How to Change and Fix a Flat Tube half-day workshop during the summer of 2020 with an enrollment of 10 or more.
4. The program supervisor will offer a How to Adjust Your Bicycle Brakes and Derailleur Cables 1-day workshop during the summer of 2020 with an enrollment of 10 or more.
5. The program supervisor will offer a Clean and Lubricate Your Bike half-day workshop during the summer of 2020 with an enrollment of 10 or more.
6. The program supervisor will offer The Nuts and Bolts of Bicycle Nuts and Bolts workshop during the summer of 2020 summer with an enrollment of 10 or more.
7. The program supervisor will offer a Wheel Truing Basics 1-day workshop during the summer of 2020 with an enrollment of 10 or more.

These objectives indeed offer seven classes in basic bicycle maintenance and repair, thus fulfilling the aspirations of the goal. Assuming the program supervisor and the fitness and wellness supervisor agree to accept this list, it becomes the metric for determining accomplishment of the goal. Often, the two supervisors will discuss and maybe revise these based on their discussion. Preparing SMART program management goals and objectives is an important skill that programmers must develop to provide direction effectively for the development and management of program services. When properly prepared, they network and coordinate programming operations and provide metrics for determining and documenting accomplishment of the outputs of the organization. Remember, however, that they have not yet developed program design goals; Chapter 9 discusses this. Now complete Exercise 7.1.

Using Goals and Objectives to Establish Programming Standards

The organization can also use program management goals and objectives to establish operational standards. McCarville (1993) indicated, "Standards provide precise standards that staff members may use to monitor their own success in providing programs and services" (p. 36). Exhibit 7.1 (page 132) describes program planning standards and outcomes for the operation of recreation services for the

Develop a hierarchy of goals and objectives for the following strategy from those presented earlier in this chapter:

3. Build community, promote wellness, and ensure equal access for all.

Prepare one MBO statement for implementing this in a specific fiscal year.

Then prepare two objectives for implementing this MBO statement.

Then prepare two statements for implementing each objective at the next level of the organization.

Trade your statements with another student and analyze each other's work. Consider and discuss the following points:

- Are each of the statements SMART?
- Do the statements have operational clarity?
- Is there a clear hierarchical order to the statements that becomes progressively more specific?

City of Eau Claire, Wisconsin. Using standards and outcomes in this manner helps direct the program that will be developed at each recreation center.

Program management goals such as those in Exhibit 7.1 (page 132) ensure that program operations at Eau Claire Parks, Recreation, and Forestry Department are organized and controlled with a minimum level of programming. They establish standards and outcomes for program content, evaluation, and review. Similar approaches direct the management of day camps, swimming pools, craft centers, and the like. In experience-producing organizations, these types of goals are analogous to the production goals in manufacturing organizations. Organizations can use program management goals as quality assurance guidelines to direct program production at a number of similar facilities or programming entities. Now complete Exercise 7.2 (page 135).

A Codification Approach to Networked Goals and Objectives

Another way to network agency goals and objectives is through codification. Introduced in Chapter 6, the Commission for Accreditation of Park and Recreation Agencies (CAPRA) has 10 major categories of standards that use a codification system to measure compliance with a given standard. Standard 6.0, Programs and Services Management, consists of five subcategories, each of which is assigned a number. The City of Eau Claire's Parks, Recreation, and Forestry Department Comprehensive Recreation Program Plan (2013–2017) in Exhibit 7.1 (page 132) illustrates how succeeding levels of goals and objectives are codified.

Exhibit 7.1. Parks, Recreation, and Forestry Planning Standards and Outcomes

The City of Eau Claire's *Parks, Recreation, and Forestry Department Comprehensive Recreation Program Plan* (2013–2017) identifies standards and target outcomes to establish general practices for programming.

CITY OF EAU CLAIRE
PARKS, RECREATION, AND FORESTRY
RECREATION PROGRAMMING PLAN

Recreation Program Standards and Outcomes

The Recreation Division has moved from general program objectives to more specific program target outcomes, as defined in the Recreation Program Plan and as identified in the *Prime Times* activities and services publication. Programming outcomes have been established for each activity offered. The Recreation Division team reviews and updates the program outcomes prior to each publication or twice annually.

Recreation Programming Target Outcomes
   a. Encouraging people to try new things, develop new skills, or maintain existing skills.
   b. Promoting affordable healthy options on concession menus, in vending machines, and for program snacks.
   c. Offering programming that can improve a participant's health, strength, endurance, and well-being.
   d. Cultivating social skills, including leadership, team building, following directions, sportsmanship, and cooperation.
   e. Creating a safer community in and around water through learn-to-swim programming.
   f. Providing a connection to the natural environment.
   g. Creating positive activities and fun environments that allow creative expression for youth.
   h. Facilitating gatherings and bringing the community together.
   i. Developing friendships through social interaction and similar interests.
   j. Promoting individual and community development.
   k. Offering a range of options for different income levels and different abilities.
   l. Adapting to new demographics and preferences.
   m. Offering programs that are responsive to community demands or interest.
   n. Evaluating programs, services, and facilities measured through analysis and evaluation results.

Selection of Program Content

The Recreation Division selects program content based on specific activities and opportunities with an understanding of individual differences and the culture of the community. The Internal Needs Index outlines programs for each age segment of the population, the scope of the program (e.g., skill development, physical development, relaxation, cultural, club, or tournament), the participation level (e.g., single, small group, or large group), the degree of involvement, and the primary function (e.g., physical, educational, social, or creative). The Recreation Division solicits customer feedback through program evaluations to ensure that the community is pleased with the program offerings and programs and that services are added, removed, or modified to reflect the culture, ages, interests, and skill progression of patrons. The 2010 census information and School District Annual Reports are useful in determining the makeup of the community and assisting in determining programs and services that reflect community needs, demographics, and economic status. These documents are located in Recreation Superintendents Operations Manual.

Exhibit 7.1. (continued)

Examples of programs with a system of progression include:
- Red Cross Learn to Swim (parent–child, otter, seal, dolphin, Levels 1–6)
- USTA Quick Start Tennis Program (Levels 1, 2, 3)
- USA Hockey Learn to Skate
- Hockey Programs (mini mites, mites, squirt, peewee, bantam)
- Youth Sport Programs (instructional and league)
- Instructional (canoeing, diving, cooking, golf, tumbling)
- League Play (baseball, basketball, flag football, soccer)
- Adult Programs (instructional and league)
- Instructional (dance)
- League Play (softball, volleyball)

Examples of programs selected to reflect the culture and interest of the community include:
- Doggie Swim Fest
- Outdoor Ice Rinks
- Winter After Hours
- July 4th Celebration
- Grandparents Day at Fairfax Pool
- Par-te-Rec/Camp Summertime (specialized recreation)
- Hobbs Events (lunch break open skate, teen skate, turkey skate)
- Fairfax Events (dollar swims, water safety fest, splash party)

The criteria below have been established as general practices for evaluating programs, facilities, services, and new opportunities. Selection content and criteria include:
- Offer new programs based on professional industry trends
- Evaluate activities and events annually to determine the succession of each program
- Evaluate activities for programming duplication within the community
- Create partnerships and cooperative programming opportunities within the community
- Establish healthy guidelines for programs and facilities
- Set affordable fees that meet the recovery requirement as set by City Council
- Program at existing Parks and Recreation facilities to become solvent
- Focus on desired outcomes and end results for programs and facilities
- Balance business operation with commitment to service
- Market programs and facilities to increase enrollment and revenues
- Review the vision with upper management to align with the organization's direction

Recreation Program Planning Schedule of Review

Recreation Division Team Meeting

These topics and documents are reviewed, analyzed, and updated during Recreation Division team meetings directed by the superintendent of recreation. Recreation Division meetings are scheduled weekly. Items listed may be presented at any meeting during the month specified.

Exhibit 7.1. (continued)

January
Review and Update:
  Recreation Program Standards and Outcomes
  Selection of Program Content
  Scope of Program Opportunities
  Community Education for Leisure
  Participation Barriers

February
Marketing Approach:
  - Review Advertising Methods
  - Update Primary Contact Databases
  - Review Creating Identity
  - Review Promoting Wellness
Technology Utilization:
  - Review Software Programs
  - Review Web-Based Information
  - Review and Update Social Media Plan

March
Review and Update:
  Participant Involvement
  Self-Directed Programs and Services
  Leader-Directed Programs and Services
  Facilitated Programs and Services
  Fee-Based Programs and Services
  Cooperative Programming and Collaboration
  Outreach to Underserved Populations

April
Review and Update:
  Volunteer Recruitment and Retention
  Safety Plans and Emergency Action Plans
  Customer Services and Responsiveness

May
Payroll Planning

June
Budget Planning
Complete CIP and Budget Information

July

August
Program Evaluation Analysis
Complete Program and Service Determinants
  Worksheet

September
Funding Resources and Pricing Strategies
  - Purchasing and Bidding Procedures
  - Fees and Charges
  - Cost Recovery
  - Funding Resources
  - Achieving Financial Sustainability

October
Update Recreation Activities Matrix
Update Program Life Cycle Analysis
Review Internal Needs Assessment
Review and Update Program Outcomes
Summary
Review Facility Inventory and Utilization

November
Update Recreation Provider Inventory
Update Athletic Facility Inventory
Review Community Demographic Profile
Review and Identify Recreation Trends

December
Review of Strategic Planning Initiatives
Review of Mission, Vision, and Values
Review of Plan Summary and Recommendations
Team Development
  - Establish Goals
  - Review Job Descriptions
  - Review Recruitment Procedures
  - Update Orientation Schedules
  - Establish Training Opportunities

Note. From City of Eau Claire (n.d.).

Develop a series of program standards for the operation of a chain of commercial rec-reation facilities. Each facility has a nursery, a weight room, an exercise machine room, an indoor swimming pool, a running track, a concession and lounge area, 12 racquetball courts, and separate shower and locker facilities for men and women. Each facility is family oriented; 85% of the membership in each facility is made up of families.

After writing the program standards, discuss the following questions:

- Are the standards comprehensive and explicit enough to guide less capable staff members? That is, if the standards are met, will a facility have an acceptable program?
- Is there enough flexibility to allow creative staff members leeway to develop a program further?
- Are the standards written to recognize differences among facilities with regard to the number of members, the number of staff, and the size of the budget?

To demonstrate how programs may be codified in this manner, we use the mission and program offerings of Easter Seals of Central Illinois. The wording used by the agency has been retained and is an example of how different features are called different terms in practice. The following is the agency's statement of purpose, and this is what we have called a mission statement:

Easter Seals provides exceptional services to ensure that people with disabilities and their families have equal opportunity to live, learn, work and play in their communities. Our purpose is to change the way the world defines and views disability by making profound, positive differences in people's lives every day. (Easter Seals of Central Illinois, n.d.)

The following are the agency's programmatic goals, which we call 3–5-year strategic directions. Their statement of purpose is operationalized with the following programmatic goals:

1. To provide hands-on, comprehensive, vital programs and support to help people reach their full potential (live).
2. To provide programs designed to help children and adults learn, and often re-learn, basic functions master skills needed to develop and thrive, and be sharp and active as they age (learn).
3. To offer a range of training, placement and related services that help people prepare for the workforce (work).

4. To offer fun, healthy programs for children, adults and caregivers to relax, connect with friends and engage in constructive activities (play). (Easter Seals of Central Illinois, n.d.)

These goals define how Easter Seals of Central Illinois will accomplish its mission. The board of directors and community board accept the accomplishment of these goals as proof that the agency has accomplished its mission. Other goals could have been selected, but these were chosen for a variety of reasons, including client needs, staff skills, agency resources, and unique opportunities available to the agency.

Notice that these goals do not have time limits or measurement devices—they are not SMART. They are typical of short-range planning goals developed to provide programmatic direction to an agency for a 3- to 5-year period. These same goals may continue as part of the agency mission for a number of years if periodic review and evaluation determine that they are still desirable for the agency.

Figure 7.1 shows the four goals, each having been assigned a code number from 1.0 through 4.0. These goals thereby become the four components of the Easter Seals' program. For each component, the organization can develop additional goals that further define what is to be included in each component. Table 7.1 shows the support goals for component 4.0 Play.

From the goals in Table 7.1, the agency can begin to develop annual goals for programming purposes. For example, for 4.1.1 Timber Pointe Outdoor Center, the agency could develop the following goals:

1. To offer residential camping for children with and without disabilities during summer 2020 (4.1.1.1).
2. To offer a day camp program for children with and without disabilities during summer 2020 (4.1.1.2).
3. To offer an adventure camp (high ropes, zipline, and horseback riding) for children with and without disabilities during summer 2020 (4.1.1.3).

Figure 7.1. Easter Seals Program Goals

Table 7.1

Ongoing Play Goals 4.0

4.1 Camping and Recreation
4.1.1 Timber Pointe Outdoor Center
4.1.2 Contracted Partner Groups
4.2 Respite Family Support Services
4.2.1 Parent's Night Out
4.2.2 Individual and Family Counseling
4.2.3 Brain Paint
4.2.4 Rehabilitation Coordination

In a similar fashion, Easter Seals can further define and develop each of the goals included for its programs in the hierarchical manner discussed earlier. With the addition of a numeric coding system, the purpose of each activity, program, or other undertaking of the organization can be traced through the hierarchical structure of the goals and objectives that have been developed.

This numeric, hierarchical arrangement helps the organization in three ways. First, development of the goals and objectives helps interpret the organization's mission into desired programs for development. Second, it clears up uncertainty surrounding the management of programs and thereby gives the organization direction and focus through a sequential, logical, and orderly process of goal and objective development. Much of what is done in a leisure service organization is normatively determined based on any number of factors, including resource limitations, client interests, staff skills, abilities and interests, and unique opportunities available to the agency. The use of goals and objectives to develop program directions helps the agency interpret to its public why it exists and what it will accomplish. Third, this arrangement provides a networking structure for employee effort. Through the information and networking provided by a hierarchical arrangement of goals and objectives, employees at all levels understand their role in helping the organization achieve its mission.

It can be difficult for agencies to develop a hierarchical arrangement of goals and objectives that is logical, is constructed in the correct order from general to specific, and includes measurable statements. The codification approach offered by CAPRA brings structure that clarifies the process. The numeric coding system allows a person to quickly identify the place of a goal or objective statement and its relationship in the overall hierarchical structure. Now complete Exercise 7.3.

Exercise 7.3.
A Systems Approach to Writing Goals and Objectives

Use the list of goals and objectives prepared in Exercise 7.2 (page 135), and place them in the codified system explained in the A Codification Approach to Networked Goals and Objectives section.

- Does the use of this system help keep the process organized?
- Discuss how this system might help provide direction to the agency and help account for the services it produces.

Conclusion

Agencies can use goals and objectives to develop strategic directions derived from the mission statement. Three- to 5-year short-term strategic directions can provide short-range planning direction for the agency. Agencies can further define these directions by developing 1-year MBO statements. Additional development of SMART MBO statements with supporting goals and objectives can help agencies to achieve operational clarity, networking, and coordination of effort by staff and metrics for assessing and documenting outcomes. This chapter also discussed the use of program management goals for establishing program standards. Finally, it reintroduced the CAPRA codification system from Chapter 6 as an additional system for tracking the management of programs through the incorporation of goal and objective technology.

References

Arlington County Department of Parks and Recreation. (2016). *Strategic plan 2016–2020*. Retrieved from http://arlingtonparks.us/docs/mobile/index.html#p=1

City of Eau Claire. (2013-2017). *Parks, Recreation, and Forestry Department comprehensive recreation program plan*. Retrieved from http://www.ci.eau-claire.wi.us/home/showdocument?id=2081

Easter Seals of Central Illinois. (n.d.). Taking on disability together. Retrieved October 25, 2018, from http://www.easterseals.com/ci/

McCarville, R. E. (1993, August). Keys to quality programming. *Journal of Physical Education, Recreation, and Dance, 64*(8), 34–36, 46–47.

PART III
Targeted Program Development

Part III discusses Stage B of the Program Development Cycle and how the strategic programming directions of the organization move forward to designing programs. Part III includes five chapters. Chapter 8 discusses techniques for obtaining participant input to be incorporated into the design of a program. Chapter 9 identifies program outcomes and writing design goals that ensure their implementation. Chapter 10 explains techniques for program design, including the Framed Experience Model. Chapter 11 discusses specialized intentional design programming techniques and provides examples. Chapter 12 discusses techniques of applied creativity to use in program design.

Chapter 8: Obtaining Participant Input

Chapter 9: Writing Program Outcome and
  Design Statements

Chapter 10: Program Design

Chapter 11: From BBP to Intentionally Designed
  Leisure Experiences

Chapter 12: Creative Programming

Stage B: Targeted Program Development

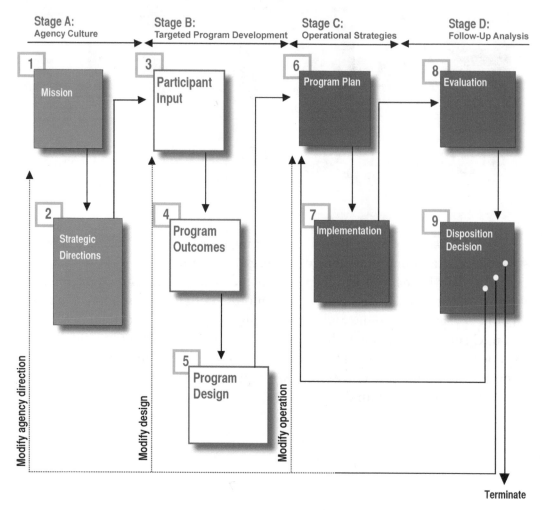

Splashing Into Fun
Photo courtesy of Cincinnati Recreation Commission. Photo by Tina Corcoran.

8 *Obtaining Participant Input*

KEY TERMS

Participant Input, Social Policy Literature, Political Science Literature, Need, Interest, Want, Intention, Normative Need, Felt Need, Expressed Need, Comparative Need, Citizen Advisory Committees, Public Meetings, Interviews, Focus Group Interview, Surveys, Marketing , Exchange, Segmentation, Target Marketing

Step 3: Participant Input

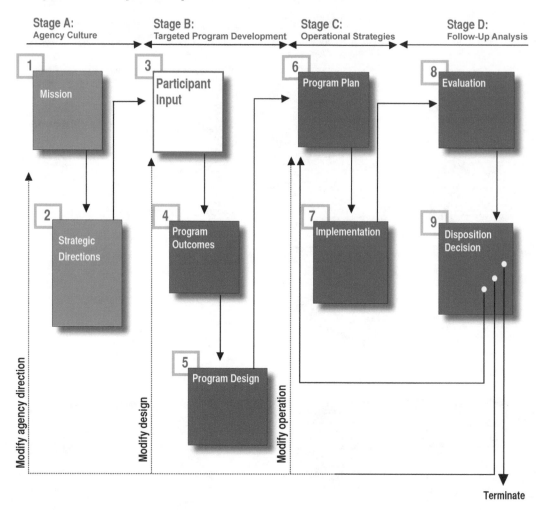

In this step, programmers seek participant input into program development. Throughout the development of the park and recreation field, practitioners have been admonished to seek input from those they serve when developing parks, facilities, experiences, and program services. Today, this is still sound advice. Although programmers may, through trial and error, serendipitously develop a successful program, the more information they have about the needs, preferences, and habits of potential participants, the higher the probability for developing a successful program.

The method for obtaining participant input differs depending on the organization. Commercial operations and not-for-profit organizations need to obtain input from participants but use different methods than public park and recreation operations. Commercial operations are most likely to use the marketing methods discussed later in the chapter, along with social media

> The more information they have about the needs, preferences, and habits of potential participants, the higher the probability for developing a successful program.

Implementing Intentionally Designed Experiences

Agencies that use the intentionally designed experience approach to programming must understand the needs and interests of their participants. This chapter covers several needs assessment methods; however, the intentionally designed experience approach lends itself well to scheduled interviews, or focus groups, as the preferred method of assessing needs for the preparation of sequenced, scripted recreation activities for the targeted audience.

input. Not-for-profit organizations are more ideology driven and often have specific services or programs they operate based on these ideologies. For example, the Y has specific program outcomes it desires from its programs for youth. Advisory boards and other more focused and personal participant input techniques are more common in not-for-profit organizations. Working in a public agency requires that the programmer respond to and assess a larger population than other leisure service organizations (i.e., the general public). In public operations, every citizen is a client; thus, programmers need to use more inclusive methods that attempt to obtain representative input from the entire population.

Several mechanisms for obtaining input from participants and other stakeholders have been developed. These include input from citizen board members who may be elected or appointed to governing or advisory boards, needs assessment strategies, and market assessment methods provided by marketing techniques. Usually, governing boards of recreation enterprises do not provide input into program development. However, they do help with setting policies that govern participation in various program services, as well as determining resource allocations that will determine which program services may eventually be developed. Advisory councils and other similar citizen advisory groups are usually more focused and are organized to give direct input into specific activity or facility development.

This chapter gives a detailed explanation about how programmers conduct needs assessment and market analyses to obtain participant input into program development. Carpenter and Howe (1985) stated, "In leisure programming, needs assessment performs two major functions: the generation of program ideas, and the facilitation of input from constituents and responsiveness to constituents by service providers" (p. 77). Embodied in this definition are two major objectives of needs assessment: (1) helping the agency determine the direction it will take in developing program services and (2) incorporating citizen input into the decision-making process.

These objectives arise from two bodies of literature that contribute to needs assessment. First, social policy literature has sought to justify the services provided to citizens by suggesting that the services fulfill identifiable needs. The concept of needs as used by McKillip (1987) exemplifies this point of view: "Needs are value judgments that a target group has problems that can be solved" (p. 7). McKillip makes clear his view that needs, and therefore decisions about them, are value laden, not objective.

How do you describe those you serve? The term you select influences how you perceive your role and the professional paradigm you use. For example, service recipients who are termed customers are part of an economic exchange model where they purchase a service from you. If you serve clients, they likely have some deficiency that your services will need to correct or address, as in a therapeutic model.

Schlatter and Chang (2018) surveyed public park and recreation programmers in the state of Illinois to ask how they describe their service recipients. The table below includes findings from the survey. Overwhelmingly, survey respondents described their service recipients as participants.

This is an interesting choice in that the term *participant* implies more than any other term that to experience leisure in a program, individuals must engage the interaction and participate in it. *Participant* is used throughout this book except in the chapter on marketing. Much of the marketing literature is from a business perspective, which uses the terms *clients*, *customers*, and *guests*.

Descriptors for Service Recipients
(Percentage of respondents indicating a descriptor was the one used in their agency)

Recipient	Frequency	%
Participant	169	63.8
Patron	47	17.7
Guest	14	5.3
Customer	12	4.5
Resident	11	4.2
Other	10	3.8
Client	2	0.8
Total	265	100.0

Note. From Schlatter and Chang (2018).

The second body of literature, which is exemplified by the work of Summers (1987), stems from political science. Summers stated,

> Citizen participation in decision making is the essence of needs assessment. It concerns grass-roots democracy and the importance of people being free and able to express their views on matters that affect their lives, families, and communities. Needs assessment is a social institution that integrates ideas from political theories of democracy with practices flowing from the mainstream of social science research. (p. 3)

He continued to say that needs assessment "is a special case of citizen participation, and participation issues are essentially questions of value" (p. 3). The second objective of needs assessment, then, is how best to incorporate citizen input when making value judgments about what needs exist and which needs should be served.

Often, programmers feel unsure about the needs assessment step of the Program Development Cycle. They are uncertain about the appropriateness and adequacy of their needs assessment methods. The whole process of seeking and incorporating participant input in public park and recreation operations is a "wicked problem" (Kolko, 2012). This does not mean it is evil, but that it is a problem without a single answer. An absolute answer is reached with a linear transformation like a math problem, such as 2 + 2 = 4. In this instance, the correctness of the answer is certain.

Needs assessment is wicked because there are a multiplicity of leisure needs, and in many cases, none are any more compelling than others. Second, a lot of people give input and may have different opinions. Often, there is no consensus or majority view. Third, the needs that emerge from the process and are recommended must compete for funding with other needs in a municipality. Recreation programs and facilities must compete with fire, police, education, and so on. A recent poll of local government officials showed that local government officials ranked parks and recreation sixth in importance among 10 public services (National Recreation and Park Association [NRPA], 2017a, p. 9). Public leisure service agencies use fees and charges to mitigate this lack of priority for funding. The average park and recreation operation in the United States now recovers 29% of its operating expenditures through revenue generation (NRPA, 2017b, p. 3) wherein users of the service pay for the service.

Needs assessment attempts to solve the problem of determining what programs should be offered. Recommended services that emerge from this process are a proposed solution to this problem. But all recommendations are tempered by what Wendt (2015) calls the "problem-solution paradox" (p. 9). That is, problems and solutions evolve jointly and must be understood and analyzed simultaneously; often recommendations and implementation of a specific program service changes the problem! So indeed, needs assessment is a wicked problem. Recognizing this, programmers must develop a better understanding of needs and assessment methods to reduce some of the uncertainty about its use. The literature has made clear several operational principles that help programmers understand needs assessment limitations and its role.

First, the literature suggests that needs are not objective entities—they are value judgments. What programs will be developed is always a matter of choice, not fact.

Second, any needs assessment identifies more needs than an agency can fulfill. Needs assessment methods eventually lead to a decision about which competing needs will be met. These decisions are also value laden. Because of this, McKillip (1987) suggested that decisions among competing needs should be based on an analysis of the cost, impact, and feasibility of alternatives. Indeed, often this is the case. Programs are chosen based on their cost, degree of impact (i.e., how many people will be served), and the feasibility of the agency being able to offer the program.

Third, because of the multiplicity of needs, needs analysis is not an optimizing strategy. That is, it will not lead to a final, objective determination about the one clear course of action that programmers should follow. At best, it will help clear up some of the uncertainty about which programs should be developed and the potential markets for various program alternatives.

Fourth, in practice, participant wants are in constant flux; thus, needs assessment should be an ongoing process. Programmers must constantly assess needs and develop programs based on current information. Social media provides a good conduit for updates and information about the current wants of participants.

Fifth, needs assessments can fulfill three roles: (1) provide data that enable the agency to better understand the individuals who will be affected by the actions of the agency, (2) assess patron response to new program proposals, and (3) help establish priorities among alternative courses of action (Summers, 1987).

Ultimately, the goal of needs assessment is to use participant input for identifying and documenting recreational needs that can be successfully met with leisure services developed by the agency. To systematically assess needs, programmers should understand the definitional and methodological issues of needs assessment.

Need Concepts

Need is one of several constructs for investigating motivation for participating in leisure (Mannell, 1999). In discussing leisure interest "finders," Witt and Groom (1979) pointed out that the literature often fails to distinguish between needs, wants, interests, demands, and other similar terms. Recreation professionals tend to use these terms interchangeably with little explanation of their meaning. Marketing literature (Kotler & Armstrong, 2018) offers a pragmatic approach to defining need and related concepts that give insight into leisure needs assessment.

Need

A *need* is a state of deprivation arising out of the basic innate biological characteristics of humans. A need is not created by society, but exists apart from and prior to society. Evidence suggests that humans have a need to participate in activities that are intrinsically rewarding, stimulate arousal, and are intrinsically motivating (e.g., see Csikszentmihalyi, 1975; Ellis, 1973; Iso-Ahola, 1980, 1982; Neulinger, 1974). The need for experiences provided in leisure and recreation is innate; programmers do not have to create it through marketing, advertising, program design, or any other technique—and the people's need for this will be served. The question is, which providers will they select for fulfilling this need?

Interest

An *interest* is an awareness or feeling about what a person would like to do or acquire. Interests are learned and are influenced by social forces. An individual's self-concept can also precipitate an interest in a specific activity.

> An *interest* is an awareness or feeling about what a person would like to do or acquire.

Want

A *want* is a culturally learned behavior pattern for satisfying specific needs. Individuals need food, but they learn to want a Big Mac, a steak, a taco, or sushi. Individuals need intrinsically rewarding and stimulating behavior, but they learn to want to participate in tennis, bowling, oil painting, or reading to satisfy the higher order, innate needs. People have few needs, but many wants. Wants are constantly being altered by social forces, including family, friends, and social institutions such as churches, schools, and the business community. Furthermore, satisfying a want often leads to the creation of additional wants (Witt & Groom, 1979). Programmers can influence, manipulate, and satisfy wants.

> A *want* is a culturally learned behavior pattern for satisfying specific needs.

Intention

An *intention* is the commitment to acquire specific satisfiers of wants under given market conditions. When intending to participate in an activity, people intend to do so at a given time, location, and price. Many people are interested in or want to scuba dive on a Caribbean island; considerably fewer intend to commit the necessary time and money to do so. For recreation program planning, it is essential for programmers to understand the number of individuals who intend to participate in a program under a defined market condition.

There is no need for specific forms of leisure participation. For example, no one has a need for softball. But humans do have a need to participate in engagements that provide them perceived freedom, intrinsic satisfaction, and the opportunity to engage in co-production of the activity. Currently, then, the notion that leisure satisfies specific needs is thought to be a learned response to engaging in specific activities (Mannell, 1999). Leisure needs assessment, then, is an attempt at determining the interests, wants, or intentions of potential participants. It is important when interpreting data from a needs assessment that programmers know whether the data reveal interests, wants, or intentions. These concepts imply varying strengths of motivation for participating in activities. Because each concept implies a different degree of motivation for participating, the patrons in each conceptual level will require varying promotional efforts that convince them to participate.

> *Intention* is the commitment to acquire specific satisfiers of wants under given market conditions.

An individual who has an "interest" in an activity has the lowest level of motivation to participate. An individual who "wants" to get into a program has a stronger motivation and is therefore more likely to participate. An individual who "intends" to participate has made a strong commitment to participate in an activity and is likely to do so if given market conditions are met. These latter individuals make up a market and create demand for an activity.

Practitioners have often been disappointed with the reliability of needs assessment data because there has not been significant correlation between what individuals indicate they intend to do and what they actually do. In many cases, this lack of reliability is caused by poor framing of the data collection questions; that is, they are not specific enough. Fishbein and Manfredo (1992) pointed out that although intention is a good predictor of specific behaviors, it is less accurate for predicting intention to reach less well-defined goals or classes of behavior. Which of the following would have the greatest predictive power?

a. Needs assessment data indicate that during the next year 1,000 community residents intend to get more physically active (a general leisure participation goal) or play in an adult sports league (a general class of behavior).

OR

b. Needs assessment data indicate that 125 men intend to participate in a company-sponsored adult softball league that would be offered the next summer on Tuesday and Thursday evenings from 6:30 to 7:30 p.m. at a price of $100 per player.

Did you conclude that *b.* provides the most powerful data with market details that if met will likely lead to a well-enrolled, successful program?

Unfortunately, many needs assessment instruments simply identify general interests or wants, rather than detailing market conditions about specific activities. Exhibit 8.1 presents examples of needs assessment questions that contrast the differences between wants and intentions. Questions about target intentions point out the additional detail needed for programmers to assess an individual's intention to participate accurately and to gather sufficient data to develop a program that can be offered under a given set of market conditions. Now complete Exercise 8.1 (page 151).

Needs From a Social Justice Viewpoint

Mercer (1973) pointed out that, from a social policy standpoint, some types of needs are more debilitating than others. Therefore, resources that alleviate these needs are more urgently needed if social justice is to be achieved. Mercer identified four types of needs: normative, felt, expressed, and comparative.

Normative Needs

Normative needs are objective standards defined by organizations and groups that are qualified to do so because of their training or position. The *Recreation, Park, and Open Space Standards and Guidelines* (Lancaster, 1983), published by the NRPA, is an example of such standards. Today, the NRPA has replaced this document with its Park Metrics program that provides data about practices in other agencies. These data may be used as benchmarks to be achieved. Many communities develop their own park and open space standards in developing a park master plan. These are desirable future states to be achieved by the community.

> *Normative needs* are objective standards defined by organizations and groups that are qualified to do so because of their training or position.

Exhibit 8.1. Questions Contrasting Wants and Intentions

Wants

The table below lists many recreational activities. Some are currently offered by the agency, and others are new activities that the agency may offer in the future. For each activity, indicate by checking the appropriate response whether you would participate in the activity if it were offered by the agency next year and, if so, whether you would pay for the cost of the activity program.

Activity	Definitely No	Probably No	Unsure	Probably Yes	Definitely Yes
Baseball	☐	☐	☐	☐	☐
Cooking	☐	☐	☐	☐	☐
Cross-country skiing	☐	☐	☐	☐	☐
Scuba diving lessons	☐	☐	☐	☐	☐
Tennis instructions	☐	☐	☐	☐	☐
Volleyball league	☐	☐	☐	☐	☐

Intentions

The following is a list of leisure activities that you may enjoy. For each activity, please tell us:
1. if you participated in the activity in this past year and/or
2. if you intend to participate in it this coming year.

For those activities in which you intend to participate next year, please tell us:
3. the frequency with which you intend to participate in a typical month (if seasonal, when the activity is in season);
4. the primary participants in the activity—that is, yourself alone, with family, or with friends;
5. the location where you usually participate (agency-owned facility or other supplier);
6. the time(s) of the day or week you prefer to participate;
7. the price at which you no longer can afford to participate; and
8. potential barriers, if any, to your participation.

Note: Below are the items that need to be included on an instrument. Although they are laid out vertically in this exhibit, they should be displayed horizontally for each activity for which information is sought.

Baseball

1.	Experienced this last year?	☐ Yes	☐ No
2.	Intend to participate this year?	☐ Yes	(Go on to 3)
		☐ No	(Go on to next activity)
3.	Expected frequency (in season)	☐ Daily	
		☐ Several times per week	
		☐ Several times per month	
		☐ Once per month	
		☐ Less often than once per month	

Exhibit 8.1. (continued)

4. Primary participants (select one)
   - ☐ Alone
   - ☐ With family
   - ☐ With friends

5. Location (select one primary location)
   - ☐ [Name of agency facility]
   - ☐ Competing facility or facilities if appropriate

6. Preferred activity times (circle all that apply)

Day	Early Morning	Mid-Morning	Lunchtime	Early Afternoon	Mid-Afternoon	Night
Monday	X	X	X	X	X	X
Tuesday	X	X	X	X	X	X
Wednesday	X	X	X	X	X	X
Thursday	X	X	X	X	X	X
Friday	X	X	X	X	X	X
Saturday	X	X	X	X	X	X
Sunday	X	X	X	X	X	X

7. Circle the number that represents the dollar amount at which you would no longer be able to afford to participate in this activity. Please use only one section depending on whether this activity is paid for on a per-participation basis or per-session basis.

   a. Activities paid for on a per-participation basis:

Could not afford to participate if there were a fee	1
$1.00 per participation	2
Over $1.00 but under $3.00 per participation	3
Over $3.00 but under $5.00 per participation	4
Over $5.00 but under $7.50 per participation	5
Over $7.50 but under $10.00 per participation	6
Over $10.00 but under $15.00 per participation	7
Over $15.00 but under $25.00 per participation	8
Over $25.00 but under $40.00 per participation	9
Over $40.00 per participation	10

   b. Activities paid for on a per-session basis:

Could not afford to participate if there were a fee	1
$5.00 per session	2
Over $5.00 but under $10.00 per session	3
Over $10.00 but under $15.00 per session	4
Over $15.00 but under $20.00 per session	5
Over $20.00 but under $25.00 per session	6
Over $25.00 but under $30.00 per session	7
Over $30.00 but under $50.00 per session	8
Over $50.00 but under $74.00 per session	9
Over $75.00 per session	10

Exhibit 8.1. (continued)

8. Potential barriers. Please check the barriers listed below that are most likely to keep you from participating in the activity. (Select no more than three)

☐ Activity unavailable near my home

☐ Lack of child care

☐ Lack of transportation

☐ Poor facility

☐ Inconvenient hours of operation

☐ Poor management of facility or program

☐ Lack of program information

☐ I am not skilled enough

☐ I am uncomfortable with other users

Note. Adapted from the Leisure Needs Survey Instrument, U.S. Navy Recreational Services Program.

Exercise 8.1.
Developing Needs Assessment Questions

In class, discuss the different kinds of information you would have collected with the two types of responses to the needs assessment questions in Exhibit 8.1. Which of these instruments would provide the most complete information for developing and designing a program? Which would be the most expensive to administer?

After the discussion, write needs assessment questions for the following three activities to be held at a public swimming pool:
- Swimming lessons
- Scuba lessons
- Public swimming

Now exchange questions with a class member and critique each other's questions. Remember to try to determine a patron's intention to participate. The more specific you can be about the activity, time, place, and price, the more likely you are to obtain reliable information.

For normative standards, the need documented is the difference between what a community may have and what the normative standard suggests it should have. The agency can reduce the amount of need in a community by increasing supply. This narrows the gap between what is and what should be provided. The agency could also raise the standard, which widens the gap between what is and what should be provided. Often this technique, not surprisingly, is called a gap analysis, the difference between what is and what should be offered.

Felt Needs

Felt needs are perceptions about what an individual believes he or she would like to do. They are analogous to wants, interests, and intentions. Felt needs may be thought of as latent demand; that is, they are demands that could be turned into consumption. Felt needs are shaped by social forces that lead individuals to conclude that they have a need for specific services or facilities. They are dynamic in that they change over time, sometimes in a very short time frame.

Expressed Needs

Expressed needs are fulfilled through participation. They are included as needs because if the supply currently fulfilling the needs was terminated, they would immediately become felt needs again, demanding attention and resources.

Comparative Needs

Comparative needs are variations in services provided or variations in access to leisure opportunities experienced by different cohorts of individuals. Variations in leisure facilities and services provided to different neighborhoods are often a major point of contention in the delivery of community recreation services. Variations in access to public recreation resources by different cohorts defined by race, gender, sexual orientation, and so on become issues of concern in social justice policy analysis, whose intention is to make access for various cohorts more equitable.

Comparative needs are also a concern in many other leisure service organizations. Two examples of comparative need problems in various agency settings are (1) variations in the opportunities provided to persons on different work shifts in corporate recreation settings and (2) variations in service access by personnel of different ranks in the military.

The debate about how to fairly distribute public recreation resources and meet identified needs continues. Since it is a wicked problem, it will likely never be fully resolved to everyone's satisfaction and the debate will continue. Concerns about social justice are further exacerbated by the government's lack of interest in them. In a recent survey, social equity/social justice concerns were ranked eighth out of eight important issues facing communities by those polled (NRPA, 2017b, p. 6).

Any solution is likely to be a "satisficing" one wherein a temporary solution is agreed to since a fully satisfying, optimizing strategy cannot be found or agreed upon. It is likely that programmers will need to deal with this issue on a continuing basis. Do not become frustrated, this is the situation for all programmers. It is the nature of wicked problems, not a failure on your part. The following section provides methods for implementing needs assessments.

Approaches to Needs Assessment

Programmers are often overly concerned about whether they are conducting needs assessments correctly. Because of their possibly ineffective needs assessment methods, they are concerned about overlooking a tremendous pool of unfulfilled needs. The inadequacy that many programmers feel stems from their not conducting a systematic random survey of the population on a routine basis. Often, this is not done for a variety of reasons, including a lack of skill or limited resources. In addition to surveys, however, several methods can be used by programmers to assess needs on an ongoing basis.

The National Park Service (n.d.) defined needs assessment as gathering information directly from the public and analyzing it. Assessment involves organizing the information collected into meaningful patterns that will lead to the development of leisure services that meet unfulfilled needs. Two methods for conducting community needs assessments include group approaches and surveys. The National Park Service identified four approaches that are frequently used in conducting leisure needs assessments: citizen advisory committees, public meetings and workshops, unstructured inputs and structured exploratory interviews, and surveys. To these we add the use of social media. This section explains these approaches.

Citizen Advisory Committees

Citizen advisory committees are comprised of community residents who are either appointed or elected to a committee that advises the agency staff or board. The notion of a "community resident" is robust and can include groups of individuals from various communities (e.g., a member of the local hiking community advises a committee on development and maintenance of trails). Advisory groups can be valuable in providing a communication link between the agency and its constituency.

Summers (1987) pointed out that agencies and citizens can misuse citizen advisory groups. Agencies can mobilize citizen groups to support their own already formulated policies under the guise of citizen input. Groups of community residents can form groups to lobby for their own program interests rather than representing the general public interest. In this latter role, advisory groups can become formidable political forces that lobby to have scarce resources directed to their own activity interests. For example, youth soccer groups could lobby for the development of additional fields and other facility improvements dedicated to soccer. However, the most positive approach to the use of citizen advisory groups assumes that because of their knowledge and interest, members will consider all dimensions of an issue and truly represent general community concerns. These groups can provide programmers with valuable insight into the program needs of patrons and provide feedback on various program and facility development options.

Public Meetings and Workshops

Public meetings are frequently used for soliciting citizen input on policy development, planning issues, budget allocations, or leisure needs and preferences. In some instances, agencies are required to conduct such meetings to satisfy a grant or legislative requirement. In conducting a public meeting, the agency establishes two-way communication with its publics and facilitates dialogue by offering an outlet for expressing views and emotions about an issue. Often during a public meeting, a programmer can assess the strength of emotion accompanying an issue that cannot be assessed with other methods.

A workshop (or planning charrette) is a more organized public meeting during which people participate in small discussion groups with a focused agenda. Facilitating citizen input with a more organized agenda often leads to more productive meetings.

With either method, citizens self-select who attends the meeting, and it is likely that those who attend will have the strongest opinions either for or against an issue. Because of this polarized representation, it can be problematic determining how closely opinions expressed at public meetings and workshops represent the views of the general population.

Interviews

An interview is a meeting in which information is obtained. Programmers can acquire needs assessment information from unscheduled and scheduled interviews.

Unscheduled interviews. While operating and supervising programs, programmers have many opportunities to obtain information from current and prospective patrons. Unscheduled interviews include the many face-to-face unsolicited comments, Tweets, and telephone calls made by constituents to programmers. While visiting and supervising program operations, programmers make themselves accessible to the public. The public will approach them and interact, providing information such as complaints, compliments, and suggestions.

These are valuable pieces of information, but they often require that the programmer be prepared to probe the comments immediately to validate and discover all information that may be useful. To provide structure to these interviews and thereby obtain the most information possible, programmers need to have a basic interview schedule prepared to obtain the most critical pieces of information. Just because they are unscheduled does not mean they should be unstructured! Exhibit 8.2 shows a list of questions that could provide structure to unscheduled interviews.

As with all unsolicited comments from self-selected individuals, it is important for programmers to ascertain how widespread a specific viewpoint is held throughout a population.

> **Exhibit 8.2. Unscheduled Interview Agenda**
> 1. Obtain the name and address of the participant.
> 2. Identify the specific program, facility, policy, or staff member about which the participant is commenting.
> 3. Ascertain if the participant is making a complaint, giving a compliment, or making a suggestion.
> 4. Make certain the participant identifies the specific issue he or she is concerned about.
> 5. Try to discover what resolution or outcome the participant would like to have.
> 6. Make note of all follow-up actions taken.

Focus groups. Scheduled interviews are arranged and structured. They are conducted with an interview schedule and are given some direction by the interviewer. Several types of group interview techniques may be used, including nominal group interviews and focus group interviews. The rest of this section gives a general description of conducting a focus group interview for needs assessment purposes.

Focus group interviews can be used for one or more of the following:
- to develop hypotheses for further testing,
- to provide information for structuring questionnaires,
- to provide overall background information on programs,
- to solicit patron impressions about new program concepts,
- to stimulate new ideas about older programs,
- to generate ideas for new programs, and
- to interpret previously obtained quantitative results.

The focus group technique involves three distinct phases: preparing for the interview, conducting the interview, and analyzing the results.

Preparing for the interview. Although it seems obvious, it is important for interviewers to prepare well before the face-to-face interview begins. Before good interview questions can be developed, the interviewer must thoroughly understand the problem being examined. Thorough preparation requires identifying a focused problem statement, developing questions that are logically deduced from the problem, and preparing topical areas that will introduce the questions. Topical areas help the interviewer keep the interview moving smoothly in a logical fashion, thus providing coherence to the process.

The reader is cautioned against trying to develop a problem statement and questions that are too broad. The focus group interviewing technique is useful because it facilitates an in-depth examination that can lead to new insights into the specific problem. Covering too many topics or too general of a topic often precludes the in-depth examination of a problem or concept that is uniquely accessed with this technique. Two examples of focus group problems and meeting agendas are provided. Exhibit 8.3 (page 157) illustrates a focus group problem and an agenda for a future recreation program at a voluntary nonprofit youth-serving agency. The second example, Exhibit 8.4 (page 158), illustrates how a tourism manager at a convention and visitors bureau used the focus group approach with local business leaders to discuss how they use social media to attract visitors to the metropolitan area. Participating leaders represented local museums, an indoor rock climbing gym, downtown and uptown business associations, shopping malls, a performing arts center, a local winery, a bed and breakfast, a local car festival, performance groups, and sport and entertainment centers.

The second part of preparing for the interview involves selecting the people to be interviewed. The authors have found that some practitioners believe an open-call public meeting is a focus group. It is not. In a focus group, only a few individuals are included in the interview, so they must be selected carefully. Programmers should consider the following points when selecting group members:

- It is important that the group is kept small enough to facilitate open communication. Between six and 10 group members would be most appropriate.
- The group should have homogeneity and contrast (Wells, 1979). It is especially important that interviewers maintain homogeneity on factors that might otherwise inhibit open communication or create conflict that could become the focus of the session. For example, well-educated, middle-class individuals may inhibit the full participation of lower class, less educated individuals in a focus group. In this case, it would be best for interviewers to interview two groups, each made up of people with similar backgrounds. Interviewers must still be inclusive in who is included in the cumulative interviews about the issue, but they do not all need to be present at the same interview. However, some spark should also be provided through contrasts in the composition of the group. For example, in a focus group interview designed to examine the operation of an indoor tennis facility, the interviewer would want to include users of the agency's tennis facility and users of a competitor's tennis facility. The interviewer must carefully constitute groups to ensure an open exchange of ideas and that the group is made up of members who can contribute to a thorough discussion of the issue including its pros and cons.
- A decision about where to conduct the interview must be made. There are generally three choices: the agency's facilities, a neutral site, or the participant's facilities, such as someone's home.

Conducting the interview. How the interview is conducted is critical to obtaining the information desired by the agency. The interview can be conducted in a directive or nondirective style. In the nondirective style, the interviewer acts as a facilitator who introduces prearranged questions, gets the group discussing them, and intervenes only to keep the discussion fruitful. Ideally, the interviewer does not participate in the discussion, although this cannot always be avoided and occasionally the interviewer must intervene to ensure that what is being discussed is factually correct.

Exhibit 8.3. Focus Group Interview Problem Statement and Agenda

Problem Statement

To determine how single-parent families with children from 6 to 12 years of age make decisions about their children's participation in summer recreation programs.

Opening Narrative

Welcome. Today we are going to discuss a topic I think you will find interesting and that you know a lot about—your children's summer recreation activities. We are interested in learning when and how decisions about summer recreation participation are made, who makes them, and what is important to you and your children about the activities selected.

Before we start, I have a couple of requests: first, that only one person speak at a time so that we can truly interact with each other; second, that you feel free to say exactly what you think—we want both positive and negative comments. Give us your true feelings.

Now, to get started, let's go around the table one at a time and have you tell us a little bit about yourself and your family. All of you are single parents—we would like to know how many children you have, their ages, their genders, and a little bit about them and each of you.

Focus Questions

1. How would your children answer the following comment: I have to participate in this program because _____. (Probe: What reason do they most frequently give about why they must be in a program?)

2. Who do your children most like to participate with in recreation activities? (Probe: Friends, siblings, schoolmates?)

3. How would you answer the following comment: I want my children in summer recreation programs because_____. (Probe: What reasons do you give your friends, neighbors, or former spouses about why your children must be in a specific recreation program?)

4. In my home,_____decides which recreation activities my children will select to participate in. (Probe: Is the decision made mostly by the children, the parent, jointly, or between the resident and nonresident parent?)

5. When do you normally make decisions about which summer recreation activities your children will be in? (Probe: How far in advance of summer do parents want to know what their children's schedules will be?)

6. How would your children answer this question: I wish I could _____ this summer. (Probe: Identify programs that children may want or programs that parents may want for them.)

7. I will not let my children be in a recreation program unless I am sure _____. (Probe: What must a program do or be before parents will allow their children to participate?) Keep the discussion going on this until all fruitful information is obtained.

In the directive style, the interviewer provides much more structure and controls the flow of discussion. The interviewer generally introduces a topic and keeps the discussion going until the topic has been covered to his or her satisfaction; the interviewer then introduces a new topic. With either style, the interviewer should

Exhibit 8.4. Focus Group Example for a Convention and Visitors Bureau

The Tourism Marketing Manager for the Bloomington-Normal Area Convention and Visitors Bureau recently held a focus group meeting with local business leaders to discuss how social media is used to attract visitors to the metropolitan area. Participating leaders represented local museums, an indoor rock climbing gym, downtown and uptown business associations, shopping malls, a performing arts center, a local winery, a bed and breakfast, a local car festival, performance groups, and sport and entertainment centers. See their focus group meeting agenda below.

Problem Statement

To determine how local businesses use social media to attract visitors to the metropolitan area.

Opening Narrative

Welcome. Today we are going to discuss how our various agencies use social media. We are interested in learning the extent to which you use Internet-based social media outlets such as Facebook, Flickr, Twitter, YouTube, and ShareThis. We want to know the struggles and benefits in using these 21st century marketing techniques.

Before I start, I have a couple of requests: 1) that only one person speaks at a time so we can truly interact with each other and 2) that you feel free to say exactly what you think. We want both positive and negative comments. Now, to get started, let's go around the table one at a time and have you tell us your name and a little bit about your own involvement with social media such as Facebook or Twitter. Thanks, and now let's move on to our focus group meeting questions!

Focus Questions

1. Describe the extent to which your business currently uses social media. (Probes: Twitter, Flickr, Twitter, YouTube, ShareThis. How many does your business use?)

2. Explain how your business began using social media. (Probes: Had you seen it presented at a conference? Did you learn about it through networking? Did you notice other businesses using it?)

3. Tell us concerns your business had when the decision was made to use social media for marketing purposes. (Probes: Did you think employees would use social media for personal reasons? Did you think it could cause computer viruses? Did you think it would be too difficult to learn?

4. What are the benefits of using social media as a marketing tool for your business? (Probes: Do you understand your customers better? Do you get more hits on your website?)

5. Describe any frustrations your business has experienced with social media. (Probes: Do you receive unprofessional postings? Were some social media more difficult to learn to use than others?)

6. Give an example of how you use social media to attract visitors to our metropolitan region. (Probes: Do you have a Facebook group that people can join? Do you have a link on your website for people to follow you on Twitter? Do you have a Calendar of Events link on your website? Do you offer giveaways or hold contests to engage the visitors?)

7. Finally, please share a tip about using social media with the rest of the group. (Probes: What hints or suggestions can you provide to other business leaders? What pitfalls should be avoided?)

Acknowledgment: The authors thank Ms. Erin Watts, Bloomington-Normal Area Convention and Visitors Bureau, for her collaboration on this exhibit.

elicit responses that are the true beliefs and feelings of the group members. The choice of style is influenced by the purpose of the interview, the content of the questions to be asked, and the group members.

Analyzing the results. Analyses can range in detail and thoroughness from a brief impressionistic summary of the principal findings to a very detailed content analysis of tape recordings from the interview. In either case, results from an interview should be organized around the original problem statement and the principal questions asked during the interview. Written results should reflect participant views, including the distribution of views, the strength of conviction, and new viewpoints revealed during the interview.

Surveys

Although the use of systematic random surveys is widely recommended in recreation literature, their use as a needs assessment method has been questioned. Heberlein (as cited in Johnson & Meiller, 1987) suggested that public involvement includes four major functions: informational, interactive, assurance, and ritualistic. The informational function includes getting information from the public. Surveys are excellent for gathering information from but poor at giving information to the public.

> Although the use of systematic random surveys is widely recommended in recreation literature, their use as a needs assessment method has been questioned.

Dillman (1987) pointed out that the uniqueness of the survey is its ability to "tell the proportion in a population who have a certain attribute and the proportion who do not" (p. 192). This makes it a powerful tool for needs assessment. Dillman also argued that it is possible for those giving the survey to conduct scientifically valid surveys and meet the need for citizen involvement if they do the survey process appropriately. However, what it takes to conduct a needs assessment survey successfully has changed dramatically because new survey methods and techniques have been developed.

A properly conducted survey is the method of choice for ensuring the most representative view of all citizens. Chapter 21—the chapter on evaluation—includes technical information about how to conduct surveys. Implementing a needs assessment survey requires simultaneously coordinating many tasks; thus, many errors may be made. Readers interested in conducting a needs assessment survey are encouraged to read Dillman (1987, pp. 192–208) for a succinct briefing on how to avoid problems with nine tasks essential to implementing a survey.

In addition to having the technical skills for creating a survey, programmers must also know how to administer the survey. Surveys sent through the mail incur costs for printing, postage, and envelopes, as well as data entry and analysis. Phone surveys require trained staff who are willing to work during the evening hours and weekends. Still, many citizens do not like being called at home for survey purposes.

Today, it is more common that survey data are collected with an online method. When done correctly, online surveys can provide excellent needs assessment information to agency managers. Some advantages of online surveys include higher response rates, convenience, elimination of data entry cost, and website integration whereby surveys are created on the agency website, which allows users to remain on the website while taking the survey. Among the more popular online survey tools are SurveyMonkey, Google Forms, and Zoomerang. There is some confusion among practicing programmers because survey methods can be used for needs assessment and for evaluation. Although the technology is the same, the focus of the questions is not. Program evaluation deals with the past and judges the worth of what was done. Needs analysis deals with future options and tries to confirm which strategic direction the agency should pursue.

Social Media

Another approach to needs assessment is the use of social media such as Facebook, Twitter, Instagram, and YouTube. Several strategies can provide useful needs information to programmers. First, they can monitor the social media activity of their competitors to gain insight on new ideas. By reading comments left by a competitor's target audience on their social media pages, programmers can see what people liked or did not like. They can read any complaints made on competitors' sites and see how the agency handles them. Also, programmers can look at competitors' YouTube videos and Instagram pictures to gain a visual understanding of their programs and services.

Second, programmers can pay attention to complaints that are posted on their agency's social media sites. A complaint posted on social media is public to the entire social media audience, and a simple misunderstanding can spiral out of control if not addressed quickly, calmly, and professionally. Typically, one staff member at the agency will handle social media complaints as a part of his or her workload. This ensures that the task is given prompt attention on an ongoing basis and all responses are coordinated through a single conduit.

The use of hashtags is another social media application for needs assessment. A word or phrase becomes a hashtag when the # symbol is placed in front of it and allows the user to categorize content. For example, searching #waterpark yields numerous related water park feeds. When clicking on a particular #waterpark hashtag, the user will see all the public content attached to it and will thus be exposed to potential new program ideas.

Finally, programmers can use social media to stay on top of trends in the field. Doing so, they help the agency stay ahead of the competition. All of these social media approaches can help programmers confirm what has been discovered through other needs assessment methods and gain insight about new ideas and leisure experiences.

Integrating the Approaches

Each approach has strengths and weaknesses. No single approach can give a completely accurate picture of the needs in a community and provide the social action that is often needed for implementing solutions. Although the method of choice, surveys are expensive and usually not conducted annually in every organization. An agency should conduct one annually if possible. Certainly, a needs assessment survey should be conducted no less often than every 3 years.

The other approaches gather other data that supplement the survey data and provide focus to a survey when it is conducted. Survey data often do not provide sufficiently detailed information for making programmatic decisions, so one of the other approaches, such as a focus group, may be used for gathering additional focused information about data initially discovered in a survey. In the latter case, exploratory methods may be used for discovering issues or needs whose distribution in the population can only be assessed through a systematic random sample survey. Input through social media usually occurs in real time, thus providing the most up-to-date, actionable information to the programmer. Programmers can use the methods identified, then, in a complementary manner to form a comprehensive needs assessment program for an agency.

Needs Assessment Questions

Programmers can ask many questions to determine wants that an agency can satisfy. Part of the uncertainty that programmers have about whether they are conducting an adequate needs analysis has to do with their lack of understanding of what constitutes needs assessment questions. The National Park Service (n.d.) identified the following questions:

- What do its constituencies believe the agency should be doing? (Setting objectives)
- What needs and wants do citizens have? What are the characteristics of those who have a particular need (want)? How many are affected? What makes individuals decide to use or not use existing services? (Identifying target markets)
- How do potential target markets react to various service alternatives that could meet these needs (wants)? (Product development)
- What price should be charged? (Searching for a suitable price point)
- How can its availability be best communicated? (Promotion)
- At what time and locations should it be offered? (Distribution) (pp. 63–64)

A needs analysis is conducted whenever programmers seek answers to these or similar questions in a systematic manner and analyze the responses. The quality of the effort will depend on how pertinent the questions are, how the data are analyzed, and how representative the data are for the service population. In conducting leisure service needs assessments, programmers can almost always identify a program need, develop the service to fulfill the need, have the program populated, and believe that needs are being fulfilled. However, they are concerned that an even greater need may not have been discovered. The solution to this is a continual ongoing assessment of needs and revisions to services based on the new information.

Marketing Leisure Experiences

Over the past 40 years, marketing techniques have been applied to the operation and management of leisure services. Crompton (1978) wrote one of the first articles that advocates the use of marketing concepts for analyzing leisure services. Crompton has continued to promote the usefulness of marketing principles as a major program management strategy for park and recreation services. Schultz, McAvoy, and Dustin (1988) expressed concern about the adoption of business management strategies as the management paradigm for providing leisure services. Along the way, research has demonstrated that "agencies have not comprehensively integrated marketing techniques into programming efforts" (Tew, Havitz, & McCarville, 1999, p. 14).

Marketing is undergoing a revolution as marketers adjust to the experience economy. Schmitt (1999) documented that marketing is moving from a focus on features and benefits (F & B marketing) to a focus on how products and services contribute to customer experiences and lifestyles. According to Schmitt, experiential marketing differs from F & B marketing on four key characteristics. It focuses on customer experiences. Instead of focusing on product benefits and features, experiential marketing focuses on consumption situations, that is, action vignettes wherein products are consumed. It is assumed that customers make purchasing decisions not only on rational grounds but also on emotional ones. Finally, because of the eclectic nature of consumption decisions, marketing research and tools must be eclectic. Marketing, then, has moved closer to methods used by programmers for many years. That is, it currently focuses more on the experiences and the methods programmers have been using to create them.

Marketing literature contains a number of concepts and methods for program development and management. Although marketing techniques are used in programming, programmers possess the unique ability to design programs that provide maximal opportunities for the leisure experience. Programmers can do this because they have been educated in how humans experience leisure in social occasions and how these occasions can best be structured to maximize the opportunity to experience leisure. This unique professional ability does not stem from training in marketing. McCarville (1999) described marketing as "a set of interrelated activities that focus on the client. The ultimate goal of this process is to discover an optimal fit between client preferences and agency capabilities, then to mobilize resources accordingly" (p. 415). This, of course, is what the other methods of needs assessment try to accomplish, but with different techniques.

A comprehensive marketing program can provide important information regarding programs that individuals desire, the price they are willing to pay, when and where they desire to participate, and how services may be promoted. Marketing activities require a focus on the clients, the clients' desires, and grouping clients with similar desires so that effective programs can be developed. To understand the contribution that marketing can make to leisure program development, programmers must understand some basic marketing concepts.

Marketing and Exchanges

First, what is marketing? Marketing is a process of influencing voluntary exchange transactions between two or more entities in which one party is the customer and the other the marketer (adapted from Zikmund & d'Amico, 2002). Crompton and Lamb (1986) stated, "Marketing is a set of activities aimed at facilitating and expediting exchanges" (p. 16). Marketing focuses on meeting identified patron needs, including their logical extension through interests, wants, and intentions. The process depends on good communication conduits between the customer and the marketer. All marketing is based on the notion that needs are met through exchange processes. Understanding the notion of exchange is critical to understanding marketing.

An exchange occurs when two or more parties satisfy their needs and wants through the exchange of something of value. In many cases, one of the items of value is money, although goodwill, satisfaction, and other intangibles are also valuable items that may be exchanged. Kotler and Andreasen (1987) identified four conditions that an exchange condition assumes:

1. There are at least two parties.
2. Each can offer something that the other perceives to be a benefit or benefits.
3. Each is capable of communication and delivery.
4. Each is free to accept or reject the offer. (p. 70)

This last point creates a concern and a justification for using marketing concepts in administering municipal recreation and not-for-profit leisure services. Because municipal and not-for-profit providers have third-party funding sources to subsidize and keep the price of leisure services artificially low, how they incorporate patron desires into their programs becomes a major issue. These agencies have a monopoly on offering low-cost leisure opportunities, so patrons are less free to accept or reject them because comparable services at lower price points may not be available. By offering services at a lower price, the agency can accomplish its social justice mission by making leisure services available to individuals who would not otherwise have access to them.

Given this situation, these agencies can adopt one of three orientations or operating philosophies (Kotler & Andreasen, 1987). First, they can adopt a product orientation and offer what they believe is good for the public. Second, they can adopt a sales orientation and try to stimulate interest in the services of the agency. Third, they can adopt a customer orientation and try to develop services that meet identified patron needs and wants. This third option has a marketing orientation. Agencies that have the financial resources to offer subsidized recreation use marketing techniques to incorporate, at the front end, patron input into the development of services. In addition, marketers are also admonished to practice "societal marketing," which advises them to consider not only individual needs and wants, but also the collective needs of society (Zikmund & d'Amico, 2002). Marketing provides a number of useful concepts and techniques for helping accomplish this end.

A Market Defined

Kotler and Armstrong (2018) stated, "A market is the set of actual and potential buyers of a product or service" (p. 33). Thus, they believe the programmer should be concerned with current and potential buyers. On the other hand, Zikmund and d'Amico (2002) stated, "A market is a group of potential customers for a particular product who are willing and able to spend money or exchange other resources to obtain the product" (p. 9). They believe one should focus on those who are ready and willing to purchase (i.e., those with the financial capability and intent to purchase). The individuals in a market desire to obtain a similar product or service that can fulfill a specific need or want. This need or want may be an experience or contribution to a lifestyle they desire. A major challenge for all marketers is convincing potential customers to become consumers of a specific product.

> The individuals in a market desire to obtain a similar product or service that can fulfill a specific need or want.

Segmenting Markets

Any market may be large or small, but it will usually be made up of identifiable subgroups called market segments. For example, fishermen make up a recreation market. This market can be segmented by subdividing all fishermen into saltwater and freshwater fishermen. The market could be further segmented into shore and boat fishermen. Further segmentation along any number of variables is possible. O'Sullivan (1991) identified five classes of descriptor variables for segmenting leisure markets: leisure needs and interests, geographic characteristics, sociodemographics, behavioral area, and synchrographics. Figure 8.1 (page 168) shows an adaptation of these, including examples of some descriptors. According to Shaw and Ivens (2005), "The new differentiators will be the customer experience and the emotions that the physical elements evoke" (p. 17).

Agencies can segment markets to identify and focus on groups of individuals with whom they may want to develop exchanges. Kotler and Armstrong (2018) defined market segmentation as "dividing a market into distinct groups of buyers who have different needs, characteristics, or behaviors and who might require separate marketing strategies or mixes" (p. 75). If the many variables identified in Exhibit 8.4 (page 158) are used, markets can be segmented almost infinitely.

How much segmentation is enough? This is a difficult question to answer. In practice, segmentation must be managed to be effective. Weinstein (1987) identified three reasons that this is true: (1) not everyone is a potential customer for every service the agency may develop; (2) an agency's service mix must be limited because of limited resources and economic efficiency; and (3) because the number of potential customers and the number of services available are limited, it is most efficient for the agency to match services with potential customers. No agency has the resources to meet all identified market segments; therefore, the agency must make strategic choices about which markets to serve. Market segmentation, then, helps agencies be more efficient in matching specific cohorts of customers with services tailored to their specific needs.

Differences in segments must have a practical significance that warrants separate marketing attention. Kotler and Armstrong (1990) suggested four criteria that must be met before segmentation is justified: measurable, accessible, sizable, and actionable.

Measurable. First, the segment must be measurable. The programmer must be able to determine its size, the ability of the population to purchase the service, and other differences in market behavior that are unique to the market segment. This is why some programmers reject marketing. Often, it is cheaper for programmers simply to offer a program and see if it succeeds than to confirm the existence of the market segment before offering the program. For example, one of the authors was once asked how to determine the market for weekend rentals of recreation equipment kits for picnics. Conducting a marketing survey for a community of 10,000 to determine the demand for the kits was more expensive than simply buying the equipment for five kits, publicizing the program, and adjusting from observed use. Because measuring many recreation markets is expensive, marketing is not the answer to every program development problem.

Accessible. Second, the market must be accessible. It is possible that some markets need services but simply cannot be reached efficiently. In a city as large as Los Angeles, there may be a market of individuals who want to play Scottish bagpipes. Because the people are widely scattered and a conduit for reaching them does not exist, the critical number needed to make up a program may never materialize. The market cannot be readily accessed.

Sizable. Third, a market segment must be substantial enough to warrant separate marketing attention. In commercial agencies, the test is whether a segment is large enough to be profitable. In not-for-profit and government operations, justifying developing services for identified market segments is more complicated. Two common tests are whether the segment is large enough to be served efficiently or whether it has a unique, demonstrable need that is part of the service mission of the agency.

Actionable. Fourth, the market segment must be actionable. Does the agency have the resources to treat the segment separately? Is the segment likely to respond to separate marketing attention, and is their unique characteristic likely to remain stable over time? In recreation, often many market segments can be identified for a single facility. For example, in a public swimming pool there are children who want to play in the water, people who want to practice springboard diving, those who simply want to swim laps for an aerobic workout, and so on. Some of these segments will be too small for the programmer to justify separate treatment. In addition, some of these uses interfere with each other. For example, swimming laps and general swim play often cannot occur simultaneously. Therefore, the agency may not be able to offer service to every segment.

> Market segments with whom the agency desires to have exchanges are termed target markets.

Target Marketing

Once the total market is segmented, the agency may adopt different strategies to complete exchanges with the various segments identified. Some segments, for reasons outlined previously, will not be served. Market segments with whom the agency desires to have exchanges are termed target markets. Crompton and Lamb (1986) defined a target market as "a relatively homogeneous group of people or organizations that have relatively similar service preferences with whom the agency seeks to exchange" (p. 112).

The major reason for segmenting markets is to determine whether the market should be targeted as a whole or whether specific segments should be handled differently. Marketers influence the target market through the marketing mix, that is, "the set of controllable marketing variables that the firm blends to produce the response desired in the target market" (Kotler & Armstrong, 1990, pp. 40–41). The variables that marketers most frequently cite as being controllable include product, price, promotion, and place.

A different market mix can be developed for each target market with which an agency seeks to have exchanges. One or more of the four market mix variables can be altered for each target market. *Product* is a generic term that describes the service, product, experience, or facility the agency is developing, making, staging, or constructing for the client. Many products could be developed. Changes in the product itself—that is, changes in the six key elements of a situated activity system—will obviously have a tremendous effect on the market mix. Recall the discussion about developing leisure products in Chapter 4.

The price at which a product is sold, including a zero price, will affect consumption. Chapters 17 to 19 detail pricing recreation services.

Promotional campaigns for the same leisure product can be designed differently for different target markets. For example, the programmer could simply alter the promotion campaign to emphasize different benefits from the same service and distribute the different publicity campaigns to the different target markets. The programmer could promote, for example, a fitness facility to two different markets, one of which is most interested in opportunities to meet new friends and the other in keeping physically fit. The two groups could use the facility at the same time but would be attracted to it for different reasons. These differences would need to be incorporated into separate promotional campaigns. Chapter 14 includes information about developing promotional campaigns.

Place involves distribution of services, including the day, time, and location of service. Changing the place of a service will often change the market of people attracted to it. Chapter 13 includes information about scheduling leisure service products.

It is important for programmers to realize that developing different market mixes for each target market is a more expensive strategy than developing a single market mix for the entire market. For this reason, they should be sure that there are enough actionable differences between market segments to justify developing separate market mixes.

Target Marketing Strategies

Kotler and Armstrong (2018) identified three target marketing strategies: undifferentiated, differentiated, and concentrated. Figure 8.1 (page 168) illustrates these. The undifferentiated strategy assumes that the entire market will be handled as a single entity or mass marketing. Any existing market segments are not recognized, and a single market mix is developed for the entire market. Or perhaps there are not enough differences between the market segments to warrant developing different market mixes. In this case, the undifferentiated strategy is justified. Often, however, agencies use this strategy for the wrong reason—they simply do not want to develop additional market mixes.

A second alternative is adopting a differentiated strategy, which means the agency will operate in two or more segments of the market and will design different market mixes for each segment. It is assumed that this strategy will lead to more exchanges with each segment because of a unique product mix for each target market. For this strategy, it is important that each product has a unique position in the market relative to other products in the same product space. These different qualities must be communicated to the target markets for this strategy to fulfill its potential benefit. Generally, this method of operation will be more expensive, but it will result in deeper market penetration (i.e., more participants).

The concentrated target marketing strategy recognizes the existence of multiple market segments but devotes the major marketing effort of the agency to developing only one market mix that may attract one or more smaller segments. With this strategy, the agency simultaneously ignores some market segments for various reasons while developing a single market mix. Programmers can adopt this strategy when the agency does not have sufficient resources to serve all identified markets or when the agency wants to serve market segments not being served by other providers. Often this is called niche marketing because only one niche is served. An example of the latter instance is the development of a public golf course with inexpensive green fees in a community that has private country clubs with limited memberships and a commercial golf course with high green fees. The public sector would thus be target marketing golf to middle- and lower-income players who cannot afford to play at the other two courses. This would be their niche, middle- and lower-income players. This example is used because the term *niche* often describes high-end products and groups. All it really means is that the target market has unique but common characteristics.

Public agencies and some not-for-profit agencies often face an ethical problem when applying the concentrated target marketing strategy—which market segments can they ignore? Which should they try to serve? Often they are tempted to serve easily accessible markets, when in reality the public system should serve the most vulnerable clients. For example, Spigner and Havitz (1993), in discussing recreation opportunities for the unemployed, pointed out that the unemployed "are rarely

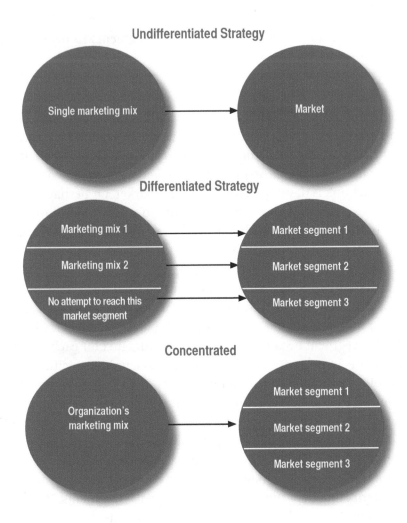

Figure 8.1. Alternate Target Marketing Strategies. Adapted from Kotler and Andreasen (1987).

singled out as a target market" (p. 52). This is one dilemma of addressing social justice concerns—individuals who constitute these markets are often the most difficult to reach.

Comparing Marketing and Programming

Marketing contributes to program development in several ways. The market mix is made up of price, promotion, place, and product. Changing any of these variables alters the market that will likely be served. Of these variables, product is the one for which programmers have unique expertise. They understand the leisure experience and how to structure leisure occasions. Thus, they are well prepared for marketing in the experience economy. Additional techniques and skills for accomplishing this are discussed elsewhere in this text.

The major contribution of marketing to recreation programming is the provision of methods for identifying needs that can be developed into programs and knowledge about exchanging the services with target markets successfully. Promotion, pricing, and place (distribution) in the consumption of leisure services are additional contributions of marketing techniques to recreation programming.

Some cautions about the misuse of marketing concepts are in order. Marketing technology provides excellent techniques for isolating market segments that are truly in need of social services. Although these techniques have been in use in recreation and leisure service agencies for over 40 years, agencies have generally used them to develop services for the average, middle-class constituent who can function in a market-driven, fee-for-service economy. Programs are rarely targeted for anyone other than the average person (Spigner & Havitz, 1993). Programmers have less often used marketing technology to help public and not-for-profit agencies focus their efforts on markets specifically targeted by their mission statements—the implementation of societal marketing. The need to accomplish this makes achieving the marketing task more complicated and difficult in public and not-for-profit agencies than in commercial and private agencies.

As target marketing techniques become more sophisticated, their summary effect is to provide the agency with the ability to manipulate the patron. Smith (1992) stated, "Privacy in the 1990s includes not only the right to control personal information about oneself and how it is used, but also the right to be free of manipulation, whether in the marketplace or by the government" (p. 19). Given the tracking of consumer preferences and behavior by Google and other e-marketers, this concern was indeed prophetic. Agencies whose missions include contributing to the public good must ensure that they are using these techniques ethically to further the legitimate interests of their patrons and community, rather than catering to the sole interests of the agency.

Finally, although the conceptual constructs of marketing are engrossing and make logical sense, their successful implementation depends on a continuing stream of relevant data. McCarville (1999) stated, "Clearly, a need for coordination exists around both the collection and dissemination of data" (p. 429). Few recreation agencies have allocated the resources to accomplish this. They often lack the personnel and infrastructure to routinely collect and analyze the data for supporting a comprehensive marketing campaign that would provide programmers with the data to develop market-based program services.

Conclusion

Developing successful programs requires the systematic collection of information from potential participants and other stakeholders for use in program development and operation. Three general methods for accomplishing this are including stakeholders on advisory groups, using needs assessment techniques, and gathering strategic marketing information. This chapter presented and explained multiple techniques for accomplishing these, including marketing. Each method provides different types of information. These techniques complement each other by providing comprehensive information about the leisure desires of the constituents of the agency.

References

Carpenter, G. M., & Howe, C. Z. (1985). *Programming leisure experiences.* New York, NY: Prentice-Hall.

Crompton, J. L. (1978). Development of a taxonomy of a leisure services delivery system. *Journal of Leisure Research, 10,* 214–218.

Crompton, J. L., & Lamb, C. W., Jr. (1986). *Marketing government and social services.* New York, NY: Wiley.

Csikszentmihalyi, M. (1975). *Beyond boredom and anxiety.* San Francisco, CA: Jossey-Bass.

Dillman, D. (1987). Elements of success. In D. E. Johnson, L. R. Meiller, L. C. Miller, & G. F. Summers (Eds.), *Needs assessment, theory, and methods* (pp. 188–209). Ames: Iowa State University Press.

Ellis, M. J. (1973, April). *Why people play.* Englewood Cliffs, NJ: Prentice-Hall.

Fishbein, M., & Manfredo, M. J. (1992). A theory of behavior change. In M. J. Manfredo (Ed.), *Influencing human behavior: Theory and applications in recreation, tourism, and natural resources management* (pp. 29–50). Urbana, IL: Sagamore.

Iso-Ahola, S. E. (1980). *The social psychology of leisure and recreation.* Dubuque, IA: Wm. C. Brown.

Iso-Ahola, S. E. (1982, February). Intrinsic motivation: An overlooked basis for evaluation. *Parks and Recreation, 17*(2), 32–33, 58.

Johnson, D. E., & Meiller, L. R. (1987). Community level surveys. In D. E. Johnson, L. R. Meiller, L. C. Miller, & G. F. Summers (Eds.), *Needs assessment, theory, and methods* (pp. 126–141). Ames: Iowa State University Press.

Knowles, M. S. (1970). *The modern practice of adult education.* New York, NY: Association Press.

Kolko, J. (2012). *Wicked problems: Problems worth solving: A handbook and call to action.* Austin, TX: AC4D.

Kotler, P., & Andreasen, A. R. (1987). *Strategic marketing for nonprofit organizations* (3rd ed.). Englewood Cliffs, NJ: Prentice-Hall.

Kotler, P., & Armstrong, G. (1990). *Marketing: An introduction* (3rd ed.). Englewood Cliffs, NJ: Prentice-Hall.

Kotler, P., & Armstrong, G. (2018). *Principles of marketing* (17th ed., Global ed.). Harlow, United Kingdom: Pearson.

Lancaster, R. A. (Ed.). (1983). *Recreation, park, and open space standards and guidelines.* Alexandria, VA: National Recreation and Park Association.

Mannell, R. C. (1999). Leisure experience and satisfaction. In E. L. Jackson & T. L. Burton (Eds.), *Leisure studies: Prospects for the twenty-first century* (pp. 235–251). State College, PA: Venture.

McCarville, R. (1999). Marketing public recreation services. In E. L. Jackson & T. L. Burton (Eds.), *Leisure studies: Prospects for the twenty-first century* (pp. 415–433). State College, PA: Venture.

McKillip, J. (1987). *Need analysis: Tools for the human services and education.* Beverly Hills, CA: Sage.

Mercer, D. (1973). The concept of recreational need. *Journal of Leisure Research, 5*(1), 37–50.

National Park Service. (n.d.). *Marketing parks and recreation.* State College, PA: Venture.

National Recreation and Park Association. (2017a). *Local government officials' perceptions of parks and recreation.* Retrieved from https://www.nrpa.org/publications-research/research-papers/local-government-officials-perceptions-of-parks-and-recreation/

National Recreation and Park Association. (2017b). *2017 NRPA agency performance review: Park and recreation agency performance benchmarks.* Ashburn, VA: Author.

Neulinger, J. (1974). *The psychology of leisure.* Springfield, IL: Charles C. Thomas.

O'Sullivan, E. L. (1991). *Marketing for parks, recreation, and leisure.* State College, PA: Venture.

Schlatter, B. E., & Chang, Y. (2018). Recreation programming practices: Unpublished survey. Illinois Park and Recreation Association.

Schmitt, B. H. (1999). *Experiential marketing.* New York, NY: Free Press.

Schultz, J. H., McAvoy, L. H., & Dustin, D. L. (1988, January). What are we in business for? *Parks and Recreation, 22*(1), 52–54.

Shaw, C., & Ivens, J. (2005). *Building great customer experiences.* New York, NY: Palgrave Macmillan.

Smith, R. E. (1992). Target marketing: Turning birds of a feather into sitting ducks. *National Forum, 72*(1), 18–21.

Spigner, C., & Havitz, M. E. (1993, November). Societal marketing or social justice: A dialogue on access to recreation for the unemployed. *Parks and Recreation, 27*(11), 51–57.

Summers, G. F. (1987). Democratic governance. In D. E. Johnson, L. R. Meiller, L. C. Miller, & G. F. Summers (Eds.), *Needs assessment, theory, and methods* (pp. 3–19). Ames: Iowa State University Press.

Tew, C. P. F. J., Havitz, M. E., & McCarville, R. E. (1999). The role of marketing in municipal recreation programming decisions: A challenge to conventional wisdom. *Journal of Park and Recreation Administration, 17*(1), 1–20.

Weinstein, A. (1987). *Market segmentation: Using demographics, psycho-graphics, and other segmentation techniques to uncover and exploit new markets.* Chicago, IL: Probus.

Wells, W. D. (1979). Group interviewing. In J. B. Higginbotham & K. K. Cox (Eds.), Focus group interviews (pp. 2–12). Chicago: American Marketing Association. (Reprinted from *Handbook of marketing research,* by R. Ferber, 1974, New York, NY: McGraw-Hill)

Wendt, T. (2015). *Design for dasein: Understanding the design of experiences.* New York, NY: Thomas Wendt.

Witt, P. A., & Groom, R. (1979). Dangers and problems associated with current approaches to developing leisure interest finders. *Therapeutic Recreation Journal, 8*(1), 19–30.

Zikmund, W. G., & d'Amico, M. (2002). *Effective marketing: Creating and keeping customers in an e-commerce world* (3rd ed.). Cincinnati, OH: South-Western.

Youth Sports Soccer League Practice
Photo courtesy of City of Grand Prairie Parks, Arts, and Recreation Department.

9 *Writing Program Design and Outcome Statements*

KEY TERMS

Program Outcomes, X Intervention Goals, Y Outcome Goals, Program Design Standards, Terminal Performance Outcomes, BBP Target Issues, BBP Activity Components

Step 4: Program Outcomes

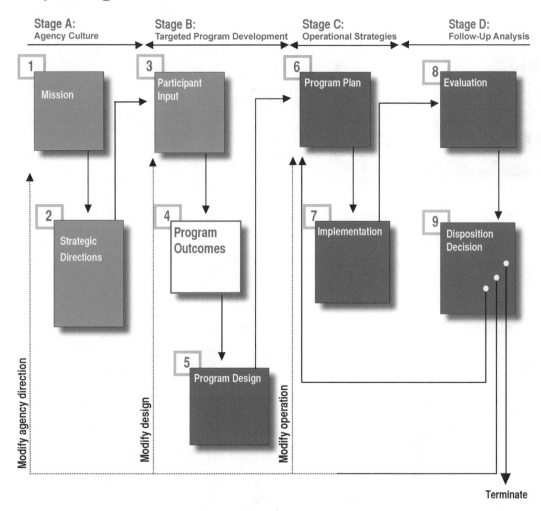

Specifying outcomes for program design is the final stratum in developing the programming strategy of an organization. At this point, the programmer transitions from strategic to operational planning, preparing a set of coordinated tasks to implement strategies identified in the strategic plans. These evolve from strategic directions and program management goals (MBO) that were developed earlier in the process. They were explained in Chapters 5 and 6. For an example of the entire hierarchy, see Figure 9.1. In this figure, Box A includes the mission statement. This establishes the overall direction of the agency, as was discussed in Chapter 6. Box B includes 3- to 5-year planning strategies. As Chapter 7 discussed, the programmer uses these to further develop its mission by defining its programmatic directions. Box C includes 1-year management by objective statements. These were also discussed in Chapter 7. At this point, the programmer integrates strategic programming strategy with budget development and commits resources to the development of a specific program. Box D includes program design statements. These help programmers to implement programming operations and provide them with direction

Box A

The Arlington County Department of Parks and Recreation promotes wellness and vitality through dynamic programs and attractive public spaces.

Box B

1. Provide excellent programs, services, places, and spaces.
2. Steward natural and historical resources.
3. Build community, promote wellness, and ensure equal access for all.
4. Manage access efficiently and effectively.
5. Cultivate an effective, dynamic workforce.

Box C

1. The Superintendent of Parks and Recreation will hire a Fitness and Wellness Supervisor within the first two months of FY 2020.
2. The Superintendent of Parks and Recreation will budget $75,000 for fitness and wellness programs during FY 2020.
3. The Superintendent of Parks and Recreation will operate 20 fitness and wellness programs during FY 2020.
   a. Fitness and Wellness will offer basic bicycle maintenance and repair classes and workshops for teens and adults during the summer of 2020, with an enrollment of 15 or more.
   b. Fitness and Wellness will offer a How to Change and Fix a Flat Tube half-day workshop during the summer of 2020 with an enrollment of 15 or more.
   c. Fitness and Wellness will offer a Clean and Lubricate Your Bike half-day workshop during the summer of 2020 with an enrollment of 15 or more.
   d. Fitness and Wellness will offer The Nuts and Bolts of Bicycle Nuts and Bolts workshop during the summer of 2020 summer with an enrollment of 15 or more.

Box D

X Interventions	Y Outcomes
1. The instructor will teach students how to change and fix a flat tire tube.	1. By the end of the workshop when requested, 90% of the students will be able to change and fix a flat tire tube.
2. After the first hour, the instructor will allow each student to demonstrate removing a flat tire tube from the bicycle wheel.	2. By the end of the first hour when requested, 90% of the students will be able to remove a flat tire tube from the wheel.
3. After the second hour, the instructor will allow each student to demonstrate how to repair a flat tire tube.	3. After the second hour when requested, 90% of the students will be able to demonstrate how to repair a flat tire tube.
4. After the third hour, the instructor will allow each student to demonstrate how to reinstall the bicycle wheel.	4. After the third hour when requested, 90% of the students will demonstrate how to reinstall the wheel.
	a. Line up the dropouts in the fork with the axle of the wheel.
	b. Slowly lower the fork onto the axle.
	c. Hold the quick-release lever in place as you tighten the bolt.
	d. Reconnect the brakes and make sure they're working.

Figure 9.1. An Example of Networked Goals and Objectives

for design, staging, and evaluation. They are discussed in this chapter, and the reader will find that this chapter includes a lot of exercises. The best way someone can learn to write goal and objective statements is to practice doing it with tutored guidance.

Outcome Statements (Y Statements)

There are two types of program design statements. Box D of Figure 9.1 (page 175) includes examples. The intervention, or X statements, specify how staff will stage events and intervene to accomplish participant outcomes (i.e., the Y statements). During program staging, intervention activities occur before outcomes. But in the design phase, it is best for programmers to follow Dr. Stephen Covey's famous axiom, "Begin with the end in mind." Thus, the final level of statements involves writing terminal performance outcomes, Y statements, which should be developed before intervention statements. They describe in detail the outcomes participants will experience (i.e., what is supposed to happen to people as a result of participating in a program). They describe the experience the designer intends to produce so its occurrence can be imagined. Writing them requires a shift in the usual focus of goal development from what staff will do to participant outcomes (i.e., what will happen to individuals as a result of their participation in the program?). They describe in rich, descriptive detail all of the outcomes to be produced, including emotional as well as more traditional outcomes.

These statements come from numerous sources. Shaw and Ivens (2005) explained the importance of understanding customer expectations as one source, "The implication is that you need to understand your customer's expectations" (p. 23). They identified several sources from which participants develop their expectations:
- Our expectations are built from previous experiences.
- We learn from reading things in papers.
- From previous experiences that are similar, we translate what they are like.
- We learn from what people have told us.
- We learn from what we have read in magazines, seen on television or films, and so on. (Shaw & Ivens, 2005, p. 23)

The authors of this book add that people also develop expectations from surfing websites and through their social media links. An additional source of possible outcomes is the programmer's own data gathering efforts. This is the point in the process at which programmers use the information they have developed from user surveys and other marketing investigations about the needs and wants of their constituents, as discussed in Chapter 8.

Programmers are cautioned that needs assessments may only provide enough information for the development of a partial list of design outcomes. Programmers often complete the list of outcomes with additional data from their organizational environment, knowledge about their clientele, and previous professional experiences. For example, an assessment makes apparent the need for a program that serves mothers with preschool children during the morning hours and gives them a noncompetitive activity that allows the mothers to socialize. This need is obviously not a program, but it could serve as a partial list of outcomes to be achieved in a program. In this example, the programmer would need to add more outcomes and then design implementations to stage a program to solve the original design problem.

But not all outcomes come from constituents. People cannot express a desire for a program or experience they have never had or learned about. Thus, new programs may have designed outcomes that originate from the programmer's creativity and innovation. Additionally, often program outcomes originate from the mission of the agency. This is the case when the agency intends to provide transformational services wherein the outcome of a program service will result in changes in people's lives, behaviors, or knowledge. For example, "Pop Warner exists to use football, cheerleading, dance and a respect for education to develop strong, smart, responsible, healthy young men and women. We give them experiences that build their appreciation for and understanding of leadership, teamwork, and discipline" ("Why There," para. 1). Thus, one would expect that each program they offer would have at least one outcome that intends participants acquire skill in or increase proficiency in football, cheerleading, or dance, as stated in the mission.

Exhibit 9.1 provides another example of design outcomes. These goals outline an Egg Hunt designed so that each child can find an egg (or at least go home with an egg) and can search without competition from parents hunting with their children, but in a way that permits parents to observe and photograph their own children. The program will also provide opportunities to visit the Bunny. The program designer outlines as an outcome each experience he or she believes is critical to the overall experience of the program. Collectively, these outcomes define the program design problem. The program designer then designs and stages interventions, or X statements, to ensure the accomplishment of each outcome.

Exhibit 9.1. Program Design Outcomes—Egg Hunt

Key experiences to be staged:

- To facilitate each child finding an egg
- To provide opportunities for children to visit the Bunny
- To keep parents from hunting eggs
- To help parents enjoy seeing their children hunt eggs

Design problems frequently involve developing programs for a specific facility. For example, unused time at a bowling alley, recreation center, swimming pool, or ice rink may need to be filled with a program service. In these instances, the organizational need of filling a facility becomes the primary impetus for developing a program. Programmers then add patron input from a needs assessment to the design problem and design a program to meet articulated client needs and to fulfill the organizational need of increasing use of the facility.

Precise and descriptive terminal performance outcomes facilitate designing and staging the experience intended. They define the program design problem; that is, a program needs to be designed to facilitate the experiences outlined in the intended outcomes for participants, and they should be SMART. How specific these statements need to be depends on the nature of a program and the outcomes intended. When the outcomes of a program focus on transformations or changes in each individual, the outcomes must be individualized and more focused. For example, compare the outcomes in Exhibit 9.2 with those in Exhibit 9.3. The outcomes for the concert series are more general and involve outcomes not focused on changes in the behavior of individuals. In contrast, the outcomes for the baseball clinic are stated in terms of outcomes for individuals to achieve. In both cases, the outcomes serve as a framework for program design. Outcomes in Exhibit 9.1 (page 177) provide an example of outcomes for participants (children) and spectators (parents). Decisions about what to include or exclude in staging the programs are guided by the outcomes intended, the Y statements. The next section also discusses individualized terminal performance outcomes. Now complete Exercise 9.1.

Exhibit 9.2. Program Outcomes for a Concert in the Park Series

- To provide a series of concerts featuring live music at no charge to the public
- To stage the concerts in an easily accessible downtown park
- To feature the natural setting of the park as part of staging the experience
- To feature a band that will play a variety of musical styles
- To create a festive picnic atmosphere at each concert
- To create an atmosphere conducive to family relational building

---

Exhibit 9.3. Performance Outcomes for a Baseball Clinic

When tested by staff at the end of the clinic:
- Participants will be able to correctly answer 70% or more of written questions on baseball rules.
- Participants will be able to correctly answer 70% or more of written questions on baseball strategy.
- Participants' batting averages will have increased by .050 or more.
- Seventy percent or more of the participants will indicate that their skill at playing their chosen position will have increased significantly.

Exercise 9.1.
Goal Networking

The program design outcomes in Exhibit 9.1 are the final set in a complete network of goals and objectives. Returning to the material in Chapters 6 and 7, discuss how these program design outcomes likely developed through the organization from mission, through strategic directions and MBO statements, to program design outcomes. In doing so, consider the following questions:

- Can you develop the 3- to 5-year, short-range planning directions and the 1-year, management by objective–type statements associated with this program?
- Can you see how this series of goals and objectives are networked throughout the agency's organizational structure?
- Do you understand how a goal for one level of the organization can become an objective for another level of the organization?
- Do you understand how the program design outcomes provide direction in decisions about staging the event?

Individualized Terminal Performance Outcomes

The most specific Y program design statement is a terminal performance outcome that states an observable behavior to be performed by a participant. This level of focus is needed when programs are being designed to provide instruction, to provide therapy, or to implement outcome-based programming. Exhibit 9.3 presents examples of terminal performance outcomes for a baseball clinic, an instructional program wherein the performance of each child is the focus of the programmer's effort.

The condition specified in Exhibit 9.3, "when tested by staff at the end of the clinic," indicates when the participants are expected to exhibit the behaviors that are the outcome of participation. In the first outcome, the observable behavior is an exam score and the metric is a score of 70% or more correct answers. An implicit assumption of this process is that the abilities demonstrated resulted from the participant's involvement in the program designed and staged by the programmer.

Box D of Figure 9.1 (page 175) shows another example of this technique in the goals and objectives. Specifically, Objective 3, "After the third hour when requested, 90% of the students will demonstrate how to reinstall the wheel" including (a) lining up the dropouts in the fork with the axle of the wheel, (b) slowly lowering the fork onto the axle, (c) holding the quick-release lever in place while tightening the bolt, and (d) reconnecting the brakes and making sure they're working. Collectively, the performance outcomes in Box D give the programmer direction for designing the flat tire tube repair class. They, too, are written so that they can be measured and their attainment thereby verified.

Intervention Goals (X Statements)

Programmers next develop intervention goals, that is, X statements that explain the actions programmers will stage to accomplish the outcomes intended. Box D of Figure 9.1 (page 175) includes examples of these. Traditionally, these are the type of programming intervention goals developed. They specify what the programmer and programming staff must accomplish to stage the program and achieve the outcomes specified. They must be SMART to provide metrics for assessing their accomplishment and accountability of staff responsible for their implementation.

Using the method recommended here, the programmer can focus the interventions on facilitating the outcomes specified for participants. Box D of Figure 9.1 (page 175) includes one or more X interventions that staff will implement when staging the program and that will ensure accomplishment of each outcome intended (i.e., each Y statement). Exhibit 9.3 (page 178) provides an additional example, specifying intervention goals, X statements, for the baseball clinic. Again, the statements support the outcomes intended and the activities/programs that are staged will ensure accomplishment of the outcomes intended. The examples provided may be time consuming to implement but ensure programs implement the outcomes intended and ultimately achieve the overall mission and strategy of the organization. Chapter 10 includes more about this. Now complete Exercise 9.2.

Exercise 9.2.
Programming by Design

Design outcomes for a 4th of July Independence Day theme party at a retirement village. First, list three design outcomes you want to achieve (i.e., the experiences you want those who attend to have). Second, for each outcome prepare a management goal specifying actions the program will take to ensure each outcome is accomplished.

- How might participant input be solicited and incorporated into design goals?
- Are the essential experiential elements of this program apparent from the list?
- Is the list of outcomes explicit enough to guide the development of intervention goals?
- Does the list make apparent the unique experience that will be offered in this program?

Program Design Standards

This section departs somewhat from other material in the chapter to illustrate that programmers can use goals and objectives in different ways to guide program operations. Program design can be guided by program standards developed in an agency. In this case, an agency developed a list of outcomes desired for a specific program, and these standards provide a generic design template. Exhibit 9.4 presents an example of program standards for "theme programs" used by the U.S. Army V Corps.

Theme programs are a specific form of program service that military recreation employees who work in the Army V Corps Recreation Centers are required to develop. By their standards, a theme program includes at least six of the 10 specified elements of a theme program. Obviously, they develop each program element around a single theme.

The goal in this instance is to develop a theme program. The 10 elements serve as predesignated design outcomes. If employees incorporate six of the 10 elements into the program design, they will have produced a theme program. The design of a theme program in this agency is thus guided by program standards. Incorporating patron desires into the final design will increase the probability of developing a successful program. Exhibit 9.5 (page 182) shows an example of 10 program design outcomes developed with this concept. Now complete Exercise 9.3 (page 183).

Exhibit 9.4. Ten Elements of a Theme Program

A theme is an underlying, dominant, or recognizable concept. Programmers generally do an excellent job of developing themes for major holidays and events such as Christmas, Easter, or Independence Day. To add experiential depth to programs, this concept needs to be carried through in other programs. In a military recreation operation, a program that includes at least six of the 10 following elements will meet the standard of a theme program:
1. Activities (active games)
2. Refreshments (food and beverages)
3. Decorations or props
4. Entertainment (live)
5. Audiovisuals (films/slides/videotapes)
6. Costumes
7. Lighting (special room arrangement)
8. Prizes
9. Music (canned, for atmosphere)
10. Gimmicks (giveaways, mystery or special guests, special effects, animals, etc.)

Note. From H. Rice, Director V Corps Recreation Centers, 1986.

Exhibit 9.5. A Caribbean Christmas Theme Program

(*Note:* Research at the library how Christmas is celebrated in the Caribbean islands, and incorporate those elements.)

Program Element #1: Activities

1. Limbo contest
2. Seashell hunt
3. Straw hat decorating
4. Salsa or Caribbean dancing

Program Element #2: Refreshments

1. Fresh fruits (tropical)
2. Fruit cocktail bowl with shredded coconut
3. Other recipes researched in library or from family members of Caribbean origin

Program Element #3: Decorations or Props

1. Hanging suns (large colorful swatches of fabric stapled to walls in interesting patterns)
2. Palm trees, banana trees (potted)
3. Large seashells made of papier-mâché

Program Element #4: Entertainment

1. Steel band
2. Caribbean music group

Program Element #5: Audiovisuals

1. Movies (travelogues) of the Caribbean islands
2. Slides of scenes from the Caribbean islands
3. Recordings of Caribbean drums playing

Program Element #6: Costumes

1. White shirts open to the navel with colorful cummerbunds for men
2. Colorful sundresses for women

Program Element #7: Lighting

1. Colored spotlights with bright colors: red, orange, yellow, and so on illuminating the room

Program Element #9: Music (canned)

1. Steel drum music
2. Have a limbo expert perform

Note. Adapted from an original program concept by Darmstadt Recreation Center Staff.

Workshops are short-term educational sessions that focus on a specific topic or skill area such as gardening, digital photography, creative writing, Web publishing, or geocaching, for small groups of participants. Develop programming standards for 1-day workshops in an agency. These standards should specify the general expectation for every program in the agency that is called a 1-day workshop. When finished, discuss the following questions:

- How will participant input be solicited and incorporated into the final program design?
- Does the description give the workshop a unique programming format in the agency?
- Do your workshop goals give enough guidance and direction to programmers who wish to develop workshops?

Conclusion

To design a program, the programmer must specify the interventions that will be staged (X statements) to implement the program and create the leisure experience intended (Y statements). At this point, it is important for programmers to develop SMART Y statements that vividly describe the experience to be created. They can follow this with developing SMART X statements, program design goals that specify the staging activities that staff will implement to ensure accomplishment of the outcomes intended. This chapter provided an example of the use of goals and objectives in the development of program standards and management of program services. Thorough work at this point in developing SMART outcomes and program implementation goals will expedite the program design process covered in the next chapter.

References

Shaw, C., & Ivens, J. (2005). *Building great customer experiences.* New York, NY: Palgrave Macmillan.

Spokane Pop Warner. (n.d.). [Homepage]. Retrieved November 1, 2018, from https://www.spokanepopwarner.org/

Additional Reading

Gronlund, N. E. (1970). *Stating behavioral objectives for classroom instruction.* New York, NY: Macmillan.

Movies in the Park
City of Long Beach, Department of Parks, Recreation, and Marine.
Photo by Long Beach Parks, Recreation, and Marine.

10 *Program Design*

KEY TERMS

Program Design, Definition of Program Design, Co-Creation of Experiences, Framed Experience Model, Encounter, Visualization, Imagined Interactions, Design Tactics, Candidate Plans, Frame, Artistic Factors, Technical Factors, Transition, Framed Experience Design

Step 5: Program Design

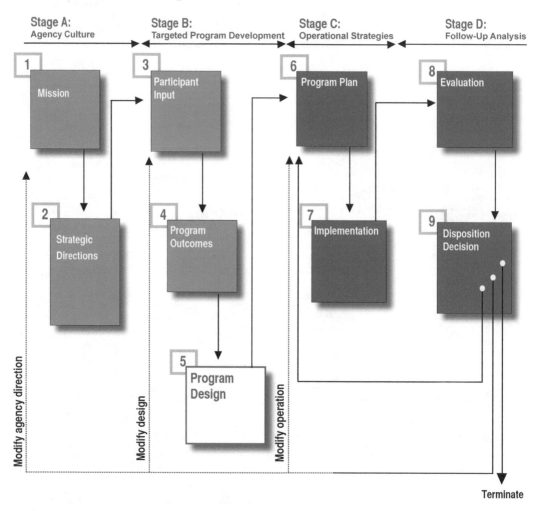

Program design is a transitional step in which programmers plan the details of how to stage a program to facilitate a leisure experience for participants. Figure 10.1 shows the general process of design. This stage is the final step in Stage 2 of the Program Development Cycle. In this step, the programmer uses data collected in Stages 1 and 2, including the agency's mission, strategic direction, participants' needs and wants, and intended program outcomes.

During program design, the programmer designs an interactive situated activity system that will animate a program to move it through time and orchestrate its flow (Edginton, Hanson, & Edginton, 1992), by manipulating the six key elements discussed in Chapter 3 and altering the pattern of attention required from participants so there is variety in the content and intensity of consciousness demanded in the series of encounters that make up the program. Staging and implementing the design prepared in this step produces a managed experience pattern. Hull, Stewart, and Yi (1992) provided evidence for this phenomenon, noting, while discussing a hiking experience, that "a recreation experience is dynamic: It fluctuates over the course of the engagement. Moods change. Scenic beauty varies. The degree of absorption in one's activity fluctuates" (p. 249). Furthermore, they documented that these experience patterns not only vary throughout the experience, but that subsets of participants have different experiences. Thus, the same program provides different individuals with different experiences. They speculated that recreation experience patterns may be influenced by the management of the recreation site (i.e., staging of a program). Program design, then, is the process of staging a program and thus facilitating this notion of a managed experience pattern.

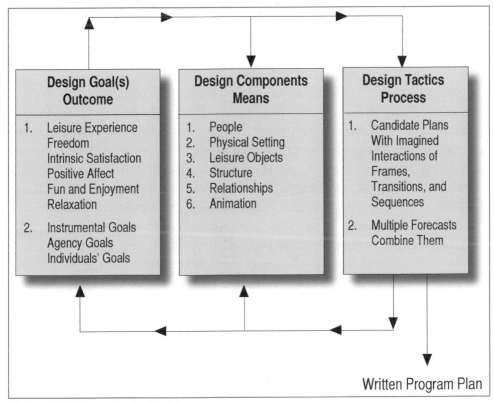

Figure 10.1. Program Design Model

Designing Leisure Experiences

Simon suggested that design is intervention to create or change something (as cited in Mintzberg, 2009, p. 54). *Program design is a strategy for planning interventions in social encounters that make up leisure experiences. Programmers plan the step-by-step action scenarios and configurations of the six key elements of a situated activity system that will frame encounters and guide participants through the social interactions necessary for facilitating the leisure experience intended by the designer.* We might add, if the programmer's previous work has been accomplished correctly, the program will also include features expressly desired by the participants.

Experience design has not received serious attention in the literature. Much education and literature on event planning, tourism management, recreation management, sport management, and arts management focuses on operations management of the experiences provided, not their design. An insightful analogy that demonstrates the role of operations management to design is the relationship of a construction manager to an architect. The construction manager manages the operation of constructing a building designed by the architect. Similarly, a programmer manages the staging of an experience (operating a program) as directed by the program designer. But there is a void of attention and responsibility for completing a thorough design of an experience prior to its operation. Often, design decisions are simply cobbled together as they arise in the process of staging an experience. The design thus achieved is often incomplete, not focused on theme, and not focused on the contribution each framed encounter should make toward achieving design goals. Design implemented in this manner lacks the comprehensiveness that could be achieved if it were executed a priori rather than during the implementation process.

Discussions of design are often limited to specific parts of events, such as graphic design, color selection, floral design, and presentation of food. Berridge (2007) provided a useful analogy for understanding the breadth of experience design. Imagine a large white cube, a venue for an experience to occur. It is void of all six elements of the situated activity system. Design is the process of making the decisions for filling this void space. From the universe of all that is possible to include, design is the process of selecting those things necessary for achieving the experience as envisioned by the designer. This design process is more comprehensive than that normally attributed to concepts of design focused on artistic, engineering, and physical layout decisions. It focuses on the experiences of participants and how the programmer's designed intervention choices might influence these.

Designing Interactive Experiences

Designing experiences that facilitate the opportunity for participants to co-create them is more challenging than designing experiences that only operationalize Phases 1 or 2 of the interaction ritual, discussed in Chapter 2. It is a different paradigm of production. In Phase 3, the experience stager gives up some control of the experience to minded, self-reflexive individuals, who help co-create outcomes. Although the programmer can predict the interactions likely to occur, these are not certain and thus the outcome is not certain.

A technology for designing interactive experiences can be drawn from several bodies of literature. Experience results from an individual's summary impression of participating in the interactions of a series of staged encounters. Each encounter, or situated activity system (Goffman, 1961), consists of six structural elements that the designer can manipulate. Chapter 3 discussed these in detail. As a reminder, the six elements include the people interacting in the occasion, the venue or physical setting, the objects that fill and are acted on in the occasion, social conventions that structure and guide interaction, the relationships of individuals in the occasion, and how interactions are guided (i.e., the animation of the occasion).

Building Blocks of a Framed Experience Model of Program Design[1]

The Framed Experience Model proposed here assumes that experience is co-created through individuals interacting in a series of framed encounters that are designed and staged by the program or event designer. A frame is the smallest unit of interaction that can be designed, and it exists as long as it occupies the conscious attention of participants. Berridge (2007) suggested that event and experience design and staging is a "predicative skill" (p. 163); thus, each frame includes a prediction of what will occur given the resources and manipulations the experience designer plans for a frame. Accomplishing this requires familiarity with several concepts and techniques that constitute the building blocks of the Framed Experience Model: encounters, the use of visualization to experiment with and rehearse proposed animation plans, frames, transitions, and consideration and inclusion of artistic and technical factors in experience design. The designer concludes these techniques by framing an experience design to animate the experience.

Encounter

Experience is the cumulative memory—cognitive, kinesthetic, and emotional—that results from direct observation and/or participation in a series of encounters. An encounter is a focused occasion of interaction (Goffman, 1961) that occurs when co-present individuals interact to a co-created end. In encounters, the interaction ritual is enacted, as described in Chapter 2. An encounter is the smallest unit of joint behavior and thus the focus of an experience designer's intervention and manipulation.

As discussed, the designer cannot manage all points of contact, so in leisure experience design the designer determines what points of contact to frame to guide participants to the intended design outcomes. This is especially important in large events and tourist trips, as many side encounters initiated by participants become part of the experience. In these cases, it is essential that the programmer designs enough encounters that the experience has a unique form and signature to it. For example, Renaissance festivals are large events with many interactive possibilities. The programmer would want to ensure, by design and staging, that everyone who came to the event would have a shared set of encounters that would define their participation in the festival. Although each participant would also have a unique set of collateral (Holt, 2014) encounters, all would experience the defining set of encounters designed and staged by the programmer. Through this process, programs provide lasting memories with a unique signature.

Visualization

Many endeavors allow for rehearsal of interactions in advance of operation. For example, a director can block and rehearse a play prior to its performance. A football

---

[1]This is original material. Both the term and process are original to this book.

RESEARCH UPDATE

Who uses visualization? In a recent survey of recreation programmers in Illinois, over 75% of the respondents across all categories reported using visualization often when planning programs and events.

Respondents	%
Females	78.8
Males	78.6
0–5 years of programming experience	76.8
6–10 years of programming experience	76.0
11–15 years of programming experience	79.4
Certified	77.7

Note. From Schlatter and Chang (2018).

coach can practice plays in advance of a game and prepare players for what is expected to happen in the game. A choreographer can rehearse a dance before its performance. But there is no such opportunity for staging many leisure experiences and events. Participants show up and interact for the first time in real time.

Visualization, sometimes referred to as imagined interactions, is a simulation heuristic that programmers can use to vicariously experience a program in advance of its operation. Research conducted by one of the authors and reported in the Research Update box in this chapter verifies that more than 75% of practicing professionals confirm that they use visualization in their work. In the process, programmers determine the specific interventions that they need to implement when staging the program to reach the design goals. According to Beach (1990), "Tactics are specific actions that are intended to facilitate implementation of a plan and to produce progress toward their goal" (p. 8). Interventions, then, are design tactics, the actions that the programmer must implement to stage the animation of a program, that is, to operate it. In the previous chapter, we identified these as Program Management Goals or Interventions—X Statements.

Design tactics are developed through imagined interactions, "a type of instrumental thought process as well as a type of simulation heuristic" (Honeycutt, 1991, p. 122). The notion of imagined interactions stems from symbolic interaction theory, discussed in Chapter 2. Mead (1934) identified the ability of humans to carry on an internalized conversation with themselves as a distinguishing feature of human intelligence. The notion that we are self-reflexive indicates we are capable of becoming objects in our own minds and thereby taking the role of others in an effort to understand how they see us. This internal dialogue can be focused on imagined interactions with others. Edwards, Honeycutt, and Zagacki (1988) indicated,

> This type of mental activity is important, because one may consciously take the role of others, imagining how they might respond to one's messages within particular situations, and thus one can imagine and test the consequences of alternative messages prior to communication. (p. 24)

They concluded that imagined interactions are one mechanism allowing individuals to plan and measure social action.

Visualization allows the designer to ask and answer what-if questions about various candidate plans for each encounter proposed, as well as experiment with different sequences of encounters. A priori use of this rehearsal technique (i.e., projective imagery) rectifies many potential staging problems prior to operation. Using projective imagery, the programmer simulates the possible social interactions of a program in his or her mind and experiments with various configurations of the encounters that make up the program and various combinations of the key situating elements of each encounter. With these images, the programmer rehearses and models candidate plans (i.e., alternate design tactics that they could use to stage program implementation). Analogy with a previous sequence of events or with imagined future events is a major underlying representational system that is often used. Kaufmann's (1988) work on the use of mental imagery in problem solving support its use. He stated, "In imagery we try to imagine what will happen under actual or hypothetical perceptual conditions (rather than inferring it through logical transformations)" (p. 234). The images are heuristic, and thus, the programmer creates them to experiment with what-if questions about various combinations that could be used. Their selection is also volitional (self-directed), and the programmer thereby uses directed consciousness to select different combinations of elements for experimentation and eventual adoption.

> Once several candidate plans have been developed, they compete with each other for adoption as the final solution.

These alternate candidate plans facilitate projecting different outcomes with different configurations. The programmer gives each candidate plan conscious attention and develops it until it is a feasible solution to the design problem (i.e., it facilitates the experience intended from participating). To achieve this, the programmer imagines multiple forecasts of candidate plans to develop alternate staging scenarios. Chapter 12 discusses techniques for pushing the formulation of multiple forecasts. Once several candidate plans have been developed, they compete with each other for adoption as the final solution. In addition, programmers can alter these by combining selected parts of different candidate plans and combining them into a final plan.

Implementing and Manipulating Imagined Interactions

To implement this process, visualize the operation of the program, that is, how the interaction scenarios of a program might be staged. This involves more than sight and can include all of the senses (Green, 1976). It may also produce feelings (Penfield, 1961, as cited in Green, 1976). Thus, you vicariously experience the sense of a program as if you are there, are going through it step-by-step, and are feeling the emotion of participating. Now complete Exercise 10.1.

To succeed, you need to learn a variety of visualization skills. First, discover how you personally organize visualizing. Individuals tend to use their personal default process for implementing this behavior and organize it in only one way. Therefore, you must consciously force yourself to visualize a program differently. Several techniques for accomplishing this follow.

Visualization occurs from one of two perspectives: external or internal (Weinberg, 1988). During external visualization, you become an object to yourself. For example, you may observe yourself participating as the leader of an event. It is analogous to watching a videotape of you leading the event. You aim to experiment with various leadership styles and strategies, to forecast the optimal style for the event. During internal visualization, you attempt to be at a program and to experience it vicariously from beginning to end. You aim to understand how the program will affect a participant, that is, what it is like to participate in this program. You normally assume one of these two perspectives when imaging and must consciously convert to the other to use visualization thoroughly to design a program.

Exercise 10.1.
Using All Five Senses

Objective:
To develop the ability to use all five senses to vicariously experience a program.

Step 1:
One way to practice using all five senses is to visualize a fond memory from your childhood, such as a holiday visit to a relative's (aunt's, uncle's, or grandparent's) home. Hear the sounds of the family socializing after the meal, recall the tastes and smells of the food, visualize the home, and recall what it was like to touch special objects associated with the holiday.

Step 2:
Next, use the five senses to recall a recent program that you conducted. Our senses make it possible to be there, see it, feel it, smell it, hear it, and experience the emotion of a program. You can use these skills to recall events previously experienced or to anticipate future occurrences.

You may also force yourself to change your physical viewpoint of the program. What will it look like from an aerial view? What if you reversed the sequential order of the program? You might take a side view of it or an under-the-ground view. What will it look like to a child who is 36 inches tall? Attempt to see the program from a different geographic location or physical position.

> During internal visualization, you attempt to be at a program and to experience it vicariously from beginning to end.

It is also useful to change the social role you are using to visualize the interactions of the program. Changing from leader to participant is one such change. But you must also internally visualize the program from the roles of other program participants, such as parents, spectators, the program manager, and referees. It is important that you are thorough in this step so that you can predict and deal with all possible difficulties and problems in the design of the program, rather than during its operation. Now complete Exercise 10.2.

Exercise 10.2.
Visual Imaging From Different Perspectives
(Rossman & Schlatter © 2001)

Directions: Use this instrument to record comments about any changes you'd make as a result of the vicarious rehearsals you've made of your program.

Description of Visual Imaging Perspectives	Comments
Entire Program Use external imaging to visualize the entire operation of a program.	
Participant's Perspective Use internal imaging to experience the program from the participant's perspective.	
Perspective of Others Use internal imaging to experience the program from the perspective of each of the other participants who may be in the program (i.e., parents, spectators, referees, and so on).	
Entire Program Use external imaging and visualize the entire program from the program manager's perspective.	
Comprehensive Visualization Use internal and external imaging to visualize the program from all perspectives.	

Animating the Program Design

A useful icon for experimenting with candidate plans is the vignette of a cartoon strip (Ableson, 1976). As illustrated in Figure 10.2, a program is a series of frames and transitions between frames that occur in a temporal sequence (Goffman, 1974). Each frame is an encounter (i.e., an interactional episode made up of a single configuration of the six key situating elements of program production).

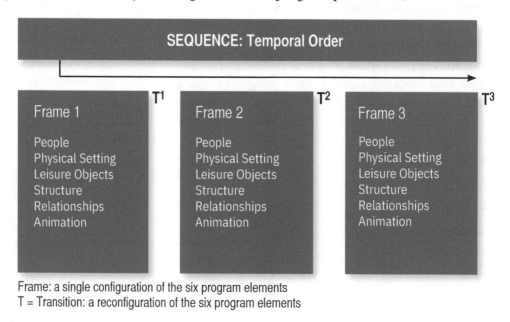

Frame: a single configuration of the six program elements
T = Transition: a reconfiguration of the six program elements

Figure 10.2. Program Frames and Transitions

Again, the length of time that a frame exists is the amount of time the elements in the frame occupy the conscious attention of program participants. To carry through with the theatrical metaphor used earlier, consider each frame as a scene that the programmer must stage appropriately to accomplish the design outcomes of the program. Film producers often use a similar technique called story boarding to frame each important scene of a film for staging. Each frame, then, represents a single episode, and a program consists of numerous episodes that occur in temporal order.

The programmer can use the icons of a cartoon strip or story boarding to graphically depict a temporal sequence of experience frames. Using these techniques, the programmer can rewrite the experience in each frame or change the temporal order at will. Each candidate plan that is visualized is a rewritten vignette. Animation of the overall experience comes about when

- the key situating elements in each frame are changed,
- the temporal order of frames is rearranged, and
- interventions for essential transitions are directed.

This succession of changes and the need for patrons to consciously attend to, interpret, and co-produce them results in interaction and thereby animates a program.

Five Preplanned Forecasts

The number of visualizations that are possible can be overwhelming. However, experience with program operations can provide programmers with a useful guide for getting started. The following are five preplanned visualization forecasts that programmers can use to formulate candidate plans for a program:

1. Use external imaging to visualize the entire operation of a program. This is like seeing a movie of it.
2. Use internal imaging to experience the program from the participant's perspective.
3. Use internal imaging to experience the program from the perspective of every other participant who may be in the program, for example, spectators, parents, and referees.
4. Use external imaging and again visualize the entire operation of the reconfigured program from the program manager's perspective.
5. Use external and internal imaging to visualize the final program with imagined interactions, changing roles from observer to participant, and give special attention to evaluating how the staged program operation, as currently configured, addresses the design goals developed earlier.

Evaluating Candidate Plans

How does a programmer determine which candidate plan to adopt, or which to alter and combine into the design tactics to be implemented? How well a candidate plan solves the design problem (i.e., implements by the outcomes intended) is a primary criterion. How well the candidate plan facilitates a leisure experience for the participant is also a primary criterion. Thus, the programmer adopts the candidate plan that facilitates perceived freedom by creating choices; that facilitates intrinsic satisfaction; that provides opportunities for positive affect; and that makes the program fun, relaxing, and entertaining. Second, the programmer also considers adopting candidate plans that best contribute to accomplishing specific patron, agency, or community program goals.

Frame

A frame is a conceptual representation of a co-created encounter that includes all a leisure experience designer needs to consider when designing an interaction. Figure 10.3 (page 196) provides a graphic representation of a frame. A frame includes the outcomes intended, the interventions that facilitate the outcomes, the key interactional elements to be acted on, the artistic factors that enhance the experience, and the technical service quality factors that need to be tracked throughout the encounter. Frames are connected by transitions between frames.

Designing a frame begins with stating the outcomes intended from interacting in the specific encounter. These are represented in Figure 10.3 (page 196) by Y statements. The outcomes intended may be emotional, cognitive, or kinesthetic. The intended outcomes for each frame should be drawn from and should implement

FRAME # _____

Name of Program: _____

Overall Outcomes (Intentions) _____

_____

INTERVENTIONS

Things you do!

X_1 _____

X_2 _____

X_3 _____

ENCOUNTER

Key Interactional Elements

Your agenda for intervention and manipulation!

PEOPLE
PHYSICAL SETTING
LEISURE OBJECTS
STRUCTURES
RELATIONSHIPS
ANIMATION

OUTCOMES

What happens to participants as a result of your interventions and participants' co-production!

Y_1 _____

Y_2 _____

Y_3 _____

Do these contribute to the overall outcomes intended?

ARTISTIC FACTORS

Program Enhancements

Themeing

Deepening

Sensitizing

Customizing

Characterizing

Memorabilia

Framing and Sequencing

Wowing

Empathy/Understanding

NOTES ON KEY INTERVENTIONS
to be implemented during staging

X_1
_____
_____
_____

X_2
_____
_____
_____

X_3 _____

_____
_____
_____

TECHNICAL FACTORS

Service Quality

Courtesy of Cast

Tangibles

Reliability

Responsiveness

Eliminating Negatives

Competence

Assurance/Credibility

Recovery

Effectiveness of Communication

Security

Figure 10.3. Encounter Frame. © 2011 J. Robert Rossman.

one or more of the overall intended outcomes for the program or event (i.e., the cumulative experience). This a priori conceptualization of the outcome(s) from the experience is critical to the overall success of design. Russell Banks, a senior associate with Gensler design group, indicated that "his team won't put pen to paper without agreement on the design criteria and what success will be evaluated on" ("Shared Vision," 2009). Disney Imagineers ("Imagineering," 2009) discussed this process of concept development, indicating that it soon moves to "the team envisioning what the visitor experience might be as they approach the attraction, enter the attraction, and what happens during the attraction." Each describes what will happen to people as a result of participating, that is, the unique leisure experience being designed as the intended outcome of the staging process. Again, since the designer is not likely to provide direction at all points of contact during an experience, it is important that the points of contact that are framed indeed implement specific outcomes that help accomplish overall design goals.

Next, the programmer identifies the interventions or manipulations that must occur during staging for the outcomes intended in each frame to be achieved. Figure 10.3 shows these as X statements. There are myriad choices possible, and design is the process of selecting those that will be implemented from the universe of all that could be implemented. These choices should primarily be guided by the contribution of the interventions or manipulations to implementing the outcomes intended with consideration of other factors such as risk, feasibility of implementation, budget constraints, and other similar restrictions. It is here where creativity is demonstrated as the designer develops novel interventions, manipulations, and choices available to participants in an experience. Applied creativity is discussed in Chapter 12 but is used in the program design process here.

Programmers can implement interventions through any of the six key elements that situate an experience, discussed in Chapter 3 (for additional elaboration about these design elements and their usefulness, refer to Berridge, 2007, Chapter 10). The options for manipulation are great, and when programmers consider various permutations of their combinations, the options are almost infinite. Thus, any designed leisure experience is a series of choices for participants among these alternate design elements, whether the experience designer makes them intentionally or not. However, making these choices intentionally with specific purposes in mind so they contribute to and facilitate intended outcomes is the essence of intentional design.

Artistic and Technical Factors

In the design of each frame, the programmer needs to consider artistic and technical factors of experience design (Ellis & Rossman, 2008). Intentional choices about which factors should be included or enhanced will improve the experience intended.

Artistic Factors

Artistic factors are a collection of staging techniques that the programmer can implement to enhance interactive engagement for participants or to guide these engagements to intended design outcomes, thereby strengthening engagement and improving an experience. Table 10.1 provides a list of artistic factors with brief explanations. Generally, these are best practices used by the authors or discussed in the extant literature on experience design. Not all are used in every frame or even every experience. Part of the experience designer's art is knowing which to use for creating the unique outcomes intended.

Table 10.1

Artistic Factors

Factor	Description
Theme	Was theme effectively utilized throughout the duration of the experience as well as in each of the six elements of the situated activity system?
Deepening	Were all of the three phases of the leisure experience programmed (i.e., anticipation, participation, and reflection?)
Sensitizing	Were all of the five senses used?
Customizing	How was the experience customized for participants?
Characterizing	Was the cast in character throughout the experience?
Memorabilia	How was the memory of the experience sustained through memorabilia?
Framing and Sequencing	Was the framing and animation of the event appropriate (e.g., an appropriate venue, appropriate social objects, appropriate decorations, music)?
Wowing	Were there any surprises, value-added features included in the event? Did it exceed the expectations of participants?
Empathizing and Understanding	Did staff show empathy and understanding to the plight of participants?

Note. Adapted from Ellis and Rossman (2008).

Not all artistic factors will be discussed here, but a couple of examples will be provided. Generally, experience designers do an excellent job with theme for major events that are pre-themed (e.g., Valentine's Day). On this day, many recognizable symbols contribute to theme including the colors red and white, icons of hearts, arrows, lace, cupid, and the word *love*, plus two often given gifts, chocolates and red roses. The consistent tieback of all design elements to theme in other experiences is comparatively neglected when weighed against their use in Valentine's Day, Christmas, and other major themed experiences.

Similarly, experience designers often do not use all sensory stimuli available to enhance and intensify the interactive engagement of an experience. Usually visual stimuli are well tended, as are sound and taste when food service is involved. But tactile stimulation is frequently neglected, and sometimes odors beyond those contributed by food are neglected. Yet, when students are asked to deconstruct some of their most memorable experiences, tactile stimulation and odors are often the triggers that help them recall the pleasant memories of these experiences. One student recalled the tactile stimulation of the closeness of attending a rock concert including being in the mosh pit. This often neglected tactile stimulant helped her recall the rock concert experience. This is also an example of participant co-created, collateral experiences that were likely not a part of the planned interventions. The list of artistic factors is long and not all apply to every event, but each provides additional interactive possibilities that enhance outcomes.

Technical Factors

Technical factors are service quality factors that contend with how people expect service providers to treat them in an encounter. They sort out aspects of service quality delivery and are drawn from the popular SERVQUAL model of customer service performance (Parasuraman, Berry, & Zeithaml, 1991; Parasuraman, Zeithaml, & Berry, 1988). Table 10.2 lists technical factors with brief explanations of each. Some factors need conscious attention and inclusion in a designed frame, while others are often not an issue unless service provision drops below minimal expectations and the resulting void attracts the attention of participants.

Table 10.2
Technical Factors

Technical factor	Description
Courtesy of Cast	Were the cast friendly and courteous? Were there voids in this feature?
Tangibles	Was the physical environment neat, orderly, clean, appropriately climate controlled, and comfortable?
Reliability	Was the experience staged effectively (i.e., Were your expectations met? Were expectations created by program flyers or advertisements met?)
Responsiveness	Did the cast members react to guest requests promptly and appropriately?
Empath and Understanding of Participants	Did cast members show understanding of the needs and perspectives of participants?
Competence	Were cast members (staff) competent and well trained for their positions?
Assurance/Credibility	Did cast members instill confidence in their abilities to meet guest needs?
Recovery	If mistakes occurred, how well did the cast recover? Remember, experiences are staged and consumed concurrently. Some errors are predictable. Because of this, staff should be prepared to recover gracefully. Did they?
Effectiveness of Communication	Was communication effective?
Security	Did the participants feel physically, socially, and emotionally safe?
Critical Incidents	Did any unanticipated experiences occur that were so eventful (distressing, disgusting, or wowing) that you will feel compelled to describe them to your friends and family members?

Note. Adapted from Ellis and Rossman (2008).

These factors reflect participant satisfaction with the service provided and the experience staged, including interactions with staff and environment. Increasingly, customers are becoming more choosey. Their expectations about desired levels of service emanate from their service experiences elsewhere, their previous experiences with an organization, and reports from friends, family, and social media about prior service encounters. Participants' evaluation of service quality factors is thought to operate similarly to Herzberg's two-factor theory of motivation. Good service does not lead to satisfaction and will not earn an operation kudos, as participants expect good service and believe they are entitled to it. However, an omission on any factor may lead to dissatisfaction with the service encounter. Participants expect good service, believe they are entitled to it, and will terminate a service encounter if they believe the service they are receiving is below standard. Thus, the experience designer must be cognizant of these factors during design and track implementation while staging an experience.

Transitions

An experience is a series of framed encounters joined by transitions. Figure 10.4 shows a graphic for planning transitions. Transitions can be soft or hard. Soft transitions do not need a lot of the designer's attention; these transitions are readily apparent to participants (i.e., they understand how to transition to the next frame). A hard transition needs to be designed and staged because it is not apparent to participants how to transition to the next frame.

A good transition sustains theme (and at the least, certainly does not break theme), helps shift mood or intensity of participation, helps sustain engagement or provide a moment of relief or reflection as appropriate, and positions participants for participation in the next frame (Roark & Evans, 2010). Programmers often neglect transitions during the design phase of an experience and do not realize their necessity until noticing their absence while staging an experience. Prerehearsal of staging an experience by visualizing and vicariously experiencing it in advance is essential to avoiding these omissions. Figure 10.4 may help the experience designer consider and deal with transitions during the design process so as not to deal with these for the first time while staging an experience.

A Framed Experience Design

In a total experience design, the programmer animates predicted interaction by sequencing a series of designed frames connected by transitions. Figure 10.5 (page 202) shows an example of a framed experience design for An Evening of American Folk Music.

The experience is comprised of five frames that represent the key points of contact that the experience designer believes need design and staging. This program was created for a club of individuals who are interested in playing and singing American folk music and meet in a different venue every 4 to 6 weeks.

TRANSITION # _____

Check One:

Soft Transition   or   **Hard Transition**

_____   _____

| Transition is apparent to participants with little need for intervened direction. **STOP** | | Transition is not apparent and will need directed intervention. **CONTINUE** |

INTERVENTIONS Xs

Explain the actions you will take through people, to the physical setting, with leisure objects, structures, relationships, or animation cues to make this happen— the Xs.

OUTCOMES Ys

Describe outcomes desired from this transition.

DESIRED OUTCOMES

- Sustain theme
- Help shift mood or intensity
- Continue engagement or provide a moment of relief or reflection as appropriate
- Set up convenient participation in the next frame

Figure 10.4. Transition. © 2011 J. Robert Rossman.

Figure 10.5. A Framed Experience Design for an Evening of American Folk Music

Frame 1—Reception

People	X1	Y1
Physical Setting	X2	Y2
Leisure Objects		
Social Structure	X3	
Relationships		
Animation		Y3

Y1 Renew friendships
Y2 Learn layout, anticipate using venue
Y3 Newcomers are welcomed to group
X1 Returning participants greet each other
X2 Map/flyer of venue is distributed
X3 Greeters for newcomers are assigned

T3: Hard—On cue, participants move to initial designated areas.

To set up F4, participants should be given instructions about rotation throughout the evening.

To set up T4, participants should be given instruction about their return to the initial assembly area for Frame 5.

T1: Soft—Call attention of assembly.

Frame 2—Welcome & Orientation

People		Y1
Physical Setting		
Leisure Objects		
Social Structure	X1	
Relationships		
Animation		Y2

Y1 Participants know everyone and are familiar with the venue
Y2 Participants know evening's routine
X1 Welcome all, introduce guests and venue
X2 Review map and explain how groups will rotate this evening so everyone gigs with different musicians

T2: Soft—Participants are in position

Frame 3—Performance

People		Y1
Physical Setting		
Leisure Objects	X1	
Social Structure		
Relationships		
Animation		

Y1 Participants are entertained and instructed by the virtuosity of the guest performer
X1 Introduce guest performer, who then performs

Frame 4—Gigs
Change groups 2–4 times in the course of a 60–75-minute program

People		Y1
Physical Setting		
Leisure Objects	X1	
Social Structure	X2	
Relationships		
Animation	X3	

Y1 Participants are engaged in playing instruments and singing folk music
X1 Instruments and scores are played
X2 Music used is varied in each gigging group
X3 On cue, individuals rotate to different groups to play and sing (gig)

T4: On cue—Participants return to original assembly area.

Frame 5—Finale

People		Y1
Physical Setting		
Leisure Objects	X1	
Social Structure	X2	
Relationships		
Animation	X3	Y2

Y1 & Y2 Playing instruments and singing folk music to build camaraderie of group, memories, and commitment to return
X1 Instruments and voices
X2 A finale involving familiar music and the entire group
X3 Playing instruments and singing

Note. Although Transition graphics are not displayed, the information in them was used to design each transition.

To design a frame, the programmer begins by specifying the outcomes intended to result from participation in the interactions of the encounter represented by the frame. The programmer draws these intentions from the overall outcome goals of the experience. Knowing the outcomes necessary for accomplishing the intended goals of an experience provides motivation and intention in the design of interventions to be staged and enacted in the process of interacting in an encounter. Table 10.3 lists the intended outcomes for this experience.

Table 10.3
Experience Goals for An Evening of American Folk Music

- Develop and sustain a club of individuals interested in learning and performing folk music.
  - Program design outcomes for each meeting of the club:
    - Provide opportunities to learn folk music.
    - Provide opportunities to perform folk music.
    - Provide opportunities to build fellowship with other folk music enthusiasts in the community.

Frame 1—Reception

During the first framed encounter, participants are received into the group and venue. Continuing participants will likely want to renew their friendships and acquaintances, while newcomers will need to be greeted and socialized into the group. As part of the staging design, the programmer designates individuals to initiate contact with newcomers and make certain they feel welcomed into the group. Additionally, since the group often meets in different venues, the experience designer can implement additional designed interventions such as distributing diagrams of the venue, taking steps to build anticipation for using the evening's venue, and providing participants an opportunity to learn its layout.

Although much more may happen during this first encounter due to variations in how individuals choose to interact, the programmer directs interventions toward ensuring three critical outcomes occur: developing familiarity with the venue, building anticipation for using the venue that evening, and providing opportunity for developing camaraderie within the group for continuing and new members. Thus, the designer does not try to control all elements, but instead institutes sufficient interventions to ensure realization of overall goals for an encounter while allowing participants the opportunity and freedom to pursue other engagements of their choosing. These collateral side engagements allow a personalized and unique experience for each participant, and this is why individuals who attend the same event often report different outcomes. But the designer's goal is to ensure the accomplishment of a singular shared experience through their design.

Transition 1

The first transition is a soft one only requiring that the attention of the assembly be obtained. Many transitions are soft, readily apparent to participants, and thus require little design. The hard transitions that are not apparent to participants often have not received forethought and design attention from the experience designer and may lead to problems during staging. A thorough review of each transition during design is the best protection from encountering operational problems with inadequate transitions during staging.

Frame 2—Welcome and Orientation

This frame represents the second major encounter of the experience. The primary outcome intended is for participants to feel welcomed and socialized into the group. The programmer achieves this by formally welcoming everyone and introducing newcomers to the larger group. Additionally, the programmer can review the diagram of the evening's venue and how the program will be animated that evening. Both of these activities put participants at ease by creating a level of familiarity with the venue, participants, and procedures. The programmer can achieve further socialization for new participants by assigning them a host for the evening.

Transition 2

Since participants are already in place, this, too, is a soft transition. The programmer shifts the focus of attention from the welcome and orientation to the guest performer for the evening.

Frame 3—Performance

A performance each evening provides an interesting frame to the overall experience. Performers are often group members, but sometimes other people from outside the group perform. The performance is intended to be entertaining and educational. The virtuosity of the performer instructs and inspires other group members. Usually, the performer focuses on some picking, plucking, or strumming technique, a specific genre of folk music, or special techniques for playing a specific musical instrument.

Transition 3

Transition 3 is a hard transition. Participants move from the current assembly area to different areas in the venue and reassemble in smaller groups to play folk music together (gig). After gigging for 20 to 30 minutes, they move again to different gigging groups so they have an opportunity to play different music with different musicians. Depending on the amount of time available, this basic transition may occur two to four times during the evening.

Frame 4—Gigs

Each gig is a focused session of playing and singing folk music. The composition of gigging groups is important, as the proficiency of the musicians varies. The programmer ensures that individuals have some opportunity to play with musicians of similar proficiency and interests, as well as in groups of mixed abilities. This requires careful planning in advance so that each musician has a varied and motivational experience throughout the evening.

Transition 4

The final transition is relatively easy for the programmer to accomplish. The programmer instructs participants to return to the original assembly area at the conclusion of their last gigging session. The programmer realizes the need to do this and learns to prepare the gigging leaders to accomplish this through careful, a priori design.

Frame 5—Finale

The finale allows the programmer to provide closure and departure from an experience. Closure draws together the experience for participants, helping them review and collect their positive memories of the experience. In this program, the final frame involves the entire group playing and singing a few pieces all can play. This process builds group camaraderie, helps participants recall memories of the evening, reinforces memories of the evening, and motivates individuals to commit to return again. A good wrap-up and send-off has been achieved.

Discussion

An experience is a complex interactional form. After the programmer analyzes an experience thoroughly and deconstructs it into its component, sequenced frames, this seems obvious. To create a memorable outcome, program designers need to identify the key frames that define the experience, make it memorable, and give the program a unique signature. The programmer must design and stage each key frame appropriately for every operation of an experience. This requires significant advance design work and attention to details during the staging of an experience.

A good experience design allows the designer to alter the basic design to create variety during subsequent offerings of the experience. Now visualize possible variations on the basic design of An Evening of American Folk Music. Obviously, the frequent use of different venues creates variation. The implications for staging each venue require a review and alterations as warranted for the reception and gigging frames. A different performer each evening allows for a variety of instruments, types of music, and vocal styles. Although there is a performance each evening, the permutations of this frame can provide infinite variety.

Moving individuals to a series of gigging groups each evening creates good variety, as does changing the style of music pursued in each group. Providing opportunities for participants to play with individuals of different ability provides great interest and engagement, but, for example, less skilled players may find it challenging to play with advanced players, and other participants may find satisfaction in their competence when playing with players of similar ability.

Finally, the programmer can change the order of frames some evenings. For example, the performance frame could sometimes be the concluding frame, thereby providing an inspirational performance for the finale that participants anticipate throughout the evening and that provides a motivating memory that encourages participants to return in the future. Thus, this basic experience design has many options for variation without the need for complete redesign. Good design allows reordering of frames for the achievement of variation in a program. See Case Study 10.1 (page 208), WHALE WATCH® Kaikoura, New Zealand, at the end of the chapter for an example of a program that must anticipate that each staging will be different.

Conclusion

Experiencing a program can be conceptualized as participating in a vignette of sequenced encounters. Each encounter consists of planned frames of interaction wherein the programmer gives conscious attention to various configurations of the six key elements of a situated activity system. Program design must be conducted from this knowledge base—the programmer understands and intervenes in social interaction by using the six situating elements to stage each frame, to reorder frames, and to design key transitions between frames. Programmers can use visualization techniques to simulate the interactions within frames and of the total program. They can use these in the design process to develop and experiment with a variety of candidate plans that they will eventually combine into a single set of design tactics that solve the design problem by achieving the outcomes intended.

The Framed Experience Model for designing memorable leisure experiences assumes that these desirable experiences will most likely occur when participants co-create them. Producing experiences that facilitate co-creation with participants is a more complicated production paradigm requiring a technology that permits the design and staging of instances of behavior wherein experience is created through participant interaction. The Framed Experience Model provides programmers the wherewithal to accomplish this, by focusing design efforts on episodes of interaction (i.e., encounters) that provide focused experiences wherein overall program outcomes can be implemented. The technique also facilitates a general overview of the entire experience so individual encounters cumulate in the experience intended by the designer.

References

Ableson, R. P. (1976). Script processing in attitude formation and decision making. In J. S. Carrol & J. W. Payne (Eds.), *Cognition and social behavior*. Hillsdale, NJ: Erlbaum.

Beach, L. R. (1990). *Image theory: Decision making in personal and organizational contexts*. New York, NY: John Wiley and Sons.

Berridge, G. (2007). *Events design and experience*. Burlington, MA: Butterworth-Heinemann.

Edginton, C. R., Hanson, C. J., & Edginton, S. R. (1992). *Leisure programming: Concepts, trends, and professional practice* (2nd ed.). Dubuque, IA: Wm. C. Brown.

Edwards, R., Honeycutt, J. M., & Zagacki, K. S. (1988, Winter). Imagined interaction as an element of social cognition. *Western Journal of Speech Communication, 52,* 23–45.

Ellis, G. D., & Rossman, J. R. (2008). Creating value for participants through experience staging: Parks, recreation, and tourism in the experience industry. *Journal of Park and Recreation Administration, 26*(4), 1–20.

Goffman, E. (1961). *Encounters*. Indianapolis, IN: Bobbs-Merrill.

Goffman, E. (1974). *Frame analysis: An essay on the organization of experience.* New York, NY: Harper Colophon Books.

Green, H. (1976). *Mind and image: An essay on art and architecture.* Lexington: University of Kentucky Press.

Holt, N. A. (2014, February). *Capitalizing on collateral learning.* Keynote address presented at the 2014 Academy of Leisure Sciences Teaching Institute, Pacific Grove, CA.

Honeycutt, J. M. (1991). Imagined interactions, imagery, and mindfulness/mindlessness. In R. G. Kuzendorf (Ed.), *Mental imagery* (pp. 121–128). New York, NY: Plenum Press.

Hull, R. B., IV, Stewart, W. P., & Yi, Y. K. (1992). Experience patterns: Capturing the dynamic nature of a leisure experience. *Journal of Leisure Research, 24,* 240–252.

Imagineering. (2009, August 9). *Event Design.* Retrieved from http://www.eventdesignmag.com/viewmedia.asp?prmMID=628&prmID=1

Kaufmann, G. (1988). Mental imagery and problem solving. In M. Denis, J. Engelkamp, & J. T. E. Richardson (Eds.), *Cognitive and neuropsychological approaches to mental imagery* (pp. 231–239). Dordrecht, Netherlands: Martinus Nijhoff.

Mead, G. H. (1934). *Mind, self, and society.* Chicago, IL: University of Chicago Press.

Mintzberg, H. M. (2009). *Henry Mintzberg managing.* San Francisco, CA: Berrett-Koehler.

Parasuraman, A., Berry, L. L., & Zeithaml, V. A. (1991). Refinement and reassessment of the SERVQUAL scale. *Journal of Retailing, 69,* 420–451.

Parasuraman, A., Zeithaml, V. A., & Berry, L. L. (1988). SERVQUAL: A multiple-item scale for measuring consumer perceptions of service quality. *Journal of Retailing, 64,* 12–37.

Roark, M. F., & Evans, F. (2010). *Play it, measure it: Experiences designed to elicit specific youth outcomes.* Monterey, CA: Healthy Living.

Schlatter, B. E., & Chang, Y. (2018). Recreation programming practices: Unpublished survey. Illinois Park and Recreation Association.

Shared vision. (2009, July 6). *Event Design.* Retrieved from http://www.eventdesignmag.com/viewmedia.asp?prmMID=626&prmID=1

Weinberg, R. S. (1988). *The mental advantage: Developing your psychological skills in tennis.* Champaign, IL: Leisure Press.

Case Study 10.1. WHALE WATCH® Kaikoura, New Zealand

Watching whales is an exciting but seasonal activity in many parts of the world because whales migrate and can only be seen when they pass various land points. Because of a canyon in the ocean close to Kaikoura, New Zealand, a resident population of male sperm whales can be seen most days. A permanent tourist attraction that takes visitors to see whales has been operating since 1989.

The whole operation is appropriately themed with whale motifs including the visitor reception center, the buses that transport visitors to the boat docks, and the boats themselves. The boats have been custom designed with one purpose in mind, watching whales. They are modern, well equipped, and very comfortable. Their design affords everyone on board a good vantage point for observing whales.

The attraction is an excellent example of staging a program in the experience industry wherein the order of frames presented can change with every trip. Although there is a resident population of sperm whales, they dive and surface at different times of the day and in different locations. So it is not certain that a whale will be spotted on every trip. The company offers partial refunds if their customers do not see a whale during a trip, sort of a customer assurance package. On some days, in addition to whales, customers may be treated to sightings of migrating whales and other sea life in the area.

Staff cannot be sure when a whale or other migrating sea life will be sighted. Thus, the cumulative experience on each trip is somewhat serendipitous. Staging each trip is a perfect example of the staff expecting and being prepared to present frames as they emerge while having prepared frames to present for dealing with expected downtime when there is no sea life for customers to observe. To accomplish this, the staff skillfully give the experience substance and continuity by using all four realms of experience—active and passive engagement, entertainment, aesthetics, and education. They build anticipation for whale sightings with video clips that are shown en route to the observation area and between times when whales are sighted. Some educate about whales in general. Others are entertaining, showing unusual behavior of whales that have been in the area. Some passively engage customers by showing whales known to be in the area. The resident whales are named and the company has videos of previous sightings of these whales, which can be shown as a follow-up to the sighting of a specific whale.

It is difficult for the operation to actively involve visitors in finding whales, because it takes experience and equipment, but the program does provide active opportunities for their customers to observe whales in their natural environment. This unusual experience is deepened by a well-designed program and a staff skillful at staging all four experience realms. The hosts on each trip skillfully move the participants' attention through events as they emerge or are presented by the staff. Holding the diverse elements of the program together to create a whole, unified experience fully depends on their communication skills. Remove this feature and the tour becomes a boat ride where customers occasionally observe whales and other sea life.

Orchestra Bringing Holiday Cheer to Guests at the Tony Shotwell Life Center
During Cookies With Santa Program
Photo Courtesy of City of Grand Prairie Parks, Arts, and Recreation Department

11

From BBP to Intentionally Designed Leisure Experiences

KEY TERMS

Benefits-Based Programming, Issue and Target Goals, Processing,
Outcome-Based Programming, Intentionally Designed Experiences,
Black Box of Programming

Step 5: Program Design

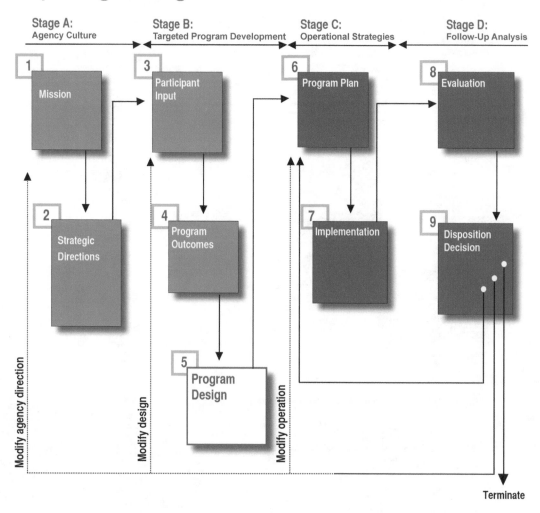

Programmers use many approaches to design and stage recreation programs, one of which is benefits-based programming (BBP). Developed to address the overall effects, benefits, and changes to participants as a result of being in a recreation program, BBP was promoted by the National Recreation and Park Association (NRPA) during the 1990s and early 2000s (Allen & McGovern, 1996; Allen, Stevens, & Harwell, 1996; Allen, Stevens, & Lee, 2000; Crompton & Witt, 1997; Witt, 1993–1999). The premise of BBP was that intentionally designed recreation programs could address specific pro-social outcomes such as resiliency among youth as well as other populations. This chapter discusses BBP and several derivations of this approach that have emerged in recent years including outcome-based programming (OBP) and intentionally designed experiences (IDEs).

Benefits-Based Programming

Although no longer actively promoted by NRPA, BBP is still used by municipal organizations and nonprofits because of its utility in providing solid evidence of beneficial program outcomes that are communicated to stakeholders through marketing (Wells et al., 2008). There are four steps to BBP: identify target issues, design meaningful programs, measure the beneficial outcomes of those programs, and communicate the outcomes to stakeholders (Allen & McGovern, 1996; Forest, 1999).

In the first step of BBP, agency stakeholders target problems or societal issues for a specific audience such as youth or senior citizens. The statement of the issue and resulting target goals become the focus of the program. A key point is that benefits-based programs alone cannot address an issue entirely. Widespread community involvement will be needed for stakeholders to confront all facets of a social issue. Program goals that emanate from the issue must validate and be logically connected to the issue. Now complete Exercise 11.1.

Exercise 11.1.
Identifying Issue and Target Goals

Read the following issue and accompanying information, and answer the discussion questions.

A community college president noted that growing numbers of senior citizens are taking classes at the college. Several seniors approached the president about the apparent lack of fitness activities geared toward seniors. The president called a meeting between herself, the seniors, and the campus recreation director. The campus recreation director decided to use the BBP approach to develop a senior fitness program.

Discussion Questions
1. What is the issue as identified by the president, senior citizens, and campus recreation director?
2. Identify 3–4 program goals that will address the issue identified in the first question.

The second step involves the design of meaningful programs that address the target issue through performance objectives, activity development, processing, and monitoring. The more activities that are structured and intentionally designed, the greater the likelihood participants will achieve the desired program outcomes. Processing the effect of completed activities with participants is essential to this step and is carried out by program leaders. Effective processing can help participants recognize how their feelings about what they learned in the activity can be transferred to real-life situations (Haas & Sibthorp, 2004). Processing can be done formally or informally, depending on the type of activity, setting, and participant. Figure 11.1 (page 212) lists 12 questions that programmers can use when leading a processing or debriefing session (Allen & McGovern, 1996). Last, through monitoring, programmers gain feedback on the extent of achievement of performance objectives.

In the third step, programmers evaluate program outcomes in relation to the target issues and goals. When possible, they should use valid and reliable evaluation instruments; otherwise, they will need to develop appropriate indicators. If evaluation findings indicate that participants successfully addressed the target goals, then programmers can claim the achievement of those positive social outcomes.

Communicating outcomes to stakeholders is the final step of BBP. Utilizing marketing for disseminating program outcomes to the public, funding sources, and stakeholders legitimizes the relevance of recreation programs and improves communities. Examples of BBP successes include improved community conditions or the realization of a psychological expectation. Methods for communicating the outcomes range from news releases, annual reports, and promotional materials, to speaking engagements and websites.

Asking the right questions is often the key to good processing. The following questions can help activity leaders become more comfortable with processing:

How did you feel when you had to trust someone else to keep you safe?
How did you decide whom you would trust?
What did it feel like to cooperate with other members in your group?
How did you (your group) make decisions?
How well did you do?
What did you say to yourself?
In what ways did you criticize or support yourself?
What type of feedback did you receive or give to others?
In what ways do you differ from other group members?
What was your greatest success today?
How can you use something you learned today in other situations?
What did you learn about yourself during this activity that you want to work on in the future?

Figure 11.1. The Right Words. From Allen and McGovern (1996).

Outcome-Based Programming

Similar to BBP, OBP employs inputs, activities and processes, outputs, and outcomes to create programs that produce beneficial results to participants and society at large (McNamara, n.d.). Inputs are the items needed to run a program, such as staff, money, equipment, and resources. Activities are the processes, such as teaching, guiding, coaching, and encouraging, used for staging a program that meets participants' programmatic needs. Outputs are units of service, such as the number of people served by a program or the number of games played in a sports league. Outcomes, the last component, illustrate the overall changes in behavior, skill, or attitude that participants experienced as a result of the program. Additional terms in OBP include *outcome targets* (percentage of participants expected to achieve an outcome) and *outcome indicators* (long-term indications of the success of the program).

OBP approaches have been used with success in after-school programs, outdoor adventure settings, and camp environments. The Afterschool Alliance (2011) noted that the most successful features of after-school programs include prepared staff, intentional programming techniques, promotion of the arts, community partnerships, student participation with sustained assessment, and safe and appropriate venues. In this context, intentional programming employs clear goals and associated activities that enhance children's school involvement and build their social skills. Such approaches offer useful methods for after-school-program professionals to document how participant involvement has led to outcomes such as positive self-concept, making good choices, and making friends (Afterschool Alliance, 2011; Durlak & Weissberg, 2007; Granger & William T. Grant Foundation, 2008; Roark, Gillard, Evans, Wells, & Blauer, 2012), all of which may lead to continued funding for after-school programs.

Intentionally Designed Experiences

Facilitating sequenced, scripted recreation activities for youth is the focus of IDEs (Roark & Evans, 2010). In this approach, the programmer designs the recreation activity to bring about a participant outcome and measures it using an outcome questionnaire. IDEs have been used successfully in camp settings, parks and recreation departments, outdoor experiential programs, scouting, religious organizations, and other youth-focused programs.

Participant outcomes center on the fun of an activity within the contexts of wanting to meet new people, making friends, or being in a group. Upon completion of a sequenced, scripted IDE, the youth complete a brief questionnaire that measures the effect of the program on a 5-point scale (Roark & Evans, 2010). Participants read each item and select a response choice that ranges from 1 (*no fun*) to 5 (*lots of fun*). The appeal of this approach is that a score of 3 or higher means a positive outcome occurred. By quantifying program outcomes in this manner, organizations can effectively communicate results to stakeholders or use them for marketing and fund-raising purposes (Roark & Evans, 2010).

Roark and Evans (2010) provided examples of what an IDE looks like and how it operates in *Play It, Measure It*. They described the pirate experience, for example, in terms of its theme, developmental outcome, setting and formation, participants, duration, energy level, materials, and preparation. A special invitation to participate in the program generates excitement and anticipation among participants. Facilitators are encouraged to use the scripts that accompany each activity to ensure that key points and descriptions are not overlooked. This ensures reliability of the programming process regardless of who delivers it. Transition descriptions that offer guidance to the facilitators and ensure a smooth transition from one activity to the next are also central to IDEs. When the activity has ended, participants answer a 2- to 5-minute questionnaire that measures gains in an outcome such as friendship or teamwork.

Nature-based camp settings often provide environments that allow for a sense of escape from the usual. Compared to daily short-term recreation programs, a residential camp experience may last for a considerably longer amount of time (e.g., 1 week, 2 weeks, or 1 month). Such sustained participation has a higher probability of goal achievement. Camps that are structured with rituals, traditions, and ceremonies provide opportunities for campers to learn and practice these positive engagements for an extended period. When these experiences include living in social groups, it becomes possible for the programmer to establish strong cohesion among the participants (Garst, Browne, & Bialeschki, 2011).

Free or unstructured time is also unique to the camp environment. BBP providers argue that structured program are the most successful, thus discouraging providing free or unstructured time in programs. In many cases, the programs they operate are of short duration, not allowing for providing unstructured time in addition to programmed activities. Camp researchers contend that unstructured opportunities may afford opportunities for meaningful activity wherein skills learned in structured settings can be enjoyed and performed. Ultimately, for complete success, campers will need to exhibit these positive behaviors on their own apart from participating in structured programs. Providing flexible program structures allows programmers to tailor activities to children's individual needs (Durlak & Weissberg, 2007). Therefore, camps may be uniquely situated to effect positive youth outcomes through intentionally provided unstructured time (Garst et al., 2011).

Another example of an IDE is the SAFE approach, which employs activities that are Sequenced, Active, Focused, and Explicit (SAFE; Durlak & Weissberg, 2007). SAFE centers on personal and social skills program components and employs interactive activities, explicit facilitation scripts, and focused participant goals to address prosocial behaviors. When using SAFE in after-school program settings, facilitators also use sustained monitoring techniques to demonstrate that their interactive activities lead to stated program outcomes among participants. Similar to BBP, OBP, and IDEs, the SAFE approach, through the ability to accurately measure and report such evidence, can make a convincing case to funding sources that after-school programs are worthwhile of continued social and financial investment (Durlak & Weissberg, 2007).

Studies on Intentionally Designed Experience Approaches

Roark et al. (2012) studied the effect of IDEs on the development of friendship skills and fun among youth in an after-school program, using symbolic interaction theory (SIT). As Chapter 2 described, symbolic interaction theory attempts to understand behavior at the level of face-to-face interaction through interpretations of objects, symbols, words, and meanings (Blumer, 1969). Roark et al. examined the effect of three content- and process-oriented approaches to IDEs: the SAFE approach (Durlak & Weissberg, 2007), the Situated Activity System approach (Rossman & Schlatter, 2011), and a General Design approach. The study findings indicated that all three IDEs increased friendship skills and were perceived to be fun by participants.

In a later study, Gillard and Roark (2017) investigated the extent to which intentional staff training affected camper friendship skills. Specifically, they studied changes in campers' self-reported outcomes over three summers. In the first summer, staff received no training in camper friendship skills. In the second summer, staff received 45 minutes of specialized, intentional training, and in the last summer, staff received a 90-minute training session, along with a mid-summer booster session. A comparison of camper outcomes between the 45-minute friendship skills training for staff and no training for staff indicated that intentional training affected camper outcomes. However, a comparison of camper outcomes between a 45-minute training and 90-minute training plus a booster training session did not show significant differences, suggesting that a mid-summer staff training might not be needed. Overall, the study illustrates that intentional staff training can positively affect participant outcomes.

Unpacking the "Black Box" of Programming

Research on program outcomes rarely considers which aspects of a program or structured activity contributed to those outcomes. Sibthorp, Paisley, and Gookin (2007) dubbed this phenomenon "black box" programming (p. 1), wherein it is assumed that mere participation in a program will lead to outcomes with little regard for understanding the specifics that led to program successes. Mainieri and Anderson (2015) used implementation evaluation to evaluate how well a structured camp curriculum was delivered, as well as its overall quality. They measured quality through observations of a program during its operation, using the Youth Quality Program Assessment (High/Scope Educational Research Foundation, 2005) instrument. Through interviews with facilitators of the camp's structured programs, Mainieri and Anderson uncovered mechanisms that were believed to contribute to the overall success of the program. Those mechanisms included the implementation of a carefully structured curriculum, camper engagement, adjustments made by facilitators during program delivery, and acknowledgment by campers when the material presented to them over time became intuitive. In sum, by combining intentional programming techniques with implementation evaluation, the programmer can unpack the black box of programming and better understand how programs affect positive outcomes among participants. Now try Exercise 11.2 (page 216).

Readers whose area of focus within the profession is therapeutic recreation may have already noted the prescriptive nature of BBP and the related approaches to program planning described in this chapter. Prescriptive programmers plan outcome-based activities designed for a specific purpose and a specific user group. This approach contrasts the homogenized approach that recreation and park agencies often use to design generic programs for participants in general. The Framed Experience Model of programming, explained in Chapter 10, encourages more focus on programming to specific outcomes than do other programming methods for

Too often programmers assume that participants will accomplish program outcomes simply by attending the structured activity or program. There is often much more to it than that! Think about a recent program that you helped facilitate. Perhaps it was an obedience dog-training program for teens or a bicycle maintenance repair class for adults. Answer the following questions to gain a better understanding of the extent to which programs affect positive outcomes among participants.

1. Name a recent program you have facilitated or helped facilitate: _____
2. List 3 outcomes of the program you listed above:
   a.
   b.
   c.
3. Answer the following questions about the structure of your program.
   a. Did the program follow a carefully structured curriculum? Yes No
   b. Did you make adjustments to the program during its delivery? Yes No
   c. Did you employ the use of scripted activities as described in the text? Yes No
   d. Did you keep track of participant skill acquisition during the program? Yes No
   e. Did participants acknowledge in debriefings or evaluations that program outcomes were accomplished? Yes No

Discussion

This exercise is not intended as a comprehensive example of unpacking the "Black Box" of programming. Rather, the purpose is to raise an awareness among programmers that it is naïve to assume that outcomes will be accomplished through mere participant attendance at a program. In Question 3, answering yes more than no suggests that you take the time to structure and facilitate activities for your intended participants. Still, readers should consider using mechanisms such as the Youth Quality Program Assessment to gain a more comprehensive understanding of how programs affect positive changes in participants.

general recreation operations. However, it does not focus on specific populations or behavioral change as BBP models do. Allen et al. (1996) contended that purposeful, outcome-oriented programming results in more resilient participants, which is the overall goal of BBP approaches. The point is that BBP approaches, although prescriptive in nature, can effectively be tailored to address the issues of any user group, not just those commonly associated with therapeutic recreation settings.

Conclusion

Implementing IDEs is labor intensive, requiring considerable record keeping, report writing, and monitoring before, during, and after the program. Programmers new to this approach may be overwhelmed at the level of depth and involvement required on their part to plan, implement, and evaluate effective programs. New and seasoned programmers will find that specific chapters in this text will equip them with the knowledge and skills necessary to incorporate outcome-based approaches into their programming efforts.

The adoption of the IDE approach to program planning has myriad benefits. First, it offers a useful framework for planning purposeful and successful programs, and it is an effective conduit for communicating program outcomes to stakeholders and funding sources. An underlying assumption of using this approach is that readers already possess an understanding of recreation programming. As illustrated in the first three chapters of this book, designing leisure experiences requires a sound understanding of programming theory and competence in a variety of complex skills and techniques. This chapter provided an overview of benefits-based approaches to recreation programming including BBP, OBP, and IDEs. It also discussed current research on the effectiveness of IDEs and implementation evaluation.

References

Afterschool Alliance. (2011). *Quality afterschool: Helping programs achieve it and strengthening policies to support it* (Afterschool Alert Issue Brief No. 47). Retrieved from http://www.afterschoolalliance.org/issue_briefs/issue_quality_47.pdf

Allen, L., & McGovern, T. D. (1996). *Implementing a benefits-based recreation program.* Paper presented at the NRPA Congress for Recreation and Parks, Kansas City, MO.

Allen, L., Stevens, B., & Harwell, R. (1996). Benefits-based management activity planning model for youth in at-risk environments. *Journal of Park and Recreation Administration, 14*(3), 10–19.

Allen, L., Stevens, B., & Lee, C. (2000). Benefits-based programming: Making an impact on youth. *Journal of Park and Recreation Administration, 18*(1), 34–49.

Blumer, H. (1969). *Symbolic interactionism: Perspective and method.* Englewoods Cliffs, NJ: Prentice-Hall.

Crompton, J. L., & Witt, P. A. (1997, October). Repositioning: The key to building community support. *Parks and Recreation, 32*(10), 4.

Durlak, J. A., & Weissberg, R. P. (2007). *The impact of after-school programs that promote personal and social skills.* Retrieved from Collaborative for Academic, Social, and Emotional Learning website: https://casel.org/wp-content/uploads/2016/06/the-impact-of-after-school-programs-that-promote-personal-and-social-skills.pdf

Forest, K. K. (1999). Benefits-based programming. *Illinois Parks and Recreation, 30*(5), 41–42.

Garst, B. A., Browne, L. P., & Bialeschki, M. D. (2011, Summer). Youth development and the camp experience. *New Directions for Youth Development, 2011*(130), 73–87.

Gillard, A., & Roark, M. F. (2017). Does staff training on camper friendship skills make a difference to campers with serious illness? *Journal of Park and Recreation Administration, 35*(4), 1–12.

Granger, R. C., & William T. Grant Foundation. (2008). After-school programs and academics: Implications for policy and research. *Social Policy Report: Giving Child and Youth Development Knowledge Away, 22*(2), 3–19.

Haas, C., & Sibthorp, J. (2004). Making the benefits last. *Parks and Recreation, 6*(24), 26–32.

High/Scope Educational Research Foundation. (2005). *Youth program quality assessment.* Ypsilanti, MI: High/Scope Press.

Mainieri, T., & Anderson, D. (2015). Exploring the "black box" of programming: Applying systematic implementation evaluation to a structured camp curriculum. *Journal of Experiential Education, 38*(2), 144–161.

McNamara, C. (n.d.). Basic guide to outcomes-based evaluation for nonprofit organizations with very limited resources. Retrieved November 8, 2018, from http://www.managementhelp.org/evaluatn/outcomes.htm

Roark, M. F., & Evans, F. (2010). *Play it, measure it.* Monterey, CA: Healthy Learning.

Roark, M. F., Gillard, A., Evans, F., Wells, S. A., & Blauer, M. M. (2012). Effect on intentionally designed experiences on friendship skills of youth: An application of symbolic interaction theory. *Journal of Park and Recreation Administration, 30*(3), 24–36.

Rossman, J. R., & Schlatter, B. E. (2011). *Recreation programming: Designing and staging leisure experiences* (6th ed.). Urbana, IL: Sagamore.

Sibthorp, J., Paisley, K., & Gookin, J. (2007). Exploring participant development through adventure-based programming: A model from the National Outdoor Leadership School. *Leisure Sciences, 29,* 1–18.

Wells, M. S., Arthur-Banning, S. G., Paisley, K. P., Ellis, G. D., Roark, M. F., & Fisher, K. (2008). Good (youth) sports: Using benefits-based programming to increase sportsmanship. *Journal of Park and Recreation Administration, 26*(1), 1–21.

Witt, P. A. (1993–1999). *Development of methods to evaluate recreation programs.* Funded by the National Recreation and Park Association.

Open Gym
City of Aurora Department of Parks, Recreation, and Open Space. Photo by Sherri-Jo Stowell.

12 *Creative Programming*

KEY TERMS

Creative Programming, Applied Creativity, Innovation,
Diagram of the Creative Program Design Process, Problem Definition,
Generation of Approaches, Exploration/Interpretation

Step 5: Program Design

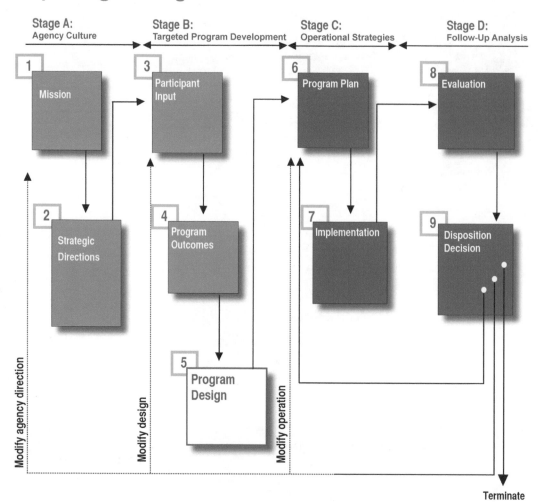

Throughout the experience industry, there is a constant pressure for innovation, that is, creatively developing new products and services, and innovative methods for implementing them. New opportunities emerge that cannot be solved with current approaches. Many organizations have "idea centers" where employees from throughout the organization are sent to create and innovate (Ward, 1985). Programmers, too, must create new leisure services with fresh programs and innovative ways of staging them.

Creatively programming is different from program planning. In the latter, the programmer examines existing alternate solutions to a problem and then selects the best solution. This methodology stems from problem-solving literature that identifies the following steps: problem definition, identification of alternatives, evaluation of alternatives, implementation of the alternative selected, and finally, evaluation of the solution implemented. Creative programmers not only synthesize the facts available and identify alternate solutions, but also consciously create additional programmatic solutions for the identified design problem. Furthermore, they develop innovative procedures for program staging. Thus, programmers can apply creativity during program design and while developing the staging plan.

Understanding Applied Creativity

Are you a creative person? Can you find creative solutions to programming problems? Can you develop innovative implementation procedures? Kelley and Kelley (2013) asserted, "In our experience, *everybody* is the creative type" (p. 5). In all likelihood, you can be creative if you put forth enough effort with the techniques outlined in this chapter.

What is creativity? Although many definitions of creativity exist, there is little consensus about its definition. On the one hand, it refers to that rare gift of genius and insight that enables a person to unlock great mysteries of the universe. This cannot be taught. On the other hand, creativity also refers to the ability to overcome problems by approaching them in novel ways and by systematically developing innovative solutions to them. According to Tudor Richard (as cited in Howard, 1985), the opposite of this type of creativity is "stuckness," habitual thinking that generates the same solutions to problems. Creativity training will not produce a Michelangelo, but it can help programmers escape from "stuckness" and develop more novel solutions to programming problems.

> Creativity also refers to the ability to overcome problems by approaching them in novel ways.

Von Oech (1990) suggested that to be creative, a person must first have a broad base of knowledge about a subject. This knowledge base does not guarantee creativity, but is a prerequisite to it. What you have learned thus far in this text certainly has provided you a broad base of knowledge about programming. Second, by using techniques that manipulate this knowledge and experience, a person is opened to new ideas and thoughts about the subject. He calls getting unstuck "opening our mental locks" that keep us from seeing things differently.

Finke, Ward, and Smith (1992) developed a model of creativity based on their research. It is called the Geneplore Model, illustrated in Figure 12.1 (page 222). Creativity is modeled as an iteration between generating preinventive structures with special properties and reinterpreting their meaning in a new context. This iterative process occurs within the constraints of the program being developed. They concluded that creativity is the result of not one but several mental processes that lead to creative insight and discovery (Finke et al., 1992). Applied creativity, then, requires the development of a kit bag of techniques.

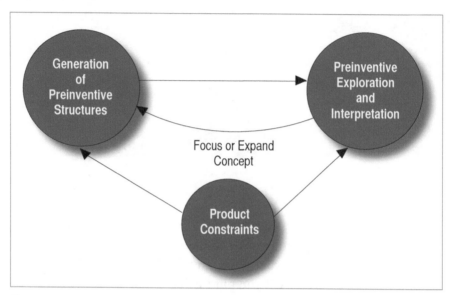

Figure 12.1. The Geneplore Model. From Finke, Ward, and Smith (1992).

Although the search for the origins of creativity and the mental processes that give rise to it continues, programmers operate in the present and thus develop innovative programs for people to enjoy tomorrow. Ackoff and Vergara (1981) offered a pragmatic definition of creativity for use in organizations' efforts:

> We define creativity in problem solving and planning as the ability of a subject in a choice situation to modify self-imposed constraints so as to enable him to select courses of action or produce outcomes that he or she would not otherwise select or produce, and are more efficient for or valuable to him or her than any he or she would otherwise have chosen. (p. 9)

The processes and techniques for developing creative programs, then, must provide programmers, first, with the means to unlearn and, second, with the ability to see things in a new way. Specifically, they must prevent programmers from imposing their default responses to identified problems—the blocks to innovation. These result from training or routinized responses to the same or similar problems. After removing default blocks, programmers need techniques that facilitate the generation of novel ideas. In this case, novel means an idea programmers would not normally have developed given their previous assumptions and methods of operation. These may seem like modest goals, but in many cases, programmers' thinking and methods of operating have become so routinized that they do not realize how stuck they are!

Creativity in Developing Programs

Several unique factors of recreation programs are relevant to the use of creativity. First, programmers face a unique problem-solving mode. There are few widely recognized and accepted protocols for operating leisure programs. The literature of the field does not include step-by-step implementation procedures for specific programs. Thus, the creative problem-solving situation faced by the programmer is one in which few established procedures allow for computational transformations based on rule-governed interferences, such as deductive or inductive reasoning (Kaufmann, 1988). The engineering discipline would likely use computational transformations, but recreation programming would not. As discussed, designing leisure experiences is a wicked problem.

The programming problem to be solved, then, is most likely novel, complex, and ambiguous because of the many approaches that may work in the correct context. Programmers are more likely to solve these kinds of problems by using an analogical technique—simulated mental models of what might happen—rather than inferring what will happen through computational transformations. The mental imagery techniques outlined in Chapter 10 are examples of analogical transformation techniques.

Second, remember from Chapter 3 that a situated activity system comprises six key elements and that a change in any one will result in a different program. Creating a new program does not necessarily require beginning completely anew. A change in any one element results in a new program; thus, the programmer's

> A change in any one element results in a new program.

goal in being creative is to change at least one element in a way that will make a difference.

Finally, a program is new if its its patron group has not previously experienced it. So *new* does not necessarily mean it is new to the programmer, the staff, or the world; rather, it means it is new to the patron group.

Creative Program Design Process

Is there a method to creativity? How does a person organize efforts to systematically approach creativity? Wallas (1926) identified four stages of the creative process: preparation, incubation, illumination, and verification. The first edition of this book presented these stages as a linear model of creativity. Based on the work of Finke et al. (1992), the model has been revised, and the work of these authors, as well as the work of Wallas, has been used to develop the model presented in Figure 12.2.

The model is not linear; rather, it assumes that creativity and innovation occur as the cumulative result of activity conducted in four phases: problem definition, generation of approaches, exploration and interpretation, and innovation. Individuals iterate between the phases as insights become apparent. Having a good definition of the problem or well-developed program design outcomes facilitates the creative process. Thus, prior to implementing techniques that facilitate the generation of novel approaches, the programmer must frame the problem appropriately and thereby prepare to solve the right problem. Commonly called creativity, this iterative process includes de-constructing the generation of approaches and an investigation and exploration of their applicability. The programmer harvests the cumulative effort of these phases to produce novel approaches for solving the program design problem.

> Having a good definition of the problem or well-developed program design outcomes facilitates the creative process.

The first three phases—problem definition, idea generation, and interpretation of the ideas—should lead to creative, novel ideas. However, the programmer must transform these into something tangible and useful. Experimenting with various prototypes and examining how well they solve the design problem is a recommended strategy. This is innovation—verifying the applicability of the novel ideas generated for solving the program design problem and experimenting with methods of implementing them.

The entire process is constrained by known limitations of the program. These could include constraints or predefinitions of any of the six situating elements (Chapter 3). For example, the programmer attempts to develop an innovative program for the use of an older, existing recreation center. Ideally in this case, the programmer has total creative freedom beyond the constraining fact that an existing facility must be used.

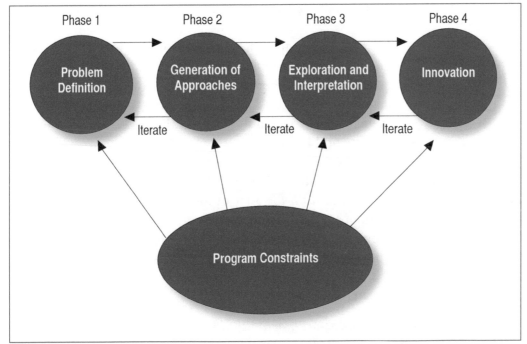

Figure 12.2. Creative Program Design Process. Adapted from Wallas (1926) and Finke, Ward, and Smith (1992).

Four Phases of the Creative Process

Phase 1: Problem Definition

The major goal during Phase 1 is to develop a statement of the problem, that is, the difference between the way things are and the way the programmer believes they ought to be or desires them to be in the future. In the initial effort, the programmer ensures the real problem is understood by asking a series of focusing questions. What is known? What is unknown? What assumptions underlie the problem? What if different assumptions are made? The programmer asks these and other similar questions. Additional focus results from data about the program. These are gathered from a variety of sources including a completed needs assessment, a market study, observed incongruities in current operations, observations of successful or unsuccessful program operations, and other similar sources.

Once gathered, the data must be analyzed. To completely analyze the problem, the programmer explicates the problem completely by breaking it down into its parts and determining the relationship among the parts and all parts to the whole. Time spent in this step is well invested, for it is unlikely that the programmer will develop a good solution to a problem that is not well understood.

Programmers can use many techniques to further their understanding of a problem. One of the key efforts is to "unlearn" what they already "know"—to remove those mental blocks that keep them from seeing things in a new way (Von Oech,

1990). Pablo Picasso once said, "Every act of creation is first of all an act of destruction."

> "Every act of creation is first of all an act of destruction."
> –Pablo Picasso

To facilitate this, programmers use techniques that force them to look at things in a different way by changing the question, using different words to ask the same question, or denying there is a problem in the first place. Programmers might use these techniques to see if the answers provide insight into the problem.

Try questioning the basic assumptions of your organization by playing "Fools and the Rules" (Von Oech, 1990), in which "You take your holiest sacred cow and sacrifice it on the altar of foolishness" (p. 148). The idea is to use humor to make fun of agency products, rules, or policies and to expose their basic assumptions and possible flaws. Here is an example of this technique given to one of the authors by Julia Dunn (personal communication, 1991):

Rule: We will have state-of-the-art programs.

Fool: *Who needs state-of-the-art programs? They create state-of-the-art problems. Why not let someone else be the innovator and we'll copy what they've done. It would be cheaper.*

Redefining the problem often triggers a solution. Consider this example:

One of the authors was once involved in deciding what was to be done with a piece of playground equipment at a park–school site. A rather large number of children had fallen from the two slides on a large, integrated wooden play unit. The local school principal and a PTA committee had decided that the slides were the problem and thus needed to be removed. The author was asked to meet with them to discuss the problem. Before the meeting, however, the author observed children using the equipment.

From these observations, it was apparent that the problem was the placement of the two slides and the large number of children who wanted to play on them. The slides were placed so that the children could slide down one and immediately get in line to slide down the second one. Going down the second slide put the children in a position to get in line to use the first slide again. Thus, the two slides were actually being used as one, and there were simply too many children to be accommodated by this arrangement.

After the analysis, the problem was redefined as having insufficient slides and incorrect slide placement. A twofold solution was proposed: (1) move one slide so that the two could not be used in a circular manner, and (2) add a third slide, thereby increasing the number of opportunities to slide. The solution was innovative compared with removing the slides, and it was developed primarily through analyzing and restating the problem. This solution has worked for many years.

"It's a consequence of the human-centered approach. It's a consequence of the fact that somebody came up with a problem, but when you go in to understand the problem by understanding human factors, talking with the people, the problems are messy" (David Kelley in an interview with Camacho, 2016). We realize the paradox created by advising you on one hand to be as specific and measurable as possible in developing program design statements and now to be as unspecific as possible. Accountability is enhanced by specificity and creativity is enhanced by being unspecific. Ultimately, you must achieve both. Human-centered, empathetic data collection is the crux of the programmer's efforts in this phase. Programmers who know and deeply understand their participants are better informed to generate good problem statements likely of being solved. This seems like a "we do it better" argument, but results indicate this is true. Techniques and efforts aimed at human-centered design more frequently lead to successful innovation.

> They are written with the fewest restrictions possible and thus enhance, rather than inhibit, the generation of novel approaches.

The final effort in this phase is to develop a statement of the problem. How detailed this statement will be depends on the known constraints of the program being developed. The best problem statements have emergent properties (Finke et al., 1992). They are written with the fewest restrictions possible and thus enhance, rather than inhibit, the generation of novel approaches. The problem statement includes clear implications for the key needs to be addressed and the key program elements to be manipulated. Consider these problem statements:

1. To develop a 1-week special event to serve as the finale of a summer sports camp for boys and girls 8 to 12 years old.
2. To develop a program for working mothers with children 1 to 3 years of age to provide them with quality interaction time with their children.

We hope you like #2. The second example leaves the most room for creative discovery and innovation because it is a less specific problem statement. The constraints imposed by a specific program will partly determine the restrictiveness of a problem statement. Too often, more is included than is necessary, which inhibits creativity. These statements are different from SMART goals and objectives, which are more restrictive and confining in their structure.

Phase 2: Generation of Approaches

The major goal during Phase 2 is to generate novel approaches. Some of the key creative efforts include to be impractical and irrational, to be playful, to suspend judgment and facilitate a free flow of imagination, and to relax and spend time (Von Oech, 1990). There is some disagreement about how the programmer's time is best spent in this phase. There is a trade-off between using techniques that force the generation of many ideas and those that focus efforts on producing a few good ideas. One theory suggests that if you generate enough ideas, you will surely include one good enough to solve your problem. However, a second school of thought suggests that you should be more contemplative, mull over ideas, and use critical judgment to generate a few good ideas. Buffington (1987) suggested that the best problem solvers "creatively worry and carry a problem around with them even while doing other tasks" (p. 121). They produce quality over quantity. After all, you only need the one good idea that will solve your problem. You must develop a style that works for you.

Miller (1988) identified two methods of thinking—linear and intuitive—either of which can lead to the generation of good approaches. Linear thinking helps us "organize information in ways that give us new 'entry points' for solving problems" (p. 116). The use of logical, incremental, sequential thinking leads the programmer to look for novel solutions. In contrast to this, intuitive techniques provide the means for the programmer to make inferential insights that facilitate a conceptual leap to a whole solution.

Programmers need to develop a variety of techniques that facilitate the discovery of approaches that they would normally not consider. We will provide you with some techniques that have worked for us. However, go to the sources referenced at the end of this chapter to identify other techniques that may work for you, because the correct technique is a matter of personal style and the type of problem being addressed.

The use of matrix analysis (Miller, 1988) is an excellent example of linear thinking. The Programmer's Evaluation Cube (Exhibit 6.4, page 110) is a three-dimensional matrix that shows the programmer, through logical extension, where to look for new program ideas. By cross tabulating life cycle stages, program formats, and activity types, the programmer documents existing services and concurrently identifies voids to be filled with new services.

Brainstorming is a common technique used in this phase for generating a large number of ideas. Divergent thinking is characterized by five distinct skills: fluency—the ability to generate a large number of solutions; flexibility—the ability to use many approaches or strategies in solving a problem, and a willingness to change directions; originality—the ability to produce clever, unique, and unusual solutions; elaboration—the ability to expand, develop, particularize, and embellish ideas; and irrationality—the ability to allow the right, irrational, creative side of the brain to dominate thinking. Divergent thinking techniques attempt to systematize the ability to accomplish these skills. However, realizing what we are attempting to accomplish enhances our ability to get the job done. Exhibit 12.1 provides explanations of two divergent thinking techniques.

Rather than employing techniques that force us to innovate, to get unstuck, to get out of our routine, and to come up with the next logical extension, some of us succeed by engaging in the "creative worrying" identified earlier. We consciously sets aside a time for the mind to wander completely and to be free of the conceptual discipline imposed by analytical and linear thinking techniques.

Exhibit 12.1. Divergent Thinking Techniques

Brainstorming is one of the most widely known and widely used divergent thinking techniques. It is organized ideation by groups whose goal is to generate as many ideas regarding a design problem as possible within a given time limit. Ideas are generated in an atmosphere of "suspended judgment," that is, the goodness or badness of any idea is suspended during idea generation. Brainstorming sessions are conducted with the belief that generating a large quantity of ideas will produce good ideas for problem solutions.

To conduct a brainstorming session, the leader clearly defines the problem to the group before starting the session. It is best if the individuals making up the group have diverse backgrounds so that idea generation will not be stifled by groupthink. When the session begins, group members say anything that comes to mind as a possible solution to the identified problem. The group leader records all ideas as they are given. Everyone can piggyback on a previous idea by adding to it, combining it with others, and so forth. During brainstorming sessions, the following principles should be followed:

- Suspended judgment. To encourage as many ideas as possible, critical evaluation of their feasibility and worth are temporarily suspended.

- Encourage quantity. The more ideas that are generated, the more likely you are to get the one that will solve the problem.

- Piggyback. Encourage individuals to cross-fertilize, add to, innovate from, or combine with the ideas already generated.

- Encourage wild ideas. Encourage people to reveal their wildest ideas and not prejudge their feasibility or acceptability by the group.

Brainwriting is a modification of brainstorming; participants write down their ideas rather than give them orally. Participants do not identify their own papers. After a given time, papers are exchanged and each person modifies, combines, or in some way builds on the work of the previous writer. The exchange of papers continues until all apparent possibilities are exhausted.

This technique works better than brainstorming for some groups. This is especially true for groups that may have dominant members or for groups in which unequals, in terms of job position, may be working together.

Paul MacCready, who developed the *Gossamer Albatross*, the first human-powered airplane to successfully cross the English Channel, was aware of how others were attempting to solve the problem by building a very small aircraft, barely capable of carrying a pilot. He sat the problem aside and went on vacation. While observing birds in flight, particularly birds soaring, he thought that the solution was to make the plane large rather than small so there would be enough wing surface to provide the lift needed to get the craft airborne. Super-light plastics provided the material needed for building a large, but still lightweight, aircraft. Once airborne, the craft was more of a glider than an aircraft. Yet technically it was a man-powered aircraft. Waiting, contemplating, and reinterpreting seemingly incongruent data are also successful strategies for developing novel approaches.

Analogies are examples of intuitive thinking. They require the programmer to find a correspondence between dissimilar things by thinking in a way that makes the familiar strange and the strange familiar. Reconciling these incongruities produces insights into novel associations. For example, Von Oech (1990) recommended imagining how others would solve the problem. What analogies might result if Superman rather than you were going to develop the program? How might a surgeon, an airline pilot, or an army tank commander approach the program? What questions would they ask; what assumptions would they make; what tools, equipment, and places would they use; or what processes would they employ?

One of the authors has asked students to compare (identify the similarities and differences between) operating a recreation program and giving a stand-up comedy routine. Some of their answers were:

They both play to an audience.
They have their ups and downs.
They must be novel to sustain interest.
Both depend on a good leader.
Either can fail!
A good plan or script is essential for success in either.

A continuing effort throughout this phase is to keep focused on the correct problem. It is recommended that programmers continually define and redefine the problem based on new insights gained through their efforts in Phase 2. This process helps focus the unconscious thought process on the critical issues that the programmer needs to solve the problem successfully. This sharpens and keeps on target unconscious thinking. The check may reveal some insight or direction that will provide the adaptations or innovations that can unify the direction of further thoughts. Often, programmers need to keep redefining the problem until developing a more suitable problem statement. Now complete Exercise 12.1.

Exercise 12.1.
Redefining Problem Statements

When confronted with a new problem, we usually attempt to fit it into a familiar problem and then proceed to solve it. Identify a problem statement and then use the series of questions below to aid in moving the problem to a more familiar basis. In attempting to refine a problem, ask some of the following questions:

- Have you seen the problem before, perhaps in a slightly different form?
- Have you seen a problem with a similar unknown?
- Identify a solution to a similar problem.
- Can you use its results or its methods?
- Can you use different words to describe the problem?
- Can you solve any part of the problem?
- Try the fit of a solution of a related problem. Although it may be more general, more specific, or analogous to your current problem, see if it will work!

Phase 3: Exploration and Interpretation

The primary goal in Phase 3 is to synthesize the approaches generated in Phase 2 into an acceptable solution. The programmer accomplishes this by exploring and interpreting the feasibility of the ideas generated in the previous phase for solving the programming problem. This, too, can be difficult. Sometimes programmers do not recognize a solution even though it is before them, because they simply have not discovered the cognitive structure that allows the pieces to come together as a solution. The creative efforts in this phase require programmers to rearrange ideas to make seemingly diverse elements converge. Various types of analogies and projective imagery (discussed in Chapter 10) may be useful for completing this phase.

Another method involves the programmer using several analogical positions to shift the context of an experience to test the applicability of approaches. Try each of these analogies:

Personal analogy. Place yourself at the center of the program, and identify how each novel approach would contribute to your leisure experience in a program. What are the paradoxes, the problems, or the conflicts? How might they be combined and resolved?

Direct analogy. Draw a direct comparison to another event. How would the novel approaches you have developed be used in a trip to the moon? How would they be used to stage an arts festival or the Olympics? How would they be used in the NCAA Final Four tournament or the Super Bowl?

Symbolic analogy. Try to find the symbolic essence of the approaches. For example, when one of the authors lived in Texas, the state celebrated its sesquicentennial. Since these events occur so infrequently, it is not certain what events are appropriate for celebrating a sesquicentennial. The essence of the event, though, seemed to be to celebrate patriotism and political liberty. Most community celebrations included events similar to those normally operated on the Fourth of July. There were symbolic similarities between the two events.

Fantasy analogy. In this case, you can go beyond objective reality into fantasy. What would the program be like if it were operated for the Flintstone family? What would a *Star Wars* production of your program be like? How would members of the *Modern Family* or *Big Bang Theory* casts like your program?

Programmers can also expand the conceptual space to frame the program problem. For example, instead of conceptualizing a citywide annual softball tournament, they can think about planning a national or international tournament. Thinking of a larger, more encompassing event may lead programmers to new contexts and viewpoints.

After giving this your best effort, flip and get dissatisfied with everything. Change it all to see what happens! Apply Osborn's (1963) manipulative verbs to accomplish this. Ask: What if I adapt, modify, magnify, minify, substitute, rearrange, reverse, or combine the concepts? By applying these verbs, you can rearrange, combine, and recombine your approaches to investigate their feasibility.

When do you stop? Von Oech (1990) offered important advice about this—accept that there may be more than one right answer. Often, education and training are organized around finding the correct answer to a question, as if there is only one! Because of this, Von Oech recommended finding the second right answer. Thus, the effort continues until you find a second solution that is the approximate equivalent of the first right answer. If you find one that is better, keep going, of course!

Phase 4: Innovation

The primary goal during Phase 4 is to be innovative and shape the proposed solution into a feasible program. Programmers first verify that their final proposal truly solves the program design problem. Then they screen the program to determine its feasibility for implementation. Discoveries during this phase may require some redesign of the program or development of a new method of operation.

Design thinking, discussed earlier, encourages prototyping possible solutions so that the programmer can test them. In this case, the programmer would expect to have a series of failures through trial-and-error learning by staging different versions or parts of a new program. Liedtka and Ogilvie (2011) offered, "Rapid prototyping is the creation of visual (and sometimes experiential) manifestation of concepts. It is an iterative set of activities, done quickly, aimed at transforming the concepts generated in the **What if** stage into feasible, testable models" (p. 141). Visualization is one such technique, but operating a smaller version of a special event with likely eventual participants would be a more grounded example allowing for testing several versions prior to offering a final version. The point is to be action rather than planning oriented and to try various versions or parts of a program.

Simonds (1961) designed five preplanned scenarios that programmers can use to verify the conceptual harmony of the final design. This harmony results from the integration of all working relationships, functions, and elements so that each complements the other and the overall design. During this process, programmers often again use projective imagery to vicariously experience the program and to model its operation.

Simonds's five scenarios are outward and inward plan progression, expansion and contraction of the plan concept, satellite plan verification, integral planning, and proving the plan.

In examining the outward and inward progression of a design, programmers consider the effect of each design element from the innermost point of its generation to its final outcome. Conversely, programmers ensure that each design element in the final design is a logical conclusion of the outermost components and implications of the overall design. For example, in outward progression, the programmer could examine the effect on the participant's overall experience of waiting in line for 30 minutes before an event. What effect would this have on the participant's overall leisure experience? It is well documented that standing in line creates anxiety. This type of anxiety would interfere with a leisure experience, so the programmer would develop some other method of queuing to meet the design goal.

In inward progression, programmers consider the outermost components of the design and logically progress into the minute details of the design to ensure that they are consistent. For example, if a programmer advertises a noncompetitive volleyball tournament, but then stages it in a gym with a center arena, spectator seating surrounding a center court, and a public address system announcing the score after each point, the operational details of the event would be inconsistent with the overall design concept. Although these are extreme examples, failure to verify the details of a plan in this thorough, detailed manner often leads to operations that are inconsistent with original design intentions.

In expansion and contraction of the plan, the programmer expands the areas of consideration to the farthest extensional aspects of the plan and contracts each part down to its most trivial detail. In doing this, the programmer attempts to develop worst-case and best-case scenarios of program operation to anticipate and plan for the most probable events. Consider the role of weather in the design of an outdoor program. If the possibility of good weather is extended to rainy weather, how does this affect program design? Will it alter the equipment used, the location, or the date, or will it require that the program be called off? What if too many or too few participants show up? Does this need to be known in advance? What are the implications of these scenarios? When applied thoroughly, this expansion and contraction technique raises many questions that programmers need to plan for during the design or staging process.

In the satellite plan verification scenario, the programmer examines the relationship of each part of the plan to the whole plan. Each element of the plan design must be in harmony with the whole design concept. In leisure program design, the programmer considers the wholeness of a program including aspects such as registration procedures, cleanup procedures, the location and timing of refreshments, and so on. To be thorough, the programmer examines the choices made for each of the six elements of a situated activity system, discussed in Chapter 3, to ensure that each contributes appropriately and complementary to solving the identified design problem.

Integral planning puts further order and conceptual harmony into the program design with a final check of the key program frames, the key activating elements that are assumed to be central to each frame, the key transitions planned, and the appropriateness of their sequential order. Some frames and transitions and some of the situating elements are more critical to accomplishing the design goals than others are. This is the final opportunity for the programmer to take steps to ensure that these key design features have been incorporated into the design and the operational plan (which will be discussed in Chapter 13) to maximize the probability that the experience intended will occur.

As one example, look again at the Egg Hunt discussed previously. Although there were many considerations, two key design frames were integral to this event. First, each child needed to find an egg, and second, parents needed to be able to watch their children hunt, but be kept from helping them. Once these key design frames were identified, all other design elements considered for inclusion were evaluated by the degree to which they would maximize the probability of these two elements occurring. In integral planning, then, the programmer attempts to ensure that the design includes the elements integral to accomplishing the overall design goals.

Finally, Simonds (1961) suggested proving the plan and determining if the design created indeed corresponds to the original design concept. The programmer makes the final solution an accurate reflection of the original problem statement. Easy mistakes for programmers to make when manipulating elements is inventing new needs, inflating the importance of one, or de-emphasizing another. Once again, to test this the programmer vicariously experiences the program step-by-step as if participating in it, seeing it, and touching it. Through projective imagery, programmers imagine themselves not as designers, but as participants—an older participant, a younger participant, or a participant of a different ethnic group or socioeconomic background.

Throughout the verification process, the programmer remains faithful to the original programming problem. If the design does not solve the original problem, the programmer has not succeeded. Accomplishing the original design goal involves correlating established and prioritized relationships of the major determinants (design elements, goals, objectives, etc.) with the whole. The detailed scenarios discussed will direct the designer in successfully searching for all relationships and interactions among the six situating elements of program production. Now complete Exercise 12.2 (page 236).

For the final effort in this phase, the programmer screens the program to ensure it is feasible to implement and that it is truly innovative, that is, sufficiently different from current offerings. Figure 12.3 shows an instrument for conducting this screening. The programmer scores each component on the instrument and then sums the scores. Programs that score 28 points or more are considered to be feasible to implement and innovative enough to be worth the effort.

Conclusion

Creativity is an iterative process for identifying novel approaches to programs and innovative methods for operating them. Programmers use it to create alternative solutions for programming problems, and it should be a routine part of the program design and planning steps of the Program Development Cycle.

> Creativity is an iterative process for identifying novel approaches to programs and innovative methods for operating them.

The four distinct phases of the creative process include identifiable techniques to facilitate the programmer's efforts. Throughout the process, the programmer continuously returns to the problem itself to ensure it is correctly defined and that the assumptions made about the constraints are valid. In many cases, the selection of techniques for facilitating the programmer's effort is a matter of personal choice and style. Thus, the programmer must develop a kit bag of techniques to apply until identifying one that works in a given situation.

Creative program design is hard work and requires the application of many diverse skills. However, if the techniques and processes presented in this chapter are thoroughly applied to program design problems, programmers will be able to develop innovative programs for their constituents. Good luck!

Program Characteristic	Score			
	4 Excellent	3 Good	2 Fair	1 Poor
1 Provides Benefits to Target Patrons				
2 Is Significantly Different From Other Programs				
3 Can Be Produced Economically				
4 Can Be Marketed Economically				
5 Fits in With Rec. Dept. Image				
6 Rec. Dept. Personnel Have the Needed Skills to Produce and Promote It				
7 Rec. Dept. Personnel Have Time Needed to Produce and Promote It				
8 Adequate Facilities Are Available				
9 Contributes to Agency Mission				
10 Material Resources Are Readily Available				

Subtotals

Total Score

Programs scoring 28 or more points are innovative and feasible

Figure 12.3. Program Screening Instrument. Adapted from a form used by U.S. Navy Recreational Services Unit.

Exercise 12.2.
Let's Get Creative!

Directions: Read the following problem statement and work through the creative design process model. Answer the questions as you go. Use a PENCIL!

Problem Definition

Write problem statement here:

What don't we know about the problem statement?

1.
2.
3.

What do we know about the problem statement?

1.
2.
3.

Rules and Fools:
Rule:

Fool 1:

Fool 2:

Fool 3:

Generation of Approaches

Brainwrite a list of ideas. Suspend judgment, be impractical and irrational, be playful, etc.

1.
2.
3.
4.
5.
6.
7.
8.
9.
10.

Given the above list, do you want to redefine the problem statement?
(circle one)

Yes (if yes, rewrite below) No

New statement:

Exercise 12.2. (continued)

Exploration and Interpretation

Test out your favorite approach from the following four perspectives:

Personal analogy (imagine yourself doing the event)

1. What's fun about it?

2. What's potentially bothersome?

Direct analogy (compare this to another event)

1. Name other event

2. Would this be **more** or **less** fun (circle one)? Why?

3. Would this idea be **more** or **less** challenging? Why?

Symbolic analogy

1. Name the symbolic elements in your idea.

2. Name a program with similar symbolic elements.

3. Which idea is better? Why?

Fantasy analogy

1. Choose two fantasy populations.

2. Is one of these a possible theme for your idea or not? Why?

Given these explorations, do you want to select another idea or stick with the one you've chosen? If you switch, erase the above and start again.

Innovation

Which idea do you want to consider given your progress through this creative design model?

Now go to the Program Screening Instrument in Figure 12.3 (page 235) and work through the form with your idea.

Evaluation of this learning exercise:

1. How has this exercise helped you develop your creative skills?

2. Which part(s) was/were most helpful regarding your ability to be creative?

References

Ackoff, R. L., & Vergara, E. (1981). Creativity in problem solving and planning: A review. *European Journal of Operational Research, 7*, 1–13.

Buffington, P. W. (1987, February). *Sky: Delta Airlines Inflight Magazine.*

Camacho, M. (2016). David Kelley: From design to design thinking at Stanford and IDEO. *She Ji: The Journal of Design, Economics, and Innovation, 2*, 88–101.

Finke, R. A., Ward, T. B., & Smith, S. M. (1992). *Creative cognition: Theory, research, and applications.* Cambridge, MA: MIT Press.

Howard, N. A. (1985, March). How to generate bright new ideas. *Success, 1985*, 54.

Kaufmann, G. (1988). Mental imagery and problem solving. In M. Dennis, J. Engelkamp, & J. T. E. Richardson (Eds.), *Cognitive and neuropsychological approaches to mental imagery* (pp. 231–239). Dordrecht, Netherlands: Martinus Nijhoff.

Kelley, T., & Kelley, D. (2013). *Creative confidence.* New York, NY: Crown Business.

Liedtka, J., & Ogilvie, T. (2011). *Designing for growth: A design thinking took kit for managers.* New York, NY: Columbia Business School Publishing.

Miller, W. C. (1988). Techniques for stimulating new ideas: A matter of fluency. In R. L. Kuhn (Ed.), *Handbook for creative innovative managers.* New York, NY: McGraw-Hill.

Osborn, A. F. (1963). *Applied imagination.* New York, NY: Scribner and Sons.

Schlatter, B. E., & Chang., Y. (2018). Recreation programming practices: Unpublished survey. Illinois Park and Recreation Association.

Simonds, J. O. (1961). *Landscape architecture.* New York, NY: McGraw-Hill.

Von Oech, R. (1990). *A whack on the side of the head: How can you be more creative?* New York, NY: Warner Books.

Wallas, G. (1926). *The art of thought.* New York, NY: Harcourt, Brace.

Ward, B. (1985, June). Centers of imagination. *Sky: Delta Airlines Inflight Magazine.*

Additional Readings

Alexander, C. (1970, March). Changes in form. *Architectural Design, 1970*, 122–125.

Broadbent, G. H. (1966). Creativity. In S. A. Gregory (Ed.), *The design method.* London, England: Butterworths.

Gordon, W. J. (1961). *Synectics: The development of creative capacity.* New York, NY: Harper and Brothers.

Howard, N. A., Hoffer, W., Ingber, D., Raudsepp, E., Niemark, J., & Johnson, H. (1985, March). Creativity: A special report. *Success, 1985*, 54–61.

Jones, J. C. (1980). *Design methods: Seeds of human futures.* New York, NY: Wiley.

Smith, E. T. (1985, September 30). Are you creative? *Business Week*, pp. 80–84.

Weisberg, R. W. (1986). *Genius and other myths.* New York, NY: W. H. Freeman.

PART IV

Operational Strategies

Part IV explains Stage C, Operational Strategies, of the Program Development Cycle. The programmer prepares a written program design that has been developed for a targeted population, to share it with all who will help implement the program. When preparing the plan, the programmer deals with the realities and limitations of agency resources and alters the plan to fit the resources available or additional resources found through fees and charges or a program sponsor. During this stage, the programmer completes the preparations for staging the program and implements the program.

Chapter 13 explains how to write a program plan. The next six chapters deal with staging the program. This is the step where programmers spend the majority of their effort, thus the need for multiple chapters that explain the many tasks needed for staging a program. It is easy for programmers to justify spending time on this step, because it involves completing tasks that have an obvious, direct relationship with producing program services. However, they must guard against allowing this step to dominate their time to the exclusion of other steps in the cycle.

Furthermore, some believe that all program failures are traceable to inadequate implementation. Inadequate implementation could be the cause of failure, but there are other possible explanations. For example, failure could be traceable to an inadequate analysis of needs and the consequent development of a program service for which there is simply no demand. The programmer is cautioned, then, that spending too much time on program implementation and too little time on the other steps of the Program Development Cycle may create operational problems for the programmer and the agency.

Chapter 14 includes the techniques that recreation agencies use to promote program services. Chapter 15 covers how to queue and register individuals. Chapter 16 discusses staffing and supervising program services. Chapter 17 talks about issues involved in developing an agency's program pricing policy. Chapter 18 outlines methods for determining program costs. Chapter 19 discusses establishing a price for a program.

Chapter 13: Preparing the Program Plan

Chapter 14: Techniques for Program Promotion

Chapter 15: Registration Procedures

Chapter 16: Staffing and Supervising Program Operations

Chapter 17: Developing a Program Pricing Philosophy

Chapter 18: Determining Program Costs

Chapter 19: Pricing Program Services

Stage C: Operational Strategies

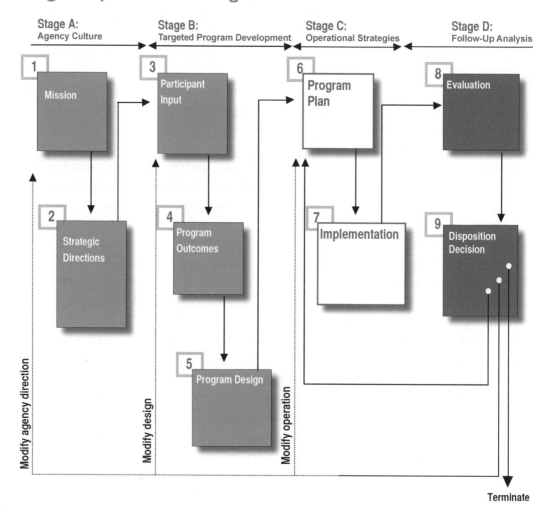

Learning to Fish
Photo Courtesy of City of Grand Prairie Parks, Arts and Recreation Department.

13 *Preparing the Program Plan*

KEY TERMS

Program Plan, Management Plan, Flow Chart, Animation Plan, Program Scheduling, Facility Scheduling

Step 6: Program Plan

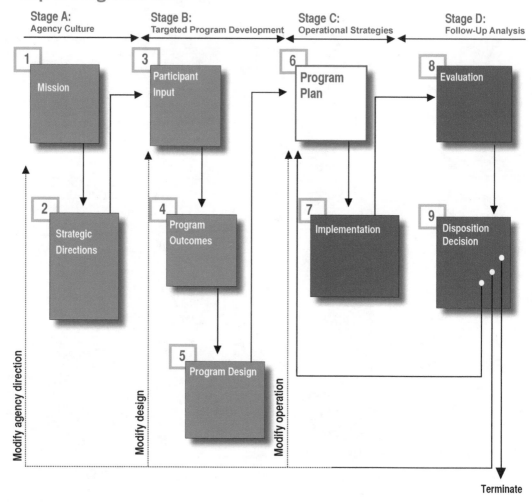

In most instances, programmers cannot produce a program single-handedly. To produce a program as the designer intends, they communicate details of the design and staging to other staff members who will help implement it. Through a written program plan, programmers communicate the role of each person involved in producing a program. Clear communication through the program plan is necessary for successful implementation.

> To produce a program as the designer intends, programmers communicate details of the design and staging to other staff members who will help implement it.

The written program plan is analogous to the architect's blueprint or the project manager's network diagram. Through a blueprint, an architect communicates to various workers their roles and functions in completing a structure as designed by the architect. Project managers in many professional areas, such as construction planning, movie production, and political campaigns, execute projects with a written plan that outlines the activities to be accomplished, role assignments for those responsible for various aspects of the plan, and a timeline for their completion.

Once the program design is well thought out and clear in the programmer's mind (this is accomplished with the techniques covered in Chapters 7, 9, 10, and 11), the programmer prepares a written program plan. Although the program may seem well designed and clear, writing down the plan in detail often exposes design flaws that must be corrected. One benefit of writing a program plan is that flaws can be discovered and corrected before implementation. Even though the planning step is illustrated as separate from the design step, programmers often iterate between the two while writing the plan and the need for redesign becomes apparent.

Successful programs are operated or experienced four times. First, the designer vicariously experiences them during the design step. Second, in writing the program plan, the designer again vicariously experiences the program and develops the interaction scenarios necessary for animating. Third, the program is operated. Fourth, in evaluating the program, the designer relives it vicariously through regressive imagery and models it with proposed modifications for improvement using projective imagery.

The written plan is a working document that is subject to ongoing revision. It provides

- a record of information about the current development status of the program,
- a record of the resources for operating the program, and
- a reference for use during future operations of the program. (Adapted from Kliem, 1986)

Program Plan

This section explains the steps in the program plan outline, as presented in Exhibit 13.1 (page 244).

Exhibit 13.1. The Program Plan

1. Program Title
2. Agency Mission and Programming Strategy
3. Need for the Program
4. Terminal Performance Outcomes
5. Staging the Program
   a. Venue Arrangements
   b. Special Arrangements
   c. Inclusion Plan
   d. Equipment, Supplies, and Material Needs
   e. Promotion Plan
   f. Budget and Pricing Information
   g. Registration Plan
   h. Staffing and Staff Orientation Plan
   i. Management Plan
   j. Cancellation Plan
   k. Setup
   l. Risk Management Plan
   m. Animation Plan
   n. Program Wrap-Up
6. Program Evaluation
7. Disposition Decision Plan

Note: The authors are grateful to Crossley and Jamieson (1997) for some of the concepts and ideas included in this exhibit.

Program Title

This section of the program plan includes the name of the program, the sponsoring agency, and a descriptive introductory paragraph indicating the who, what, when, where, why, and how of the program. After reading this paragraph, the reader should have basic familiarity with the leisure experience to be created by the program.

Agency Mission and Programming Strategy

The program plan also includes a statement of the agency's mission and the programming strategy this program will implement. These make it apparent why the agency is involved in producing this program.

Need for the Program

The program plan includes a statement of the need for this program. It answers the questions, why is this program needed, and how was this need determined?

Terminal Performance Outcomes of the Program

The program plan also includes specific outcome statements about the accomplishments intended for the program, the Y statements identified and discussed earlier in the text. As discussed, the outcome statements specify what leisure experiences the program is supposed to create and the participant outcomes expected. If the programmer uses an outcome-based approach, the outcomes intended should be individualized (i.e., specified for each participant).

Staging the Program

This section of the program plan provides a detailed set of instructions about staging the program (i.e., how the program is to be implemented and operated). There is always a question of how much detail should be included. At a minimum, the program management goals, the X statements of interventions necessary, should be included. Unfortunately, programmers too often provide so little detail that only someone who has previously observed the program being operated could use the "details" to reproduce the program. At a minimum, programmers must provide enough details so that another programmer from a different agency could reproduce the program. Generally, if you have any doubt about the need to include additional detail or description, include it.

Venue arrangements. Venues are locales for staging leisure experiences and include buildings, special facilities, and park areas. Examples of frequently used program areas are recreation centers, gymnasiums, theatres, or parklands; playgrounds or athletic fields; and water resources such as swimming pools, lakes, or beaches. The program plan notes any unique facility attributes needed for the program.

> Venues are locales for staging leisure experiences and include buildings, special facilities, and park areas.

The program plan specifies how arrangements can be made for the venue. In many cases, the programmer uses agency venues, in which case the program will need to be placed on the schedule for the venue. In some cases, programmers use venues owned by other agencies. At the least, they are likely to need to schedule the venue with their own agency's scheduling system. In other cases, they may need to secure a reservation, make a deposit, or obtain a contract to use facilities owned by a different agency. The program plan also includes maps that indicate the location of the venue and diagrams of the areas and facilities.

Special arrangements. Some programs require special arrangements with agencies or businesses outside of the recreation agency. It is advantageous for programmers to make such arrangements or reservations early in the planning process to ensure availability. Organizations commonly use contractual agreements when making provisions for venues, transportation, entertainment, and concessions. Other arrangements may require the procurement of camping permits, insurance, or special maintenance services.

Inclusion plan. Individuals with disabilities have the right to participate in programs with the general population. Research has determined that communities are increasing the number of inclusive options for individuals with disabilities (Devine & Kotowski, 1999). Agencies are required to provide reasonable accommodation in all programs, for those with disabilities. In a recent survey, agencies ranked the lack of funding for providing these opportunities, constraints on staff due to a lack of adequate support resources, the lack of an adequately trained staff, and negative staff attitudes as the highest limitations that prevented them from implementing inclusive services (Devine & Kotowski, 1999). In most cases, the agency will need to figure out how to accomplish inclusiveness regardless of its difficulty.

> Communities are increasing the number of inclusive options for individuals with disabilities.

Accommodations that reduce the barriers to participation may be provided in many ways, depending on the disability of the individual desiring to participate and the type of program service being offered. The types of accommodation most frequently provided by agencies include pool lifts, the relocation of classes to accessible facilities, the provision of adaptive equipment, the provision of sign interpreters, and the development of inclusion plans (reported by 50% or more of the agencies in a survey conducted by Devine & Kotowski, 1999). Until programmers identify the specific disabilities of individuals who wish to participate, they may find it difficult to develop this part of the plan. However, in advance of such requests, programmers help develop a sensitivity to providing inclusive services in the agency and community, the policy infrastructure to support inclusion services, adequate funding to support these services, and the resources likely to be needed for provision of inclusive services.

In a 2012 white paper prepared by Rossman, agencies reported that one of their obstacles in partnering with health service agencies was the inability of staff to write adequate charting notes. To obtain funding from many of these funding sources, the agency had to prepare acceptable documentation notes about the progress of individual clients. This is an important skill that is needed for agencies to find funding partners for providing inclusive services for some disabilities.

Equipment, supplies, and material needs. The program plan also includes a list of equipment, supplies, and materials needed for operating the program. These were previously discussed in Chapter 4, but will be briefly reiterated here. Equipment is a nonconsumable product that can be used by people to participate in leisure; thus, it includes items that can be used more than once—usually for several operations of a program. Equipment covers everything from tents and basketballs to lifeguard rescue buoys. Supplies are items such as chalk, paper, paint, writing implements, clay, food, paper cups, and coffee filters that are consumed during program operations. Materials are items such as cement or lumber that are used in the construction of something of a permanent nature. The program plan notes any special supply or material needs, notes their availability, and indicates a source. It also identifies supplies and materials that may need to be acquired through a bidding process or that take some lead time to obtain.

Promotion plan. This section of the program plan explicates the target market for the program and the plan for promoting the program to this market. It includes details about the types of promotional materials, their distribution, and the timeline for implementing the promotion plan. Chapter 14 discusses developing promotional materials.

Budget and pricing information. Here the program plan includes the budget for the program, including revenues, income projections, expenses, and how the price for participation was determined. Chapters 18 and 19 discuss the budgeting and pricing of programs.

Registration plan. This section of the program plan details registration procedures. It specifies when registration will occur, who will conduct it, where it will occur, and how it will be conducted. If there are any special registration requirements for this program, this section specifies them. For example, only individuals who hold American Camp Association certification as Campcrafters may be permitted to register for a wilderness camping program. Chapter 15 discusses how to conduct registration.

Staffing and staff orientation plan. This section of the program plan determines and specifies the number and qualifications of the staff needed for operating the program. It also specifies procedures for hiring, orienting, and training staff. Chapter 16 discusses staffing. Similarly, if volunteers are necessary for the program, the program plan should include information on recruiting, training, and supervising them.

Management plan. Programs are rarely implemented by a single individual. Program operation most often requires the coordinated effort of many individuals. The operation of one-off programs such as events and festivals is most analogous to project management. According to Moder, Phillips, and Davis (1983), "A project is a set of tasks or activities related to the achievement of some planned objective, normally where the objective is unique or nonrepetitive" (p. 3). A project is not usually repeated in an identical manner on an ongoing basis as is product production wherein the same product is produced repeatedly. Checklists and flowcharts identify the activities for completing a project and scheduling their completion in an acceptable time span, given a finite set of resources. The Management Plan section in this chapter discusses the accomplishment of this in programming.

Cancellation plan. The program plan also details what will happen in the event of program cancellation. Many alternatives could be considered, but contingencies need to be specified and prepared. Cancellations often occur because of weather, but may also occur because of illness or some other unforeseen incident. When an employee cannot lead or supervise a workshop, class, or another scheduled event, the contingency plan specifies possible substitutes so that the program does not have to be cancelled. However, some programs require the presence of employees who possess special qualifications or certifications, such as a lifeguard. In situations in which customer safety is at stake and there are no qualified substitutes, cancellation is the safest option.

For outdoor events, the program plan could specify an alternate indoor location. Often, the plan will provide an alternate date for outdoor programs that are cancelled because of unfavorable weather. If weather conditions are unsettled, the programmer should delay making a decision to cancel a program until the last moment possible. If bad weather clears shortly before the scheduled starting time of a program, patrons will appear and expect service. To avoid bad public relations, program staff must be ready to operate the event or be at the event location to redirect patrons to an alternate place or date. The major point here is that the programmer must cancel an event and manage its cancellation—events will not cancel themselves.

> When an employee cannot lead or supervise a workshop, class, or another scheduled event, the contingency plan specifies possible substitutes.

For events for which patrons paid a fee, it is best for programmers to let patrons know how their fee will be refunded, at the time of cancellation. Failure to inform patrons about refunds at the cancellation of an event will lead to many inquiries about this issue.

Setup. The program plan specifies detailed plans for program setup including a drawn *stage plan* illustrating an aerial view of the physical layout of the venue. It is essential that the venue be set up and ready for operations when patrons arrive. However, depending on the program and venue, setup can be time consuming and may involve many individuals. Therefore, programmers should allow for plenty of lead time and, if needed, plenty of assistance to complete program setup.

Setup may involve creating a specific atmosphere in a particular location, such as decorating a gymnasium with a tropical theme for a teen dance. It may also involve collecting equipment and supplies for a program, such as a day hike. For special events, programmers may need to request setup assistance from the maintenance staff through a work request form. Although these vary from agency to agency, work request forms generally contain the same information. The person completing the form fills in the date and time of the event and provides a detailed and explicit description and diagram of the work to be done. If setup arrangements are critical to the success of a program, it is best for the programmer to be present during setup.

Risk management plan. Although many recreation and leisure services agencies employ risk management coordinators to manage the overall safety and well-being of participants and agency personnel, they also have a general expectation that all employees will be safety conscious and maintain a safe venue and safe operation of programs. Participants must also assume some of the normal risks of participating in specific types of recreation, be advised about these normal risks of participation before starting a program, and sign off that they have been informed and accept the risks. Risk management coordinators work with board members, administrators, programmers, and leaders in preparing risk management plans.

Programmers should address the following risk management components in their plans: reporting and record keeping, facilities inspection and hazard abatement procedures, participant safety briefing and preparation, staff supervision, and emergency procedures (Kraus & Curtis, 2000). Exhibit 13.2 gives examples of how programmers might cover each of these components.

Exhibit 13.2. Incorporating Risk Management Components Into the Program Plan

The following are examples of how programmers might address risk management components.

Reporting and Record Keeping—Programmers should make sure that

- participants or parents/guardians have read and signed all required forms, including waivers, releases, and assumption of risk, and
- program leaders know where to find and are capable of completing and filling out all risk management forms, including accident and incident reports.

Facilities Inspections and Hazard Abatement—Programmers should make sure that

- appropriate staff inspect all required equipment and facilities before each session,
- broken equipment is identified and either repaired or removed immediately, and
- routine maintenance procedures on the program area are completed in a timely fashion.

Participant Safety Briefing—Programmers should make sure that

- appropriate participant behavioral expectations regarding the program and equipment usage are established and enforced, and
- participants are informed of behavioral expectations.

Staff Supervision—Programmers should make sure that

- programs have adequate staff–participant ratios,
- staff understand sexual harassment laws, and
- staff know their supervisory responsibilities pursuant to the program.

Emergency Procedures—Programmers should make sure that

- emergency procedures are clearly posted,
- program leaders know what to do in case of an emergency, and
- if appropriate, participants know what to do in case of an emergency.

Note: The authors are grateful to Kraus and Curtis (2000) for some of the concepts and ideas that are included in this exhibit.

Animation plan. The program plan also includes a description of the key animation frames, transitions, and scenarios. Chapter 10 discusses animation, and the Animation Plan section in this chapter discusses the animation plan further.

Program wrap-up. In this step, programmers ensure the return of equipment and the return of venues to their pre-event state. They also prepare and send thank-you letters, post-event news releases, and other follow-up correspondence. This step may also include the distribution of awards, trophies, and/or certificates. Remember, this is the reflection phase of participation, which provides an opportunity for capturing the reflections of participants and leads them to anticipating the next operational cycle of the program.

Program Evaluation Plan

The program plan outlines specific instruments and techniques for evaluating the program. Chapters 20 and 21 present techniques and instruments for conducting program evaluations.

Disposition Decision Plan

The program plan also includes a basis on which programmers can determine the future of the program. Chapter 22 details the accomplishment of this.

Management Plan

After the program has been conceptualized and designed, it is necessary for programmers to develop a management plan that outlines the implementation of the event. The Flow Chart Method (FCM; Murphy & Howard, 1977) has been discussed in the recreation programming literature as an effective method for managing the implementation of recreation programs. The method provides a specific technique for identifying, sequentially ordering, and prioritizing the tasks that must be completed for program implementation.

Flow Chart Method

The FCM provides an elementary network diagram (Murphy & Howard, 1977; Russell, 1982) that can be used for managing a program. According to Kliem (1986), "A network diagram is a graphic representation of a series of activities and events depicting the various aspects of a project and the order in which these activities and events must occur" (p. 35). Used properly, the FCM reduces the possibility of careless mistakes or omissions in the program planning process. Russell (1982) identified the FCM as the most useful to her as a practitioner. This management technique serves the needs of most recreation programs.

The two following sections explain the steps that the programmer must complete to implement the FCM for a summer day camp program. Exhibit 13.3 illustrates the steps in a checklist. Exhibit 13.4 (page 252) illustrates the steps in a flowchart.

Exhibit 13.3. Checklist for Implementation of a Summer Day Camp Program

Major Function	Task	Time Required to Complete (Weeks)	Deadline
Program Design	Design program	2	1/15
Site Selection	Select sites	2	1/30
Staffing	Prepare position announcements	2	2/28
	Announce staff positions	1	4/1
	Prepare staff manual	6	3/30
	Interview applicants	2	4/21
Promotion	Plan promotional flyer	2	2/1
	Send flyer to printer	1	3/1
	Distribute flyers	1	3/30
	Submit news release	1	5/15
Equipment, Supplies, and Materials	Research suppliers	1	3/1
	Order equipment, supplies, and materials	1	3/15
	Monitor equipment, supplies, and materials (reorder if needed)	3	4/15
	Deliver to sites	1	6/18
Registration	Plan registration process	2	4/30
	Program registration	1	5/15
	Assign campers	1	5/30
Staff Training	Staff training	1	6/18
Program Operation	Summer Neighborhood Day Camp Program	8	8/13
Evaluation	Plan evaluation methods	1	5/15
	Collect evaluation data	1	8/13
	Evaluation report	1	8/20

Developing the Checklist

1. Divide the program into its major functions. These major functions generally include staff, facilities, promotion, program design, registration, and so on.
2. Analyze each major function independently by generating a list of tasks or activities that must be addressed. It is not required in this step that the tasks be placed in any particular order. A list of the staff functions could include updating the staff manual, recruiting, interviewing, hiring, conducting orientation, and evaluating.

Exhibit 13.4. Flowchart for Summer Day Camp Program

Program Design   1/15—Design program

Site Selection   1/30—Select sites
Staffing   2/28—Prepare position announcements
                                          4/1—Announce staff positions
                                  3/30—Prepare staff manual
                                          4/21—Interview applicants
Promotion   2/1—Plan promotional flyer
                                  3/1—Send flyer to printer
                                  3/30—Distribute flyers
                                          5/15—Submit news release

	Jan	Feb	Mar	Apr	May	Jun	Jul	Aug

Equipment, Supplies, and Materials   3/1—Research suppliers
                                  3/15—Place order
                                          4/15—Monitor order
                                                  6/18—Deliver to sites
Registration   4/30—Plan registration process
                                          5/15—Conduct program registration
                                          5/30—Assign campers
Staff Training   6/18—Conduct staff training
Program Operation   8/13—Camp
Evaluation   5/15—Plan evaluation methods
                                                  8/13—Collect data
                                                  8/20—Prepare evaluation report

3. Prioritize each activity within the major functions by projecting the amount of time required to complete the task and establishing a deadline for that task (Exhibit 13.3, page 251). For example, the staffing function of interviewing applicants will take 2 weeks to complete, and the deadline for that activity has been determined as April 21 of the current year.

Developing the Flowchart

4. For the final step, programmers chart all of the activities on a flowchart (Exhibit 13.4). The length of the flowchart will be the sum of the time estimates determined for each function in the previous step. For example, if the programmer determines that 6 months would be needed to adequately

plan, implement, and evaluate a special event, then approximately 6 months should be allotted in the flowchart. Last, each activity on the flowchart should include a completion date. Murphy and Howard (1977) stated, "The placement of all these activities on the time line (or flowchart) is the most difficult and time-consuming, but also the most important, step in the application of FCM" (p. 200).

After establishing the flowchart, programmers use it as a guide to map the progress of the plan. They can estimate the effect of proposed or necessary changes on the program. Important to note, however, is that while all programmers should utilize checklists, not all programs will need flowcharts. Smaller programs that can be planned in a shorter time frame, for example, a month or two, can successfully be outlined with only a checklist. Programs that require extensive planning over 6 to 9 months or more will benefit from the graphic representation provided by a flowchart. Thus, a flowchart makes an excellent record of work accomplished and a good guideline for use in the next operation of the program. Now complete Exercise 13.1.

Animation Plan

Through the animation plan, the program designer shares with other staff members the frames of interactions, the transitions, and the sequences for creating a specific experience for patrons. The animation plan is analogous to the playwright's script or the sport coach's playbook. These documents communicate to a number of individuals their roles in producing a scenario of actions called a play. Actors, stage technicians, the director, and others take direction from the playwright's script to produce the play as it was designed and written. The players in different sport positions take direction from a coach's playbook about the scenario of actions that must occur for execution of a play.

In a similar way, the animation plan for a leisure program describes step-by-step, frame by frame, the movement of patrons through the program experience. A thorough understanding of the intended leisure experience and its facilitation is crucial for preparing the animation plan.

Exercise 13.1.
Practicing the Flow Chart Method

In groups of three, select a program and practice the FCM by following the four steps below. Refer to Exhibits 13.3 and 13.4 as guidelines for the exercise.

- Divide the program into its major functions.
- Analyze each major function independently by generating a random list of necessary tasks or activities that must be addressed.
- Prioritize each activity within the major functions by projecting the amount of time required to complete the task and establishing a deadline for that task.
- Place all of the activities on a flowchart.

This plan contains many cause-and-effect predictions of the program designer. The designer assumes that if X happens, patrons will respond in a predictable manner. For example, if there are identifiable places to form lines, the designer assumes patrons will queue in the designated area. All animation plans are predictions based on the programmer's knowledge of the patrons to be served; this information comes from data acquired through research or previous experiences with similar patrons.

Exhibit 13.5 contains an animation plan for a Fourth of July Balloon Ascension. The plan details what will happen to patrons and how staff members will interact with them to stage the experience intended. How detailed an animation plan will be depends on the complexity and size of a program. It should be detailed enough that staff members understand the total program and their role in staging the leisure experience intended. Now complete Exercise 13.2 (page 258).

Exhibit 13.5. Animation Plan for Balloon Ascension

Terminal Program Outcomes
- Special Event Staff will stage on July 4 a non-skill-based Fourth of July Balloon Ascension that will attract 500 or more individuals.
- The Special Event Staff will market and stage the event to attract families, as evidenced by 90% or more of the participants arriving as family units (mixed groups of adults and children).

Schedule
The Balloon Ascension is scheduled for 11:00 a.m. Staff should report at 6:00 a.m. to begin filling balloons with helium. Gates will open at 10:00 a.m. Most patrons will begin arriving at 10:30 a.m. Patriotic music will begin at 10:00 a.m. The event will be completed by 11:30 a.m.

Staff Orientation
Patrons who attend the Balloon Ascension will most likely be family units, so there will be many parents with small children. There will also be unaccompanied children from about 12 to 15 years of age. Since this is primarily a family event, there are usually few disciplinary problems. Patrons come fully expecting to be able to help their children launch their balloons in a pleasant, enjoyable atmosphere. Your job is to help them in a low-key, courteous manner to obtain a card and a balloon, tie the card to the balloon, and be in the appropriate area to launch their balloon on time.

Because we have a large number of staff members at this event to personalize leader–patron contact, we will not use the PA system except to help create an upbeat atmosphere with taped patriotic music and to announce the final instructions and countdown to launch. You will give directions and encourage interactions by speaking to small groups of individuals and keeping them informed about what must occur.

The day will probably be very hot. You may become easily irritated with patrons who do not understand instructions or procedures. It is likely that you will have to explain the same point over and over. Be sure you know how the event will operate and be prepared to answer questions. Patrons' pleasure at the event will depend on your courteous treatment of them. It will require effort to remain pleasant, but all staff members are expected to do so.

Exhibit 13.5 (continued)

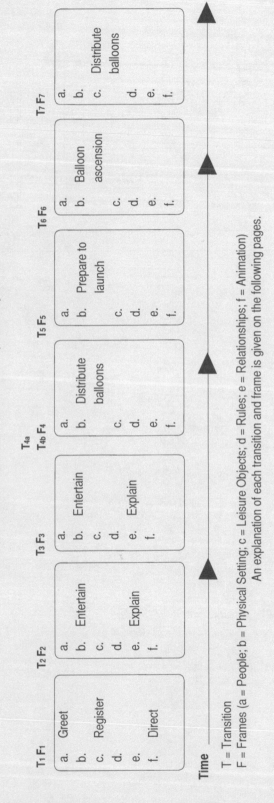

Scenario of Frames and Transitions (With Key Elements)

T = Transition

F = Frames (a = People; b = Physical Setting; c = Leisure Objects; d = Rules; e = Relationships; f = Animation)

An explanation of each transition and frame is given on the following pages.

Exhibit 13.5 (continued)

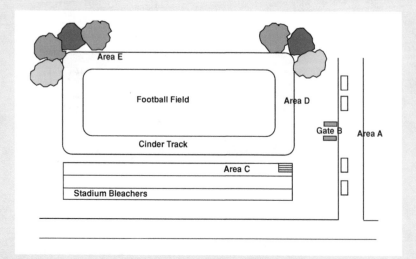

Animation of Program Production Elements

T1 Patrons are directed to the tables in Area A by staff assigned to this area.

F1

a. Patrons are greeted at the tables by staff.
b.
c. Postcards are completed for each participant.
d.
e. Staff will make an effort to address family units.
f. People are directed to Gate B.

T2 At Gate B patrons are directed to be seated in Area C.

F2[a] For those in Area C:

a. Families are seated together and are advised by staff in the area that at approximately 10:45 they will proceed to the track and be given their balloon, which must be tied securely to the card.
b. The U.S. flag will be flying from the flagpole, and the whole area decorated with red, white, and blue banners and streamers.
c. Patriotic music will be played and flyers announcing the remainder of the community-sponsored Fourth of July events will be distributed.
d. Emphasize that everyone will launch their balloons at the same time, on signal after a countdown.
e. Encourage parents to help make certain that balloons are tied securely to cards.

Exhibit 13.5 (continued)

T3   At approximately 10:45, Gate B is closed and patrons arriving from Area A are queued outside Gate B.

F3   For those queued in Area B:

a.   Staff will reassure the families in line that they will be admitted and that there are sufficient balloons for all.
b.
c.   Patriotic music will be played and flyers announcing the remainder of the community-sponsored Fourth of July events will be distributed.
d.   Emphasize that everyone will launch their balloons at the same time, on signal after a countdown.
e.   Encourage parents to help make certain that balloons are tied securely to cards.

T4[a]   Staff will move patrons seated in Area C, row by row, to Area D.

T4[b]   Once all of the patrons in Area C have been moved through Area D to Area E, Gate B will be opened and those in the queue outside Gate B will be moved through Area D to Area E. This may occur sooner if the queue outside Gate B gets too long and the staff in Area D seem to have the capacity to handle more patrons.

F4   At Area D:

a.   Staff will greet families when possible. Helium-filled balloons will be distributed to all participants with cards—only one per participant.
b.
c.   Getting balloons and tying cards to balloons are the focus of attention. Patriotic music continues.
d.   Emphasize that everyone will launch their balloons at the same time, on signal after a countdown.
e.   Encourage parents to help make certain that balloons are tied securely to cards.
f.   Everyone must be moved through Area D and onto Area E.

T5   It is important that staff effectively and courteously move the first patrons from Area D to the end of Area E, or there will not be room for all patrons. This will be accomplished by individual requests from staff members, not by PA announcements.

F5   At Area E:

a.   Parents prepare their children to launch their balloons.
b.   Staff should keep patrons on the track and off the grass infield.
c.   Getting balloons to launch is the primary focus of this frame.
d.   Staff should encourage patrons to hold onto the balloon until the signal to launch is given.
e.   Encourage parents to help their children with the activity.

Exhibit 13.5 (continued)

T6 After all of the balloons are distributed and people are assembled in Area E, the PA announcer will stop the patriotic music and give people final instructions about the event. They will then give a countdown, and at the end of the countdown an air horn will sound. This is the signal to launch.

F6 At Area F—after the launch:

a. Parents and their children will stand and watch the balloons fly away for about 3–5 minutes after launch.
b. Staff should keep patrons on the track and off the grass infield.
c. Watching the balloons ascend is the primary focus of this frame.

T7 As balloons fly out of sight and the patrons get ready to leave, they should be directed to Gate B. Staff should attempt to keep them on the track during this process. At Area D, each child will receive a balloon to take home. It is important for staff to assure parents that there are enough balloons for everyone so there is not a rush to Gate B.

F7 At Area D and Gate B

a. Staff and patron interaction is fostered by giving each child a balloon as everyone leaves. Flyers announcing the rest of the community Fourth of July events are also made available.
b. Patriotic music begins again. Getting a balloon to take home is a key in this frame.

Exercise 13.2.
Animation Plan

Get into groups of five students. Each group should prepare an animation plan for a 1-hour Valentine party to be held in your classroom. Discuss the following questions:

- Is the plan sufficiently detailed?
- Do staff members understand the leisure experience you are trying to create and their role in facilitating it?
- Does the plan explain how patrons will move through each activity and from one activity to the next?

Scheduling Programs

Developing a comprehensive schedule of programs in an agency is an important task. Appropriate scheduling maximizes attendance, increases patron satisfaction, and efficiently uses agency venues. Programmers must consider four elements simultaneously in scheduling program services: balance, impact, location, and timing.

Balance

A program schedule needs to be balanced along two dimensions. First, it is wise for programmers to avoid simultaneously scheduling similar activities that appeal to the same target group of patrons. To avoid overlap, they must be familiar with all of the agency's program services and with programs being offered by other providers in a given service area. Second, scheduling a balanced variety of activity types at a given time maximizes the attendance at all activities. For example, at a given time, it would be best for programmers to schedule an art, drama, individual sport, team sport, and fitness activity, rather than five team sport activities.

Impact

In developing a schedule, programmers should understand how different activities scheduled in close proximity to each other affect patron enjoyment. For example, scheduling a Valentine Dance for teenagers and a Valentine Dance for senior citizens at the same time in different rooms of the same facility would not be a good idea. Each group would adversely affect the enjoyment of the other because of incompatible age groups, unacceptable sound volume choices for each group, incompatible activity requirements for the same space, and similar problems.

Location

The location of a program will affect attendance. Individuals seek out programs that are accessible. Access promotes use; therefore, it is wise for programmers to schedule programs at locations that are accessible to the target population.

Timing

The time when a program is offered will partly account for attendance at the program. When scheduling a time for a program, programmers should know the personal schedules of typical target patrons. Any program competes for all other available uses of patrons' time, so programmers need to know the time use habits of patrons to make wise decisions about when to hold a program.

Information about program balance is developed from acceptable practice in the profession. Offering a balanced program is generally recommended, although documented local interest and past participation history would justify offering an unbalanced set of program offerings. Programmers derive information about avoiding adverse effects through a thorough understanding of and previous experience with an event.

In scheduling the location and timing of events, the programmer has two choices. First, market research data or needs analysis data should include questions that will enable the programming staff to determine when individuals are available and where they are located. Obviously, scheduling programs when patrons can participate in them and close to their residences is the best option. Second, facilities are not always available at the appropriate time or patrons' schedules are unknown. In these instances, the programmer develops a program schedule based on availability or past practice with the target population.

Scheduling Program Cycles

The time frame for cycling program changes and for periods of operation varies from agency to agency. Community customs and accepted practice most often determine the cycle used. This section explains the usual program scheduling cycles.

Annual

To develop an annual schedule, programmers first obtain a calendar with lots of space for making entries for each day. They scan the calendar and mark the days on which obvious programming events fall. Christmas, Easter, Independence Day, Jewish holidays, Memorial Day, and Thanksgiving are examples of days when special programs will most likely be operated. Additionally, they identify any special days or seasons for which local custom dictates the need for a special program. For example, flower festivals during the spring or fall are popular in many communities, Cinco de Mayo (May 5) is the day that individuals of Mexican descent celebrate their victory in the Battle of Puebla, and Juneteenth (June 19) is the day many African Americans in Texas celebrate the implementation of the Emancipation Proclamation. Additional programming ideas can be obtained from *Chase's Calendar of Events*, a comprehensive day-by-day directory of special days, weeks, and months.

It is also important to block out programming seasons. Many public park and recreation systems organize their program offerings around winter, spring, summer, and fall. They need to specify dates on which these seasons start and end. Other periods around which program seasons can be scheduled include every 2 weeks, every 4 weeks, monthly, every 6 weeks, bimonthly, and so on. After identifying operating seasons for the year, programmers can specify program services that will fill each season.

It is equally important for programmers to identify dates that must be avoided. Local custom dictates these dates. For example, in many communities Wednesday night is church night. Because of this, schools and public recreation departments avoid scheduling events on Wednesday nights.

Other Scheduling Cycles

As suggested, many agencies schedule their programming cycles according to the seasons of the year. This arrangement usually makes good sense because many recreational activities are dictated by the weather.

Some recreation operations can run only seasonally. For example, marinas, ski resorts, outdoor ice-skating rinks, golf courses in many parts of the country, and water parks are usually seasonal operations. In these cases, the programmer first specifies when the operation will open and close, when developing a program schedule.

In some settings, other events dictate scheduling cycles. In employee recreation, for example, production schedules sometimes influence the organization of workers' time and therefore when patrons will be available for programs. On some military training bases, recreation scheduling seasons conform closely to the training schedule. If service personnel are rotated in and out of a base after completing a 10-week training course, then the recreation department's programming cycles coordinate with this schedule.

In a similar manner, different agencies schedule program services with other cycling frames, including monthly, weekly, daily, or hourly scheduling. Regardless of the time frame, the general method of scheduling is similar. Now complete Exercise 13.3 (page 262).

Facility Scheduling

Scheduling a facility is one of the easiest tasks for programmers to complete. However, an ineffective scheduling system leads to double-booking, with much patron displeasure and bad public relations for the agency. To be able to schedule competently, programmers need to have a good scheduling system and pay constant attention to implementing the operational details of the system.

The most foolproof system involves creating a scheduling matrix appropriate for the facility. The matrix includes each facility and each hour that it may be scheduled. It shows blank spaces that represent the potential hours available for programs. Exhibit 13.6 (page 263) shows a matrix for a small neighborhood recreation center with two rooms.

When scheduling the specific facility, the programmer writes the name of the individual, group, or program that will occupy the space onto the schedule in the appropriate place. In this way, each space can be scheduled only once. To avoid confusion, the organization should have only one scheduling matrix. All methods, even computerized scheduling programs, use this simple, basic procedure.

Use a calendar for the month of December in the current year. Develop a program schedule for December for two facilities.

The first facility is a private health club with a swimming pool, weight room, running track, 16 racquetball courts, a snack bar, and a nursery. The facility is usually open from 6 a.m. through midnight Monday through Saturday and from 9 a.m. through midnight on Sunday. Membership in the health club consists of mostly families with school-age children.

The second facility is a recreation center on a military base. The facility includes a game room with a pool table and a table tennis table; a hall for banquets, dances, card playing and so forth, complete with a catering kitchen; a snack bar with video games; and a TV lounge. Eighty percent of the base population will be on leave beginning December 20. Those remaining after that will be mostly young singles. The commander wants the recreation center open and operating every day of the month.

Discuss the following:
- What data do you need to collect first?
- What are the most obvious dates for scheduling special programs?

Facility Scheduling Trends

- Digital signage is rapidly replacing the posting of paper facility schedules on bulletin boards.
- Rental forms are increasingly available online, as well as online facility schedule viewers to check for conflicts.
- Links to street maps, parking, and directions to facilities are commonly posted with facility rental information.
- Rental forms may be submitted by e-mail or printed and sent by U.S. mail.

How, then, can scheduling go wrong? Inattention to detail is the most frequent error. Busy staff members may give out a reservation but fail to write it on the master schedule. This error often results in double-booking. It is obviously important for the agency to have a system designed so that each space available can be scheduled only once. Normally, recreation operations do not overbook facilities for which they take reservations.

The most detailed scheduling matrix used in recreation operations is a facility schedule. Exhibit 13.7 (page 264) shows a scheduling matrix for a racquetball club. Properly scheduling such a facility requires a schedule for each day of operation, with an hourly schedule for each court in the facility. Programmers can develop other facility schedules using a similar system.

Exhibit 13.6. Recreation Center Schedule

Upper-Level Room

Time	M	T	W	H	F	SA	SU
8:00							
9:00							
10:00							
11:00							
12:00							
1:00							
2:00							
3:00							
4:00							
5:00							
6:00							
7:00							
8:00							
9:00							
10:00							
11:00							

Lower-Level Room

Time	M	T	W	H	F	SA	SU
8:00							
9:00							
10:00							
11:00							
12:00							
1:00							
2:00							
3:00							
4:00							
5:00							
6:00							
7:00							
8:00							
9:00							
10:00							
11:00							

Exhibit 13.7. Raquetball Court Scheduling Matrix

Day:					Date:			
	Court							
Time	**1**	**2**	**3**	**4**	**5**	**6**	**7**	**8**
6:00 a.m.								
7:00 a.m.								
8:00 a.m.								
9:00 a.m.								
10:00 a.m.								
11:00 a.m.								
12:00 p.m.								
1:00 p.m.								
2:00 p.m.								
3:00 p.m.								
4:00 p.m.								
5:00 p.m.								
6:00 p.m.								
7:00 p.m.								
8:00 p.m.								
9:00 p.m.								
10:00 p.m.								
11:00 p.m.								

In scheduling a facility, programmers must not ignore the need for facility maintenance, custodial care, and setup and teardown time. An attractive, clean, well-maintained facility contributes to patron satisfaction. However, to accommodate the level of maintenance and custodial care desired, the agency must schedule an appropriate amount of time for these operations.

Conclusion

Programmers use the program plan to share the staging of an event (i.e., the operational details of what must occur) so that patrons can have the leisure experience intended. Writing the plan requires that the designer clarify design and operational details. A written program plan contains enough detail that a different programmer can duplicate the program.

A management plan provides organizational details for the many activities that must be accomplished for the programmer to implement the program. Management planning identifies all activities that must be completed for the programmer to implement the program and places them in the order in which they need to occur. The FCM is the most frequently used technique for implementing recreation services.

A unique component of a recreation program plan is the animation plan. This plan explicates the scenario of interactions—including the contents of each frame, the transitions, and their sequence—that must occur for patrons to have the leisure experience intended.

For maximum attendance and efficient use of facilities, programmers needs to set up an overall design in the scheduling of recreation program services. They can use a variety of time frames for scheduling programs. Documented patron preferences are the best data for use in scheduling. They can accomplish facility scheduling by developing a scheduling matrix appropriate for the facility.

References

Crossley, J. C., & Jamieson, L. (1997). *Introduction to commercial and entrepreneurial recreation* (Rev. ed.). Champaign, IL: Sagamore.

Devine, M. A., & Kotowski, L. (1999). Inclusive leisure services: Results of a national survey of park and recreation departments. *Journal of Park and Recreation Administration, 17*(4), 56–72.

Kliem, R. L. (1986). *The secrets of successful project management.* New York, NY: Wiley.

Kraus, R. G., & Curtis, J. E. (2000). *Creative management in recreation, parks, and leisure services* (6th ed.). Boston, MA: McGraw-Hill.

Moder, J. J., Phillips, C. R., & Davis, E. W. (1983). *Project management with CPM, PERT, and precedence diagramming* (3rd ed.). New York, NY: Van Nostrand Reinhold.

Murphy, J., & Howard, D. (1977). *Delivery of community leisure services: A holistic approach.* Philadelphia, PA: Lea and Febiger.

Rossman, J. R. (2012). *White paper: The agile organization: Transforming your agency to survive and thrive in any economy.* Arlington, VA: National Recreation and Park Association.

Russell, R. V. (1982). *Planning programs in recreation.* St. Louis, MO: C.V. Mosby.

Having Fun at Summer Camp
Photo courtesy of Elmhurst Park District. Photo by Kassandra Collins.

14 *Techniques for Program Promotion*

KEY TERMS

Promotion, Communication, Persuasion, Channel, Brochure Copy, News Release, Flyer, Electronic Communication, Promotional Technologies

Step 7: Implementation

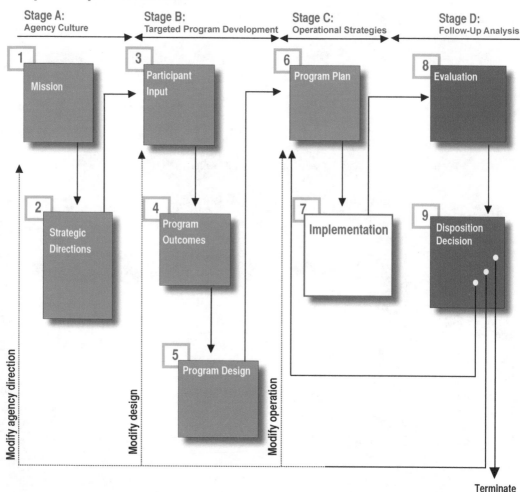

Howard and Crompton (1980) defined promotion as "basically communication that seeks to inform, persuade, or remind members of a potential client group of an agency's programs and services" (p. 448). To this list, Crompton and Lamb (1986) added "to educate." Kotler and Andreasen (1987) suggested that "any communication process involves a message sender and a message receiver (a target audience)" (p. 506). To truly communicate in promoting program services, the programmer must not only be concerned with the form and content of the message to be sent, but also must understand the educational and cultural background of those who are intended to receive the message.

Promotion will be more successful if accompanied by services that have been developed within a marketing framework (Russell & Verrill, 1986). A good promotional campaign cannot sustain participation in services that are not well designed and based on identified participants' wants. Only one of the four primary marketing elements—promotion—must also be supported with a product that is well designed, delivered at the right time and place, and made available at the appropriate price.

An agency's promotional campaign, then, involves fulfilling one or more of the following functions: to inform, to educate, to persuade, or to remind. There is some disagreement about which of these functions is most appropriate for a leisure service agency to use to attract participants. Which strategies will dominate an agency's promotional campaign depends on the type of leisure service organization offering the program and the location of the program in the program life cycle (more on this in Chapter 22).

Persuasion

Persuasion is a different activity than the other three forms of promotion because it aims to bring about a change in attitude or behavior (Manfredo & Bright, 1991). Persuasive communication theory suggests that individuals can be persuaded with central or peripheral methods (Ajzen, 1992). The central method assumes participants exercise a high degree of information processing through rational behavior that involves a thorough examination and evaluation of the ideas and information presented, which results in selecting the best alternative from all that are possible.

> An agency's promotional campaign, then, involves fulfilling one or more of the following functions: to inform, to educate, to persuade, or to remind.

The peripheral method assumes that participants do not thoroughly process information, because of a lack of interest, ability, or time. In this instance, persuasion occurs with factors tangential to the content of the message, for example, the credibility of the presenter or the communication channel.

Most practitioners today recommend using advertising strategies that account for both methods (Manfredo, Bright, & Haas, 1992), because participants likely use both methods for processing information about leisure participation. For example, a person may carefully decide to begin participating in an exercise program and be persuaded to do so with information provided from several sources, which shows a high degree of rational processing. However, after deciding to participate, the person may spend little time selecting a health club to join. In fact, the decision may be based on an advertised testimonial from a local professional athlete featured in the health club's advertisement, a decision that shows a low degree of information processing.

> Persuasion is a different activity than the other three forms of promotion because it aims to bring about a change in attitude or behavior.

The persuasiveness of any form of communication will be affected by comprehension of the advertisement, effects of prior knowledge, involvement with the topic, repetition of the message, credibility of the source, and attitudes toward the advertisement (Manfredo et al., 1992). Current information about persuasive communication is too voluminous to reiterate here. However, several myths that persist must be dispelled. First, too much material is written at a reading level above the ability of the intended recipients, and consequently, they cannot comprehend it. The programmer must know the target market well to correct this.

Second, information acquired from direct experience has the most salience and will therefore be the most difficult for programmers to alter. Inexperienced or infrequent participants of a given activity will be easier to influence than experienced, frequent users. This is also why it is critical that programmers ensure the agency is ready to provide a service effectively and efficiently prior to launching it. The knowledge and image that accompany a bad experience with an agency's service, acquired from direct experience, is difficult for programmers to alter.

Third, continued repetition of an advertisement does not increase the recipient's favorableness toward the advertisement in a linear fashion. There is usually an initial increase in favorableness, followed by a point of diminishing returns when it declines. The dynamics of this variation depend on a number of factors, including the type of advertisement, the complexity of it, and the attitude of the recipient about the advertisement (Manfredo et al., 1992).

Persuasion is usually accomplished through advertising, which is not neutral. Advertising is at least a mildly aggressive attempt to persuade someone to purchase the sponsor's product or service (Russell & Verrill, 1986). Commercial recreation operations often use an aggressive advertising campaign to attract customers to use their services instead of the services of another supplier; that is, they try to increase their market share.

Communication Channels

The promotion should bring the agency's services to the attention of the intended audience, that is, its target market. Kotler and Andreasen (1987) explained that "a channel is a conduit for bringing together a marketer and a target customer at some place and time for the purpose of facilitating a transaction" (p. 473). Leisure service agencies normally use at least two channels to promote their programs.

One channel is aimed at the general public. Because of a commitment to equity of access, municipal leisure service agencies in particular inform all potential participants about available services, thus allowing and encouraging general access to programs. Although commercial recreation operations may conduct a promotional campaign directed at the general public, equal access to program information, in these cases, is a marketing rather than an equity decision.

A second channel is a more targeted effort directed to the target market for the service. This second channel informs and reminds the individuals who are most likely to participate in the program. Targeting a promotional campaign is considered more cost effective because it places information about a program in the hands of the individuals most likely to purchase or use the service.

The usual medium for the channel directed to the general public is a publication such as an agency brochure that includes the agency's services for a given period. These publications educate the public about the agency, its services, and its facilities. Agencies often mail their brochures to community residents and generally make them available on their website in a downloadable format. Additionally, they may send news releases to a local newspaper. The usual medium for the more targeted effort is an in-house-produced, single-page flyer that they distribute at recreation centers, at their main office, at neighborhood locations, and perhaps through mail or e-mail to previous participants of the same or similar programs. Agencies have increasingly been using digital signage and social media platforms to deliver material that would have previously been placed in a single-page printed flyer.

Some larger agencies employ communication specialists, who often develop organization-wide policies requiring that they either write or review all communications from the agency. This ensures a unified message and brand for the agency. Even medium-sized agencies may become overwhelmed by the amount of communication and often leave the initial preparation of copy to the employee offering the service. Thus, to promote program services effectively, programmers need to be proficient at writing copy that describes their programs and services for inclusion in a general agency publication. They must also be proficient at preparing public service news releases for the local press and be able to produce single-page flyers to promote a program. Requiring that these communication pieces be reviewed by a communication specialist usually means they will need to be prepared with a longer lead time than would otherwise be needed. This review requirement may be an overlay policy that is required for what is explained in the following three sections. The remainder of this chapter discusses techniques for producing each major conduit for communication.

Writing Brochure Copy

Writing copy that effectively promotes a program is challenging. Unfortunately, many agencies only simply inform participants about their services, because information copy is the easiest to write. Copy that simply informs participants does not usually include any more than the basic five Ws and the H that reporters use to ensure the completeness of a story, that is, who, what, when, where, why, and how (Ryan & Tankard, 1977).

Well-written copy captures the expectations of the target market and conveys how the program will provide benefits by meeting these expectations (Leffel, 1983). Consider the two pieces of copy for a Zumba class in Exhibit 14.1 (page 273). One piece of copy was taken from a seasonal brochure published by a municipal recreation

> Well-written copy also captures the expectations of the target market and conveys how the program will provide benefits by meeting these expectations.

department. The other was taken from a publication of a commercial recreation operation. (We have altered both sets of copy to protect the identities of the agencies.) Can you guess which is from the commercial agency? Which one captures the interest of the reader? Which one communicates the benefits to be derived from participation? Does either overstate what a participant could reasonably expect to accomplish in a few hours of instruction? What else do you notice about the copy?

Writing creative copy is an art. It is therefore difficult to offer cookbook solutions about writing good copy. Foster (1990) offered nine guidelines for preparing creative copy:

1. Clarity—simple, clear sentences and words are preferred.
2. Details—providing detail creates familiarity with a program.
3. Use the senses—using references to the senses keeps a reader's interest and humanizes the content of the copy.
4. Use personal experiences—use both your own and those of your satisfied customers to create interest and association with a program and its benefits.
5. Use conversational speech—reading dialogue creates a sense of "being there" and sharing in an experience.
6. Opposition—contrasting long with short sentences, fast with slow pace of reading, and so on, creates interest.
7. General versus detail—anchor detail (usually unknown information) to more general information that is more likely known.
8. Repeat—repeat and repeat words, phrases, and details that are strong and add support to one's point when repeated.
9. Parallel construction of sentences and phrases—this is a more sophisticated form of repetition that can be used for additional emphasis. (pp. 29–31)

Writing concise, informative, and interesting copy for a promotional brochure requires practice, practice, and more practice. Now complete Exercise 14.1.

Preparing News Releases

Writing news releases requires preparing longer copy than that for promotional brochures or flyers. Space in newspapers for items considered news is free to the sponsoring agency. However, when news releases are submitted, the writer competes for a limited amount of space with other organizations seeking publicity. To increase the probability that a news release will be published, the programmer should know and meet the newspaper's deadlines and prepare well-written copy.

Many newspapers rewrite news releases submitted by programmers. Expect your wonderfully written copy to be rewritten. Newspaper editors know that the same news release has probably been submitted to several outlets, and they do not

Exhibit 14.1. Sample Promotional Copy

Copy Example 1

Zumba®

Come have fun with Zumba®! Learn how to do the Latin-inspired dance fitness class under the guidance of a knowledgeable Zumba® instructor. No running shoes or cross trainer shoes. Instructor: Esperanza Perez. Class: Z4756. Day: T/TH. Time: 6:30–7:30 am. Length: 8 weeks. Start: October 6. Fee: $50.

Copy Example 2

Zumba® - Come join the party!

Zumba®, the fun and easy way to get in shape, is for people all levels and all ages. Zumba® is taught in a manner that creates a welcoming workout atmosphere where everyone feels accepted regardless of age, ability, and/or fitness level. Zumba's® balanced workout mixes fast and slow Latin rhythms with resistance training movements. All you need is some dance shoes (not tennis or running shoes), a T-shirt, and comfortable shorts or sweat pants. An individual program for your specific needs and goals will be designed for you. You will develop a clear understanding of necessary fitness and body-toning moves through dancing routines that include Merengue, Salsa, Mambo, and much more!

Your Zumba® fitness instructor, Esperanza Perez, is trained in both Zumba® Gold (for teaching the true beginner) and Zumba® Toning (for teaching body-sculpting techniques and strength training). A Zumba® instructor for 10 years, Esperanza is known in the region for leading 5 Biggest Loser Competitions through Zumba®! Dates: October 10, 12, 17, 19, 24, 27, 31, November 2, 7, 9, 14, 16, 21, 23, 28, 30. 6:00–7:00 am. Fee: $84.

Exercise 14.1.
Writing Brochure Copy

Write at least four pieces of brochure copy for a pastry baking class. In one, emphasize the setting in which the program will occur. In the second, call attention to the opportunity for sociability that the program will present. In the third, highlight the opportunity for personal achievement that the program will present. Write one more with an emphasis of your choice.

Program Facts

Who: Program participants and the instructor, Allison Kuzera, head pastry chef for the Fairmont Hotel, Clarksberry bake-off winner for 2019, and state fair bake-off winter for 2020!

What: Holiday pastry baking class, including cookies, fruit cakes, and ethnic breads.

When: One night per week, 6:30–9:30 p.m. for the six weeks before Christmas.

Where: In the test kitchen of the Fairmont Hotel.

Why: To become better at baking, to prepare excellent holiday baked goods, to make Christmas presents for family, friends, and others.

How: Sign up by November 1, 2020, at the Recreation Department office; class fee is $65, including all supplies.

want the same copy to appear in their own paper. However, many smaller papers do not have sufficient staff to rewrite news releases, so the copy prepared will often appear verbatim in these outlets. In fact, well-written copy that requires little or no rewrite will probably be given priority and published because of tight production schedules. News organizations live by the clock. If you do not meet their deadlines, the materials submitted will not be published, no matter how well written or important.

> News organizations live by the clock. If you do not meet their deadlines, the materials submitted will not be published, no matter how well written or important.

Preparing a news release involves writing copy in a specific style and preparing the copy according to standard news writing conventions. All news stories should be brief but accurate. They should have a good lead and be written in the inverted pyramid form of writing. The lead is the first paragraph or two of a story that immediately lets the reader know the topic of the story. Ryan and Tankard (1977) suggested, "Good, straight news leads quickly satisfy a reader's need and desire for information, and attract a reader to the rest of the story" (p. 101).

The inverted pyramid form of writing requires that the most important pieces of information be placed at the beginning of a story. The assumption is that the reader may stop reading at any point. The story should therefore be written so that the reader has the pertinent facts early in the piece and each succeeding paragraph contains progressively less important information.

Formatting a news story is also important. A newsroom is a busy place, and a great deal of copy crosses an editor's desk each day. Each story should therefore have a slug placed in the top left corner of each page of the story. The slug includes the writer's name, address, e-mail address, and phone number; the title of the story; a release date for the story; and the approximate number of words. All news releases should be double-spaced to allow room for the editor's proofing marks and corrections. If the story is longer than one page, the bottom of each page, except for the last page, should end with "more." The end of the story is signified by "end." Exhibit 14.2 shows a sample news release for a balloon flying contest. After reading the news release, complete Exercise 14.2.

It is important for programmers to be selective in the types of materials they submit to newspapers. Not everything done in the agency is newsworthy. The programmer is most likely to have material published if it meets one or more of the following news values (Ryan & Tankard, 1977):
- News events that involve local events with local people. Almost all news releases by not-for-profit recreation agencies meet this requirement.
- News releases that are timely. For example, an announcement of a Turkey Trot race has a high likelihood of being included in a series of articles about Thanksgiving.

Exhibit 14.2. Sample News Release

NEWS RELEASE
Anytown Park and Recreation Department

Fred Bloom
Recreation Supervisor
(xxx) 565-2651
30th Annual 4th of July Balloon Fly
Release any time after June 20, 2020
Approximately 220 words

30th Annual Fourth of July Balloon Fly

Silver balloons will be used when Anytown Park and Recreation Department conducts its 30th annual Fourth of July Balloon Flying Contest. The Balloon Fly will take place at Veterans Park, 5th and Locust, at 11 a.m. Registration will begin at 10 a.m. There is no charge, and all children through 16 years of age may participate.

Last year, the winning balloon flew over 300 miles to eastern Arizona. The farthest any balloon has ever flown over the past 24 years is 500 miles. In 1976, a balloon flew the 500 miles to western New Mexico in about 12 hours.

The silver balloons being used this year to celebrate the 30th anniversary of the event are several mils thicker than the balloons usually used. The extra thickness will allow the balloons to remain airborne longer and thus fly farther. According to Sid Kinder, Assistant Director of the Park and Recreation Department, "We expect to set a new record this year."

Usually about 1,500 balloons are released each year. Mr. Kinder said, "This event is very popular with families. We want everyone to know that all children are welcome and every one of them will get a balloon to release." In case of rain, the event will be held at the same time and place on the following Saturday morning, July 11, 2020.

Exercise 14.2.
Preparing News Releases

In class, critique the news release included in Exhibit 14.2 by answering the following questions:

- Does the news release have a good lead?
- Is the news release written in the inverted pyramid style?
- Does the news release invite participation?

Now rewrite the news release.

- News releases that involve prominent individuals or institutions. When the mayor of a local community joins a fitness program at a local YMCA, an event that would not normally be newsworthy (i.e., someone joining the fitness program) becomes so.
- Stories involving a large number of people and that have human interest are newsworthy. Tot swimming programs always generate interesting copy and excellent pictures for a news story.
- Stories that involve novel happenings are almost always newsworthy. Agencies that have zoos have an almost unlimited supply of novel, interesting stories.

Successfully obtaining space in newspapers requires that the programmer selectively submit newsworthy items that are well written in a journalistic style. Some newspapers have policies about distributing space to local agencies and organizations. It is therefore important for the agency to understand what it most needs to do to get published in the local paper. A frank discussion with the news editor about the most essential pieces of information that need published in the paper is often necessary so that the agency uses its allocation wisely.

Preparing Flyers

Flyer Production

Almost all agencies use in-house-produced flyers to promote their programs. The quality of these flyers varies among and within agencies. The quality of a program flyer that promotes a service often depends on the revenue of the program.

Regardless of the agency, programmers will likely need to be skilled in producing single-page promotional flyers. To produce them, the programmer will do the design, artwork, layout, and copywriting, and may even have to reproduce the flyer.

Flyer Design

Nelson (1981) stated, "Designing means creative action that fulfills its purpose" (p. 112). When designing a flyer, programmers should remember its purpose to inform, educate, remind, or persuade individuals to participate in a program. The design should include attractive artwork, good layout, well-written copy with complete information, and excellent quality production. Unfortunately, many flyers produced in-house are often of poor quality and give participants a bad image of the agency and its programs. Taking the effort to produce well-designed flyers is essential to an agency's overall promotional campaign.

To design flyers, many programmers use desktop publishing software applications such as Microsoft Publisher and Adobe Spark. These applications include templates; however, many practitioners look at flyers from other agencies for design ideas. When preparing a flyer, programmers often select

> It is important that the images contribute to the purpose of the flyer.

the images first because these become the central theme around which they develop the rest of the flyer. It is important that the images contribute to the purpose of the flyer. Many practitioners consult Google Images or Pinterest when searching for suitable images. Other websites such as Shutterstock and iStock offer a wide range of quality images for purchase. Agencies are increasingly using photographs of past programs and events for their flyers, as well. For photos that feature agency participants, it is essential for programmers to follow policies related to photo releases. Software programs such as Photoshop and Illustrator allow the programmer to manipulate images, for example, by resizing and cropping. To find interesting fonts online for flyer copy, consider the DaFont website. Thus, programmers can easily produce attractive flyer copy in a short time using software applications and images. Exhibit 14.3 (page 278) is an example of a flyer with copy and illustrations produced with Microsoft Publisher.

Formal and Informal Balance

The flyer should be at rest with itself, leaving the reader with an overall pleasing visual image. Balance can be achieved through formal or informal balance. In formal balance, everything done on one half of the flyer repeats on the other half. Formal balance can be achieved with symmetry.

Informal balance is asymmetrical. An asymmetrical layout that is balanced is a more difficult undertaking for someone who is inexperienced at layout. The objective is still an overall pleasing visual image, but it is more difficult for the designer to achieve. Informal balance can be achieved through arranging the various design elements in different ways until an overall visual balance is achieved. Neither copy nor illustrations should be finalized until the desired balance is obtained.

Proportion of Elements

Proportion is the relationship of sizes of the various design elements to each other and to the overall flyer. For example, what is the proportion of illustration to copy? What is the proportion of the title lettering to the rest of the flyer? What is the proportion of white space, that is, the ratio of space left blank to the space printed with copy or illustrations? Ideally, the flyer should have enough white space that it looks uncluttered.

To achieve the most pleasing overall look, the programmer should avoid arranging spaces with obvious mathematical relationships. Dividing a flyer into halves or quadrants is less interesting than other ways of dividing space. Unequal divisions of space result in the most interesting flyers.

Sequence of Presentation

The layout determines how the reader progresses through the flyer while reading it. The layout presents the copy and the illustrations in a logical sequence that leads the reader through the flyer to a conclusion or final point. In Western civilization, individuals naturally progress through written material by reading from left to right and from top to bottom. The layout should accommodate this habit.

Exhibit 14.3. Sample Program Flyer

🍁 NEWTOWN PARKS AND RECREATION DEPARTMENT

BLUES STYLE GUITAR CLASS

PLAY BLUES STYLE GUITAR WITH EASE!
LEARN THE FUNDAMENTAL 12-BAR BLUES,
TURNAROUNDS, AND ENDINGS, AND HOW
TO IMPROVISE IN OUR 10-WEEK PROGRAM.
BASIC BLUES CHORD PROGRESSIONS WILL
BE TAUGHT, AS WELL AS FINGER-PICKING
TECHNIQUES FOR THE RIGHT HAND.

FOR MORE INFORMATION OR SPECIAL ACCOMMODATIONS, PLEASE CONTACT
NEWTON PARKS AND RECREATION DEPARTMENT AT 498-2249

Learn a skill
that will bring a lifetime of
enjoyment &
satisfaction

NEWTON COMMUNITY CENTER
4TH AND VINE
NEWTON, AL 48620

PHONE: 493-498-2249
FAX: 439-569-8530

$100 FOR 10 LESSONS

NEWTOWN COMMUNITY CENTER

SATURDAYS, JAN 4-MAR 8

FROM 10:00-11:30AM

INSTRUCTOR: NOELLE SELKOW

REGISTER ONLINE AT WWW.NEWTOWN.ORG

To add interest, however, programmers can redirect how the eye will move through a flyer by taking advantage of other likely sequences of eye movement. Nelson (1981) suggested, "The eye moves naturally, too, from big elements to little elements, from black elements to lighter elements, from color to non-color, from unusual shapes to usual shapes" (p. 119). With either type of sequence, the programmer wants to enable the eye to progress smoothly through the contents of the flyer.

Unity of Content

The illustrations, copy, and overall look of a flyer should make a harmonious presentation. The flyer should make a single statement to the reader and not create visual or rhetorical dissonance. An example of visual dissonance would be the inclusion of photographs and line drawing on the same flyer. Using two styles of type—for example, Old English and Western—on the same flyer would create visual dissonance. Undesirable rhetorical dissonance would be created through the use of different verb tenses in different sections of the copy or through writing in different points of view (i.e., first, second, third person) in various sections of the copy.

Emphasis

Certain elements of the flyer should be emphasized: the headline, artwork, or copy. For flyers with several pieces of artwork, one should dominate. For those with several copy blocks, one should receive primary emphasis. When nothing on a flyer is emphasized, everything and nothing stand out! When laying out a flyer, programmers should take control of what will be emphasized, ensure it is the dominant feature, and make certain nothing else upstages it.

Nelson (1981) suggested that the best test of good layout is removing one element. The relationship of elements should be so strong that after one is removed, all others need to be repositioned. If this is not the case, the original layout was not properly designed.

Writing Copy

Copy for flyers is similar to copy for the general circulation brochure. But brochure copy will normally be written in paragraph form and clustered together, whereas flyer copy may be split apart and dispersed throughout the flyer. It is important, therefore, that the programmer not split apart the sentences of the brochure copy and display it on the flyer. Normally, the programmer needs to expand brochure copy into complete, logical passages that can then be distributed throughout the flyer and intermingled with artwork and other illustrations.

Production Methods

Many agencies use laser printers for producing a small number of flyers. In any case, the programmer will need to produce a good, clean copy. This means that the flyer used for reproduction will need to have good contrast between the font used and the background. What you present for reproduction is what you get! Printing will not cover up sloppy work, bad layout, or poorly written copy. Print shops offer cost-effective options for high quantity orders. Flyers, brochures, poster files, and the like can easily be uploaded to the print shop, where high-quality prints can be produced on digital printers.

Although an agency's promotional campaign may involve more than what has been discussed above and include oversight by a communication specialist, in most cases programmers will be expected to write clear, concise copy describing their programs. This copy will be included in agency brochures, news releases, and flyers. Promoting a program, then, is one of the first processes in implementing a program. The promotional campaign for any program must be started well in advance of registration for the program. Finally, well-written and well-designed promotional materials should be made available to the target market on a timely basis; otherwise, they will be of little benefit in promoting programs.

Innovative Promotional Technologies

Like many other industries, the leisure service industry has begun to embrace technological advances for promoting their programs. This section describes how technology enhances program promotion through use of the Web, social media, e-mail, specialty publications, tourism and chamber of commerce offices, and cable TV public access programs. The authors are grateful to Slottag (1999) for some of the information included in this section.

Web

The idea for the World Wide Web began in Switzerland in 1989 at the CERN (translated from French as the European Particle Physics Laboratory). Researcher Tim Berners-Lee wanted to create an efficient and easy environment for information sharing among geographically separated research teams. Two years later, the Web arrived. The Web is generally used for graphic design of information, dissemination of research, browsing and ordering of products, client and customer support, and display of creative arts (December & Randall, 1994).

Nearly all leisure service agencies and businesses have websites, many of which are expansive and interactive. Readers are encouraged to visit Summit Metro Parks' homepage at http://www.summitmetroparks.org/Home.aspx. By browsing websites, customers can learn about and register for programs and services, contact agency staff, see images of venues, download annual reports and brochures, and become involved through volunteering. Websites, if designed well, are excellent promotional tools. They must be maintained with up-to-date information so that they are a current source of information. Agencies will have to decide who will design the website. Many find that it is more efficient to contract out the service because of the amount of time consumed by design and maintenance. In addition to websites, recreation and tourism agencies use a variety of social media to communicate with their constituents. The following section explains some of the common social media used and tips for their effective use.

Social Media

Professionals continue to harness the power of social media at their agencies, using Facebook, Instagram, YouTube, and Twitter. An agency's website often includes links to its social media platforms. An appealing feature of an agency's Facebook page is the ability to interact with constituents through posting. For example, posting that tonight's T-ball game is cancelled is an inexpensive and straightforward way to inform parents who follow the agency on their mobile devices. Further, if parents have questions or additional information to provide about the cancellation, they can simply respond to the post. Facebook also allows the posting of pictures, video clips, and links to other websites.

Instagram is a social media platform that showcases the agency through photographs. Followers can "like" and/or comment on a photo. YouTube allows subscribers to watch the agency-created videos to get an idea of the agency's programs and events. Examples include video clips from a concert or tournament, interviews with community members, or award ceremonies. Twitter basically permits someone to answer the question, what's happening? using 140 characters or less. Recreation businesses may have a Follow Us on Twitter link inviting constituents to follow them. Similar to Facebook, Twitter can be used by the agency as an effective means of communicating information to its followers.

Social media accounts provide fun and creative ways of promoting an agency and its services. Schenck (2018) outlined legal and departmental considerations for establishing agency social media policies that will protect citizens and the agency. Legal considerations for agency social media accounts should always be discussed with the agency's legal counsel, especially for photographs and contests. Often, photographs found through Internet searches can only be used with permission from the photographer. The agency must also obtain permission to share photos of citizens, including minors, participating in its programs. Many agencies include a photo release statement on their program registration form to address this concern. Social media contests that promote and support a recreation agency must adhere to the terms of service outlined by the specific platform (Schenck, 2018).

The organization should establish policies that protect citizens and the agency itself. To ensure a consistent agency message and avoid conflicting and confusing communication, the agency can limit the number of staff who can post messages. The policy can outline procedures for handling public criticisms that are posted on the agency's social media platforms, as well as for deleting negative comments (Schenck, 2018). Other policies can ban employees from "playing" on Facebook and other social media during work hours. Social media has the potential to affect an agency positively, and well-written policies help them achieve that goal.

While social media can be a useful communication conduit for agencies, it is important for programmers to ask constituents which are most effective for getting the word out so that managers do not waste time managing four or five sites when one or two would be sufficient. Moreover, as the baby boomer workforce retires and young "wired into technology" professionals replace them, the influence of social media will continue growing in recreation agencies. Future recreation professionals will perform aspects of their work duties on mobile devices, and social media will no doubt be included. Agency policies will likely change as young professionals continue to incorporate social media into the workplace.

E-Mail

E-mail marketing remains the most effective marketing tool compared to social media platforms (Dysart, 2017). E-mail is fast and cheap, whether for sending a news release to editors or for delivering a message overseas. Also, e-mail is the first thing people check on their devices each morning, followed by social media platforms such as Facebook and Twitter (Dysart, 2017).

Obtaining permission to use someone's e-mail address often occurs during program registration, whereby customers are invited to check a series of boxes to subscribe to agency communications such as newsletters and upcoming events. These subscriptions position agencies well to send targeted communication to their customers.

Websites, business cards, and agency letterhead often include an e-mail address where the public can contact the agency. Additionally, the programmer can set up electronic mailing lists. These are established for a group of persons who are interested in a particular topic, for example, competitive tennis. The tennis players can use the electronic mailing list as a discussion forum, or the agency can use it to inform players of upcoming events and activities. Assuming the responsibility for developing and maintaining leisure interest electronic mailing lists is an extension of the traditional role agencies have assumed for nurturing leisure interest groups.

Specialty Publications

Newspapers, magazines, blog posts, and newsletters targeted to niche markets, such as senior citizens and special interest groups, are excellent places for promoting programs and activities. Writing copy for these publications may require more preparation because the article will need to focus specifically on the target market, as opposed to the general population. With modern production software, these publications can be produced efficiently, and an agency can publish niche publications more effectively. One warning—committing to a regularly produced piece can become burdensome in the long run. Once you start publishing, your readers will expect you to continue. So ensure it is really needed and that you have time to produce the copy on a weekly or monthly basis.

Tourism Offices and Chambers of Commerce

Leisure service agencies and businesses have opportunities to display promotional items at tourism offices and the local chamber of commerce. They can also post events and programs on the Web calendars of these organizations, as well as establish Web links between these organizations and other leisure service agencies.

Cable TV Public Access Programs

Some agencies choose to seek airtime on cable TV public access programs. Depending on the cable company, the on-camera presentation may be produced by the agency or the cable company itself. It is best for the agency to publicize the channel and the showtime to attract as many viewers as possible.

For these promotional technologies, programmers need to hone their writing skills, because now more than ever, agencies and their program promotions are being examined by citizens through multiple conduits. A website, in particular, makes an agency public to the world.

Conclusion

Developing the material for a promotional campaign is an early step in program implementation. Standard methods of promotion include a website, an agency brochure, news releases, and individual program flyers. In most agencies, programmers do much of the copywriting and other promotional work, with the exception of website design. To be effective, promotional materials must be well written and the promotional campaign executed in a timely manner. Social media outlets such as Facebook, Instagram, YouTube, and Twitter are equally important to promotion. Before adopting these innovative promotional techniques, programmers should ensure that all forms of communication are well coordinated to provide consistent, current information about the agency and bounded by sound policies. Projecting a consistent brand and message in all media enhances customer relations and promotes the agency as intended.

References

Ajzen, I. (1992). Persuasive communication theory in social psychology: A historical perspective. In M. J. Manfredo (Ed.), *Influencing human behavior: Theory and application in recreation, tourism, and natural resource management* (pp. 1–28). Urbana, IL: Sagamore.

Crompton, J. L., & Lamb, C. W., Jr. (1986). *Marketing government and social services.* New York, NY: Wiley.

December, J., & Randall, N. (1994). *The World Wide Web unleashed.* Indianapolis, IN: Sams.

Dysart, J. (2017, May). Email marketing: Still the killer app to beat for park and recreation agencies. *Parks and Recreation, 52*(5), 18–19.

Foster, K. (1990). *How to create newspaper ads.* Manhattan, KS: Learning Resources Network.

Howard, D. R., & Crompton, J. L. (1980). *Financing, managing, and marketing recreation and park resources.* Dubuque, IA: Wm. C. Brown.

Kotler, P., & Andreasen, A. R. (1987). *Strategic marketing for nonprofit organizations* (3rd ed.). Englewood Cliffs, NJ: Prentice-Hall.

Leffel, L. G. (1983). *Designing brochures for results.* Manhattan, KS: Learning Resources Network.

Manfredo, M. J., & Bright, A. D. (1991). A model for assessing the effects of communication on recreationists. *Journal of Leisure Research, 23,* 1–20.

Manfredo, M. J., Bright, A. D., & Haas, G. E. (1992). Research in tourism advertising. In M. J. Manfredo (Ed.), *Influencing human behavior: Theory and applications in recreation, tourism, and natural resource management.* Champaign, IL: Sagamore.

Nelson, R. P. (1981). *The design of advertising* (4th ed.). Dubuque, IA: Wm. C. Brown.

Russell, T., & Verrill, G. (1986). *Otto Kleppner's advertising procedure* (9th ed.). Englewood Cliffs, NJ: Prentice-Hall.

Ryan, M., & Tankard, J. W., Jr. (1977). *Basic news reporting.* Palo Alto, CA: Mayfield.

Schenck, L. (2018, January). Creating social media policies for your parks and rec department. *Parks and Recreation, 53*(1), 44–46.

Slottag, R. (1999). Embracing the age of niche marketing. *Illinois Parks and Recreation, 30*(4), 43–44.

Chickahominy Riverfront Park
Courtesy James City County Parks and Recreation. Scott Brown Photography.

15 *Registration Procedures*

KEY TERMS

Registration, Central Location Method—Walk-in, Program Location Method—Walk-in, Mail-in Method, Telephone Method, Fax-in Method, Web-based Method, Combination of Methods, Registration Form, Liability Release Form, Queuing, Types of Queues

Step 7: Implementation

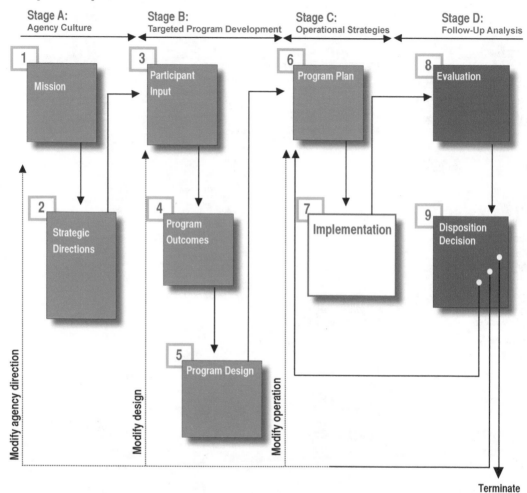

Registering individuals involves developing a list of persons qualified to be in a program. It is an inconvenient process for staff and participants and therefore should not be undertaken unless such a list is necessary. There are trade-offs between participant convenience and having a manageable, well-organized registration with adequate cash-collection procedures. Registration is usually the participant's second contact with an organization, and it is important that it is conducted well and conveniently. Registration for the agency should result in accurate class lists for each program and a confirmation of enrollment provided to each participant. Collecting fees and implementing good cash control with proper accounting of funds is a major consideration of conducting registration. For example, one of the most convenient registration methods is having participants register with the program leader at the first class meeting. Although this method may maximize convenience, having cash collection occurring in many locations makes it difficult to follow best practice cash-control procedures. Credit cards and electronic transfer of funds have made collecting registration fees easier and less risky since there is no cash drawer needed when these methods are used for collecting fees.

Five Reasons for Conducting Registration

Most frequently, agencies conduct registration for programs that require a participation fee, but registration is also useful for purposes other than documenting who has paid for a service. This section explains five instances when agencies need to register participants in programs.

Participants Must Pay a Fee to Be in the Program

These programs require registration because only those who have paid the fee are allowed to be in the program.

Program Has a Limited Number of Spaces

> Agencies conduct registration for programs that require a participation fee, but registration is also useful for purposes other than documenting who has paid for a service.

If a program has a limited capacity, it is wise for the agency to have people register even if it is not charging a fee. Participants thus secure one of a limited number of spaces by their position in a queue or some other qualifying method.

For example, the Park District of Oak Park, Illinois, operates an annual Egg Hunt that is designed to handle an estimated 1,050 children. To accommodate the estimated demand, the park district operates three hunts during the day with 350 children per hunt. Although each hunt is free of charge, parents must obtain a ticket in advance for their children to participate in a specific hunt. In this way, queuing is arranged 1 month in advance and determines who can be admitted to each hunt. Thus, being "qualified" simply means that a person has obtained one of a limited number of tickets for a hunt.

Spaces in a program may also be limited because of the carrying capacity of the facility. In outdoor recreation, agencies often restrict the number of participants permitted into some wilderness areas, because of the physical limits of the ecological systems or because the perception of an area as a wilderness would be impaired with too many people in the area. Sometimes, then, agencies need to limit participation to maintain the leisure experience. Thus, individuals need to register to obtain one of the limited spaces available.

Places in the Program Are Expensive to Provide

Because of this, agencies need to know the number of people who will partici-pate. In some events, they also need to know how many people will attend so that they can make proper arrangements. Dances with sit-down seating and parties in-volving a caterer are examples of such events. In these programs, agencies often use some type of invitation with an RSVP system or other registration system to enable the programmer to have a reasonable estimate of the number of people who will attend.

Admission to a Program Requires Some Special Qualifying Procedure

Some programs are open only to those with special qualifications. In these cases, agencies develop a list of those qualified. In sports, for example, tryouts help agencies to place players into leagues or programs appropriate for their skill levels. In outdoor adventure programming, programmers often ensure that individuals have requisite skills. For example, participants may be required to demonstrate a level of swimming proficiency before being permitted to participate in a canoe trip.

Agency Needs Specific Information From Participants

Sometimes, the special qualification may simply be that the participant has provided the agency with certain information. Some recreation centers require all participants to register during their first visit to the center. Registration is free, but people must register and provide their name, address, e-mail address, phone num-ber, and an emergency contact, and in many cases, they must sign a liability release waiver similar to the one used by the City of Santa Clara, California, Parks and Recreation Department (see Exhibit 15.1).

Registration Methods

Online Method

Online registration is likely the most common method of registration used to-day. After completing registration online, participants receive confirmation and a receipt. This asynchronous method is especially convenient compared to the other methods because registrants are not limited to open hours of registration operation. They can register 24 hours a day, 7 days a week. It has the following advantages and disadvantages:

Advantages
- This method allows participants to register whenever they desire.
- Participants receive automatic confirmation of registration.
- This form of registration is easy for persons who are familiar with computers.
- Agencies collect considerable information about their participants with on-line registration without having to use staff to input the data.
- Fee collection is with bank or credit cards; therefore, cash control is not needed.

Exhibit 15.1. Sample Registration and Liability Form

REGISTRATION FORM

City of Santa Clara Parks & Recreation Department

For Mail-In Registration:
- Complete this registration form and sign liability release on the other side.
- Make payment for the full amount due:
  Check or money order to "City of Santa Clara." Cash or credit card can be processed in person at the CRC, Teen Center, or Youth Activity Center prior to submitting mail-in packet.
- Provide proof of residency:
  Pre-printed check, current utility bill, copy of valid driver's license, or current Santa Clara Unified school report card.
- Families may submit registrations in the same envelope if they wish to be processed together; send a separate registration form and proof of residency for each family.

Residential Status: (check one)
- Santa Clara City resident/property owner
- Santa Clara Unified School District
- Non-resident

Submit registration packets to:
Community Recreation Center Registration
969 Kiely Blvd., Santa Clara, CA 95051
Registration questions: (408) 615-3140

Parent/Adult Contact (Main Account Holder) Information:

New Account? Yes ____ No ____

Name _____   _____
　　　　Last　　　　　　　　　　　First

Birth Date (month/day/year format)

Address _____ City _____ State _____ Zip _____

Cell No. (___) _____ Home No. (___) _____ Work No. (___) _____
o I would like to receive text updates (e.g. cancelled class, reminders, etc.) from the City of Santa Clara. Cellular provider: _____

Provide your email address (for Online Registration access or program updates) _____
o I would like to receive City of Santa Clara email updates with information about events and programs.

First Local Emergency Contact: _____   _____
　　　　　　　　　　　　　　　　Last　　　　　　　　First
Cell No. (___) _____ Home No. (___) _____ Work No. (___) _____

Second Local Emergency Contact: _____   _____
　　　　　　　　　　　　　　　　　Last　　　　　　　First
Cell No. (___) _____ Home No. (___) _____ Work No. (___) _____

Participant's First & Last Name	Gender	Birth Date	Course/Activity Name	Course/Activity Numbers	Fee	
Example: Sally Jones	F	7/1/75	Oil/Acrylic Painting	11861	00	00
				Subtotal		
				Deduct Current Credit Balance		
				Total Fees Due		

Please indicate any allergies, disabilities/special needs, or accommodations needed below. The instructor or staff may contact you for further information.

Participant's name: _____
Needs/instructions: _____
_____

Participant's name: _____
Needs/instructions: _____
_____

Complete liability release on other side of this page.

REGISTRATION FORM

Note: Taken from the City of Santa Clara Spring/Summer 2018 Recreation Activity Guide Recreation Activities Guide, Santa Clara, CA. This form is used for illustration purposes only. No warranty is given regarding the legal appropriateness of this form for the reader's use, and the reader is cautioned not to copy this form. Any such form should be developed and approved by the agency's legal counsel.

Exhibit 15.1. (continued)

RELEASE OF LIABILITY & ASSUMPTION OF RISK

In consideration of the acceptance by the City of the application for entry into the classes or activities listed on the Registration Form on the reverse side of this Agreement and entry to and use of any facilities or equipment as part of these classes or activities, I hereby waive, release and discharge any and all claims for damages for death, personal injury, or property damage which I may have, or which may hereafter accrue to me as a result of my participation in said classes or activities. This release Agreement is intended to discharge in advance the City of Santa Clara, its City Council, officers, agents, and employees, the Santa Clara Unified School District, its School Board, officers, agents and employees from and against any and all liability arising out of or connected with my participation in said classes or activities and entry to and use of any facilities or equipment, even though that liability may arise out of NEGLIGENCE or CARELESSNESS, on the part of the persons or entities mentioned above.

I HAVE READ THE DESCRIPTION IN THIS CATALOG OF EACH CLASS OR ACTIVITY FOR WHICH I HAVE REGISTERED, AND I AM AWARE THAT THESE CLASSES OR ACTIVITIES MAY SUBJECT ME TO PHYSICAL RISKS AND DANGERS. NEVERTHELESS, I VOLUNTARILY AGREE TO ASSUME ANY AND ALL RISKS OF INJURY OR DEATH, AND TO RELEASE, DISCHARGE, AND HOLD HARMLESS ALL OF THE ENTITIES OR PERSONS MENTIONED ABOVE WHO, THROUGH NEGLIGENCE OR CARELESSNESS, MIGHT OTHERWISE BE LIABLE TO ME, OR MY HEIRS, PERSONAL REPRESENTATIVES, RELATIVES, SPOUSE OR ASSIGNS.

It is understood and agreed that this waiver, release, and assumption of risk is to be binding on my HEIRS, PERSONAL REPRESENTATIVES, RELATIVES, SPOUSE and ASSIGNS and is intended to be as broad and inclusive as is permitted by the laws of the State of California and that if any portion of this Agreement is held invalid, it is agreed that the balance shall, notwithstanding, continue in full legal force and effect.

I have carefully READ this Agreement and fully understand its content. All participants registered in classes or activities, including minors 13-17 years of age, must sign this Agreement. Adults participating in Parent-Child Activities must sign below as adult participants in addition to the parent portion of this release Agreement.

Date: _____

ADULT PARTICIPANTS, INCLUDING THOSE PARTICIPATING IN PARENT-CHILD CLASSES, SIGN BELOW

Signature: _____   Print Name: _____

Signature: _____   Print Name: _____

PARTICIPANTS, AGE 13-17, SIGN BELOW

Signature: _____   Print Name: _____

Signature: _____   Print Name: _____

Signature: _____   Print Name: _____

To be completed by parent or guardian of minor participants

I have fully read this Agreement and fully understand its content. Furthermore, the significance of this release of liability and assumption of risk agreement has been EXPLAINED TO THE MINOR.

I certify that I have custody or am the legal guardian of said minor and that I and/or my minor child are physically able to participate in recreation . In the event I or said minor requires medical treatment while under the supervision of City staff and/or agents, I authorize said staff to provide and/or authorize medical treatment. I expect City staff to contact me immediately in the event emergency medical treatment is required for said minor, but this contact is not necessary to administer emergency aid. I will pay for all medical treatment which I or said minor may require. I hereby grant permission to City to include pictures and/or video of me and/or said minor during department activities for brochures or other publicity. I understand I will not receive any compensation for use of such pictures or video.

Signature of parent or guardian: _____ Date: _____

Print parent/guardian name: _____

Address: _____

Please indicate whether you are signing as: ☐ Parent ☐ Guardian

RELEASE OF LIABILITY & ASSUMPTION OF RISK

Note: Taken from the City of Santa Clara Spring/Summer 2018 Recreation Activity Guide Recreation Activities Guide, Santa Clara, CA. This form is used for illustration purposes only. No warranty is given regarding the legal appropriateness of this form for the reader's use, and the reader is cautioned not to copy this form. Any such form should be developed and approved by the agency's legal counsel.

Disadvantages

- Web-based registration can be a problem for individuals without computer service; however, access is generally available to the public from libraries. An agency will need to determine the extent to which this is a problem for its service population.
- Poorly designed and maintained websites can result in poor public relations. Staff must maintain careful and diligent attention to the Web-based registration system to ensure it works properly throughout the registration period, is accurate and up to date, and is accessible.
- Forgotten passwords can cause disruptions to agency staff. Participants can inundate staff with phone calls or e-mails about retrieving their passwords. Providing online password resets vastly ameliorates this problem.

Central Location Method—Walk-In

In the central location method, all registration for many programs occurs at a central location, such as a recreation center, school building, or other facility. Parking should be adequate for the number of people anticipated, queuing should be well organized, and staff members conducting the registration should be well oriented and trained to answer participants' questions. Registration workers should be trained so they can provide correct information. If an employee cannot answer a question correctly when first asked, he or she can offer to call the participant after obtaining the correct information. It can be damaging to the agency if staff answer questions incorrectly.

In a very large operation, it is often wise for the agency to specialize operations and have a station-to-station method of completing registration. It is especially important for the agency to centralize cash collections so that the money collected goes to the proper accounts. Centralized registration has the following advantages and disadvantages:

> In the central location method, all registration for many programs occurs at a central location.

Advantages

- All registration is accomplished at one time and in one place.
- Centralized registrations are the easiest for the agency to advertise and supervise, and with the critical mass of registrants, agencies can make registrations an event celebrating the agency and its programs.
- A centrally located staff member can serve participants better by answering questions about all of the agency's programs from one well-publicized location.
- The central location method also makes possible centralized cash collections and excellent cash control. This minimizes the opportunity for embezzlement; enables security of cash, as many thousands of dollars may be collected; and makes it easier for agencies to supervise the posting of payments to the proper accounts.

Disadvantages

- Participants do not see the program meeting place or meet the program staff. These meetings often raise people's level of anticipation about participating in a program. These interactions may also lead to additional registrations from people who initially may not have been aware of a program, did not realize what a program involved, or for some other reason did not initially register for a program.
- Attracting all registrants to one location can mean long lines with accompanying frustrations if the registration procedures and queues are not well planned and managed.
- With so many program ledgers and without good accounting procedures in place, staff can mix up registration fee accounts.

Program Location Method—Walk-In

In the program location method, registration occurs at the program site, such as a swimming pool, tennis court, or playground. This method has the following advantages and disadvantages:

> In the program location method, registration occurs at the program site.

Advantages
- Registrants become familiar with the program site.
- Registration affords a good opportunity for participants to meet and interact with program staff.

These first two advantages are important features for registering young children. This method gives them an opportunity to become familiar with the setting and the program staff before participating on their own for the first time.
- There is no delay in registering while waiting for people who are registering for other programs. These delays often occur in the central location method of registration.

Disadvantages
- This method requires travel time between various registration locations and standing in more than one queue for participants who are registering for several programs.
- Decentralized registration is more difficult to supervise.
- Problems associated with cash collection and cash control increase when registration occurs in several locations.

Mail-In Method

In the mail-in method of registration, participants complete a registration form and mail it, along with payment, to the agency. This centralized system is accessible to people throughout the community. It has the following advantages and disadvantages:

Advantages
- This method is convenient because it requires very little of a participant's time.
- The mail-in method allows flexibility in scheduling staff to process registrations.
- Because the payment accepted with mail-in registration is something other than cash, this method eliminates the need for the agency to supervise cash collections.

Disadvantages
- This method allows no interaction between agency staff and participants.
- To receive answers to questions, participants must place a phone call to the agency.
- Participants do not see the location of the program until the first session.
- If the agency accepts credit card payments, a return receipt will need to be mailed or e-mailed.

Telephone Method

With this method, participants simply telephone the agency to register for a program. It is often used in smaller agencies or local registrations at a community recreation center and usually does not include using an automatic phone registration system. Thus, the system is only available during hours the agency is open and staffed with employees to answer the phone. Usually, all calls are directed to a central location. This method has the following advantages and disadvantages:

> With this method, participants simply telephone the agency to register for a program.

Advantages
- Staff members can keep accurate, up-to-date records of the number of spaces filled and open at any given time.
- The agency does not have to manage a physical queue. If demand for registration is heavy, however, the agency needs to implement some method of queuing phone calls. The agency could obtain electronic equipment that will automatically answer and queue phone calls.

Disadvantages
- There is no face-to-face interaction between participants and the program staff.
- Participants do not see the program location until the program begins.
- If a fee is involved in registering for the program, collection is a problem unless the agency accepts credit card payments for fees.
- If the agency accepts credit card payments, it will need to mail or e-mail a return receipt.

- When registrants do not pay the fee at registration, registrants may not appear when the program begins, and they generally should not be allowed to participate until they pay.

Fax-In Method

In the fax-in method of registration, participants complete the registration form, the same as in the mail-in method, but must supply their credit card information on the fax form. They then fax the completed registration form to the agency's facsimile machine. This method has the following advantages and disadvantages:

Advantages
- This is a convenient method for participants, who can fax their registration at any time.
- Because the facsimile machine can receive messages at any time of the day, it expands the time the agency is "open" to receive registrations with no increase in staffing costs.
- The agency does not need to manage a queue, and because the facsimile machine can receive only one transmission at a time, there is an order of receipt of registrations.

Disadvantages
- Participants and staff do not interact; thus, the agency has no opportunity to answer questions or give out additional information about the program.
- The program participants do not see the program location until the first class session.
- If the agency charges a fee for the program, it must allow credit cards or must bill the participants. In either case, this method usually requires the agency to mail or e-mail a bill or a credit card receipt to participants.

Combination of Methods

Agencies often permit participants to register using some or all of the methods outlined. Typically, agencies combine the central location or program location methods with the mail-in, telephone, Web-based, or fax methods. The City of Moline Parks and Recreation Department, Moline, Illinois, uses a centralized registration location in the public works building for walk-in, mail-in, phone-in, online, and fax-in registrations, thus enabling the department to coordinate registrations from one location. Using a combination of methods offers the following advantages and disadvantages:

Advantages
- Participants have the greatest flexibility and opportunity in completing their registration.
- In making registration convenient, the agency maximizes its chances of fully enrolling its programs.

Disadvantages

- When the agency accepts registrations at several locations, lists can be confused and programs overenrolled unless registration is carefully coordinated. Agencies can use remote computer terminals with a centralized database for maintaining program rosters, as one solution. Agencies can allocate a given number of spaces in each program to each registration location, as another solution. In this case, staff members at any one location can accept only a given number of registrants unless a central coordinator approves additional spaces.
- Participants may be confused about which registration method to use when several methods are available.

It is important for agencies to indicate how they will queue registrations when using a combination of methods. For example, does a participant who has phoned to register receive priority over someone standing in a queue in the outer office? How does the agency queue mail-in registrations compared with walk-in and faxed registrations? What happens with mail-in registrations that are received before or after a deadline? Carefully developed and advertised registration policies provide guidance for these situations.

Registration Form

Most agencies put their brochures and registration forms on the Web for their participants. For printed activity guides, however, Dobmeyer (1986) believes the registration form should be placed inside the last page of the brochure. This placement allows the agency to use the prime space in the front of the publication to promote programs. Participants thus reach the form when they are most likely ready to complete it. When this is done, messages informing participants about the location of the registration form, for example, "For registration information, please see page XX," should appear throughout the brochure. In addition, using the last page usually means the returned registration form will also include the mailing label, which contains information that can be used for marketing purposes.

Some agencies place the registration form in the center of the brochure as a center pull-out that is printed on clay-coated paper inserted among the rest of the pages that are printed on recycled newsprint. This seems to be an equally effective placement because the recipient of the brochure is almost forced to open to the center section first because of the stiffness of the paper relative to the remainder of the brochure.

What to Include?

The two mutually exclusive objectives in designing the registration form include keeping it simple for participants to complete and obtaining as much information as possible for use in identifying participants and marketing. Current practice is keeping it simple and easy for participants to register for a program. To facilitate this, agencies can design registration forms that request only information that is needed and easily supplied by the participants. Exhibit 15.1 (page 289) shows a sample registration form that includes

- today's date;
- the registrant's name, address, e-mail address, and day and evening phone;
- the program(s) the participant wants to register for;
- the fee for each program;
- to whom the check should be written;
- what to expect after he or she registers (e.g., will the participant receive a confirmation or should the person consider him- or herself registered unless notified differently);
- a liability release form;
- information about the method of payment; and
- instructions about where to send the registration.

Depending on the type of agency involved, some of this information may be omitted or may be handled differently. In a club, such as a YWCA or a commercial club with an existing membership list, participants may not need to supply more than the enrollments desired and their names and membership numbers. In these cases, treating them like members—people who are well known to the agency—and thus avoiding the need to supply information again enhances the relationship. Club members may not be required to make payment at registration. In these situations, club members often have an open account with the agency and pay it monthly.

To maintain the illusion that completing the form is easy, agencies can keep the form as short and brief as possible. This can be difficult in some situations. For example, public agencies often mail their brochures to households, and the registration form must be long enough to accommodate a family that is likely to have multiple registrants in multiple programs. The inclusion of credit card information and a release of liability also increases the size and reduces the ease of completing a registration form.

Liability Release Form

Because the law regards anyone registered in an agency's program as an invitee (Peterson & Hronek, 1992), the agency is held to the highest legal standard of care in operating its programs. Thus, the completion of liability release forms as a part of registration is standard procedure. The release form in Exhibit 15.1 (page 289) is located on the reverse side of the registration form used by the City of Santa Clara, California, and thus is a physical part of it. It asks participants to read, sign, and date the Release of Liability and Assumption of Risk Agreement stating that they understand the risks posed by the activities and that they agree to waive and release all claims for damages they may encounter from the programs. Note also that the City of Santa Clara requires minors between the ages of 13 and 17 to sign that they have read and understand the agreement, in addition to their parent or guardian.

Distribution

The obvious key for distributing the advertising brochure is getting it to the market for the program. Depending on the agency involved, this may include different groups of individuals. For example, local and regional government agencies, because of their responsibility to all citizens in a community, try to distribute the brochure to all citizens. Many will use the bulk mail method, utilizing the "Postal Participant, Local" addressing method. With this method, the agency presorts the brochures, and mail carriers leave one in each mailbox on their route. However, the post office allows between 2 and 5 days for the carrier to deliver this type of mail; therefore, citizens in various parts of town receive them at different times—up to 5 days apart. This may create problems with the timing of registration and equity of access. If the agency uses this method, the start date of registration must be after all residents have received the brochure.

Mailing the brochure with a pay-per-piece method ensures that participants receive the brochure at almost the same time. Organizations that accept registrations from members and nonmembers usually mail a brochure to their members and then use different conduits for distributing additional brochures. Tracking registrations from various distribution locations and methods is an important marketing effort, and the agency should use some type of method for coding the brochures in each distribution conduit so it can identify the effectiveness of each.

Timing of Registration

Ideally, registration should be possible when the participant receives the brochure. However, this may become a major issue if everyone does not receive the brochure at the same time. Increasingly, agencies are producing and mailing brochures electronically as PDFs, ensuring that patrons will receive these when notified through e-mail, Facebook, Twitter, and the like. Still, many agencies indicate a starting date for accepting registrations to ensure all patrons have equal access to register. In addition, in many municipal operations and some YMCAs and YWCAs, agencies give residents or members a priority registration period. Clearly communicating the date at which each group (e.g., residents, nonresidents, members, or the general public) can begin registering is important.

Fees

In registering for a program, participants make a commitment to participate, which is intensified when they are required to pay a fee at registration. Most agency policies deem that participants are not registered until they pay the fee. The policy should specify the fee for each program, and the form should make it easy for participants to total the fees. However, because of the use of line-item accounting practices, some governmental agencies require a separate check for each program so that they can return the fee for any class that is closed. Alternatives to this method include accepting one check and informing the participant that any refunds could take up to 30 to 60 days or, in lieu of a refund, providing them with a voucher that they can use for a future enrollment. These alternatives are less desirable for the participant than returning the money.

The administration of differential pricing is important. If club members or community residents receive a lower price than nonmembers or nonresidents, the agency should state this. The method of communication can enhance it as a benefit and reduce its adverse effect. For example, one community states the price for participating and then states the discounted price for residents. This wording clearly presents the price difference as a benefit to residents and a penalty to no one.

Credit Cards

The acceptance of credit card payments for registration can broaden an agency's customer base. Agencies and individuals appreciate the speed of credit card transactions, plus there will be less cash on the premises as an attraction for potential criminals. A problem with using credit cards is that the credit card companies charge 3% to 5% of total sales as a fee. Many municipal government operations resist using credit cards, because most municipal fees are mandatory and it makes no sense to give away 3% to 5% of the fees. However, fees for recreation and leisure services are not mandatory, and most practitioners agree that allowing customers to use credit cards to pay for services will most likely increase sales volume.

Cancellations and Refunds

Before operating a program, most agencies require a minimum participant enrollment. Programmers should ensure the inclusion of this operational procedure in the advertising brochure. Additionally, they ensure that participants know the agency's procedures when registrations for a class do not reach minimum enrollment. Agencies should give full refunds for classes that are canceled by the agency.

Likewise, programmers ensure participants know what the agency will do with their registration if the class is full when their registration arrives. Some agencies place them on a waiting list until the class begins. In this case, the agency notifies the participant that he or she has not been registered but instead placed on a waiting list. Agencies need to implement clear, ongoing communication to maintain customer confidence and satisfaction about these issues.

Agencies should also make known their policy regarding the cancellation of a participant's spot in a nonfee program. No-shows can be an especially difficult problem in a program with a limited amount of spaces, when demand is high, and when no fee has been charged for the program. Some restaurants keep lists of people who make reservations and then do not show up. After a certain number of no-show incidents, they no longer accept reservations from offending individuals.

As another solution, the agency can charge a refundable reservation fee at registration and return the fee to those who attend. Forfeit fees in athletic leagues are a good example of this technique, which agencies could implement more frequently in other programs to solve the problem of no-shows. In one case, an agency charged a refundable $10 fee to those registering for a downhill slalom ski course that occured at the end of an all-day winter snow festival. In previous years, many individuals had registered and then did not run the slalom course because their scores from previous events during the day did not position them to do well with the slalom run. But staff members were waiting in freezing temperatures at the end of the course for all who had initially registered for the slalom run. When the agency implemented the refundable fee policy, almost all who registered participated in the slalom run to receive their $10 refund. With this technique, only those who do not participate pay. In essence, they were charged a penalty for putting an unreasonable burden on the agency's staff. No-show penalties also penalize individuals for taking and not using spots in a program and thus denying someone else the spot.

Transfers

Some agencies allow participants who are already registered to transfer their registration to another class with available space prior to the beginning of a program. When using this option, programmers need to state the terms of the offer, for example, that this may be done up to 1 week prior to the start of the program, or whatever the policy states.

Guarantees

Some agencies offer a guarantee of satisfaction with their programs. If dissatisfied, a customer may receive a voucher for another program or a full refund. Often, some activity fees, such as golf fees or athletic league fees for teams, are exempt from this policy.

Registration Software

Many agencies purchase registration software to conduct the registration process. When making registration software purchases, agencies should check with consulting groups that can provide valuable advice and ask the right questions about registration needs. Trade shows and conference exhibitions provide hands-on experience for agencies to get the feel for how a registration program works. Software companies often provide demonstration links for agencies to become familiar with their products. Popular recreation registration software systems include RecTrac by Vermont Systems and ACTIVE Network.

Registration software allows for online registration, produces registration lists, keeps track of enrollment numbers, produces lists of underenrolled classes, maintains waiting lists for overenrolled classes, and tracks sales, expenses, and net revenue. It can also generate analytical marketing reports that allow the agency to track a wide range of sociodemographic variables that can be cross-tabulated to facilitate target marketing to specific groups. Agencies can also use registration software for facility reservations, pass management, league scheduling, equipment and site reservations, trip reservations, court reservations, locker rentals, and golf tee times. They can use it to create a client database to store everything from names, addresses, and phone numbers, to e-mail addresses, dietary needs, and emergency contact information. Thus, registration data can support the agency's marketing effort with current registrants. Remember, however, this database does not include nonusers.

Technology in Program Registration

Using computer software, programmers can

- monitor class rosters and waiting lists;
- maintain accident report records and liability waivers;
- use mail merge functions to target specific populations or previous customers;
- track age and ability restrictions, instructors, and resident and nonresident restrictions; and
- process payments, refunds, transfers, and cancellations.

Operating Registration

The quality of registration operation sends a message to participants about the quality of the agency and its programs. A reminder once again, the brochure is the first contact with the participant; registration is usually the second and also the first participant-initiated contact. Good customer service is essential at this stage of the service encounter for the agency to keep the participant satisfied. Following are recommendations about how to deal with recurring issues that occur in operating registrations.

> The quality of registration operation sends a message to participants about the quality of the agency and its programs.

Registration Considerations

- Provide enough staff to handle the anticipated number of registrants. Supervisory staff should keep track of how long it takes individuals to register and should adjust as needed so that registrations can be completed in a reasonable amount of time.
- Schedule registration at a time consistent with local customs. Early mornings, evenings, or other time slots when participants are available should all be scheduled.
- Completely orient and train staff before registration:
    a. Emphasize the need to be courteous to participants.
    b. Try to have established objective methods for handling potential points of disagreement. For example, if registrants must show that they are residents of the community, determine in advance how this point is to be established. Must the participant have a driver's license with an appropriate address or a voter registration card? Do not leave it up to the registration staff to improvise methods for verifying age, height, weight, skill level, residency, and so forth.

c. Fully inform registration personnel about program details, waiting lists, fee payment policies and methods, refund procedures, nonresident registration policies, and the like.

d. Have details about each program available for the registration staff. Agencies often become too lax and do not require that contract leaders completely inform the agency about program details. Remember, in the eyes of the public, this is the agency's program, and the public expects agency personnel to know the details of its operation.

- Establish well-defined and well-organized queues.
- Provide simple and clear registration forms. Arrange for individuals to have completed as much of the registration form as possible before receiving the attention of registration personnel.
- Carefully instruct cashiers how to accept payment and properly record and account for each type of program fee.
- Provide additional, well-oriented staff to answer agency telephones immediately before, during, and shortly after the registration period.
- Provide adequate pens and space for writing at the registration location. Now complete Exercise 15.1.

Exercise 15.1.
Panel Discussion on Registration

Background Information: Based on their previous volunteer and work experiences, students will gather into three groups that represent the public, private, and commercial sectors. Or, if students haven't had such experiences to date, invite representative professionals into the class.

Discussion Questions

1. Describe how registration is done in the agencies in the three representative areas.

   Public sector

   Private sector

   Commercial sector

2. Based on the findings from Question 1, what are the similarities and differences in registration procedures among the three sectors?

Queuing Procedures

Queuing is simply standing in line waiting for a turn to be served. There is an old story about the British: When two or more British people get together, the first thing they must determine is how the queue will be organized. Often, programmers do not think of managing a queue until it has gotten out of control.

That queues can get out of control and become a major problem was made clear by the poorly conceived queuing system at a Who rock concert in Cincinnati, Ohio, on December 3, 1979. Riverfront Coliseum management sold a limited number of reserved seats. Approximately 80% of seats were unreserved "festival seating" (Stuart, 1979). Instead of taking care of the order in which to serve people at the point of sale, the management let the audience scramble for desirable seats the night of the concert. Because of the group's popularity, the audience began gathering for the 8 p.m. concert in mid-afternoon. It was the usual practice for the facility to open its doors 2 hours before a concert. On this evening, however, The Who were late in setting up their equipment, so the doors did not open until about 7 p.m. In addition, all of the doors around the facility did not open at the same time. The crowd at the end of the facility that was delayed in opening became unruly and charged the doors for admission. In the ensuing melee, 11 young people were trampled and killed (Thomas, 1979).

Although some queues continued to be problems, a well-publicized one occurred almost 20 years later (November 2008) when a Walmart worker was killed in a stampede by an out-of-control mob on Black Friday. Two years later, the Occupational Safety and Health Administration put retailers on notice that they risk financial penalties if they do not implement good crowd control procedures (Sixel, 2010). Poorly conceived queuing, then, can create major problems.

Some evidence suggests that standing in a queue can be an anxiety-producing experience (Mann, 1973). Traditionally, programmers ignored queues and assumed that the program began when the participants entered the facility or came into the program. Programmers did not worry about the queue.

Standing in a queue may be the participant's first self-initiated contact with a program. Successfully managing queues requires that programmers adequately deal with the first two laws of service delivery (Maister, 1985): satisfaction equals perception minus expectations, and it is hard to play catch-up ball. The participants' satisfaction depends on their level of expectation and their perception of performance. As long as their perception of performance equals or exceeds their expectations, they will be satisfied. However, if it does not, they will be dissatisfied and it will be difficult for the programmer to ameliorate this dissatisfaction with the agency's performance in operating the program. Some evidence shows that queues for concerts, movies, sporting events, and other leisure events are perceived as occasions for socializing (Mann, 1973), so participants usually arrive expecting to have a positive, satisfying experience. The key is for the agency to operate registrations in a satisfactory manner so that a program does not begin in a deficit condition of participant dissatisfaction.

To better manage queues, programmers need to understand the sociological principles that underlie the behavior of people in queues. Mann (1973) pointed out that queues are governed by the "rule of distributive justice," which was first outlined by Homans (1961). According to Mann, the rule as applied to queuing suggests that if a person is willing to invest large amounts of time and suffering in an activity—that is, standing in a line— there should be an appropriate reward—that is, preferential treatment. If individuals in a queue believe the queue is fair, they must perceive "a direct correspondence between inputs (time spent waiting) and outcome (preferential service)" (Mann, 1973, p. 48). Violating this principle creates stress and anxiety.

> If a person is willing to invest large amounts of time and suffering in an activity—that is, standing in a line—there should be an appropriate reward.

Four sources of stress and anxiety are associated with being in queues. First, there is the problem of queue jumping. This practice is a breach of distributive justice and a threat to the social order of a queue. Second, individuals are responsible for guarding their own territory. People in the queue are expected to remain vigilant and protect the queue position directly in front of them from queue jumpers. Their stress level rises when someone jumps the queue directly in front of them. When this happens, the individual bears the responsibility of dealing with the queue jumper and protecting the position. Third, people must make sure they are standing in the right queue for the service desired. When there are several queues for different services, poorly identified queues can be a source of anxiety and stress. Finally, there is the problem of how long a person will have to wait before receiving service. Not knowing the wait time can produce stress.

If the agency reduces stress and anxiety of queuing, it eliminates queuing as a possible source of participant dissatisfaction with the event. Furthermore, a well-managed queue contributes to the overall satisfaction with a leisure experience. Program implementation begins with the queue. The burden of managing it rests with the recreation staff. The operation of the queue, then, needs to be well planned.

Four Types of Queues

The first step in managing stress-free, enjoyable queues is defining them with barriers or other physical guides and reducing the possibility of queue jumping. Four types of queues can be established (Mann, 1973): a single line with a single service, multiple lines with multiple services, a single line with multiple services, and station-to-station services. In the United States, the single line with a single service and mul-

> A well-managed queue can contribute to the overall satisfaction with a leisure experience.

tiple lines with multiple services queue types seem to be the most popular. These two types work well if the agency can deliver the service in a similar amount of time to each participant. However, the multiple line, each with its own service station, approach can be terribly stress producing. Because of the differential service needs of each participant, some lines move more rapidly or slowly than others. The solution is the single line with multiple services approach. This approach seems to be gaining popularity in the United States, partly because it better implements the rule of distributive justice. It is the method of choice for large registrations in which participants may register for one or more programs for themselves, a whole family, or a group of people.

The station-to-station method of queuing is effective when participants must undertake a series of steps to complete a transaction. This method essentially links together various combinations of the first three methods. Programmers ensure that no unacceptable, stress-producing bottlenecks occur in this type of queue.

Programmers can also implement several other procedures to ensure stress-free, enjoyable queues. The remainder of this section discusses these.

Register the order of arrival, using a recognized system. A take-a-number or similar system determines the order of service. It also eliminates the need for a physical queue and its associated problems.

Improve the speed of service. The programmer can improve the speed of service by having more service stations or by reducing the burden of completing the transaction. For example, do participants have to write their name, address, e-mail address, and phone number on a separate card for each program they enter? Must they write a check for each program? Eliminating repetitive actions speeds up service and requires no additional personnel.

Assure participants of the certainty of service. If participants know that enough services are available to meet their needs, much of the stress will be alleviated. Guaranteeing this will not always be possible. However, if queue managers know that the amount of service is adequate, they should let the participants know that their waiting is not in vain. A corollary to this is letting queuers know as soon as possible when they cannot expect service so that they can stop investing their time in the queue.

Start service for participants while they are in line. An in-process wait seems shorter than a preprocess wait (Maister, 1985), so programmers should create as soon as possible the perception that service has started. For example, they can distribute registration forms, instructions about the event, instructions about the queue, and brochures about other events. Station-to-station queues often create this perception, because individuals move through a series of encounters that provide service at each step.

Post the time required in the queue. Programmers need to inform queuers about how soon they can expect service. The Disney organization does an excellent job of informing participants about the waiting time before they can gain access to an attraction. For example, in many queues they post signs that state "Approximate Waiting Time Is 30 Minutes." A pizza restaurant in Champaign, Illinois, posts in its queue a sign informing participants that "From this point, you will be eating pizza in approximately 10 minutes." Providing this information creates reasonable expectations for queuers about how long it will take in the queue before receiving service. This step eliminates unreasonable expectations, complaints, and unnecessary anxiety.

Have the queue move forward toward the point of service. When designing the queue, programmers need to ensure that queuers are moving toward the point of service or at least have the illusion of progressing toward it. This builds anticipation and relieves anxiety.

Make the queue fun. Programmers can incorporate standing in a queue into the leisure event. This is a desirable goal and can decrease stress and make queuing part of the experience. For example, at Disneyland the queue area for each attraction is thematically developed as part of the attraction and designed to build excitement for the forthcoming experience. When one author was a faculty member at the University of Illinois, the football team received a bid to play in the Liberty Bowl in Memphis, Tennessee. The local Liberty Bowl committee treated queuers waiting for tickets to hot coffee, donuts, and entertainment from a pep band. Their efforts certainly turned a boring queue into an enjoyable event that built excitement for the Liberty Bowl. Implementing similar activities can make queues a positive component of the event. Now complete Exercise 15.2.

Exercise 15.2.
Ensuring Stress-Free, Enjoyable Queues

Directions: As a class, provide real-life examples of the seven ways to create stress-free, enjoyable queues.

Ways to Create Stress-Free, Enjoyable Queues	Recreation Example	Theme Park Example
1. Register the order of arrival using a recognized system.		
2. Improve the speed of service (multiple stations, room to complete forms.		
3. Assure participants of the certainty of service.		
4. Start service for participants while they are in line.		
5. Post time required in the queue.		
6. Have the queue move forward toward the point of service.		
7. Make the queue fun.		

Giveaways

> Giveaways should be well managed and offer sufficient service to all.

Giveaways should be well managed and offer sufficient service to all. Public agencies need to consider if they want to participate in a giveaway when service for all who desire it is not possible or if the event is not properly organized and operated. Sponsors who wish to participate in giveaways at public agency events should be required to provide enough service for all and to follow queuing guidelines developed by the agency to ensure an orderly and fair queue. In some cases, agencies deal with this by announcing in advance that the giveaway will only be available to the first XX number of people.

While employed in a public agency, one author was once involved with a group of puppeteers who performed in a park one Sunday afternoon. Their performance was excellent. Some 150 to 200 children watched the performance while seated on the lawn in front of the stage. Parents stood in a semicircle behind the children. At the end of the performance, a cast member came onto the stage with a box of candy suckers and announced that the children in the audience would be treated to a sucker. All of the children immediately stood up and began pressing forward. Many were very small and were getting crushed against the stage. Children who had already received a sucker could not leave the scene because they were trapped against the stage by the children still trying to press forward. The worst that happened was that some parents were anxious and upset, and some children were crying and frightened, although no one was injured. Two points about this event need to be made. First, the puppet performance was excellent and there was no need for the addition of a sucker giveaway at the event. Second, the way the giveaway was handled damaged what was, up to that point, an excellent event.

> If not handled properly, giveaways can be a detriment to an event rather than a positive contribution.

If not handled properly, giveaways can be a detriment to an event rather than a positive contribution. Giveaways that do not have sufficient service for all can also create problems. People who are not served usually feel that the queue was unfair and feel disappointed. An agency suffers adverse publicity when it allows incomplete or poorly managed giveaways to occur under its auspices.

Pre-Queues and No Queues

Two final issues to be discussed are pre-queues and no queues. Despite well-developed agency plans for queues, participants often take matters into their own hands and begin pre-queues before the start of the official agency queue. Programmers need to anticipate this possibility and be prepared to deal with it. They must decide whether to recognize the order established by the pre-queue and how to recognize it. No matter how well a programmer plans, an uncomfortable interface always occurs when the time comes to transition between the pre-queue and the official queue. Some agencies have therefore stopped using a queue for determining the order of admission to events and now use a system of random drawing for admission positions. The NCAA has done this for Final Four public tickets. The demand is simply too great and queue management too much of a hassle to do otherwise. A number of college campuses have also implemented such a system for admission to rock concerts and other high-demand events.

Some people object to a random draw system because it eliminates the rule of distributive justice. All who enter the drawing have an equal chance of being admitted to the event. Without a queue, those who strongly desire admission do not have the opportunity to invest their time in a queue and receive the appropriate reward (preferential treatment).

The management of the queue sends messages to participants about the quality of the program. It is usually the first face-to-face contact the agency has with the participant. Queuing needs to be considered a part of the program, and programmers should deal with it during the implementation stage. They need to manage it to maximize its positive contribution to participant satisfaction with a program.

Conclusion

Implementing registration includes efficiently registering participants at a location and time convenient for them. Each registration method has advantages and disadvantages. Programmers need to handle myriad details well to complete a successful registration. Registration software packages can help agencies implement registration and follow-up marketing efforts. Understanding queuing behavior is essential for programmers to properly manage queues. Queues that are fairly and efficiently managed at registration and at program locations contribute to participant satisfaction with services.

References

Dobmeyer, E. (1986). *Registration techniques*. Manhattan, KS: Learning Resources Network.

Homans, G. C. (1961). *Social behavior: Its elementary forms*. New York, NY: Harcourt.

Maister, D. H. (1985). The psychology of waiting in lines. In J. A. Czepiel, M. R. Solomon, & C. F. Surprenant (Eds.), *The service encounter* (pp. 176–183). Lexington, MA: Lexington Books, D. C. Heath.

Mann, L. (1973). Learning to live with lines. In J. Helmer & N. A. Edginton (Eds.), *Urbanmen: The psychology of urban survival* (pp. 42–61). New York, NY: Macmillan.

Peterson, J. A., & Hronek, B. B. (1992). *Risk management: For park, recreation, and leisure services* (2nd ed.). Champaign, IL: Sagamore.

Sixel, L. M. (2010, November 18). Working; Regulators tell retailers to keep mobs in check. *Houston Chronicle*, pp. D1, 4.

Stuart, R. (1979, December 5). Cincinnati officials order inquiry into concert crush that killed 11. *New York Times*, pp. 1, D21.

Thomas, R. M., Jr. (1979, December 4). 11 killed and 8 badly hurt in crush before rock concert in Cincinnati. *New York Times*, pp. 1, 13.

Documents With Limited Circulation

Documents and brochures from the following agencies were cited in this chapter:

Recreation and Community Services Department, 1 West Campbell Ave. #C31, Campbell, CA 95008

We're All Smiles
Photo Courtesy of Cincinnati Recreation Commission. Photo by Bunny Arszman.

16 *Staffing and Supervising Program Operations*

KEY TERMS

Staffing, Position Analysis, KSAs, Job Description, Recruitment, Selection, BFOQs, Orientation, Training, Appraisal, Compensation, Contracting for Personal Services, Supervising Operations

Step 7: Implementation

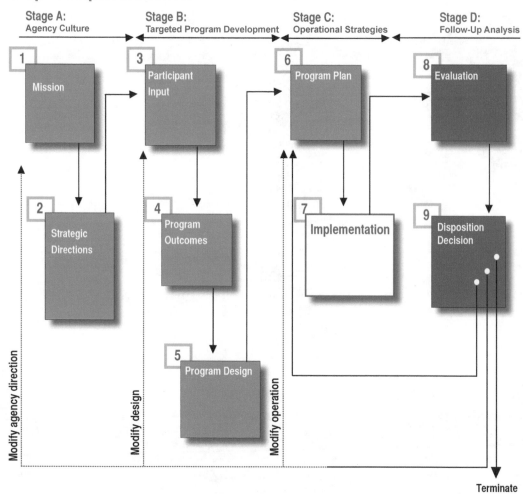

Staffing recreation services involves recruiting, selecting, orienting, training, deploying, supervising, appraising, compensating, and contracting the staff needed for staging programs. Many leisure service organizations have a *blended workforce* including permanent full-time, part-time, temporary and seasonal employees, and independent contractors. Many agencies also recruit, train, and supervise docents and volunteers. This chapter outlines the essential elements of the employment process and discusses personnel management problems and techniques associated with supervising program operations.

> Staffing recreation services involves recruiting, selecting, orienting, training, deploying, supervising, appraising, compensating, and contracting the staff needed for staging programs.

Most recreation agencies have well-developed written policies for managing full-time personnel in the agency and usually a human resources department to oversee them. Unfortunately, this is not always true for part-time and seasonal employees, even though leisure service agencies typically employ a large number of these employees to operate their recreation facilities and programs. In many agencies, part-time and seasonal workers accomplish most of the face-to-face delivery of the recreation service. This is the case in many commercial recreation operations, municipalities, not-for-profit organizations, church recreation, sport organizations, and other organizations that operate recreation services.

Research has (McKinney & Chandler, 1991) suggested that this practice has become popular because it increases staffing flexibility and lowers labor costs. With part-time and seasonal workers, programmers can match the number of staff members hired to their needs on a seasonal basis. In addition, because the interest in many recreation activities is cyclical, programmers can hire staff to lead and teach the activities currently being demanded with no commitment to their future employment.

However, this practice creates issues. First, part-time staff members are less loyal to the organization and its programs (McKinney & Chandler, 1991) and thus may not promote the long-term interests of the organization by building customer loyalty. Participants rarely know if an employee is part or full time, so they judge the organization as a whole based on the performance of all members of the blended workforce, regardless of employment status. Second, the rate of employee turnover among part-time and seasonal workers is higher. This results in a need for the agency to recruit and train new employees frequently. Both of these issues lead to a third problem: the need for full-time programmers to closely supervise the work performance of recently hired employees.

In many cases, programmers cannot personally deliver all of the recreation services under their direction. As a successful professional football coach once said, "It does not matter how much I know about how to play football. What matters is how much the players on the field know about playing football." He was implying that he had a tremendous role in teaching and preparing the players to play the game. The same is true for the delivery of recreation services. Other researchers have found that seasonal employees are more happy and motivated when supervisory practices create a work environment that is challenging and provides employees the skills needed to perform at the level desired (Henderson & Bialeschki, 1993). Thus, operating successful programs often depends on how well the programmer can recruit, train, deploy, and supervise the blended workforce. The remainder of this chapter provides a general overview of the tasks that programmers must accomplish to successfully staff and supervise recreation operations.[1]

Job Analysis

Staffing begins with understanding the mission and strategic directions of the agency. Agencies need to recruit and hire staff who can fulfill the mission and deliver program services that implement the strategic directions. In most instances, organized recreation services are people-to-people services involving face-to-face interactions between participants and staff in leadership, instructor, or customer service roles. It is essential, therefore, that the agency places qualified and well-trained staff members in these roles.

To acquire an adequate staff, an agency first completes a job analysis, "a systematic investigation of the tasks, duties, and responsibilities of a job, and the necessary knowledge, skills, and abilities someone needs to perform the job adequately" (Mathis & Jackson, 1982, p. 143). A job analysis contains all of the information necessary, including a detailed statement of work behaviors and other information relevant to the job, for the supervisor to develop and administer the job. From the job analysis, an important fundamental document, the agency derives a job description, orientation, needs, training needs, and information for employee appraisals.

The Position Analysis Questionnaire (PAQ) developed by McCormick, Shaw, and DeNisi (1979) provides an outline of job divisions for organizing a job analysis. The PAQ identifies six job divisions that characterize most jobs. McCormick et al. also identified 194 job elements that can be categorized within these six divisions. Exhibit 16.1 shows the six divisions and examples of job elements characteristic of a recreation leader's job.

Each job in an agency requires different knowledge, skills, and abilities (KSAs), and programmers need information about each of these to prepare a job analysis. Knowledge is a body of information a person must possess and apply directly to the performance of the job. For example, knowledge about water chemistry would be required for a pool operator. Skill is the possession of a demonstrable competence for performing a learned psychomotor act. Skill in water rescue techniques would be required for a lifeguard. Ability is the current competence of a person to perform a behavior that can be observed or that results in an observable product. An ability to develop and write a weekly playground program plan would be required of a playground leader.

---

[1] For a more comprehensive treatment of personnel matters, see *Human Resource Management in Recreation, Sport, and Leisure Services*, by M. L. Arnold, R. Glover, and C. Beeler, 2012, Urbana, IL: Sagamore-Venture.

Exhibit 16.1. Recreation Worker Job Analysis

1. **Information Input.** Where and how does the worker get the information used in performing the job?

   Examples: Attend staff orientation and training
   Use policy manuals
   Receive verbal instructions

2. **Mental Process.** What reasoning, decision-making, and information-processing activities are involved in performing the job?

   Examples: Interact with parents in youth sport programs
   Enforce safety rules to prevent injury
   Modify activities to meet the needs of specific groups including people with disabilities

3. **Work Output.** What physical activities does the worker perform, and what tools or devices does he or she use?

   Examples: Instruct participants in a variety of activities
   Organize and set up equipment used in recreational activities and sports
   Administer basic first aid
   Use computers for data entry, facility scheduling, and participant communication

4. **Relationships With Other Persons.** What relationships with other people are required in performing the job?

   Examples: Lead and instruct recreation activities to a variety of participants
   Communicate to parents and caregivers
   Cooperate with administrative and maintenance staff

5. **Job Context.** In what physical or social context is the work performed?

   Examples: Work in outdoor settings
   Work in a fun and social environment
   Work in constant interaction with participants, parents, coaches, and support staff

6. **Other Characteristics.** What activities, conditions, or characteristics other than those already described are relevant to the job?

   Examples: May work weekends or irregular hours or may be seasonally employed
   Must possess tactful communication skills
   Often work without direct supervision

Note. Adapted from McCormick, Shaw, and DeNisi (1979).

Other job elements that need review and consideration include the amount of decision making and problem solving an employee may be responsible for accomplishing. If a position includes such responsibilities, what are the consequences to the agency if there is an error? How much autonomy will the employee pose in their day-to-day work? Will they need to function without an immediate supervisor? Will they have financial responsibilities for collecting cash, budgeting, or purchasing materials and supplies? Programmers need to identify and accurately describe all of these and more in a PAQ so subsequent documents derived from them are valid.

Although an agency may have a personnel department, preparation of the PAQ is often assigned to the program supervisor requesting the position. Therefore, programmers should fully understand and be able to articulate the job elements necessary for performing a job. Incumbents in a similar position in a different agency are often good sources of information about what is required for doing a specific job.

Job Description

Programmers can use job analysis data to write a job description, which is a summary of the duties and responsibilities of the job. The job description is not as detailed as the job analysis, but it must represent the principal components of the job, give an applicant a good indication of the major responsibilities, and note the qualifications a person must possess to be a successful candidate for the job. Exhibit 16.2 includes a general outline of a job description.

Exhibit 16.3 shows a sample job description for an event planner; it was developed using the outline in Exhibit 16.2. Notice that the job description outlines the nature of the position, the requirements for employment, the nature of the work to be performed, the type of supervision to be performed, and special requirements. The personnel department in an agency usually has a specific outline for developing job descriptions. Any outline likely includes components similar to those in this example. Exhibit 16.4 (page 316) shows a sample job description for a front desk attendant in a health or racquet club. Compare these two descriptions to see how the jobs differ. After comparing the descriptions, complete Exercise 16.1 (page 317).

Exhibit 16.2. General Outline of a Job Description

Function Statement
A general statement of the responsibilities of the position.

Supervision
A statement specifying to whom the employee is responsible.

Domains
Statements outlining the major areas of responsibility of the employee.

Task Statements
A list of work behaviors that distinguish the position.

Worker Traits
A list of the knowledge, skills, and abilities that are essential for the position.

Desired Education Experience
A statement of the education, training, and/experience required or desired for the position.

Special Requirements
A list of any special knowledge, certifications, or other specific requirements for the job.

Exhibit 16.3. Job Description—Event Planner

Basic Function and Responsibility

Under general supervision and direction, event planners oversee multiple operations at one time, face numerous deadlines, and orchestrate the activities of several groups of people. They design, organize, coordinate conferences, conventions, meetings, seminars, exhibitions, trade shows, festivals, and other events.

Supervision

Event planners may work on a freelance basis or for an event planning company where they are responsible to the CEO of the company.

Domains

Design and oversee conferences, meetings, and other special events.

Manage logistical details in fast-paced and demanding environments for different groups of people.

Task Statements

Coordinate event logistics including facilities, catering, signage, translation, printing, and security.

Arrange attendee accommodations and transportation.

Establish and monitor budgets to support events.

Worker Traits

Be creative and well organized.

Be able to visualize events from start to finish.

Possess excellent presentation skills for communicating information effectively and persuasively.

Knowledge of media relations.

Knowledge of marketing for event promotion.

Desired Education and Experience

Bachelor's degree in tourism, hospitality administration, or related field is required.

Previous experience in managing events is desirable.

Specialized knowledge of budgets, multimedia equipment, and room setup required.

Special Requirements

Must possess a valid vehicle operator's license.

Applicants with certification in first aid will be given priority.

Exhibit 16.4. Job Description—Front Desk Attendant

Basic Function and Responsibility

Under general supervision and direction, front desk attendants oversee the operation and smooth functioning of the club, including greeting participants, explaining rules and policies, taking reservations, making sales, and other duties as assigned.

Supervision

Front desk attendants are supervised by the management personnel on duty.

Domains

Public relations.

Operate facility.

Sales.

Task Statements

Greets participants by name and issues equipment.

Makes reservations for equipment and facilities.

Makes sales of equipment and club services.

Explains club rules and policies.

Checks in users and assigns court space or equipment.

Worker Traits

Knowledge of club policies and rules.

Knowledge of game rules and techniques.

Knowledge of club equipment and facilities.

Skill in learning and remembering club members by name.

Ability to deal tactfully and effectively in enforcing club rules and policies.

Ability to explain and interpret club policies.

Ability to make sales.

Desired Educational Experience

Completion of college-level courses in recreational leadership or appropriate physical education courses is required (or desired).

Previous experience in the operation of recreation facilities or hospitality facilities is desirable.

Specialized knowledge of specific club activities is desirable.

Special Requirements

Applicants with certification in first aid will be given priority.

In class, use the outline of a job description in Exhibit 16.2 and develop a job description for a part-time or seasonal recreation worker's position. Critique each other's job descriptions by considering the following questions:

- Is the job description specific enough?
- Does the job description make clear the duties and requirements of the position?
- Are the items included representative of the complete job?

Recruitment

Recreation agencies recruit a large pool of part-time and seasonal employees to meet their needs throughout the year. Often, they also recruit and train a docent or volunteer corps. When an agency employs a large number of part-time and seasonal workers, turnover often happens frequently. Because of this, recruitment, orientation, and training often occur continually in an agency.

Recruitment involves obtaining a pool of candidates who are qualified to assume the agency's positions. Programmers cannot assume that the right employees will simply appear when needed. Recruitment needs to be accomplished prior to the need for an employee's services. You know you will need new employees, and the idea is to have a pool of qualified applicants who are ready to assume agency positions when they need to be filled. Agencies recruit from within and outside their organization.

> Recruitment involves obtaining a pool of candidates who are qualified to assume the agency's positions.

Internal Recruitment

Internal recruitment is an important strategy of hiring employees for an organization. However, if overused, it can lead to charges that employment practices in the agency are "closed" and "you need to know someone" in the organization to get a job there. If true, these practices may lead to legal problems for the agency. Even if these charges are not true, the belief that they are will eventually diminish the number of applicants and hamper the agency's ability to attract a sufficiently large pool of qualified applicants.

Despite these problems, internal recruitment is still an important strategy of hiring employees and can be implemented in several ways. The promotion or transfer of existing employees is one method of internal recruitment. Promotion and transfer to more desirable or higher paying jobs is a strong motivator for current employees. It is also more cost effective for the agency to use employees who have been oriented and are already familiar with policies and operational procedures than to train new employees. Internal promotion and transfer can be initiated by the supervisor or requested by part-time and seasonal employees to whom a list of current openings has been distributed.

Agencies also accomplish recruitment by using current and former employees to recruit new employees. They should only use this method in conjunction with a widely distributed, open announcement of available positions to the public at large. However, current and former employees are often part of a network of individuals who have the requisite knowledge, skills, and abilities to be good recreation workers. For example, members of the "tennis community" are likely to become tennis instructors or assume court management positions. Do not overlook the potential usefulness of these networks.

As a final internal recruitment method, agencies can examine previous applicants for positions currently available in the agency. Technically this is not an internal recruitment method, but it does make good use of resources invested previously in obtaining a pool of applicants. If the agency has a sufficiently large pool of good applicants, it will always have applications on file when needed. Generally, most programmers keep a file of such applicants indexed by their ability to lead or instruct specific recreation activities.

External Recruitment

External recruitment involves an organized effort to attract employees from outside the organization. A mandatory part of external recruitment is announcing the availability of positions to the general public. This should be done through the local print and broadcast media and through issuing and posting job announcements. In addition, external recruitment involves an organized and focused effort by the agency to make known the availability of positions to individuals who are likely to be qualified, that is, to target recruitment efforts. Recruiting in high schools for summer leaders is one example. Recruiting in junior college and senior college recreation, physical education, tourism, and hospitality curricula is another targeted recruitment source for seasonal and part-time employees. Still other sources might be church youth groups, recreation clubs or hobby groups, and other recreation agencies.

Another external recruitment resource is LinkedIn, a professional social networking outlet for professionals to connect with others in the field. Users post information about their educational background including résumés and professional interests. LinkedIn includes a jobs section where agencies can advertise and recruit individuals to open positions. Users can use the platform to apply for jobs. Like Facebook, LinkedIn requires its users to connect with others to build their network. To summarize, external recruitment approaches use announcements to the general public and a targeted recruitment effort focused on groups of individuals who are likely to possess the knowledge, skills, and abilities to be good recreation employees.

Selection

In many cases, agencies eliminate individuals in the applicant pool from further consideration because they do not meet basic requirements of the position. These could include an unfavorable background check, an unacceptable result from a drug test, or failure to meet the basic bona fide occupational qualifications (BFOQs are the criteria that are legally permitted in making the hiring decision) of the position.

Agencies should complete background checks for job applicants and potential volunteers. Employees and volunteers involved with programming often represent the face of the organization, and without them, many agencies could not function. Taking proper steps to properly vet potential employees and volunteers will protect the agency, community, and participants. The National Recreation and Park Association (2018) has partnered with the Background Investigation Bureau (BIB) to help with this process and recommends checking the following information when credentialing volunteers: "address trace, county criminal record check, criminal record database, and national sex offender registry" (p. 68). Persons found guilty of felonies, sex offenses, or misdemeanors should be disqualified and not allowed to serve as a volunteer (National Recreation and Park Association, 2018). Web-based screening platforms provide fast results and ensure safe environments for all.

> External recruitment involves an organized effort to attract employees from outside the organization.

After completing this initial screening process, the programmer selects which applicants to hire. Selection techniques usually involve a test, an interview, or both. In any case, the criteria on which selection is made must be valid indicators of the qualifications needed for performing the job. There are technical requirements for ensuring that tests used for hiring purposes are valid and that the questions used in interviews are legal and pertain to job performance. An explanation of these validation procedures is beyond the scope of this book.

Under the laws enforced by the U.S. Equal Employment Opportunity Commission (EEOC, n.d.), it is illegal for agencies to discriminate against someone (applicant or employee) based on race, color, religion, sex (including gender identity, sexual orientation, and pregnancy), national origin, age (40 or older), disability or genetic information. It is also illegal for agencies to retaliate against a person who complained about discrimination, filed a charge of discrimination, or participated in an employment discrimination investigation or lawsuit (EEOC, n.d.).

Exceptions to this legislation are permitted, but the burden of demonstrating a necessary and valid exception rests with the employer. The EEOC rigorously defends these criteria, and the reader is advised to not attempt such a claim without first consulting with legal counsel.

Onboarding

Onboarding is the general process of transitioning a newly hired individual to an employee ready for a duty assignment. It includes ensuring an employee's intake paperwork has been completed, applicable benefits have begun, and the employee has completed orientation.

Taking on a new job creates personal anxiety, so it is important that the onboarding process is welcoming to new employees and ensures they feel comfortable in their new position. Full-time employees make a number of important decisions about which benefits to select, likely including medical insurance and retirement programs, among others. The organization's human resources department will likely handle many onboarding activities. In some organizations, human resources conducts a general orientation to the organization, and individual departments complete the orientation, focusing on their specific department's operations and the new employee's work assignments.

Orientation

All new employees, including part time and seasonal ones, should receive an orientation to the agency. Volunteers should also receive an orientation to the agency. Orientations create an initial favorable impression of the agency for the employees, help them adjust to the demands of their position, and enhance their acceptance in the agency. For many young people hired in part-time and seasonal recreation positions, the job will be their first work experience. They often need special help in adjusting to simply having a job, as well as in developing loyalty to the organization.

Generally, the orientation covers three types of information. First, it outlines the nature of the organization. What is the mission of the organization? Who is the employee working for? What is this organization trying to accomplish? What is the employee's role in helping the organization accomplish its goals? What is the structure of the organization, and where is the employee located in this structure? This explanation should make clear to whom the employee reports, that is, the employee's supervisor.

Second, the orientation outlines the nature of a typical workday. What can employees expect their workday to be like on this job? What is a typical order of events in a workday? What kinds of tasks will they do in a typical day? From the orientation, the employees should have a good idea of what to expect during a typical workday.

> The goals of an orientation are to create an initial favorable impression of the agency for the employees, to help them adjust to the demands of their position, and to enhance their acceptance in the agency.

Finally, the orientation covers work rules, policies, and procedures for employees to follow to successfully function in the agency. Often, work rules, personnel policies, and procedures that apply to all of the agency's employees are covered at a general orientation session conducted by the human resources department. However, the task of covering job-specific policies, procedures, and special skills that employees need to know to perform the job is usually the responsibility of the supervisor. Generally, covering specific job functions and responsibilities is considered training rather than orientation and will be covered in the next section.

Depending on the size of an organization and the diversity of jobs, the following may be covered in orientation or training. Employees who will deal with the public face-to-face or who are assigned to park locations where they may be alone or working with other part-time and seasonal workers need training in emergency procedures before assuming a duty assignment. This is a must, and failure to do so could cause undue harm to participants and place the agency in a litigious situation. Many part-time and seasonal employees are given an orientation and some training and then placed in a position where they are closely supervised and given on-the-job training while performing duties. But this procedure will only work if they are closely and continuously supervised.

It is easy to subject new employees to information overload during orientation. Often, all of the information covered will be familiar to the programmer and new to the employee. Because of this, an orientation program should also include, within 1 to 2 weeks of the original orientation, a time for the new employees to meet and ask questions about what they may not have thoroughly learned or understood at the initial orientation.

Training

Training is the process whereby employees acquire the knowledge, skills, abilities, concepts, and attitudes to fulfill the responsibilities of their positions in the agency. The amount and content of training depends on job responsibilities and how much of the required knowledge, skills, abilities, concepts, and attitudes employees already possess at the time they are hired.

Part-time and seasonal employees often have fewer skills and need more training than full-time employees to fulfill their job responsibilities in the manner the agency desires. The Disney organization is firmly committed to thoroughly training part-time and seasonal workers (Pope, 1987). It never allows workers to learn on the job, but ensures that they thoroughly know a job before a duty assignment. Part-time and seasonal employees often need instruction in operating specialized equipment and apparatus. Training in leadership skills, recreation planning, and game rules is also often needed.

> Training is the process whereby employees acquire the knowledge, skills, abilities, concepts, and attitudes to fulfill the responsibilities of their positions in the agency.

Training ensures that staff members have the activity skills necessary for the program they have been hired to lead, direct, or supervise. When training part-time and seasonal recreation employees, agencies need to convey the type of recreation service they desire to offer and good customer service practices, for example, how employees should treat participants in face-to-face interactions. The experience a participant has in large part depends on face-to-face interactions with recreation workers. For example, some organizations require their staff to greet people, preferably by name, as they enter a facility. Or employees may need to give people a good departure experience from the facility. Some performance arts venues have their ushers in the hallway delivering a thank-you message while patrons exit the facility. Training in the appropriate face-to-face demeanor to use while interacting with participants to obtain compliance with policies and rules are only part of the training that part-time and seasonal recreation workers need.

Employees may also need training in the specific skills of their position. Exhibit 16.5 gives an outline of a training program for staff members responsible for supervising a recreation area or building. The program instructs employees in agency expectations and specific procedures for supervising an area or facility. It defines the role and functions of the task and prepares individuals to fill the role. It also points out how employees can implement good customer service.

Common formats for preparing employees include in-service training, conferences, and webinars. In-service training can be provided for employees during their employment. The agency selects topics in response to needs and voids in observed employee performance. Conferences are professional gatherings of practitioners, academics, and researchers where information is disseminated through keynote speakers, research and educational sessions, and meetings. Webinars are Web-based seminars, presentations, lectures, and workshops that are transmitted over the Internet by insurance agencies or professional organizations. Agencies often use webinars to train employees in the areas of sexual harassment, workplace violence, and mandated crime reporting, among others. A key feature of a webinar is its interactive elements—the ability to give, receive, and discuss information. With tight fiscal resources, webinars will likely become more viable alternatives for professional development because they reduce costs for traveling to conferences.

Training and retraining are important and time-consuming tasks for programmers. The types of training needed often become obvious as they observe staff operate programs and facilities. A general rule is that if the programmer wants something accomplished a specific way, the training process must include instructions for performing the procedure. Well-trained employees are essential to a successful program and it is well worth the time and money to train them.

Performance Appraisal

Appraisal involves evaluating employees' performance of their responsibilities. Programmers can acquire performance data with a number of methods including direct observation by the supervisor, peer evaluations completed by the employee's work partners, summary analysis of program evaluations the employee has operated, and others. Agencies most often use appraisals to determine employee eligibility for a raise and suitability for continuing employment. But they should not overlook using appraisals to identify employees who are qualified to assume different responsibilities in the agency, that is, either a lateral transfer or a promotion, and their use in determining training needs.

There are two types of appraisals: formal and informal. Supervisors conduct informal appraisal whenever they believe it is necessary. The day-to-day personal interactions of the supervisor with employees give employees feedback about how

Exhibit 16.5. Training Outline for Area Supervisors

As part of your ongoing duties, you will be assigned the responsibility to supervise park areas and facilities. This is one of the most difficult assignments you will have. When you supervise an area, your responsibility is to protect the facility, to protect the programs in operation at the facility so that participants can have the experience they desire from participation, and finally, to protect the drop-in participants of the facility. You must perform the following 10 duties to fulfill the supervisor's role:

Enforcement 1–5

1. You must actively work at supervising. Supervising time is not your break—supervision cannot be accomplished from the employee lounge or office window.

2. Circulate around the grounds or building and let your physical presence be known. Ensure all participants know there is a supervisor on duty—someone who is in charge of the facility. Wear your uniform so that you can easily be identified.

3. Protect organized programs in operation at the facility from harassment by other users (especially drop-in users) of the facility.

4. Handle any trouble or problems that erupt in the area. Be aware of locations where trouble is likely to happen, and become familiar with the participants likely to cause trouble.

5. Deal aggressively with problems likely to occur in the area. Try to anticipate problems and head them off.

Good Customer Service Practices 6–10

6. Talk to participants and encourage them to participate in organized programs. Know the answers to their questions. To do this, familiarize yourself with all of the services available from the agency.

7. Give the job your own personal touch. Make your area of responsibility a place you would like your own children, brothers and sisters, or friends to attend.

8. Try to start pickup activities. Always have a few activities to suggest to participants who seem to have run out of things to do.

9. Accept people as they are. Blacks and Whites, long-hairs and baldies, young people and old people should all receive the same courteous treatment from you. Every user is a VIP and should be treated with courtesy and respect.

10. Use the magic mirror of your smile. Handle people with a smile and in a courteous manner.

well the supervisor believes they are performing. The supervisor reacts to and comments on an employee's work during site visits, over coffee, and in similar settings, thus providing informal evaluative feedback to the employee. With young employees, frequent positive feedback assures them they are performing well and encourages them to continue with a positive attitude in the workplace. Remember, some of these individuals are young and in their first job.

The agency should also have a formal appraisal system during which the supervisor's impressions and observations of the employee's performance become a matter of written record. Four decisions need to be made before implementing a formal appraisal system.

Who Will Conduct the Appraisal?

Programmers are almost always designated as the individual responsible for appraising the performance of the part-time and seasonal staff under their supervision. However, a senior-level, seasonal staff member may be asked for input. For example, a public school teacher who is hired to direct a summer day camp may have significant input into the appraisal of younger, less experienced camp counselors. Although the programmer may have the final responsibility for appraising part-time and seasonal employees, it is important for the programmer to obtain input from employees who are qualified to make such judgments and who are in a better position to have firsthand information about an employee's performance.

It is also common practice for recreation operations to obtain input from participants about the performance of employees. Agencies often obtain participant ratings at facility operations and after program operations. These data should also play some role in the overall appraisal of the employee.

How Will the Appraisal Data Be Collected?

Programmers in most instances use an employee appraisal instrument that already exists in the agency. They should examine the instrument before the appraisal period so they know what employee behaviors they should be observing and can thus note specific behaviors during on-site observations. It is also important for supervisors to explain the appraisal system and instrument to employees before they begin work. Employees should understand the criteria on which they will be evaluated, who will do the evaluation, and how it will be used in determining raises and personnel actions.

A popular method of appraisal in organizations with many positions is an all-purpose rating scale that uses the duties and responsibilities outlined in the job description as the evaluation criteria. Exhibit 16.6 (page 326) shows an example of an all-purpose rating scale applied to the job description for an event planner (Exhibit 16.3). With this method, each position in the agency is rated in the same manner, but the appraisal criteria in each case are unique to the specific job. Now complete Exercise 16.2 (page 327).

It is also important for the programmer to record unusual incidents of an employee's performance. These include exceptional incidents and subpar, unsatisfactory performances. The programmer uses these documentation notes as the basis for comments on the permanent appraisal instrument during the formal appraisal.

If an incident is unfavorable enough to cause an unsatisfactory performance rating, it is recommended that the programmer holds a consultation review with the employee within 24 hours of the incident. During this consultation, the programmer shares the written documentation and discusses it with the employee. The employee signs off on the incident report, acknowledging that he or she has been counseled about the incident. The employee can also make a written comment on the report. In this way, personnel incidents are thoroughly documented and become a part of the employee's record. This procedure can also be used for exceptional performance. In either case, this procedure creates a written record that the programmer can use to justify any personnel action required, including promotions, demotions, raises, denial of a raise, dismissal, transfer, or recommendation for additional training.

When Will Appraisal Occur?

Frequent and timely feedback is essential for the employee appraisal system to fulfill a counseling, redirecting function in the agency. With full-time employees, agencies normally conduct an appraisal midway through the employee's probationary period and another at the end. A probationary period is a specified time an employee has to prove himself or herself to the agency. It varies in length depending on the agency and the position. At the end of the probationary period, the programmer decides either to place the employee on permanent status or to dismiss him or her. Once employees gain permanent status, the agency usually appraises them either semiannually or annually.

In many organizations, part-time and seasonal employees are never given permanent status, although they are usually appraised when their responsibilities end. For example, the performance of all summer employees would be appraised at the end of the summer program. In these instances, the performance appraisal usually determines whether the employee will be hired for the next operation of the program, that is, next summer. These practices vary by agency, so programmers will need to become familiar with policies and practices that govern part-time and seasonal employment in their agency.

How Should the Performance Appraisal Interview Be Conducted?

Programmers conduct the appraisal interview immediately after each formal performance appraisal. These interviews provide programmers with an opportunity to communicate directly with employees about their strengths and weaknesses.

Employees usually approach an appraisal interview with concern and anxiety. It is useful for the supervisor and the employee to remember that the worth of the employee as a human being is not being judged here—the worth of the employee's job performance for a specified period is being judged. The appraisal interview also provides an important opportunity for the programmer to set an agenda with employees for retraining or reorganizing how they will conduct their work. This is a primary time for counseling employees on doing their work and discovering weaknesses that may need to be corrected through additional training.

Exhibit 16.6. Employee Appraisal Instrument—Employee Performance Evaluation Report

Employee's Name: Appraisal Date:
Agency Name: Job Title:
Employment Date:
Appraisal Period: From: To:
Reason for Review: ()Mid-Probation   ()Probation   ()Annual   ()End of Season

Factors Considered in Ratings and Comments	Weight Value %		1 Unsatis-factory	4 Satis-factory	7 Above Average	10 Excep-tional	Factor Score
Demonstrates skill and creativity in planning events.	.14	×				10	1.4
Demonstrates skill in establishing and monitoring budgets to support events.	.14	×				8	1.12
Demonstrates ability to visualize events and to make necessary adjustments.	.10	×				8	.80
Promotes events to target audience.	.08	×				8	.64
Supervises event in operation.	.12	×			7		.84
Demonstrates skill in dealing tactfully and effectively with attendees.	.12	×			7		.84
Recognizes and responds to safety hazards.	.08	×			7		.56
Demonstrates skill in face-to-face leadership during the event.	.12	×				8	.96
Demonstrates skill in managing the details of event logistics.	.10	×				9	.90
TOTAL	SUM MUST EQUAL 100						Summary Rating 8.06/10

1. Assign a weight value, expressed as a decimal, for each factor.
2. Assign a score for each factor from 1 to 10.
3. Multiply weight by rating for factor score.
4. Add factor scores for summary rating.

Compensation

The three types of employee compensation include direct compensation, incentive pay, and indirect compensation. Direct compensation refers to the employee's wage or salary. Wages are usually a per hour compensation, whereas salary is usually a monthly or annual pay rate. Part-time and seasonal employees usually receive wages, whereas full-time employees may receive wages or salary. Incentive pay refers to commissions or bonuses for exceptional performance. These are rarely given in recreation and leisure positions, except in some private health clubs and tourism operations where a commission may be paid on the volume of memberships or services and products sold by an employee. Indirect compensation refers to the benefits an employee receives including medical insurance, retirement, workers' compensation insurance, and other benefits given by the agency. Most full-time recreation employees receive pay and benefits for their positions including Social Security and Medicare (Federal Insurance Contributions Act, FICA), unemployment insurance, workers' compensation insurance, health insurance, and family and medical leave. Part-time and seasonal employees usually receive pay and minimal benefits that are required for all employees including FICA that includes Social Security and Medicare insurance payments, plus workers' compensation insurance. What part-time and seasonal employees receive in addition to these will vary by agency practices and state laws.

As stated, many recreation agencies operate with a large number of part-time and seasonal employees. A low wage structure for these employees enables many recreation businesses to remain profitable. Thus, agencies often feel pressured to keep part-time and seasonal wages low.

Programmers usually bear the direct adverse effect of this strategy. They are forced to operate program services with low-wage, untrained employees whom they must train extensively and supervise closely. Even though wages are low, programmers are well advised to develop a merit-based compensation plan for part-time and seasonal employees. It is important for agencies to have a sufficiently attractive incentive pay structure to retain the employees already trained, thereby avoiding having to constantly retrain new employees.

The usual practice in incentive plans is for agencies to make all raises merit based and to require that employees spend a certain amount of time in a specific pay grade before being eligible for a raise. For example, an employee earning minimum wage may have to complete 1,000 hours (about 6 months at 40 hours/week) before being eligible to be considered for a raise. However, the raise is not automatic after 1,000 hours. The employee still must have a favorable or exceptional merit review and must spend the requisite time at the beginning pay rate. The performance appraisal determines how well the employee has performed the responsibilities of the position and his or her eligibility for a raise in pay.

Part-time wages paid by the agency must be competitive with prevailing rates for similar part-time work in the area. The availability of part-time workers in a specific geographic area will partly determine the prevailing rate. Agencies can control how selective they can be in hiring, through their position in the local part-time wage market. Obviously, offering wages on the high end of what generally prevails in the community will ensure the agency first choice of available workers.

Part-time and seasonal employees rarely receive any benefits other than those required by law. Employers are usually required to pay Social Security, Medicare, and workers' compensation insurance on every employee. Part-time and seasonal workers in recreation operations often receive the opportunity to use the employer's facilities or services free of charge or at a discounted rate. For example, employees at a water park may be admitted to the park on their day off at no charge. Agencies can offer and promote these types of benefits, which are low cost to the agency, as part of the compensation package. Sometimes these benefits provide a sufficient incremental advantage that enables the agency to attract better part-time and seasonal employees.

Contracting for Personnel Services

It is common practice for agencies to contract for the services of individuals rather than place them in the agency's employ. This can be confusing, though, because many seasonal workers receive contracts from the agency, but this does not mean they are contract employees. For example, a person may be contracted to teach a tennis class consisting of 16 one-hour lessons. The agency gives the instructor a flat rate or a percentage of the class revenue and does not place the instructor in its employ. Contract employees contract for services provided and are not employees of the agency. So the notion of a "contract employee" is an oxymoron. Because contractors are not employees, the agency does not withhold taxes or pay Social Security, Medicare insurance, or workers' compensation for them. Contractors pay these on their own when they file their taxes.

This practice can have issues. Using a contract arrangement definitely reduces direct costs for the agency because the agency does not have to pay benefits and the practice eliminates its exposure to the requirements of a number of employment laws (Moiseichik, Hunt, & Macchiarelli, 1992). However, maintaining control of the quality of contract services is sometimes difficult. The individual under contract is not an employee and thus not subject to direct supervision and control. Any irregularities in service performance or delivery become contract violations rather than personnel matters. Compliance with a contract can be enforced, but it is a more cumbersome and less direct process.

The Internal Revenue Service reviews this practice carefully since their studies have revealed that many employers "are misclassifying employees as independent contractors to avoid paying employment taxes" (Moiseichik et al., 1992, p. 63). The major employee group that has been investigated thus far is athletic league officials. At least two city recreation departments were required to pay back taxes that would have been due if the workers were correctly classified as employees. One key point of issue with athletic league officials is that the agency schedules their work. Independent contractors schedule the work themselves. For example, if you contract with a painter to paint a building, the painter decides when the work will be done.

Ensuring the contract and the contractual relationship reflect the following features increases the likelihood that a worker will be accepted as a contractor (adapted from Moiseichik et al., 1992). Agency supervisors must not control the detail and manner of how work is performed by a contractor and must not directly supervise the performance of their work. Contractors should not be subject to the agency's personnel policies and cannot be hired, fired, or disciplined under them. They are not paid through the agency's payroll system, there are no payroll deductions from their contract price, and they are paid a lump sum for the completed project or on the amount of items completed, for example, the number of games officiated. Furthermore, they supply all of their own equipment and materials; they are free to provide their services to other agencies; they are obviously in business for themselves as evidenced by a business letterhead, address, and phone; the contract period is definite; and they are free to schedule their own work—it is not scheduled by the agency.

Because of the potential tax liability of these arrangements, it is important for agencies to have a well-written contractual arrangement with these individuals. Exhibit 16.7 (page 331) shows an example of a Contract for Individual Services. The terminology in this contract focuses on the service provided rather than the person, because there are some questions about whether there can be such an entity as a "contract employee." An agency can, however, contract for the services of an individual or a group.

Because of the flexibility and savings inherent in contracting for services, this practice is likely to continue. The programmer needs to protect the agency and ensure that the agency is not using contracting to acquire services from individuals who indeed should be employees.

Supervising Operations

One of the unique requirements of operating an organization that produces leisure experiences is the need for close, ongoing supervision. "The nature of leisure services is that once the service has been delivered, it cannot be recalled," stated Edginton and Edginton (1993, p. 42). Thus, quality must be ensured at the time of delivery, and on-site observation and supervision of the leisure experience product provides a key method for accomplishing this.

Programmers must accomplish three objectives during these visits. First, programmers verify that a program is being conducted. Usually, many details must be coordinated before a program can occur. If any one of these details is not completed, the program may not occur, or it will occur with problems. If an agency uses a contracted service to deliver the program, on-site verification of program operation as a necessary part of a performance audit ensures contract compliance.

Second, programmers observe program operations to ensure they are being delivered as the agency intends and at the level of quality the agency desires. During a visit, programmers may face any of several operational problems, including program cancellation, poor staff performance, unsafe conduct of a program, malfunctions at a facility, or inadequate facility preparation. Interactions that occur with participants during these visits are what McCarville (1993) termed "key encounters." Failure to reconcile reported irritations and inconsistencies to the participant's satisfaction may result in the agency losing its patronage.

Berry and Parasuraman (1991) indicated five general dimensions that influence a customer's assessment of service quality: reliability, tangibles, responsiveness, assurance, and empathy (p. 16). On-site visits provide an opportunity for programmers to ensure the delivery of quality service. Exhibit 16.8 (page 332) includes specific activities for programmers to accomplish during these visits. These address each dimension.

Third, programmers observe on-site leadership staff and gather data to use in appraising staff performance. On-site visitations are important to staff members conducting programs, because programmers can give immediate verbal directions to staff to make necessary corrections in operations. They can also give immediate feedback about the quality of work. Observations of part-time staff members also reveal any need for additional training. Remember, however, that contractors are not subject to this type of supervisory direction.

> One of the unique requirements of operating an organization that produces leisure experiences is the need for close, ongoing supervision.

On-site supervision of leisure experience staging, that is, delivering recreation and leisure services, can accomplish several important program management functions. It is time consuming and often occurs at odd hours, but it is an essential part of the programmer's job.

Exhibit 16.7. Contract for Individual Services

Example Contract for Individual Services, Anytown, USA

Date: _____

It is agreed by and between Parks and Recreation, Anytown, USA, hereinafter referred to as "City," and _____, hereinafter referred to as "Second Party," as follows:

That Second Party agrees to perform for the City the service or services described below, and the City agrees to pay the Second Party for such services as provided below.

1. Person who will provide service:

   Name: _____ Soc.Sec. No.: _____
   Address: _____
   City: _____ Zip: _____
   Phone (Day): _____ Phone (Evening): _____

2. Description of services to be performed:
   a. _____
   b. _____
   c. _____
   d. _____
   e. _____
   f. _____
   g. _____

3. Time frame of services to be provided:
   a. Beginning _____ and continuing through _____

4. Location(s) where services will be provided:

   _____
   _____
   _____
   _____

5. The City shall pay _____ per hour/activity/project (circle one) for services rendered and no deductions shall be subtracted therefrom. The Second Party does not participate in any fringe benefits of the City, nor does the City provide liability insurance for the Second Party.

6. The Second Party is performing the above services and is acting as an independent contractor and is not an employee of the Anytown, USA.

_____

Second Party   Date

Approved and execution witnessed by:

_____

Immediate Supervisor   City of Anytown

_____

Section Supervisor   By: Parks and Recreation Director

Note. No warranty is given regarding the legal appropriateness of this statement for the reader's use. The reader is cautioned to not copy this statement, because any such statement should be developed and approved by the agency's legal counsel.

Exhibit 16.8. On-Site Visit Quality Service Activities

Dimension	Activities
Reliability	Confirm scheduled service is being operated as advertised and intended by the agency.
	Make adjustments necessary to bring service up to quality standards if warranted.
Tangibles	Confirm cleanliness of facility and equipment.
	Check safety of equipment and operational practices.
	Confirm the neatness of the appearance of personnel.
Responsiveness	Initiate contact with patrons to confirm your willingness to help them and provide prompt service or to resolve their problems.
Assurance	Present a demeanor of confidence and courtesy.
	Make certain you and your on-site staff know the answers to questions and willingly provide them to patrons.
Empathy	Present a caring, empathetic demeanor.
	Make certain on-site personnel have sufficient authority to make reasonable exceptions to policies and rules so that service can be customized to meet patron needs.

In all cases, the visiting programmer must exhibit these behaviors and confirm that on-site personnel are also exhibiting them.

Note. Adapted from Berry and Parasuraman (1991).

Conclusion

Staff members who stage leisure experiences are often part-time or seasonal employees. They must be recruited, hired, brought on board, oriented, trained, and supervised. Because experience staging is often a face-to-face interaction process, a well-trained and well-supervised staff is essential for successfully delivering leisure experiences. Conducting on-site supervision of staging delivery is a necessary quality control function that programmers must perform.

References

Berry, L. L., & Parasuraman, A. (1991). *Marketing services: Competing through quality.* New York, NY: Free Press.

Edginton, C. R., & Edginton, S. R. (1993, August). Total quality program planning. *Journal of Physical Education, Recreation, and Dance, 64*(8), 40–42, 47.

Henderson, K. A., & Bialeschki, M. D. (1993). Optimal work experiences as "flow": Implications for seasonal staff. *Journal of Park and Recreation Administration, 11*(1), 37–48.

Mathis, R. L., & Jackson, J. H. (1982). *Personnel: Contemporary perspectives and applications* (3rd ed.). St. Paul, MN: West.

McCarville, R. E. (1993, August). Keys to quality leisure programming. *Journal of Physical Education, Recreation, and Dance, 64*(8), 34–36, 46–47.

McCormick, E. J., Shaw, J. D., & DeNisi, A. S. (1979). Use of PAQ for establishing the job component validity of tests. *Journal of Applied Psychology, 64*(1), 51–56.

McKinney, W. R., & Chandler, C. L. (1991). A comparative assessment of duties between full-time and part-time recreation leaders. *Journal of Park and Recreation Administration, 9*(1), 13–29.

Moiseichik, M., Hunt, S., & Macchiarelli, D. (1992). Recreation sports officials: Contractors or employees? *Journal of Park and Recreation Administration, 10*(1), 62–70.

National Recreation and Park Association. (2018, May). Recommended guidelines for credentialing volunteers. *Parks and Recreation, 53*(5), 68.

Pope, N. W. (1987). Mickey Mouse marketing. In J. L. Crompton (Ed.), *Doing more with less in parks and recreation services* (pp. 168–176). State College, PA: Venture.

U.S. Equal Employment Opportunity Commission. (n.d.). Prohibited employment policies/practices. Retrieved October 5, 2017, from https://www.eeoc.gov/laws/practices/

Families Explore Nature During a Program at Highlands Wetlands
Photo courtesy of Westerville Parks and Recreation Department.

17 *Developing a Program Pricing Philosophy*

KEY TERMS

Program Management Accounting System (PMAS), Management Accounting, Comprehensive Pricing Policy, Service Category System, Public Programs, Merit Programs, Private Programs

Step 7: Implementation

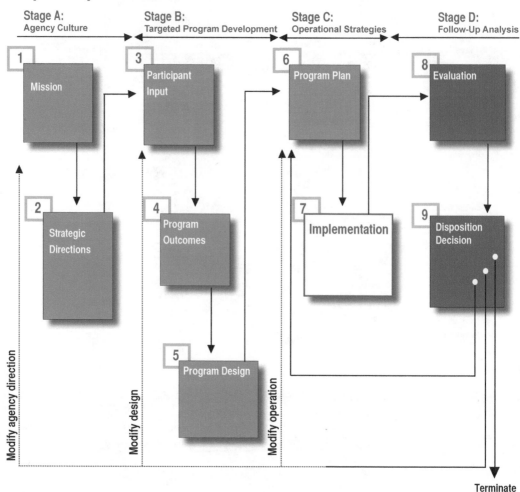

Pricing is one of the four *P*s of marketing. A marketing approach to programming requires that programmers be concerned with the costs of services and generating the revenue to pay for them, as well as designing and producing program services. Although commercial agencies have always had to charge prices that ensure the survival of the agency, more recently public and not-for-profit agencies have also become concerned with pricing issues. Over the last 6 years (2013–2018 inclusive), the percentage of operating costs recovered by public agencies has averaged 29.9%.[1] This trended down in 2016 and 2017, and in 2018, 28% of operating costs were recovered (National Recreation and Park Association [NRPA], 2018).

Although the issue of establishing a price seems, at first glance, a simple matter, the prices charged in commercial, public, or not-for-profit agencies have many implications. Charging for services can accomplish a variety of policy objectives for an agency. Howard and Crompton (1980) identified six objectives of pricing:

---

[1]This percentage was calculated from 6 years of data (2013–2018) reporting "the ratio of revenue to total operating expenses for park and recreation agencies" provided by the NRPA. Data can be accessed at https://www.nrpa.org/publications-research/parkmetrics/

the efficient use of all financial resources, fairness or equitableness, providing maximal opportunity for participation, rationing, developing positive user attitudes, and commercial sector encouragement (p. 419). A key point is that the price set for services determines who may or may not participate in an activity. Participants who cannot afford the price charged are excluded from participation. Therefore, the price established for services in any agency must be affordable by the intended target market, or the program will not reach its intended audience.

Pricing also determines the amount of revenue an agency receives and thus enables the agency to recover some or all of its production costs. The financial goals of the agency determine the contribution that the price charged has on overall agency revenue. For example, in a commercial agency, fees and charges are the sole source of revenue. Thus, they must be set to recover the production costs, plus contribute to the overhead costs and profit margin. In many not-for-profit and governmental agencies, the revenue from fees and charges represents a secondary funding source that agencies usually use to accomplish either expanding the quantity of services offered or enhancing their quality.

To better manage program pricing practices, agencies need to implement a program management accounting system (PMAS). This chapter, and Chapters 18 and 19, outlines such a system. Management accounting is distinctly different from financial accounting (Anthony & Welsch, 1981). Agencies use financial accounting to prepare information for reporting the financial performance of the organization to parties outside the organization. Agencies prepare financial accounting reports according to strict, "generally accepted accounting principles and unified by the basic equation, Assets = Liabilities + Owner's equity" (Anthony & Welsch, 1981, pp. 9–10), which ensures that each organization's report is comparable to the reports of other organizations.

> To better manage program pricing practices, agencies need to implement a program management accounting system.

A management accounting system prepares information for internal use by managers (Horngren, 1970). The information can be prepared for (1) full cost accounting, which agencies use to determine the full cost of producing a good or service in an agency; (2) differential accounting, which agencies use to examine fiscal differences between alternate courses of managerial action; and (3) responsibility accounting, which agencies use to account for the financial performance of subunits in an organization. These subunits are called responsibility centers. These areas of operational responsibility, such as individual programs or work groups, produce programs whose financial performance is isolated so that the costs and revenues associated with them can be matched and observed. To implement the recommended PMAS, agencies need to implement full cost and responsibility accounting.

While a management accounting system requires preparing accounting data beyond those needed for the financial accounting system, the management accounting system uses financial accounting information as its database. It is a reinterpretation of the same information so that program managers can use it to fulfill their responsibility to manage the organization's resources to achieve the goals and objectives of the organization (Horngren, 1970). The system also provides the data necessary for the agency to implement a procedure for systematically developing appropriate fees for programs and services.

Implementing and using a PMAS in an agency can be accomplished in six steps (see Exhibit 17.1). Some agencies may already have completed some of these steps. Realize that this system may have to be implemented in phases over several years.

Exhibit 17.1. Program Management Accounting System (PMAS)

1. The agency develops a comprehensive policy to guide its pricing decisions (covered in Chapter 17).
2. The agency identifies operational units as either line or service units (covered in Chapter 18).
3. The agency prepares line-item object-classification budgets that match revenues with expenses needed for operating a program for each of the line units identified in Step 2 (covered in Chapter 18).
4. With appropriate methods of cost allocation, the agency allocates service unit costs to line units (covered in Chapter 18).
5. The agency uses an analysis of cost, volume, and profit to calculate the full cost of service production (covered in Chapter 19).
6. The agency establishes a price for an individual service, using the conjoint implications of two data sets—the principles from the agency's comprehensive pricing policy and the production cost data developed in the cost–volume–profit analysis (covered in Chapter 19).

This chapter, and Chapters 18 and 19, outlines the way agencies can accomplish these steps. In most of the examples, we use a public recreation system as the model. We selected this type of agency because it is the most complex type of agency in which prices need to be established. Even though we use a public system as the example, any leisure service agency can use the general principles outlined.

Developing a Comprehensive Guide to Pricing Decisions— Step 1 PMAS

Howard and Crompton (1980) suggested two major pricing strategies: cost-based pricing and pricing not directly based on cost. Many agencies establish prices that are not directly based on cost. Going-rate pricing and demand-oriented pricing are two such methods. In going-rate pricing, the agency bases the price for a service on the price other providers charge for similar services. In demand-oriented pricing, the agency bases the price on "what the traffic will bear." With this latter method, the agency tries to charge all it can get or whatever the participants are most likely to pay for a service. Today this is also known as value pricing wherein the price charged directly depends on the value customers place on the product rather than its production costs. The price established with both of these techniques is not based on how much it costs the agency to provide the service; the price can be above, below, or equal to agency production costs.

Although these two methods are widely used, they are not recommended, because they lack precision in revealing where the agency has been using resources to subsidize services. The PMAS outlined is a cost-based pricing method. It assumes that knowing the full cost of service production is a prerequisite for establishing fair prices for agency services and for guiding the allocation of agency subsidies.

> Knowing the full cost of service production is a prerequisite for establishing fair prices for agency services and for guiding the allocation of agency subsidies.

An agency's pricing philosophy is determined by its role in society, the funding available to fulfill this role, and the types of services the agency offers. For example, commercial agencies market goods and services in a manner that is socially responsible and maximizes profits. Their only source of funding comes from earned income generated from the sale of goods, services, and experiences. To fulfill their role in society, they set prices that recover all production costs and contribute sufficient profit to give owners a fair return on their investment. In contrast to this, public and not-for-profit agencies generally have third-party funding in the form of tax or fund-raising income that can be used to pay for services in full, thus making them available at a zero price to the consumer, or to partly pay the costs for many services and concurrently require the user to pay part of the costs, thus providing subsidized services.

As a profession, we believe that having access to ongoing opportunities for enjoyable, fun, or peak experiences enhances the quality of life. Each provider has specific responsibilities in creating access to these opportunities. Not-for-profit organizations usually have a specific group or program they are interested in promoting. Thus, their policy-driven concerns are more focused and less comprehensive than those in the public system. Economic efficiency and consumer demand generally establish the target markets for commercial recreation enterprises. The result is that they, too, usually have a narrow range of products and a small, carefully defined target market. However, the public system has a responsibility to ensure equal access to leisure opportunities (Wicks, 1987); thus, it has a more comprehensive responsibility and it has public funds for fulfilling this social justice function. Although it is true that participation in leisure benefits the individual and society, it does not necessarily follow that each public leisure program is of immeasurable benefit (Ellerbrock, 1982). Furthermore, the system cannot meet all demand for service from tax revenues. Whom to charge, how much to charge them, whom to subsidize, and how much to subsidize them are the major philosophical issues agencies resolve in their pricing policy.

Pricing Public Recreation: Current Issues

Local public park and recreation systems in the United States have frequently found themselves in a financial dilemma while implementing fees and charges for services. Ironically, public systems that have implemented fees have often done so in a piecemeal or rushed way and have alienated participants through poorly conceptualized fee and charge systems. Yet public systems that have not implemented fees and charges often lack adequate resources to operate comprehensive recreation services, and they, too, have alienated participants through incomplete services. The issue is not one of deciding whether to charge: To have a comprehensive community recreation system, agencies must implement fees and charges to supplement tax-generated revenue. Rather, the issue is one of determining how the agency can use fees fairly to recover the costs of providing service and how the agency can use tax revenue to provide subsidized services. Wicks (1986) demonstrated that citizens hold definite yet different views regarding the services and who has priority in receiving subsidized services. In the future, agencies with a heterogeneous population will likely need to administer a differential pricing scheme for the same services for different population cohorts. When implementing a fee and charge system, then, agencies must remain sensitive to constituent views and desires regarding the distribution of tax dollars and the subsidization of various programs and client groups.

The egalitarian social philosophy that characterized the recreation movement through the first decade of the 20th century was predicated on two assumptions that today seem rather naive, or at least outdated. The first assumption was that recreation services were good for people and that providing more services led to accomplishing more good. Although this may be true, the political and economic resource base supporting ever-expanding public services was eventually exhausted. The second assumption was that all recreation programs were of equal value and in the public interest. Although public recreation officials can do many useful things with other people's money, this does not mean they have the right to tax people to meet all identified recreation needs or that they are willing to do so. The increasing diversification of program interests, the demand for program sophistication, and a diminishing willingness to pay with public dollars for services that seem to provide private benefits have led taxpayers to rebel against supporting public services, including public recreation.

In a 2017 study titled *Local Government Officials' Perceptions of Parks and Recreation,* the NRPA chronicled views of local government elected officials about funding parks and recreation. Several key findings provide insight into their views. These officials personally use their local park areas (95%) and agree that the community benefits from them (99%). Respondents rank ordered the contribution of parks and recreation to solving important community problems. They see parks and recreation as contributing to solving three community problems: community quality of life, preventing youth crime, and community health. They ranked these among their top five community priorities. But they do not believe that parks and recreation contributes significantly to solving some of their most important community issues, including attracting and retaining businesses and growth management. When asked to rank the importance of 10 local government services, they ranked parks and recreation sixth in importance among these services. They also indicated that parks and recreation is the service likely to be hit with the largest budget cut in funding when the jurisdiction suffers budgetary pressure. Support for public funding of park and recreation services would most fairly be described as moderate (NRPA, 2017).

Furthermore, public agencies have undertaken a diverse set of operations, which requires that they implement different pricing strategies. Soderberg (1988) pointed out that some agencies operate facilities that are intended to be revenue producing and must compete with similar for-profit agencies in their service area. Athletic stadiums, arenas, raceways, and similar spectator event sites are examples of revenue-producing operations. Regional tourist attractions, which are most frequently attended by tourists from out of town as opposed to community residents, also need a different pricing strategy.

Community disenchantment with public recreation, which has resulted in a withdrawal of political and financial support, has occurred not because the public questions the contribution that recreation can make to human existence, but because the public questions whether society as a whole should pay for providing recreation opportunities. The issue is, who benefits and who pays? Although a significant number of agencies institute fees and charges, in many cases this revenue only broadens the resource base for agencies to continue to provide all things to all people. However, current financial management techniques used in agencies do not keep adequate track of financial activity to truly match revenue with expenses (Howard & Selin, 1987). Consequently, managers cannot achieve congruence between pricing practices and the agency's social welfare philosophy and policies. Correcting this problem begins with developing a new philosophy concerning the role and function of recreation services, with particular focus on who benefits and who pays. Agencies also need to develop policies to implement the philosophy and financial management techniques through which they can achieve congruence between fiscal practice and agency policy.

Service Category System Philosophy

A philosophy regarding fees and charges should provide a base for differentiating services on the basis of who benefits from and who pays for the service. Economists have differentiated goods in the economy in this manner and have designated three types of goods: public, merit, and private (Howard & Crompton, 1980). Agency programs can be put into these three categories. When agencies adopt a philosophy that acknowledges these levels of goods, the social welfare philosophy of the public recreation agency shifts away from the notion that all services have equal value and should be provided

> A philosophy regarding fees and charges should provide a base for differentiating services on the basis of who benefits from and who pays for the service.

for everyone. This egalitarian philosophy is replaced with one that provides a basis for sorting out costs and benefits derived from various program services and that provides a rationale for who pays. In this conceptualization, each program type has specific characteristics that imply who pays. To develop a comprehensive fee and charge policy, agencies establish three categories for pricing programs that parallel these types of economic goods, that is, public, merit, and private programs. Each category has features that distinguish it from the other categories. The rest of this section outlines these features.

Public Programs

Public programs are the basic programs supported totally by tax dollars and available to participants free of charge. Theoretically, these programs are equally available to all. However, it is often not operationally possible for agencies to make services equally available to all. For example, a park cannot be placed equidistant from all participants. Operationally, a public program benefits all, even though only some will use the program. Its provision

> Public programs are the basic programs supported totally by tax dollars and available to participants free of charge.

is clearly in the "public interest" (Friedmann, 1973). Because the public at large derives benefit from these programs, it is assumed that their cost will be paid through public financing. Public programs, then, are available at no fee to users—they are completely subsidized services.

Ideally, the public recreation movement would like all services to be in this category. However, the diverse demands for programs almost always exceed a community's ability to pay for them. Public agencies should aim to use public tax dollars to provide a core set of free recreation programs for all citizens. Usually, public programs include provision for park areas or facilities, and low-organization events such as drop-in activities, special events, single-time block instructional workshops, and the like. Public programs usually do not require specialized leadership, the use of expensive equipment or facilities, or other high-cost components. This category varies from community to community, depending on the resources available and the community's willingness to support public recreation.

Not-for-profit organizations would offer at no cost to the user services that directly accomplish the stated social purpose of the agency. For example, scouting would not charge for the basic weekly meeting and a Boys and Girls Club would not charge a daily admission fee to its after-school program in a low-income neighborhood. A corporate recreation program may not charge for use of the basic fitness facility, because its purpose is to keep company health care costs low. A commercial facility may offer such a service as a "loss leader," that is, an activity priced below cost, to attract a specific target market to enhance profitability in another way. Examples of this include teaching introductory fitness classes at a loss to attract new customers to the facility and operating the nursery at such a facility at a loss to obtain customers during the usually low volume time of day.

Merit Programs

Merit programs are partly subsidized with tax dollars, but also have user fees attached that help agencies recover some of the production costs. Not-for-profit and commercial agencies have different sources for these subsidy dollars, but the basic concept is the same. In not-for-profit agencies, the subsidy comes from third-party funding from fundraising or donations. In commercial agencies, the funding source comes from profits from other activities. In this case, the price charged would recover part of the production costs.

> Merit programs are partly subsidized with tax dollars, but also have user fees attached that help agencies recover some of their production costs.

The benefits from merit programs can be attributed to public interest as well as private, individual gain. For example, a summer recreation program could directly benefit each child who participates and, to some extent, benefit the public at large. Partitioning out the proportion of individual and private benefits accrued from "merit goods" is obviously problematic. However, the key element of the merit-good concept is that some benefit accrues to public and private interests. Thus, it is assumed that these goods will be jointly paid for with individual and public, or third-party-generated, funds. There are widely differing philosophies about the appropriate groups that should be subsidized and the percentage of a subsidy they should receive. Operationally, merit programs include services that are partially subsidized for some reason.

Private Programs

Private programs are paid for entirely by the participants. It is assumed that the individuals using the program—not the general public—exclusively receive the benefit from private goods or private programs. In a free society, people can use their own personal resources to purchase any goods or services they believe will benefit them, including recreation services. Because the decisions are private and the benefit derived is private, it is assumed that the individual pays the full cost to acquire these services. These programs are the primary type that commercial agencies offer.

> Private programs are paid for entirely by the participants.

Summary

Collectively, public and merit programs fulfill the social justice goals and responsibilities of governmental and not-for-profit agencies. Commercial agencies that use these types of pricing philosophies do so to accomplish market positioning and targeting. Public programs are the basic free system—they are completely subsidized free services directed toward accomplishing the socially purposeful mission of the agency. Merit programs are partly subsidized services.

In allocating resources to merit programs, an agency further defines who it wants to subsidize with tax dollars or other nonuser-generated sources of revenue. Recognize that with limited resources, an agency probably cannot have all the public and merit programs for which demand can be documented. Decisions for allocating resources between these two types of services lie at the policy level and should be made by a policy-level board.

Policy Implementation

Implementing the service category system in an agency is time consuming and involves iterations among the philosophical and policy concepts presented, the accounting database of the agency, the local political process, and the limitations imposed by local resources. If agencies fail to distinguish adequately among these levels of service and continue to act as if everything they provide is in the public interest, the quality of services offered will further erode. In implementing this system, programmers first determine what the publicly provided programs in a community should and can be in view of the public resource limitations of the community. If only tax dollars were available to support services, what programs would a community choose to support?

Second, truly private and self-sustaining programs, services, and facilities need to be identified and the true costs of providing them recovered from users. Agencies should not continue to subsidize programs in public recreation systems, based on inadequate policies and poor accounting procedures. Frequently, agencies have programs they designate as "self-sustaining," but often the accounting procedures are so inadequate that agencies can identify and recover only direct costs (Howard & Selin, 1987). Indirect or overhead costs cannot be identified and continue to be subsidized with public tax dollars. This practice makes self-sustaining programs merit rather than private programs and siphons resources from program areas that the agency, from a social policy standpoint, may prefer to subsidize.

Finally, agencies need to develop policy guidelines for subsidizing the merit programs to be offered to constituents. They can make decisions about subsidizing based on many variables, such as participant characteristics, program type, and geographic service area. An agency may be required by law or charter to subsidize certain groups. Typically, communities choose to subsidize youth, teenagers, senior citizens, citizens with disabilities, and other vulnerable groups who do not have the personal resources to acquire needed services. Other communities choose to subsidize specific types of program services. For example, the U.S. Navy does not charge for any physical fitness activity, because of the priority and importance of fitness activities to its mission—combat readiness. Subsidizing program costs with tax dollars should occur only in program services that are wholly or partly in the public interest.

Before agencies can make subsidization decisions, the social welfare functions of a local recreation system must be well conceptualized. Many programs operated by public systems are truly merit goods that are presented as public or private goods. Agencies need to realize that subsidies are instruments through which they can carry out the social welfare and social justice functions of public recreation;

therefore, they should formulate comprehensive policies to ensure that they are using subsidies to achieve the results desired.

At the local level, developing policies for implementing the proposed social welfare function of local recreation systems requires agencies to review their facilities, services, and functions. Those that are truly public should be funded through public financing. Then agencies identify the private goods being offered to ensure that they are not merit goods receiving inappropriate public subsidy. Finally, agencies further develop the social welfare function of public recreation. Agencies can do this by giving clearer direction about subsidizing merit goods so that a community's social welfare desires are realized.

Exhibit 17.2 (page 346) provides an example of how one community accomplished this. In this policy, an additional category has been created. The Basic Public category equates with the public category discussed. The Extra Public category equates to the merit services discussed. The Enterprise category equates with the public category and requires recovery of all operational and capital costs so there is no public subsidy. The Private category requires recovery of all operational costs but does not require the recovery of capital costs. Based on the example provided, the Enterprise category includes activities requiring expensive, dedicated facilities, whereas the Private category includes programs that typically use more general, multiple-use facilities. Although this categorization uses some different terminology from that used in the book, any agency attempting to develop a pricing philosophy will need to deal with the basic principles outlined in this policy.

Implementing these policies in any agency requires an accounting methodology and budgeting procedure that provides data allowing for congruence between fiscal practice and policy. The PMAS outlined in Chapters 18 and 19 is such a system.

Conclusion

Systematically determining prices for an agency's programs is an important program management function. The price charged for a service often determines which participants will have access to the service. This chapter discussed issues relevant to pricing decisions. It also outlined a pricing philosophy that sorts out costs and benefits and serves as a basis for a differential pricing scheme. In addition, it outlined a step-by-step procedure for implementing a PMAS.

References

Anthony, R. N., & Welsch, G. A. (1981). *Fundamentals of management accounting*. Homewood, IL: R. D. Irwin.

Ellerbrock, M. (1982, January). Some straight talk on user fees. *Parks and Recreation, 17*(1), 59–62.

Friedmann, J. (1973). The public interest and community participation: Toward a reconstruction of public philosophy. *Journal of the American Institute of Planners, 39*(1), 2–12.

Horngren, C. T. (1970). *Accounting for management control: An introduction* (2nd ed.). New York, NY: Prentice-Hall.

Howard, D. R., & Crompton, J. L. (1980). *Financing, managing, and marketing recreation and park resources*. Dubuque, IA: W. C. Brown.

Exhibit 17.2. Categories of Park District Service

	Basic Public	Extra Public	Private	Enterprise
Definition	Services provided by the District available to all people	Additional services provided by District: an embellishment of a basic service	Private business offers this service within the District boundaries	Services that are designed to meet the ENDS policies and provide surplus funds
Who Benefits?	All age levels in the District benefit either directly or indirectly	Individual participant benefits most: all members of the community benefit somewhat	Some community members benefit: users who participate benefit	Some community members benefit: users who participate benefit
Who Pays?	The community pays through taxes: no user charges	Partially subsidized by taxes: individual users pay all direct and some indirect costs	No tax subsidy: users pay full OPERATIONAL costs, both direct and indirect	No tax subsidy: users pay at least CAPITAL and OPERATIONAL cost (direct and indirect)
Feasibility for Exclusion	Not feasible to exclude or limit individuals from service or benefit	Feasible and desirable to exclude or limit individuals	Feasible and desirable to exclude or limit individuals	Feasible and desirable to exclude or limit individuals
Examples	Celebration of the arts Winter sports Baseball fields Outdoor tennis	Adult softball Summer day camps Lighted ball fields Lighted tennis	Aerobics Karate Extended day care	Golf course Courts Plus Pro shops Refreshment stands

Notes

1. Not-for-profit organizations are not considered private businesses.

2. Director is to use discretion in setting fees until 1994 to phase in appropriate fee increases for recreation programs in each category.

3. Indirect costs = all out-of-pocket costs associated with a program: namely, wages, FICA, retirement, contractual services, continuing education, program printing and postage, athletic field electric and maintenance, and tournament fees, internal and external.

4. Indirect costs = all out-of-pocket costs, plus administrative and supervisory wages, office support staff, utilities, general postage, promotional and marketing, advertising, and registration costs. All of these are expressed by applying a 15% factor to the total of direct costs.

5. Recreation programs or facilities can be offered even if a private entrepreneur already offers a similar service within the community, provided the benefit appears to be great enough. Other services may thereby be subsidized and the tax burden relieved.

Note. From Elmhurst Park District, Elmhurst, Illinois.

Howard, D. R., & Selin, S. W. (1987). A method for establishing consumer price tolerance levels for public recreation services. *Journal of Park and Recreation Administration, 5*(3), 48–64.

National Recreation and Park Association. (2017). *Local government officials' perceptions of parks and recreation.* Retrieved from https://www.nrpa.org/contentassets/7761bd47adb142aaa62b19d00500fea3/local-officials-report.pdf

National Recreation and Park Association. (2018). *2018 NRPA agency performance review: Park and recreation agency performance benchmarks.* Retrieved from https://www.nrpa.org/siteassets/nrpa-agency-performance-review.pdf

Soderberg, P. (1988). Implementing a fee program. In G. G. Lamke & D. L. Dustin (Eds.), *User fees for public recreation? A question of equity* (pp. 1–9). San Diego, CA: San Diego State University, Institute for Leisure Behavior.

Wicks, B. E. (1986, October). *The equitable allocation of publicly provided recreation and park services: Citizens' perceptions of equity.* Paper presented at the 1986 Leisure Research Symposium, Anaheim, CA.

Wicks, B. E. (1987). The allocation of recreation and park resources: The court's intervention. *Journal of Park and Recreation Administration, 5*(3), 1–9.

Additional Readings

Crompton, J. L. (1982). Psychological dimensions of pricing leisure services. *Recreation Research Review, 9*(3), 12–20.

Crompton, J. L. (1984). How to establish a price for park and recreation services. *Trends, 21*(4), 12–21.

Manning, R., & Barker, S. (1981, September). Discrimination through user fees: Fact or fiction? *Parks and Recreation, 16*(9), 70–79.

All City Beach Day
City of Long Beach, Department of Parks, Recreation, and Marine.
Photo by Long Beach Parks, Recreation, and Marine.

18 *Determining Program Costs*

KEY TERMS

Line Units, Service Units, Line-Item, Budgets, Cost, Price, Cost Objective, Direct Costs, Indirect Costs, Cost Allocation, Cost Allocation Methods

Step 7: Implementation

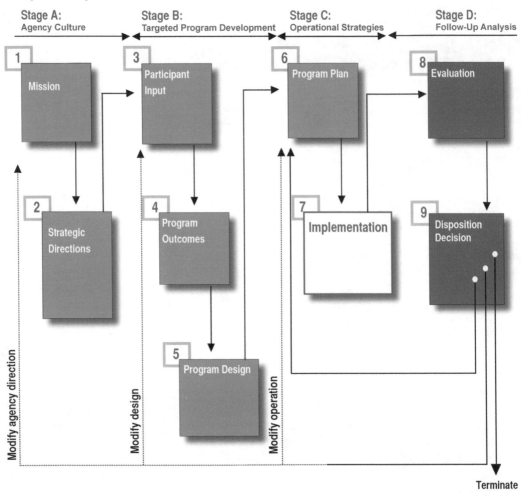

An important part of implementing the program management accounting system (PMAS) is determining the cost of program production. This chapter discusses three additional steps for determining costs.

Establishing Line and Service Units—Step 2 PMAS

In the second step of the PMAS, the agency classifies all subunits as performing either line or service functions. Managers have a good deal of discretion in defining what constitutes a unit. In any case, a unit should be headed by a manager who is responsible for its output. In most cases, the output serves either a line or a staff purpose. However, the classification of units for cost purposes does not always dovetail neatly with the arrangement of units and personnel as defined by the organizational chart. Because of this, some activities of a unit may be line functions and others may be service functions. Although

> In the second step of the PMAS, the agency classifies all subunits as performing either line or service functions.

agencies can separate line from service costs in an individual unit, it is best that they separate the line and service functions into individual units for cost analysis.

Line units are directly involved in the production and delivery of the organization's services and products. For example, recreation center staff are directly involved in producing and supervising recreation services. Their work group and its operation costs would therefore be classified as a line unit.

Service units provide services to other units and to the organization as a whole. They do not help produce the primary product or service of the organization. In a recreation and park department, the finance office would not help directly produce recreation services and would therefore be classified as a service unit. Office clerical staff would be classified as service personnel because they do not help directly produce and deliver recreation services.

The classification of an operational unit is less clear in some instances, for example, the park department in a park and recreation agency. Some of its activities, for example, cleaning recreation centers and lining ball diamonds, involve providing service to other units. Both activities support recreation center use and playing ball games. Other activities of a park department clearly result in the direct delivery of recreation services. Having well-maintained and beautiful parks for passive recreation is clearly a direct service. An example from another business makes this dilemma more clear. In most organizations, the staff function of accounting operations supports line operations. However, in an accounting firm, it is a line function.

The best advice for agencies is to understand the purpose of these data in making these classifications. This procedure is predicated on the notion that the agency exists to deliver or produce some product. (Product here is used in the generic sense and includes programs, parks, facilities, and other services produced by a park and recreation agency.) The agency's mission statement and long- and short-range goals and objectives outline its reason for existence. In this example, a park and recreation agency exists to deliver recreation and leisure services.

It is further assumed that the agency uses all of its resources to accomplish its mission. In the final goal of the PMAS, agencies account for all of their expenditures through line units, because these units are directly engaged in accomplishing the mission of the agency and in delivering its services. It is assumed that service units exist to support line units. From the viewpoint of the organization as a whole, the agency does not need to have service units except to enable line units to accomplish its mission. Collectively, the missions of all individual line units fulfill the mission of the organization as a whole. Therefore, in classifying units as line or service units, agencies ensure that the legitimate service outputs are classified as line units so they can determine the expenses of all outputs.

If providing parks for informal recreational enjoyment is a legitimate service output of the agency, then the agency should classify a portion of the park department's expenditures as a line unit output that provides this informal recreation program. For the final objective in this process, agencies determine as accurately as possible the full cost of producing each unit of agency output, that is, each program, park, facility, or other service amenity. Classification decisions that provide more accurate information regarding the full cost of each agency output are the correct and desirable decisions.

Classifying operational units as line or service units is an important step in this process. Because the manager eventually has to write off all service unit costs to the line units they serve, it is foolish to try to bury costs and hide the true production costs. The process reveals the true production costs and allows the agency to make accurate decisions about pricing and subsidization. Classification decisions that cause inaccuracies in the true cost of any one product will appear elsewhere and drive up the cost of some other product. The agency will eventually need to account for all costs incurred.

Preparing Line-Item Budgets—Step 3 PMAS

In the third step in this process, agencies prepare line-item object-classification budgets for all units, both line and service, identified in the second step. This step is not as formidable as it might seem. Most agencies already have a line-item object-classification budget. If they use a program budgeting procedure (Deppe, 1983), which assembles the budget from the lowest administrative level to the top, they already have these budgets. These budgets are the source of revenue and expenditure information from which agency budgets have been prepared.

> In the third step in this process, agencies prepare line-item object-classification budgets for all units, both line and service, identified in the second step.

This section does not demonstrate how to develop a line-item object-classification budget. Readers interested in this topic should see Deppe (1983), Edginton and Williams (1978), or Rodney and Toalson (1981) for a complete explanation of this process. This section makes clear the need for agencies to match revenues with expenses in budget preparation and explains why service unit budgets do not have a revenue side.

Although general budgeting convention dictates displaying revenues before expenses, actual budget preparation involves calculating expenses first, then identifying the amount and source of revenues that support the activity. This principle, matching all expenses with the revenues, requires staff to be concerned with the source of revenues for supporting their activities. This technique forces agencies to consider the number of dollars it will take to support an activity. It also forces them to identify the source of revenue for supporting each activity. In this latter instance, agencies begin at the time of budget preparation to identify where the revenue support for an activity originates.

Line units have an expenditure and a revenue side to their budgets. However, service units have only an expenditure side. Because service units only support line units, service unit budgets do not have a revenue side. Their only source of revenue comes from providing services to line units. Only line unit budgets, then, have a revenue side. The costs of service units must be allocated to line units.

Allocating Costs in the Agency—Step 4 PMAS

In the fourth step of the PMAS, agencies allocate all service unit costs to line unit budgets. The technique for accomplishing this is cost allocation. Before discussing cost allocation, however, we must define and differentiate terms.

Cost

The agency first distinguishes between cost and price. "Cost is a measurement, in monetary terms, of the amount of resources used for some purpose," according to Anthony and Welsch (1981, p. 10). Cost includes all dollars the agency has used to produce a program, regardless of the source of those dollars. Dollars acquired through taxation, fees, donations, and the like become costs to a program when the agency uses them to produce the program. The full cost for developing and offering a program includes all the resources the agency uses to produce the program. If an agency does not use its resources to produce Program A, then it can use those same resources to produce Program B or Program C. Producing any program causes the agency to incur a cost whether or not it recovers any of these costs through fees or third-party payments.

> In the fourth step of the PMAS, agencies allocate all service unit costs to line unit budgets.

Price

Price is the dollar amount the agency charges participants to participate in a program. The price that participants pay is a cost to the participants; that is, it is a resource they must give up to participate in the program. In some cases, such as a fully subsidized public program, participants incur zero cost. The price the agency charges for participation should be established through the conjoint implications of the full cost of production and the agency's fee and charge policy. Chapter 19 looks in more detail at pricing in the discussions accompanying Steps 5 and 6 of the PMAS.

Cost Objective

A cost objective is any activity for which the agency desires a separate measurement of cost. The functions performed by line and service units are cost objectives. In the PMAS, the agency handles service unit costs as cost objectives to identify the full costs of service unit operations. Then, through one or more cost allocation methods, the agency allocates costs of service units to line units to identify full costs of line unit operations.

In implementing cost allocation, the agency determines, as accurately as possible, the cost of providing a program or group of programs, in other words, the full cost of the cost objective. Agencies must understand two types of costs to classify and allocate them to cost objectives accurately. All costs can be classified as direct or indirect.

Direct Costs

Direct costs can be traced to a specific cost objective. They are therefore assigned to a specific cost objective as direct costs. For example, a direct cost of providing a swimming pool is the cost of chlorine. The agency purchases chlorine only because it operates a swimming pool; this is the only use for chlorine in the agency. If the agency was to no longer operate a swimming pool, it would no longer need chlorine. Chlorine, then, is a direct cost to the operation of a swimming pool. The agency would assign the cost of the chlorine as a direct cost to the swimming pool operation to determine the full cost of its operation.

> Direct costs can be traced to a specific cost objective.

Indirect Costs

Indirect costs are incurred regardless of whether the agency operates a specific program. They are created by two or more cost objectives and are therefore not traceable to a single cost objective. For example, the cost of an office computer is an indirect cost to all program services and facilities. The agency will have a computer regardless of whether it operates any one program. Even so, all programs and services absorb this cost. The agency gives up resources to acquire the computer and accounts for these resources within the budgets of all services provided. Indirect costs are often called burden or overhead costs.

> Indirect costs are incurred regardless of whether or not the agency operates a specific program.

According to Anthony and Welsch (1981), "The full cost of a cost objective is the sum of (1) its direct costs, plus (2) a fair share of its indirect costs" (p. 51). Through the accumulation of these costs, agencies determine the full cost of a specific cost objective, that is, a specific program. Exhibit 18.1 illustrates the structure of the cost of any single cost objective. The full cost of any cost objective, then, is the sum of its direct and indirect, or overhead, costs.

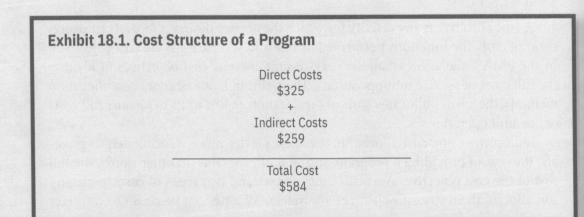

Exhibit 18.1. Cost Structure of a Program

Direct Costs
$325

+

Indirect Costs
$259

Total Cost
$584

Cost Allocation

Cost allocation is the process of identifying and assigning costs to various cost objectives. In the current case, agencies allocate indirect costs of service units as costs to line units. They can allocate other indirect costs to various cost objectives as well. The principles that follow apply to either case. In implementing cost allocation, the programmer faces a number of decisions regarding how costs can or should be allocated. Three principles guide these decisions:

1. Implementing cost allocation is an attempt at assigning indirect costs to line cost objectives in a fair and equitable manner. Aim to reflect the full costs of service production.

2. The method of cost allocation selected should accurately reflect how much of an indirect cost a specific cost objective uses or consumes. Again, try to reflect reality.

Both of these principles affect the eventual accuracy and usefulness of the data to be developed. Because many cost allocation decisions need to be made, and because managers have a good deal of discretion in making them, agencies can do so in a manner that influences the full cost of various programs. However, because the agency must eventually account for all costs in line operations, decisions initially favorable to the costs of one unit are almost always detrimental to those of some other unit. Pursuing accuracy as the guiding principle is not only the best policy; agencies often must resort to it to make everything reconcile properly.

3. Each cost allocation method includes a trade-off between accuracy and cost. For example, agencies may be able to achieve perfect accuracy of actual costs, but only at a very high cost of time and effort. Each method outlined below provides various combinations of ease of implementation and degree of accuracy. Programmers need to try to achieve as much accuracy as possible within the limits of reasonable effort. Remaining consistent over time in allocation of costs is as important as obtaining perfect accuracy, because consistency ensures reliability of data from one reporting period to another. Programmers can begin with easily obtainable but less accurate cost allocation data in the initial stages of implementing a PMAS. They can then replace these figures with more accurate cost data as they are researched and developed.

Cost Allocation Methods

Equal Share of Indirect Expenses

In this method, each functional line unit receives an equal share of indirect expenses. For example, the salary of the director of parks and recreation may be shared equally by the parks and the recreation divisions. Because there are two divisions, each assumes one half of the director's salary. Obviously, if there were three line units, each would assume one third of the salary. With this method, each unit takes up an equal share of the indirect expense to be allocated. This method is the easiest for agencies to implement, but it may also be the least accurate.

With this method, agencies make no effort to base the indirect costs a unit will assume on actual costs the unit has used. Even so, this method is often appropriate. For example, it could be argued that the director has a main responsibility of maintaining the organization's external relationships and providing overall direction to the agency. From this perspective, the time the director spends with any one unit in a given time period is irrelevant to assigning the director's salary cost. The director's functional accomplishments are equally essential to the park and the recreation units, so they must share equally in the cost of having a director on staff. It is often not practical for agencies to assign costs on a more sophisticated basis. Spending time and resources achieving increased accuracy of cost allocation in these instances may not be productive.

Percentage of Budget

With this method, agencies assign each line unit a percentage of indirect costs that equal its percentage of some overall budget figure. For example, assume the agency allocates the director's salary of $90,000 as an indirect cost to the park and the recreation units. Exhibit 18.2 displays the percentage of the overall budget assigned to these line units. In this case, the agency allocates $30,000, or 33%, of the director's salary cost to the park department budget and the remaining $60,000, or 67%, to the recreation department budget.

In this method, each functional line unit receives an equal share of indirect expenses.

When allocating costs with the percentage of budget method, the agency assumes that the actual use of the cost to be allocated is accurately characterized by the percentage of the overall budget each line unit currently consumes. Although this method is easy for agencies to implement, the accuracy of the data generated depends on the validity of the assumption. In the case of the director's salary, it could be argued that the director's time is spent in proportion to the size of each line unit's relative size in the organization. Allocating the director's salary with a method based on the relative size of each line unit is justifiable given this type of situation. The validity of these assumptions for allocation is usually best determined by on-site managers who are close enough to the situation to know how time is being spent.

Exhibit 18.2. Budget Percentage Method of Cost Allocation

Parks Budget:	$150,000	33%
Recreation Budget:	$300,000	67%
Total:	$450,000	100%

Time Budget Study

A time budget study that determines how individuals or units spend their work time provides the most accurate data for agencies to allocate costs. With this method, the agency studies the time a service unit spends on each cost objective. The agency then uses the percentage of time as the database for allocating the indirect costs of the service unit to line units. The allocation of costs is similar to the percentage of budget method, except the agency uses more accurate data to develop the percentage figures for allocating the costs.

This is an accurate method. However, conducting the study is a costly and time-consuming process. Because of this, agencies must ensure that the data to be developed warrant the research effort. After developing time budget figures, they usually continue to use the percentages generated in the initial study unless drastic alterations in work assignments or practices warrant altering the percentages. Agencies should verify time budget figures periodically on a 3- to 5-year staggered rotation schedule. In this way, they do not have to conduct these time-consuming and costly studies each budget period. They of course can alter percentages for any apparent change in operational practices.

Cost Tracking System

With this method, the agency tracks use of an item by a cost objective and charges the cost of the item to the unit using it. This method is needed particularly when the agency uses materials in addition to time to complete a job. Tracking only time, which is the case in a time budget study, often does not give an accurate enough cost estimate of the true costs to be allocated from a service unit to a line unit. In park operations, for example, agencies often need time (labor) and materials to complete a job, so they must also cost track the materials.

Agencies often use cost tracking to account for costs in an individual budget year. That is, they assign costs to the various units that used them. Agencies can use these cost tracking data, accumulated over time, during the budget preparation process to estimate the percentage of costs that they will allocate from various service units to line units.

Space or Measurement Studies

Agencies use space or measurement studies when they can determine the appropriate proportion of cost to allocate to a specific cost objective by measuring the relative proportion of overall costs of each cost objective. For example, the building shown in Exhibit 18.3 (page 358) contains 10,000 square feet of space. This space is divided into four rooms: Room A with 1,000 square feet; Room B with 3,000 square feet; Room C with 2,000 square feet; and Room D with 4,000 square feet. Implementing this method of cost allocation, the agency calculates the respective proportion of the overall space for each room. Thus, Room A contains 10% of the total building space; Room B, 30%; and so on.

Exhibit 18.3. Measurement Study Method of Cost Allocation

Room A 1,000 sq ft	Room B 3,000 sq ft
Room D 4,000 sq ft	Room C 2,000 sq ft

When allocating building operating expenses, such as electricity, water and sewer charges, gas or heating bills, and maintenance expenses, the agency can simply allocate a percentage of total costs to each room in proportion to the percentage of overall building space that each room represents. Thus, Room A would be allocated 10% of these charges; Room B, 30%; and so on.

Although the building diagrammed in Exhibit 18.3 does not include any common areas, such as hallways, a foyer, or restrooms, most buildings contain this type of space. Usually, agencies allocate expenses of the common areas to the space represented by the usable rooms in a building. In this example, then, the proportion of costs allocated to each room would not change, because the amount of usable space in the building would still be 10,000 square feet.

This method is useful in situations when agencies can accurately determine the proportion of costs to be allocated. Allocating costs for a fertilizing program in parks, for maintenance in a building, and for other similar instances is best handled in this manner.

In Step 4 of the PMAS, then, the cost allocation decisions enable agencies to allocate the indirect cost from service units to line operations. This procedure is necessary for the agency to allocate the indirect (sometimes called overhead or burden) costs of service units to the direct costs of the line operating units that deliver services and thereby produce its service output.

Conclusion

To determine program costs, agencies implement three additional steps of the PMAS. They designate all operational units as either line or service units. They prepare line-item object-classification budgets for each operational unit. They allocate indirect costs to cost objectives. This chapter discussed several methods of cost allocation appropriate for use in leisure service agencies. The PMAS recognizes program services as the line output of the agency and requires that agencies report costs in relation to their contribution to developing program services.

References[1]

Anthony, R. N., & Welsch, G. A. (1981). *Fundamentals of management accounting.* Homewood, IL: R. D. Irwin.

Deppe, T. R. (1983). *Management strategies in financing parks and recreation.* New York, NY: Wiley.

Edginton, C. R., & Williams, J. G. (1978). *Productive management of leisure service organizations.* New York, NY: Wiley.

Rodney, L. S., & Toalson, R. F. (1981). *Administration of recreation, parks, and leisure services.* New York, NY: Wiley.

---

[1]We realize some of these references are rather old. However, managerial accounting has changed most in its use of computers, which make the whole process easier and more accurate, and not in the definitions of concepts.

Fly Fishing at the Carl T. Johnson Hunt and Fish Center in Cadillac, Michigan
Photo courtesy of Michigan Department of Natural Resources. Photo by Dave Kenyon.

19 *Pricing Program Services*

KEY TERMS

Cost–Volume–Profit Analysis, Variable Costs, Fixed Costs, Changing Fixed Costs, Tabling Cost Data, Graphing Cost Data, Break-Even Point, Revenue, Revenue Line, Profit, Loss, Cost Recovery, Resistance to Prices, Establishing a Price

Step 7: Implementation

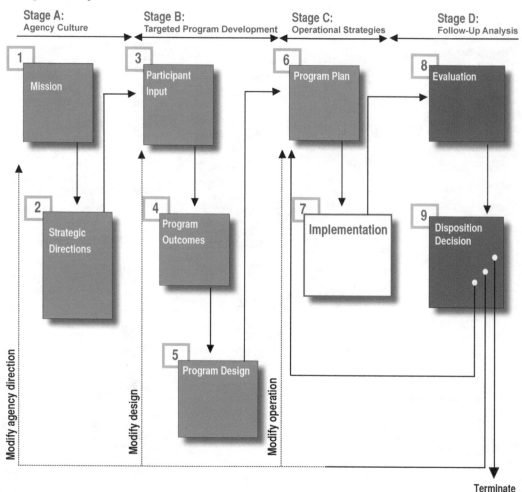

This chapter explains the final two steps of the program management accounting system (PMAS). In the fifth step, agencies isolate specific programs and calculate the actual costs of providing a service. They accomplish this with cost–volume–profit analysis, which is also called break-even analysis or contribution margin theory. The same technique has various names because of different emphases in using the technique. The implications of this will become apparent later in this chapter.

Cost–Volume–Profit Analysis—Step 5 PMAS

Cost–volume–profit analysis of an activity or segment of an enterprise permits a complete financial analysis of the expected financial results of an activity. This analysis enables the programmer to match the revenue with the expenses for an activity and to simultaneously account for changes in volume (participation level) with changes in production costs. The data generated by a cost–volume–profit analysis inform the programmer about the actual costs of providing services. With this information, it is then possible for programmers to make cost-based decisions regarding the price to be charged for services.

Classifying Costs

To implement cost–volume–profit analysis, the programmer begins by examining the expenses or costs associated with a specific activity. For programmers to use this analytical procedure, costs of a program must be classified as variable, fixed, or changing fixed.

Variable Costs

Variable costs change directly and proportionately with changes in volume. A variable cost changes by the same amount of money with the addition of each new participant or some other unit of volume (see Endnote 1 on page 376). The cost of an instruction book to be used in a class is an example of a variable cost. The agency would purchase a book for each participant and would need as many books as participants in the class. If the book costs $12, then $12 in variable costs would be added to the program for each participant who enrolls. Some programs have several variable costs. Assume that the agency purchases a book for a synchronized swim program. It may also need to purchase a swim cap and nose clip for each participant. These items sum to $20 in variable costs for the synchronized swim program. Thus, each participant added to this program would result in $20 in variable costs for the program.

> Cost–volume–profit analysis of an activity or segment of an enterprise permits a complete financial analysis of the expected financial results of an activity.

Fixed Costs

Fixed costs do not change with changes in volume (i.e., the number of participants). These costs are fixed; they remain the same throughout a program, regardless of the number of participants. There are direct and indirect fixed costs. Chapter 18 defined and explained direct and indirect costs. This is where this work in classifying direct and indirect costs is applied. Remember that the direct–indirect classification deals with the relationship of a cost to a cost objective, and the fixed–variable classification deals with the behavior of a cost in relation to changes in volume. It is therefore possible for costs to be classified as direct fixed or indirect fixed.

An example of a direct fixed cost would be the cost of renting a swimming pool for a synchronized swim program. This cost would be directly related to the specific cost objective, the synchronized swim program. It would also remain the same regardless of the number of participants in the program. Whether one or 30 people participate, the rental fee remains the same. It is therefore a fixed cost. It is probably apparent that the notion of a fixed cost has limitations. That is, the notion of a cost remaining the same is only true within certain parameters. A swimming pool has a limited capacity and can only accommodate a specific and limited number of participants, for example, 100. This parameter (i.e., 1–100 participants) is known as the relevant range.

An example of an indirect fixed cost is a proportion of some overhead cost that an agency can allocate to a specific cost objective or program. The synchronized swim program may be required to absorb some overhead increment of allocated cost, such as a share of office and administrative expenses, utilities, and advertising or marketing costs. These costs are incurred by the agency, but they are not directly traceable to a specific cost objective or program. They are fixed; they do not increase with each new participant added to a program.

Changing Fixed Costs

Changing fixed costs change in the same direction, but not proportionally, with changes in volume or the number of participants. These costs do not change in the same amount for each participant added. Most often, they change after the addition of certain numbers of participants. In the synchronized swim program, a lifeguard would be hired to guard a class of 25. The lifeguard's wage would be a direct fixed cost to this program. A second lifeguard would be needed when the program enrollment exceeded 25 participants. It would therefore be necessary for the programmer to hire a second lifeguard when the 26th person entered the class. From the 26th through the 50th participant, the agency would have the additional cost of a second lifeguard. The cost of the second lifeguard is therefore a changing fixed cost.

Because the cost of the second lifeguard does not go up with each participant added, it is not a variable cost. Because it is not fixed over the relevant range of this program—that is, 1–100 participants (which was determined in this case by the capacity of the pool)—it is not a fixed cost. It is therefore a changing fixed cost. It changes in the relevant range of the program, but remains fixed from the first through the 25th swimmer and again from the 26th through the 50th swimmer.

Presenting Cost Data

Programmers can provide analytical information about cost–volume–profit analysis by tabling the data or by placing the data in a graph. Each method has unique ways of revealing important information regarding cost behavior.

Tabling Cost Data

To illustrate this technique, we further develop the synchronized swim program example. Following are a set of facts regarding the program. (*Note:* Federal minimum wage in 2018 was $7.85 per hour. However, the minimum wage in some states is higher, and you will need to adjust for this difference in practice depending on where you work.)

1. The Delaware Recreation Center has a pool, which can be rented for $50 per hour. The pool can accommodate 100 swimmers. The rental fee also includes the use of the new stereo system with underwater speakers.
2. The synchronized swim coach to be hired will make $12 per contact hour.
3. The lifeguard to be hired will make $10 per hour and can supervise 25 swimmers.

4. A second lifeguard must be hired at $10 per hour if there are from 26–50 swimmers.
5. Each participant will use an instructional book costing $12, a swim cap costing $5, and a nose clip costing $3.
6. Each program in the aquatics division must absorb $100 in overhead expenses for administrative and supervisory wages, advertising, and marketing of the aquatics program, and office expenses for handling registration.
7. The program supervisor estimates she will spend 9 hours of her time on this program for hiring, training, and supervising the synchronized swim coach and lifeguard(s). The program director makes $15 per hour.
8. The program will operate for 10 weeks, 1 night per week, for 3 hours per night. There is an enrollment limit of 50 swimmers for the program.

First, to analyze this data, the programmer classifies each cost and determines any additional facts necessary for solving the problem. The only fact needed is the 30 hours of instruction time (3 hours per night × 1 night per week × 10 weeks = 30 hours). Table 19.1 displays the data from these facts.

Table 19.1
Synchronized Swim Cost Data

Cost Items	Actual Cost
Fixed Costs	
Direct Fixed Costs	
Synchronized Swim Coach 30 hours × $12 per hour	$360
Lifeguard 30 hours × $10 per hour	$300
Rent 30 hours × $50 per hour	$1500
Indirect Fixed Costs	
Overhead	$100
Program Supervisor 9 hours × $15 per hour	$135
Changing Fixed Costs	
Second Lifeguard (from 26th to 50th swimmer) 30 hours × $10 per hour	$300
Total Fixed Costs	**$2695**
Variable Costs	
Book	$12
Swim Cap	$3
Nose Clip	$5
Total Variable Costs Per Person	**$20**

The programmer then places the data in a cost–volume–profit table (see Table 19.2). This table shows the various volumes of participation as column headings. Choosing the levels of participation to include in such a table is somewhat arbitrary. But in this case, the table includes 50 as the largest level of volume because it is the maximum capacity of the program and 26 because it represents a breaking point for the introduction of the changing fixed cost of a second lifeguard.

The table also includes a volume level of 10 participants. An agency's operational policies and the program supervisor's previous experience with volume levels dictate choices of volume levels. For example, the agency may not operate an adult program with fewer than 10 participants. In this case, 10 represents the lowest level of activity that the table would include and also the lower limit of the relevant range. Rows in the table show various cost items and cost summaries at the volume levels specified in the columns.

The cost per participant, the final row in Table 19.2, is also known as the break-even point. At each volume specified, the cost-per-participant dollar amount represents the price that the agency must charge each participant to recover all its costs from producing the program. With this data, the programmer can determine how much it costs to produce a service. Step 6 of the PMAS discusses how the programmer uses this break-even point to set a price for a service.

Table 19.2

Synchronized Swim Program Cost–Volume–Profit Table

| Cost Items | Number of Participants | | | | | |
	10	20	26	30	40	50
Direct Fixed Cost						
Swim Coach	360	360	360	360	360	360
Lifeguard	300	300	300	300	300	300
Rent	1500	1500	1500	1500	1500	1500
Indirect Fixed Cost						
Overhead	100	100	100	100	100	100
Program Director	135	135	135	135	135	135
Changing Fixed Costs						
2nd Lifeguard			300	300	300	300
Total Fixed Cost	2395	2395	2695	2695	2695	2695
Variable Cost						
$20 per swimmer	200	400	520	600	800	1000
Total Costs	2595	2795	3215	3295	3495	3695
Cost Per Participant	260	140	124	110	88	74

Graphing Cost Data

The programmer can also place these data in a graph, which makes it possible to visually observe the behavior of each cost component. The data from the synchronized swim program in Table 19.2 have been graphed in Exhibit 19.1.

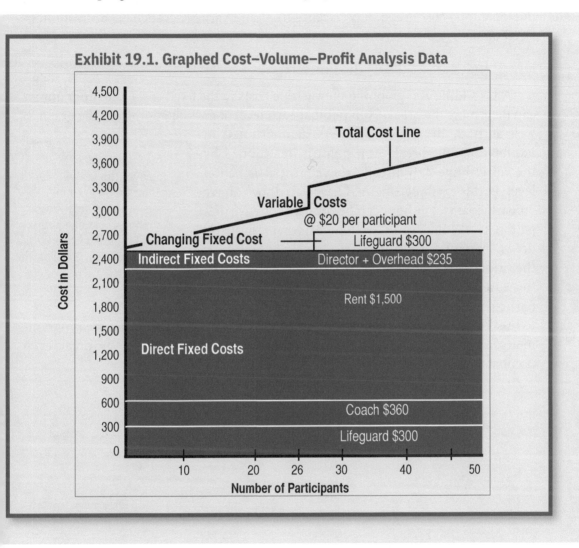

Exhibit 19.1. Graphed Cost–Volume–Profit Analysis Data

Graphed data enable the programmer to observe clearly the effect of each cost component. Direct and indirect fixed costs remain constant through the relevant range and are therefore represented by a line that is parallel to the volume line—fixed costs do not increase with increases in volume. Changing fixed costs are represented by a line that is also parallel to the volume line, but displayed on the graph in a stepped-up fashion to represent the incremental increase that is characteristic of fixed costs. Variable costs are represented by a sloped line, the steepness of which varies depending on the variable costs per person. A large amount of variable costs per person will result in a steep line, whereas a small amount of variable costs per person will result in a less steep line.

The total cost line summarizes the fixed, changing fixed, and variable costs. This line often coincides with the variable cost line on the finished graph, but only because the variable cost component was added above the fixed cost line, which was already drawn. The variable cost component of total costs can be graphed separately, as is done in Exhibit 19.2. The total cost line, then, coincides with the variable cost line on a total cost graph only because fixed and variable costs have been summarized on the graph.

Graphing the Break-Even Point

After adding and graphing the variable costs to the fixed costs, the programmer can determine the break-even point at each level of participation from the graph as well as from the tabled data. As demonstrated in Exhibit 19.3, the break-even point is determined by the vertical line A-B directly above any participation level. In this example, line A-B has been drawn above 20 participants, but lines can be drawn at any participation level. The break-even point where similarly drawn lines intersect the total cost line. In Exhibit 19.3, the break-even point for 20 participants is $2,795. In this case, the programmer would need to charge each participant $140 ($2,795 divided by 20 participants) to break even. The advantage of the graph over the tabled data is that the programmer can observe the steepness of the total cost line and quickly see the break-even point at any level of participation.

> The advantage of the graph over the tabled data is that the programmer can observe the steepness of the total cost line and quickly see the break-even point at any level of participation.

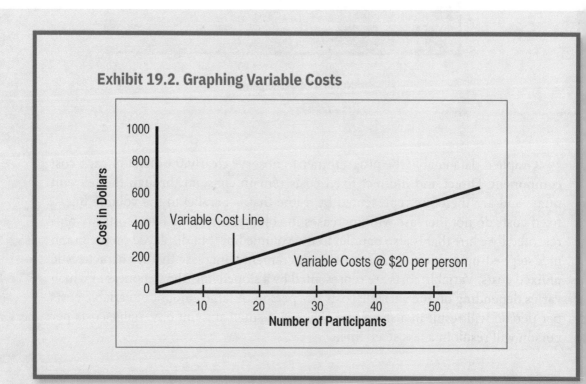

Exhibit 19.2. Graphing Variable Costs

Variable Cost Line

Variable Costs @ $20 per person

Cost in Dollars

Number of Participants

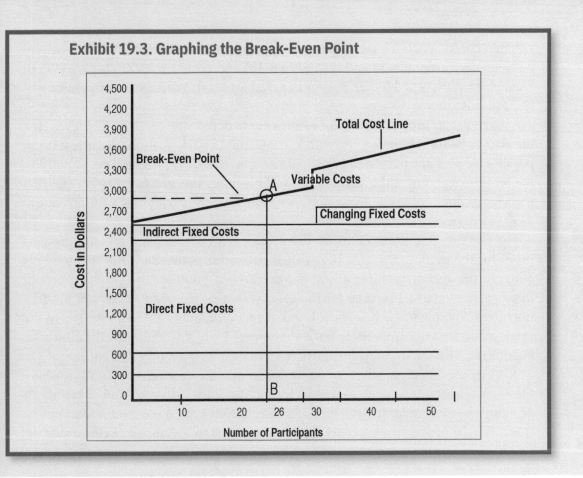

Exhibit 19.3. Graphing the Break-Even Point

Applying the Revenue Line

After completing the total cost graph, the programmer can draw revenue lines that represent various levels of revenue. Exhibit 19.4 (page 370) is a total cost graph of the synchronized swim program with the revenue line A-B added to it. Line A-B illustrates the effect of revenue at $150 per person. It is possible and advisable for programmers to draw additional revenue lines that estimate the effect of different pricing levels within the parameters of the current cost structure. The point at which line A-B crosses the total cost line is also a break-even point, that is, the point where revenue equals the cost of producing the program. With this method, the programmer can observe the effect of various prices on the minimum participation level needed for the agency to break even. With the previous method, the programmer can observe the effect of various participation levels on the price that the agency needs to charge to break even. After completing the total cost graph, the programmer can use either approach to determine a minimum price or minimum participation level. When one is determined, the other is also determined. However, the one that will take precedence in determining price and participation level is a matter of circumstances.

In Exhibit 19.4 (page 370), the break-even point occurs somewhere between the 18th and 19th participant. With 18 participants, revenue is $2,700 (i.e., $150 × 18) and costs are $2,755 (i.e., $2,395 in fixed costs, plus 18 × $20 per person in variable costs). With 18 participants, costs still exceed revenue by $55. With 19 participants, revenue is $2,850 (i.e., $150 × 19) and costs are $2,775 (i.e., $2,395 in fixed costs, plus 19 × $20 per person in variable costs). With 19 participants, revenue exceeds costs by $75.

When programmers use revenue estimates to determine participation levels, the break-even point seldom occurs with a whole unit of participation. Because it is not possible for part of a person to participate in a program, the programmer establishes the break-even point at the next highest volume level. This practice also ensures that the agency does not incur a loss. In this case, the break-even point with revenue at $150 per person is 19 persons.

In Exhibit 19.4, the area above the break-even point shaded green represents profit for the agency. The area below the break-even point shaded gray represents a loss to the agency. Volume above the break-even point on the graph will result in a profit or retained income for the agency, that is, income in excess of production costs. Volume levels below the break-even point will result in a loss, which the agency will need to compensate for with increased fees, through subsidization with tax dollars, with third-party donations, or with profits from other activities.

This latter situation often occurs in a commercial recreation operation where the agency uses one activity as a "loss leader" to draw customers into a facility or program. For example, the nursery at a tennis club may operate at a loss, but be subsidized by profits from increased court usage due to the nursery being available.

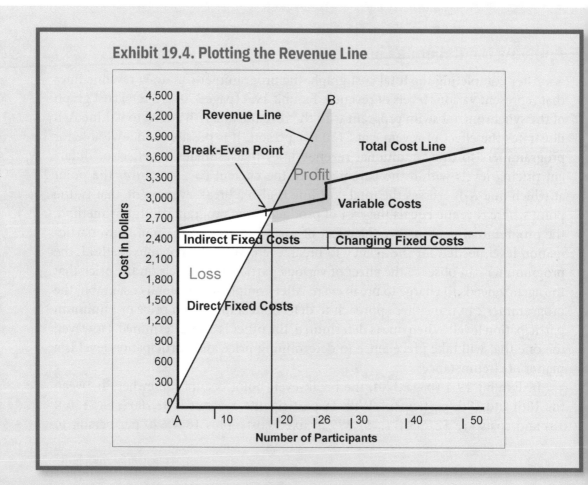

Exhibit 19.4. Plotting the Revenue Line

In practice, after determining accurate costs for program production, the programmer usually determines a price, estimates a reasonable expected volume level, and estimates total revenue earned. If the estimated total revenue is not sufficient to cover costs, then the programmer subsidizes the program cost, tries to reduce costs to match revenues, increases prices, or does not operate the program. If the program operates and revenue from participants does not cover the production costs, then the program is being subsidized by the agency. The tendency in public recreation has been to hide these costs; however, the PMAS does not allow this to happen. Programmers using this system must identify all costs and match them with revenues.

Cost–volume–profit analysis enables the programmer to isolate specific activities to match costs with revenues generated. With this technique, the programmer can determine accurately the full cost of producing services and then use this information to determine a price.

Establishing a Price—Step 6 PMAS

The sixth and final step in the PMAS involves the programmer determining the price that the agency will charge for a service. Programmers make this determination by using the data developed in the cost–volume–profit analysis, the implications of the agency's pricing policy developed in the first step, and some consideration of other factors that may mitigate the price to be established.

Cost–volume–profit analysis provides data that enable a programmer to estimate the financial performance of a specific program. A program's financial performance can be classified into one of three cases: (1) the program's revenue may be less than its production costs (representing a loss to the agency); (2) the program's revenue may equal the cost of production—the break-even point at which the agency recovers its production costs; or (3) the program's revenue may exceed production costs, which provides the agency with revenue in excess of its production costs. This excess revenue is known as a contribution margin, that is, a margin of revenue over actual production costs. The agency can apply this revenue to its profits or retained income (which is what government and not-for-profit organizations usually call this excess revenue).

In addition to the actual cost data developed through cost–volume–profit analysis, the programmer also ascertains from the service category system whether a program is a merit, a private, or a public service. A public service is offered at no cost to the public. A merit service is offered at a price that is less than that required for full-cost recovery; the price thus enables the agency to recover some of its production costs. Often, the price charged for a merit program is based on recovering only the direct costs of a program, and the agency does not attempt to recover indirect costs. A private service is offered at a price that enables the agency to recover its production costs fully.

Pricing Considerations

Before establishing the price, the programmer also anticipates possible consumer resistance to a price. Howard and Selin (1987) demonstrated that there is a price tolerance zone within which a price can be established. Furthermore, this zone varies from activity to activity, which suggests that across-the-board price increases is a poor pricing strategy. An appropriate price must be set for each activity.

For the price established, programmers also consider the attitude of the target market toward pricing. Kerr and Manfredo (1991) documented that intention to pay is most significantly influenced by past use and past fee paying. That is, individuals who are used to paying a fee for a given service and are frequent consumers of it will have the least resistance to price increases. Reiling, Criner, and Oltmanns (1988) suggested that the two most persuasive arguments that influence attitudes about paying include comparing the price proposed with commercial rates for the same service and providing data about the cost of provision (data from the cost–volume–profit analysis).

Programmers also look at price elasticity, that is, the relationship of the activity being charged to the overall price for participation. For example, when the agency operates tourist attractions, the prices at these are somewhat inelastic because the price of admission to a museum, for example, is a very small part of the total cost of a trip. Admissions to amenities constitute about 10% of the travel dollar. Thus, the $5.00 admission charge to a museum could probably be doubled without adversely affecting demand, because it would have a relatively small effect for a tourist on the overall cost of a trip to a museum. This is price elasticity, and the museum fee is an example of an inelastic price. With information from these basic sources, the programmer determines the price to charge for a program. Exhibit 19.5 includes a worksheet that brings together the data necessary for determining the price of a program. A programmer faces many possible circumstances when establishing program fees. But remember, although quantitative data about the production costs can be developed, the final price established must also be based on the agency's pricing policy, the target market's attitude toward pricing, and their ability to pay. The rest of this section outlines some of these typical circumstances.

Public Services

Agencies offer public services at no charge to the user. They do not recover any production costs from a public service. Cost–volume–profit information for public services simply informs the programmer about the costs of producing the various services provided at no charge to the public. The data help the programmer determine the comparative cost of the various public programs that the agency offers free of charge. Through an examination of the cost structure of public programs, savings and areas for cost reduction often become apparent. Cost–volume–profit analysis, then,

> Cost–volume–profit information for public services simply informs the programmer about the costs of producing the various services provided at no charge to the public.

Exhibit 19.5. Program Cost Pricing Worksheet

Programming Unit _____ Activity/Program Title _____

Fixed Costs		Changing Fixed Costs		Variable Costs (per unit)	
Personnel	(Total) $ _____	Personnel	(Total) $ _____	Personnel	(Total) $ _____
Services Contractual	(Total) $ _____	Services Contractual	(Total) $ _____	Services Contractual	(Total) $ _____
Commodities	(Total) $ _____	Commodities	(Total) $ _____	Commodities	(Total) $ _____
Materials	(Total) $ _____	Materials	(Total) $ _____	Materials	(Total) $ _____
Other Expenses	(Total) $ _____	Other Expenses	(Total) $ _____	Other Expenses	(Total) $ _____
Capital Outlay	(Total) $ _____	Capital Outlay	(Total) $ _____	Capital Outlay	(Total) $ _____

Fixed Cost Total $ _____

Add $ _____ for overhead rate*

Total Adjusted	Total Changing Fixed	Total Variable Costs
Fixed Costs $ _____	Costs $ _____	$ _____

Optional—added to recover overhead or burden costs based on cost allocation studies and agency policy.

Establishing a Price

1. Total adjusted fixed costs $ _____
2. Total changing fixed costs $ _____
3. Total variable costs per unit ($ _____) ×
   Expected number of participants (no. _____) = $ _____
4. Subtotal (add lines 1 + 2 + 3) $ _____
5. Divide subtotal (line 4) by
   expected number of participants (no. _____) = $ _____
6. Multiply result on line 5 by _____% of desired cost recovery = $ _____

The last figure (the result on line 6) represents the price that the agency needs to charge each participant in the program to achieve the desired level of cost recovery. "Percentage of cost recovery" represents the contribution the agency wants an individual participant to pay toward the cost of providing a program. Percentage of cost recovery can range from 0% to an excess of 100%. The meaning of various levels of percentage of cost recovery are outlined below.

0%: A Public Good, totally subsidized service—the user contributes nothing to the cost of providing the service.

1% to 99%: A Merit Good, users contribute a percentage of the cost of providing a service—tax dollars are used to fund the remaining percentage of costs in excess of user fee contributions.

100%: A Private Good, users contribute the full cost of providing the service—no tax dollars are used.

100% +: A Private Good, users contribute in excess of actual costs for providing the program—excess income is used to subsidize other programs.

is useful for documenting where the agency spends its resources, for identifying which groups have been receiving subsidized services, and for determining the cost of each program service provided.

Merit Services

Agencies offer merit services at a price that permits a partial recovery of agency costs. Merit services can be thought of in two ways—as programs that receive a partial subsidy or as programs that partly recover their production costs. In reality, they do both. However, which component the agency chooses to emphasize can influence how agency staff think about and treat these programs. Using cost–volume–profit analysis to examine the actual costs of producing merit programs, the programmer establishes a base from which to determine a price. Knowing the cost of producing a program does not necessarily mean the agency will charge a price that permits a full recovery of production costs. For merit services, production costs are simply the starting point in determining a price for participation.

> Using cost–volume–profit analysis to examine the actual costs of producing merit programs, the programmer establishes a base from which to determine a price.

The programmer determines the price charged for a merit service through production costs, the dollars available from other sources (primarily donations and tax dollars, depending on the type of agency) for subsidizing the program, and the agency's policies regarding the type of program under consideration. Determining a price for merit services is clearly more complicated than the programmer simply using cost–volume–profit analysis to determine actual production costs and adding on a contribution margin. The process is somewhat the opposite of adding a contribution margin for profit; in this case, the programmer subtracts a "subsidy margin" that reduces the actual price to the user. Through the subsidies allocated to merit services, the programmer implements the social justice function of the agency, so allocation of these subsidies should occur with accurate cost data. Cost–volume–profit analysis provides the programmer with accurate data to determine the actual dollar amount of a subsidy. In this way, the programmer and the agency know how much and for what programs their subsidy dollars are being used. Now complete Exercise 19.1.

Private Services

Agencies offer private services at a price that enables them to recover all their direct and indirect costs of producing the program. Cost–volume–profit analysis in private services provides the programmer with an accurate statement of the production costs. The programmer can use these figures as data for determining and justifying the price to charge for a program. In public or not-for-profit agencies, obtaining full-cost recovery for these types of services is important in that agencies do not want to use funds intended to subsidize public and merit services to subsidize services that are supposed to be self-sustaining.

Complete the following problem outside of class, then discuss your solution in class. See Endnote 2 (page 376) before you discuss the problem.

ArtFUN Inc. is investigating the possibility of providing an instructional program in ceramics. The office manager and the recreation program manager have collected the following facts:

1. The local high school has a ceramics laboratory in its art area. It has work space for 30 people and two kilns for firing students' ceramic projects. The laboratory is rented to governmental and not-for-profit agencies for $50.00 per hour and to all other users for $75.00 per hour. There is an additional firing fee for any type of user of $35 per kiln for each time it is fired.
2. A ceramics instructor earns $20 per contact hour and can handle 15 students. If there are more than 15 students, the instructor will need an assistant who earns $12 per hour.
3. The instructor has determined that each student will use $50 worth of supplies and needs a book that costs $10.
4. The office manager has determined that registration, accounting, and paperwork will require about 4 hours of staff time at $25 per hour.
5. The recreation program manager has reported that her unit will need $100 for advertising this program in the agency's brochure, and she will spend 6 hours of her time preparing, evaluating, and supervising this program. She makes $15 per hour.
6. The program will operate for 3 hours each Tuesday evening for 10 weeks.
7. The instructor indicates that each kiln will only handle projects for 15 students. A kiln will need to be fired twice during the program for each 15 students. She will need to tend to the firing for 2 hours outside of class contact time each time there is a firing, and she can handle both kilns at the same time.

Directions:

1. Identify the facts relevant for completing a break-even analysis for this program.
2. Identify the various classifications of costs and the costs associated with each.
3. Table the data including columns for the highest and fewest number of participants you would recommend, and identify where you would break even with a price of $250 per participant.

In a commercial recreation operation, knowing the full cost of production is equally important. For the agency to make a profit and stay in business, it must make a margin of profit beyond production costs. It is normal practice for agencies to use cost–volume–profit analysis to determine production cost at an estimated level of volume and then to add a margin of profit to production costs. In these cases, agencies expect each program to contribute a margin of profit to the overall profits. This increment is known as the contribution margin. For example, all programs may be offered at cost plus a 15% contribution margin to agency profit.

Public and not-for-profit agencies also use the contribution margin concept. Although not profit making, these types of agencies often develop retained income from some program services. They frequently use this retained income to subsidize merit and public services or to make up for losses incurred in the operation of less successful private services.

Conclusion

This chapter discussed methods of analyzing the relationship of cost to volume. The PMAS requires that each program service be isolated and its costs of production and revenues matched so that its financial performance can be observed. Implementing the system gives the programmer factual cost data about each program service so that cost-based pricing decisions can be made. It also enables accurate decision making regarding subsidizing programs.

Endnotes

1. Variable costs increase an equal amount with each additional unit of volume. In most leisure services, the volume unit is the individual participant. However, this is not always the case. For example, in a band contest, variable costs may depend on the number of bands entered, not the number of band members. The same is often true for calculating the costs of athletic leagues and tournaments wherein the unit of analysis is a team, not individual players.
2. If you followed instructions and are reading this before discussing the cost–volume–profit exercise in class, you are indeed fortunate. The solution to the exercise is available at https://www.sagamorepub.com/products/recreation-programming-8th-ed. Please try to solve the exercise yourself before reading the solution.

References

Howard, D. R., & Selin, S. W. (1987). A method for establishing consumer price tolerance levels for public recreation services. *Journal of Park and Recreation Administration, 5*(3), 48–64.

Kerr, G. N., & Manfredo, M. J. (1991). An attitudinal-based model of pricing for recreation services. *Journal of Leisure Research, 23*, 37–50.

Reiling, S. D., Criner, G. K., & Oltmanns, S. E. (1988). The influence of information on users' attitudes toward campground user fees. *Journal of Leisure Research, 20*, 208–217.

Additional Readings

Becker, R. H., Berrier, D., & Barker, G. D. (1985). Entrance fees and visitation levels. *Journal of Park and Recreation Administration, 3*, 28–32.

Crompton, J. L. (1981, March). How to find the price that's right. *Parks and Recreation, 16*(3), 32–40.

Ellis, T., & Norton, R. L. (1988). *Commercial recreation.* St. Louis, MO: Times Mirror/Mosby College.

Manning, R., Calliman, E., Echelberger, H., Koenemann, E., & McEvan, D. (1984). Differential fees: Raising revenue, distributing demand. *Journal of Park and Recreation Administration, 2*, 2–38.

PART V

Follow-Up Analysis

Part V discusses Stage D of the Program Development Cycle. In this stage, the programmer evaluates a program and makes a decision about the disposition of the program. Programmers need to establish the worth of program services with systematically collected evaluation evidence. They can use this evidence to document program worth, to review program operations and thus make decisions that lead to proper program management.

This section includes three chapters. Chapter 20 explains program evaluation techniques and outlines a general plan for developing program evaluations. Chapter 21 explains the development of a comprehensive evaluation system. Chapter 22 discusses making decisions about program services.

Chapter 20: Program Evaluation Techniques

Chapter 21: Developing a Comprehensive Evaluation System

Chapter 22: Making Decisions About Program Services

Stage D: Follow-Up Analysis

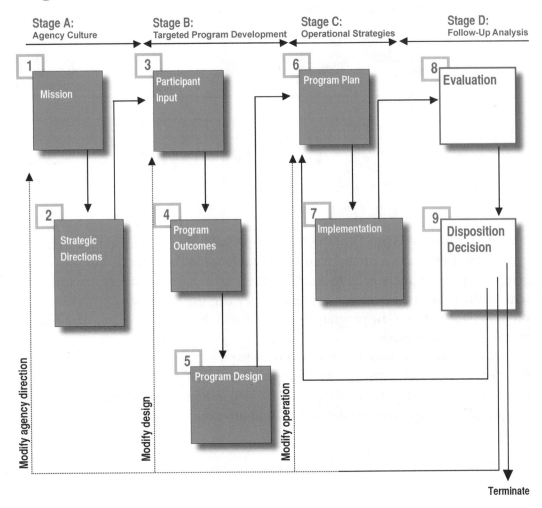

Public Art
Photo courtesy of City of Aurora Department of Parks, Recreation, and Open Space.
Photo by Sherri-Jo Stowell.

20 *Program Evaluation Techniques*

KEY TERMS

Evaluation, Evaluation Purposes, Steps of the Evaluation Planning Process,
Research Design, Sample, Sampling Techniques, Evaluation Report Passages

Implementing Intentionally Designed Experiences

The notion behind intentionally designed experiences is the ability to demonstrate positive outcomes gained from participating in carefully scripted, sequenced activities. Proper measurement and illustration of selected experiences can link play and evaluation such that program impacts will be clearly communicated to organizational stakeholders, as well as participants. The remaining chapters provide the basic framework to create an evaluation plan (Chapter 20), develop a comprehensive evaluation system (Chapter 21), and make programmatic decisions about intentionally designed experiences (Chapter 22). Readers are also advised to read *Play It, Measure It* for a specific application of evaluation using intentionally designed experiences (Roark & Evans, 2010).

Step 8: Evaluation

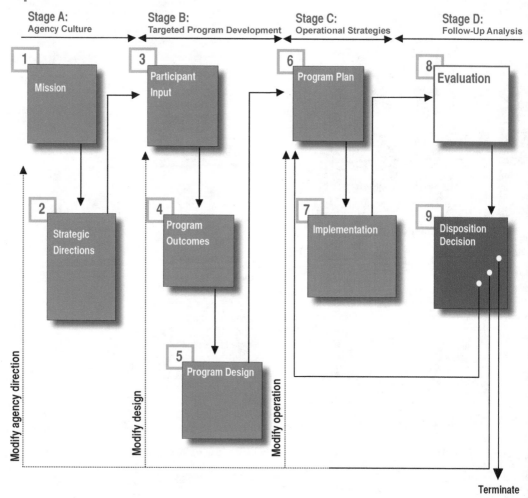

Evaluation is an elastic concept that programmers can use to describe many activities. Evaluating program services is the eighth step in the Program Development Cycle. It is the start of the follow-up analysis stage of the cycle and the antecedent to making a decision about the disposition of a program. With program evaluation data, the programmer makes a decision based on an analysis of evidence about the future of a program.

Evaluation Defined

Suchman (1967) stated, "An evaluation is basically a judgment of worth—an appraisal of value" (p. 11). Suchman's central theme is that evaluation involves making judgments of worth. Worthen and Sanders (1973) further developed this definition of evaluation, stating that "evaluation is the determination of the worth of a thing" (p. 19). They also indicated that the determination of merit or worth is the touchstone of evaluation. This latter point is important. Evaluation does not take place until a judgment of worth or value occurs. Evaluation is not simply collecting data; it also requires that a judgment of worth within the context of a value system be made with the data collected.

> Evaluation is not simply collecting data.

Henderson and Bialeschki (1995) described evaluation in terms of "assessing where we are, where we want to be, and how we can reach our desired goals" (p. 5). Methods for addressing those questions are best represented in the form of a continuum that ranges from casual, intuitive perceptions to more formal systematic approaches. The former does not require the use of systematic procedures or the presentation of objective evidence. The latter requires both and uses the scientific process to control the intrinsic subjectivity of everyday evaluation.

Many programmers evaluate their program services informally. This chapter aims to help programmers move from informal to more formal evaluation procedures. The definition of evaluation in this chapter, then, is *judging the worth of program services, based on an analysis of systematically collected evidence.*

Purposes of Evaluation

Evaluation is often imposed on programmers by a board, a third-party funding agency, or a higher level administrator. As a result, evaluation is often viewed as an add-on responsibility imposed on the programmer or as a procedure undertaken with some trepidation, because it may result in an adverse view of the programmer's efforts. The viewpoint used in this book is that evaluation is part of the programmer's ongoing responsibility of operating and managing program services—it is not an add-on responsibility. Making judgments of worth about program services can serve the programmer and the organization in establishing accountability, in program development, and in organizational management.

Establishing Accountability

Evaluation data can help the organization establish accountability by documenting program outputs and outcomes (i.e., verifying the effects of programs on participants). Documentation of benefits from program services, discussed in Chapter 11, is one example of the use of evaluation data for accountability.

Evaluation data can help verify that a program is indeed accomplishing its intended results. In the push and pull of implementing a program, programmers often make many changes from the original staging plan. Evaluation can help track outputs and outcomes of a program to help programmers verify the implementation of the original goals and intentions of the program.

Verifying outcomes with the systematically collected evidence provided by evaluation improves the credibility of the organization and its programs with its participants. It also helps position the organization more favorably within it service community. Evaluation results can be reorganized and used for public relations and publicity. Thus used, evaluation provides evidence that the programmer is an effective manager and that the organization provides services important to a community, thereby justifying the expenditures necessary for continuing services.

Program Development

With the data gathered in an evaluation, the programmer can improve and refine programs by determining what works, what does not work, and why things work the way they do. Programmers use this information to make program delivery methods more efficient, thereby saving expenses. They use evaluation data to analyze the contribution and effectiveness of each part of a program facilitating program revision. They can also use these same data to replicate effective programs and program components elsewhere.

Evaluation data can boost staff morale. Although the results of an evaluation sometimes indicate that a program is performing poorly, it is likely that most programs are doing well and will receive a favorable evaluation. Favorable evaluation reports enhance staff morale.

Evaluation, as it is currently conducted, will also result in the discovery of new needs, even though this is not the purpose of evaluation. Needs identification is part of the needs assessment step of the Program Development Cycle. However, clients often identify new needs on evaluation instruments, which can lead to new program ideas.

Organizational Management

Evaluation data can help improve organizational management. This information helps the programmer make informed decisions about how to modify programs, what services to drop, and which to continue. Programmers should make these alternate decisions with systematically collected and analyzed evaluation evidence rather than with perceptions of individuals or other less systematic methods.

Evaluation data help the manager make decisions about alternate resource allocation strategies. These are especially difficult questions in government and not-for-profit leisure service organizations because services often attract a committed core group of participants (Howard & Crompton, 1980). If an organization continues all programs that have a committed core constituency, there will be few programs to cancel. Sometimes programs are continued long after they cease to be useful to the organization. Leisure service organizations that have the benefit of annual budget increases often ignore these issues and simply add new services with the additional resources received. In a recession situation, however, they must decide which programs to eliminate. Evaluation data can provide the information and rationale necessary for the programmer to determine which services to drop. (These allocation decisions are obviously more straightforward in a commercial operation—if a program does not return a sufficient profit margin, it is eliminated.)

Programs that are continued each year without sufficient review and revision often become tired and outdated. As an organization's mission changes, a program may no longer be included in the organization's current mission even though it has a constituency. Evaluation data can provide the manager with the information and justification needed to update or terminate such programs.

Ultimately, the evaluation for each program operated must help answer the question of whether the resources needed for the program can be put to better use and allocated elsewhere in the organization. Evaluation contributes significantly to the development and management of program services and the management of leisure service organizations. Now complete Exercise 20.1.

Exercise 20.1.
Comparing Purposes of Evaluation

In class, analyze and compare the three purposes of evaluation. Consider the following points:

- How do these three purposes differ?
- How are these three purposes similar?
- How do these three purposes complement each other in a comprehensive evaluation system?

Planning an Evaluation

Evaluation is not a single activity or procedure. Most leisure service organizations do not have one evaluation procedure that can meet all of their evaluation needs. Agencies most likely have several procedures operating simultaneously to meet their diverse evaluation needs. Because of this diversity, programmers should understand how to plan an evaluation to address a specific evaluation problem and should know the issues inherent in implementing an evaluation. Grotelueschen et al. (1974) provided an outline for planning an evaluation. Programmers can use a modified form of this outline, included in Exhibit 20.1, to organize the material in this chapter. When planning an evaluation, they should follow the steps outlined in the order presented.

Exhibit 20.1. Evaluation Planner

1. Purpose: Why evaluate?
2. Audience: Who is the evaluation for? What questions do they want answered? What will they do with the information?
3. Process: How will the evaluation be conducted?
4. Issues: What questions should the evaluation address?
5. Resources: What resources are needed to conduct the evaluation?
6. Evidence: What evidence should be collected?
7. Data-gathering: How is the evidence to be collected?
8. Analysis: How can the evidence be analyzed?
9. Reporting: How can evaluation findings be reported?

Purpose: Why Evaluate?

The first question programmers will want to answer when planning an evaluation is why the evaluation is being conducted. The previous section outlined three purposes for conducting an evaluation. Although programmers may be able to address more than one of these purposes with a single evaluation, often they cannot. A single evaluation often serves only a single purpose. When attempting to serve several purposes, the programmer may never achieve the focus necessary for answering the evaluation question. The reason for specifying a purpose is to provide focus to the evaluation effort. In this way, the evaluation need identified as the reason for conducting the evaluation in the first place can be addressed. Rather than conducting one evaluation with broad, poorly focused purposes, programmers are best advised to conduct several well-focused evaluations, each specifically designed to fulfill a well-defined purpose.

In the first step then, programmers determine whether they are conducting the evaluation for program development, organizational management, or organizational accountability. As precisely as possible, they make a statement about the purpose for the evaluation. Four examples of such statements follow:

---

1. This evaluation is being conducted to determine participant-reported outcomes with program services.
2. This evaluation is being conducted to help make decisions about the disposition of this program service.
3. This evaluation is being conducted to evaluate the efficacy of our agency's social justice policies and judge the worth of our agency's distribution of program services across sociometric variables.
4. This evaluation is being conducted to document the benefits of participating in specific programs.

Audience: Who Is the Evaluation for?

Evaluation data are not generated and used in a void. Patton (1997) indicated, "People, not organizations use evaluation information" (p. 43). He further stated that the two most important factors contributing to the use of evaluation information are political considerations and the "personal factor." Political considerations relate to members of the evaluation team. When assembling the evaluation team, programmers should follow these criteria: (1) Members must have an interest in the evaluation findings, (2) members should have the power to use evaluation findings for making decisions, (3) members should believe the evaluation is worthwhile, (4) members should be concerned with how the results are used, and (5) members should be willing to commit their time and energy to the evaluation.

The second most important factor, the personal factor, "is the presence of an identifiable individual or group of people who personally care about the evaluation and the findings it generates" (Patton, 1997, p. 44). Agency personnel use evaluation data to make a judgment of worth and subsequently to make decisions based on this judgment. Identifying who will use the evaluation data and what they will do with the information is an important step in planning an evaluation.

House (1977) suggested that evaluation is a persuasive argument, rather than a scientific proof, that must respond to a specific rather than a universal audience. As House said, "Thus the situation the evaluator faces is almost always an appeal to particular audiences that [he or she] can define with some precision. If [the evaluator] cannot define [his or her] audiences, the evaluation is indeterminate" (p. 9). Compared with the epistemological rules, methods, and justifications considered accepted practice in social science research, the rules that evaluation audiences will accept are less well codified and not as universal. They are, in fact, situationally specific. Part of any evaluation thus requires uncovering the rules of acceptance, which will establish the ultimate rationale for the asserted values of a program. To accomplish this, the programmer defines with some precision the evaluation audience who will use the information and determines what questions the evaluation audience believes are important and relevant to answer.

A person's position in the organizational structure of the agency determines the types of information deemed relevant and therefore desired for evaluation (Weiss, 1973). For example, top administrators and boards generally show interest in a summary of broad issues and the effects of program services, which facilitate their decision to drop, modify, or continue a program. They also show interest in data that establish accountability for the funds being used for providing services. Program directors and middle managers are most interested in strategies that effectively meet desired ends. Direct service personnel are usually most concerned with the effects of their various face-to-face intervention techniques. Other possible users of information include external funding agencies, the public, clients, national associations, other providers of similar services, and so on. People's positions in an organization, then, determine to some degree the evaluation questions they want answered. Although it is desirable for programmers to meet the evaluation needs of the entire organization with one evaluation, this is often not be possible.

Determining the evaluation audience, and consequently the evaluation data they desire, is the second step of planning an evaluation. Identifying a specific audience is necessary for any evaluation for focusing information needs, guiding the selection of an appropriate process for conducting the evaluation, identifying salient values, and guiding interpretation of objective data to be gathered.

While planning a custom-designed evaluation, programmers must develop a priority of information needs and address as many needs as possible with the resources available to conduct the evaluation. It will probably be impossible for programmers to meet all identified needs. Therefore, it is important that they have first established those priorities that emerge from identifying the primary audience and the primary purpose for conducting the evaluation.

The answers to these first two questions about purpose and audience provide a framework for developing the remainder of the evaluation. Any process developed must fulfill the identified purpose of an evaluation and meet the information needs of a well-defined evaluation audience. Now complete Exercise 20.2.

Exercise 20.2.
Specifying the Evaluation Purpose and Audience

In class, discuss the importance of first identifying the purpose of the evaluation and the evaluation audience. Consider the following questions:

- How does specifying the purpose and audience of an evaluation help focus the evaluation?
- Why not accomplish several purposes with one evaluation?
- Why does an evaluation have to be tailored to meet the needs of a specific audience?

Process: How Will the Evaluation Be Conducted?

What techniques will the programmer use to conduct the evaluation? Howe (1980) identified six general techniques: professional judgment, measurement, discrepancy, decision-oriented, goal free, and transaction-observation. The technique selected determines how the evaluation will be conducted. Each technique uses different methods and is best suited for a specific type of evaluation. All techniques are either process models or preordinate models. Each model includes different preordained decisions and presents the evaluator with different choices and responsibilities.

Process models identify a procedure for conducting the evaluation but do not identify the criteria for making judgments of worth. An example of a process model is the use of goals and objectives. Goal and objective technology explains precisely a technique for writing goals and objectives, but the technology does not provide the original goals. Embodied in any set of goals and objectives is a point of view about what is important to accomplish and what may be ignored because it is less important. When using goals and objectives in evaluation, programmers must write the original goals; in doing so, they provide a value structure for the evaluation. When choosing a process model, then, evaluators will provide the criteria for making judgments of worth.

Preordinate models provide the techniques for accomplishing the evaluation and the criteria for making judgments of worth. An example of this type of evaluation process is the use of standards. An evaluation procedure that uses standards gives the programmer specific steps for collecting data and a set of criteria (the standards) for judging the worth of program services. Programmers are often tempted to use preordinate models, which explicate the entire technique; therefore, the programmer has little to do except implement the preestablished technique. A caution programmers must exercise in using preordinate evaluation models is ensuring that the value system embodied in the preordinate model is consistent with the purpose of evaluation identified and that the data developed from the evaluation meet the information needs of the evaluation audience.

Programmers can use the evaluation planning steps that follow in two ways. First, they can use them to analyze a preordinate model and to understand how the model deals with each planning step. Second, they can use them as a planning agenda to determine how to implement a process model or a custom-designed model.

Issues: What Questions Should the Evaluation Address?

Determining the questions to be addressed in an evaluation is a critical step. In selecting the questions, the programmer must be concerned with validity and values. To be valid, the questions must be true indicators of the values asserted for the program. For example, programmers too often use attendance figures as an indicator of the worth of a program. Attendance is a valid indicator of program impact, that is, how many and who were served. It is not a valid indicator of program quality, nor can it document program outputs, that is, what happened to the individuals in the program.

Henderson and Bialeschki (1995), in the "Five *P*s of Evaluation" (Exhibit 20.2), outlined areas for creating evaluation questions. Note that it is not advisable for programmers to evaluate everything at the same time; rather, they should select areas that relate best to the program(s) at hand. A single evaluation may focus on one or more of the Five *P*s of Evaluation. For example, a learn-to-swim program may contain questions about participants in terms of skill attainment and carryover into other areas (i.e., swimming in a lake or river). The same evaluation may contain questions about the program regarding how risk was managed in the aquatic environment and the effectiveness of the swimming instructors. Similarly, other items may address place, policies and administration, or personnel.

Resources: What Resources Are Available for Evaluation?

Every program manager must understand that evaluation costs money. At the least, it will consume staff time that could have been spent on other activities. Other expenses also associated with evaluation include printing evaluation forms, collecting and analyzing data, and preparing and distributing the evaluation report.

One resource that may exist in the agency is data that are already routinely collected. Programmers can obtain at least part of the evaluation data needed by reanalyzing or reinterpreting data that the organization has already collected. Evaluation does not always require the collection of new data. Other evaluation resources to which the agency may have access include colleagues, universities, cooperative extension agencies, and consultants. All of these potential resources can help the agency conduct evaluations.

Once the decision to evaluate is made, the questions and issues that need examined can quickly grow to a large and unmanageable number. Each piece of information obtained adds incrementally to the cost of the evaluation. Because of this, it is important that programmers provide focus to the evaluation with the procedures outlined in this section to avoid the expense of answering unimportant, irrelevant, or less important questions. It is also important that they do some cost–benefit analysis of the answers to be obtained. To determine the potential benefit of possible questions, consider the following:

> Evaluation does not always require the collection of new data.

- If this question is answered, what could be done with the information?
- Is there some management implication in obtaining an answer to this question?
- Is this information worth the cost of obtaining it?

Although having answers to many questions would be nice, program evaluation should remain focused on only questions that enable the manager to improve

> **Exhibit 20.2. Summary of Components of the Five *P*s of Evaluation**
>
> Participants
> - Motivations/satisfaction
> - Changes in attitudes as outcomes
> - Changes in knowledge as outcomes
> - Changes in skills and abilities as outcomes
> - Carryover into other situations
> - How individuals interact
>
> Program
> - Effective leadership
> - Promotion of program
> - If participants gained anything
> - Risk management
>
> Place
> - Safety concerns
> - Master planning
> - Adequate facilities
>
> Policies/Administration
> - Accountability of budget
> - Cost–benefit analysis
> - Cost-effectiveness analysis
> - Equitable provision of services
>
> Personnel
> - Performance appraisal
> - Assess training needs
> - Provide feedback for improvement
>
> *Note.* From Henderson and Bialeschki (2002). Reprinted with permission.

program development and program management or to establish accountability in a meaningful way.

Evidence: What Evidence Should Be Collected?

Evidence is any information that can be used for making judgments of worth about the issues raised in the evaluation. The evaluation effort is usually focused on the issues identified earlier in this process. Once these issues have been identified, the search for evidence begins.

Many types of evidence can be gathered, such as descriptions of personnel, participants, operational procedures, and processes; goals and objectives; costs; and program outcomes. Participant judgments about various components of a program can also be collected on open-ended or scaled questionnaires. The type of evidence that is most appropriate depends on the issues under investigation and the requirements of the evaluation audience.

A major consideration in this step of planning an evaluation is the sources and quality of the evidence. Although much evidence can be collected, the evaluator should be sure to collect the most relevant and valid evidence.

A concern in gathering evidence is that the evidence collected presents a balanced and comprehensive view of the program and its effect. Some programmers give undue attention to forcefully or articulately presented, positive or negative, extreme views about a program. The evaluator ensures that the final evaluation report is balanced and represents the typical or average view of the program. Some programmers also focus evaluation data on specific components, positive or negative, of a program rather than on judging the worth of the overall program and its components.

The programmer should be concerned about the validity and reliability of the evidence collected. Evidence should be logically accepted as a measure or indicator of the issues the evaluation addresses. The validity of the evidence in evaluation studies is often not well thought out. Validity basically asks the question, is the evidence being collected a true indicator of the issue being addressed? For example, if the programmer wants to document participant achievement when evaluating a swimming program, then a piece of evidence would be some measure of the participants' swimming skills.

> A concern in gathering evidence is that the evidence collected presents a balanced and comprehensive view of the program and its effect.

Programmers must also ensure reliability of the evidence. To be reliable, the evidence must be accurate and consistent. Reliable instruments allow programmers to obtain consistent results during each use of the instrument. For example, a rubber yardstick would not yield consistent measurement of distance and would therefore be unreliable because it would not allow for consistent results.

At some point, the programmer will try to demonstrate that participation in a program led to certain outcomes. Establishing cause and effect is one of the most difficult social science problems. It requires that programmers deal with three propositions simultaneously: time-order, covariation, and control of rival causal factors (Denzin, 1979). To establish cause and effect, programmers must establish that the cause came before the effect, that is, in a logical time-order. In evaluating program services, this is usually accomplished because the program occurs before the observation or measurement of effect. Programmers must also establish covariation between the presumed cause and effect: For every change in the cause, there should be a corresponding change in the effect. If the presumed cause leads to little or no change in the effect, the programmer cannot assert a cause-and-effect relationship. The final proposition involves controlling for rival causal factors. The programmer must be able to

> Establishing cause and effect is one of the most difficult social science problems.

demonstrate that participation in the program—not some other possible explanation—led to the observed change in the effect.

These propositions are best controlled through the use of a good research design. Although this book is not intended to be a research text, some elementary knowledge of research design can enable the evaluator to develop better evaluations. A frequently used research design is schematically represented in Exhibit 20.3. The X represents the treatment or program, and the letter O represents the observation or measurement. This research design is known as a one-shot case study (Campbell & Stanley, 1963). With this design, a program occurs, and then measurement occurs after the program. This is the typical scenario in many leisure service agencies in which program evaluations are completed at the end of a program.

Exhibit 20.3. One-Shot Case Study Research Design

X   O

Although this design controls for time-order—the treatment occurs before measurement of the presumed effect—it does not control for covariation or rival causal factors. Because there is no measurement before the program, there is no baseline data for the programmer to compare the postprogram measurement. It is therefore difficult for the programmer to demonstrate that participation led to the observations obtained in the postprogram measurements. In addition, without a preprogram test, it is difficult for programmers to assert that participation led to the obtained postprogram measurements, because they do not know if participation or some other rival causal factor led to the observed change. For example, the postprogram scores could have been a result of participants' previously obtained skills and have nothing to do with their participation in the current program.

Some of the problems with a one-shot case study design can be addressed with a one-group pretest–posttest design (Campbell & Stanley, 1963), diagrammed in Exhibit 20.4. This design introduces a pretest, and the programmer now has some baseline data with which to compare postprogram results. This design enables programmers to better demonstrate the effect of the program, because they can now document the change using measurements taken before and after participation. In this case, covariation is easier for the programmer to demonstrate. However, the problem of possible rival causal factors accounting for the change rather than the program itself still remains.

Exhibit 20.4. Pretest–Posttest Research Design

O   X   O

Programmers can deal with many of the problems associated with the previous research designs in the classical pretest–posttest control group design (Campbell & Stanley, 1963), illustrated in Exhibit 20.5. This design adds a control group (the group not receiving the treatment) to the previous design. It also features randomized assignment (R) of subjects either to the experimental group (the group receiving the treatment or participating in the program) or to the control group. If randomized assignment is not possible, the programmer attempts to identify a matched control group in which control group subjects are matched as closely as possible with program participants on all relevant variables.

Exhibit 20.5. Classical Experimental Research Design

R	O	X	O
R	O	O	

With this design, programmers can control for time-order, demonstrate covariation between the experimental treatment and the assumed result, and document the possible effects of rival causal factors. For example, if the control group shows changes in the pretest and posttest scores similar to the experimental group, they would question whether the experimental treatment (the program) was having any effect.

One problem with this design is that treatment or participation in a program is withheld from the control group. This is obviously a difficult set of circumstances in leisure service agencies. Participants register for programs to receive services, not to have them withheld! Programmers can deal with this problem, first, by using the research design diagrammed in Exhibit 20.6, instead of the design diagrammed in Exhibit 20.5. The design in Exhibit 20.6 includes all the features of the design in Exhibit 20.5, but treatment for the control group comes after the experiment. In this way, all who initially registered eventually receive the program. Administering such a scheme would require informing participants at registration that they were participating in an experiment and would be randomly assigned to different groups that will receive the program at different times.

Exhibit 20.6. Modified Classical Experimental Research Design

R	O	X	O		
R	O		O	X	O

Programmers often think that they must conduct pretest–posttest social science studies on each program operated, to evaluate services. This is not the case. They should document the effects of a program service initially, but after establishing that a specific program service leads to predictable outcomes, it is unnecessary that they document these outcomes each time. After establishing cause and effect, the programmer can return to using the first design outlined (Exhibit 20.3, page 391) and simply document that participants have had the predicted outcomes. In this way, program outcomes are continuously monitored and documented.

A final concern regarding the collection of evidence is establishing the credibility of the programmer as an evaluator. When people evaluate programs they are responsible for developing, there are inherent conflicts of interest. The credibility of the programmer as an evaluator will be compromised with no ongoing critical review and analysis of program services. If evaluation reports highlight only glowing successes, the programmer's credibility as an evaluator will be questioned.

Data Gathering: How Is Evidence to Be Collected?

This section discusses how the evidence may be obtained, how to collect data, when to collect data, how much data to obtain, and from whom to obtain data.

Techniques for Data Collection

Programmers can collect data for evaluation studies in many ways. Techniques that could be used include questionnaires, interviews, conversations, observation schedules, participant observation, anecdotal data, standardized tests, checklists, and rating scales. Programmers most frequently collect data by using questionnaires they have designed, talking to participants to obtain feedback about program services, and conducting on-site observation of programs. These strategies produce a good assortment of data for judging program worth.

However, typical data collection practices have several flaws. First, the questionnaires are usually not validated for data collection. The validity and reliability of the instrument is usually not established in any meaningful way. Second, discussions with participants and observations of ongoing programs are usually not guided by an interview or observation schedule. Evaluation practices in agencies could be greatly improved through the use of validated instruments and through increasing the reliability of the interview and observation methods.

Instrument validation is a technical matter beyond the scope of this book. However, validity begins with making a conceptual link between the issues being investigated and the questions asked on an instrument. When developing instruments, the programmer should constantly review the rationale for including each question and determine how it logically links to and is a measure of the issues being examined.

Interviewing and Observations

Interviewing and observations are less formal methods of gathering data. Most programmers handle on-site visitations to programs as public relations exercises, in which they deal with any observed problems or emergencies and chat with participants, listening to any comments—good or bad—that the participant cares to make about the program. Often, each programmer in an agency tends to look for different items to judge how well the program is being conducted, thus reducing the reliability of the evaluation system. To be useful for evaluation, observations and interviews need to be handled more systematically, that is, with more reliability.

When observing, the programmer may function as a passive, covert observer; as an active, participant-observer; or as an overt, full participant (Howe, 1993). These modes provide a variety of depths of involvement and access to the experiences of participants. In any case, the primary technique is careful observation of people's activities and recording them, that is, taking field notes.

Interviews with individuals during these visits are not simply a time to chat with participants. They should be considered guided conversations (Howe, 1993) that are driven by a structured or unstructured interview schedule and use a conversational demeanor that establishes a rapport that elicits the information needed. Both of these naturalistic evaluation methods can be made more systematic and reliable through the techniques discussed in the rest of this section.

Identify specific observation tasks or interview items. All programmers involved in interviewing or observing programs should jointly develop the necessary interview forms and observation schedules. The result of this will be the development of comprehensive schedules that incorporate the collective wisdom of all program supervisors. Furthermore, everyone who conducts an interview or observation will then examine the same items. This increases the reliability of the process. Variations will no longer be the result of who conducted the interview or made the observation.

Have detailed instructions about making observations. Uniformity of practice in conducting an interview or observation also contributes to reliability. With good instructions, it should not matter who conducts the interview or makes the observation—the results should be similar.

Staff need to be trained and prepared for making observations and conducting interviews. Having different staff each make independent observations of the same event using the jointly developed instruments and then comparing and discussing why they scored the event the way they did will improve the process. This exercise will result in consistency of results and interrater reliability.

Require immediate and detailed reports. Recording observations immediately is necessary for having accurate reports. Recalled observations are often less accurate than those recorded immediately.

Validate the observations. Information obtained through interviews or observations should always be validated. Interviewers can accomplish this by seeking out additional verification of the information from other independent sources.

Interviewers should try to discover if other participants hold the same view as those expressed by the participants interviewed. They may also try to find additional observations. In either case, determine whether the reported or observed characteristic is typical of the program or is in fact a single untypical occurrence.

Data-gathering practices currently used in many agencies are not unacceptable, but they can and should be improved. Improving them will result in more reliable and valid data on which programmers can make judgments of worth.

Selecting a Sample

Gathering data almost always involves selecting a sample. An erroneous belief among program practitioners is that selecting a sample means handing out questionnaires to whoever can be easily reached or whoever wants to complete them. Random sampling improves data in a number of ways. One of the most important is that it is the surest way of obtaining a sample that is representative of the participant group.

Given the question, how can one characterize the views of a whole population by simply getting information from a few members of the population? the answer is random sampling. Random sampling is not complicated, and after understanding the rationale for drawing a random sample, programmers will accept no substitute!

Population is a technical term for a cohort of individuals defined with some precision. For example, the members of a programming class could be defined as a population. In this case, because the class probably includes 20 to 30 individuals, the programmer would probably not draw a sample, but would conduct a census

> Random sampling is not complicated.

(a census is a data collection method wherein data are collected from every member of the population). A population could also be defined as all freshmen at a university, all undergraduates at a university, or everyone registered at a university. As the population increases in size, conducting a census becomes increasingly difficult and expensive.

The sampling problem then becomes finding out the information that would have been obtained in a census, with data gathered from a sample instead of the entire population. When collecting a sample, programmers can never be sure of obtaining the true value that would have been obtained through a census. Actually, programmers obtain an estimate of the population value. They can determine who might be included in a sample from the entire population in many ways.

> Because of this, samples selected through random selection procedures have the highest probability of being representative of the population from which they were drawn.

A sample could include only those whose names begin with *A*. It could include only those whose social security number begins with an odd number. It could include the first 500 participants to come to a swimming pool on a Sunday. Programmers can always devise a method for obtaining a sufficient number of individuals to make up a sample. The question is, are they representative of the entire population?

Random selection procedures increase the probability that the sample selected will be representative of the population from which it was drawn. This occurs because random selection is not a helter-skelter method, as is popularly believed. It is a precise method of selection in which every individual in the defined population has an equal and independent chance of being selected for the sample. Because of this, samples selected through random selection procedures have the highest probability of being representative of the population from which they were drawn. With a randomly drawn sample, programmers can generalize the findings to the population from which it was drawn. Because of the availability of websites with random number generators, obtaining a random sample has become much easier than in the past. The next sections discuss two methods for drawing a random sample: random sampling and matrix sampling.

Random Sampling

Why sample? What can sampling achieve? Programmers can achieve savings by sampling rather than completing a census. For example, it is obviously less expensive for programmers to survey 234 individuals from a population of 600 than to survey all members of the population. However, as the population size decreases, the proportion of individuals to be included in the sample must increase. With small populations, programmers must sample almost the entire population to ensure a representative sample. For example, to ensure good representation of a group of 35 individuals, the programmer would need to sample 32, approximately 91+% of the population. Yet from a population of 2,000 individuals, the programmer would only need to collect a random sample of 322 individuals, approximately 16% of the population.[1]

These sampling realities make it difficult for programmers to decide when to sample rather than conduct a census. Many programs involve registrations of 35 or fewer participants. So much data collection in evaluation of program operations involves completing a census rather than a sample. It is somewhat unclear when sampling becomes economical (i.e., there are savings to be had from sampling rather than completing a census). With a population of 400, the programmer only needs to obtain a sample of 196 individuals, about half of the population. Populations larger than 400 individuals provide opportunities for additional saving because the percentage of the population that needs to be randomly sampled continues to decrease

---

[1]All recommendations about sample size in this section are from Krejcie and Morgan (1970). This work has been repeatedly cited as the source for sample size recommendations of many published tables on this subject. Using a Web browser and entering "Krejcie, R. V., & Morgan, D.W. 1970" will direct the reader to many of these charts that recommend sample sizes for different populations. Most are based on the following parameters. These tables are used to determine the needed size of a sample (S; i.e., the recommended sample size is the number of cases needed for use in statistical analysis and is the yield required from your sampling procedure), randomly chosen (i.e., each subject has an equal and independent chance of selection) from an identified finite population (N; i.e., one you can define and access) so the sample proportion p will be within ± .05 of the population proportion P (i.e., the sample mirrors the population along all relevant characteristics with in ± .05 of the actual value) with a .95 level of confidence (i.e., upon repeated samplings, the one obtained will likely be obtained 95% of the time).

as the size of the population increases. With the introduction of websites with random number generators, drawing a random sample has become easier, and in some instances, drawing a random sample is the method of choice.

Drawing a random sample involves several steps. First, it is necessary for programmers to have a consecutively numbered sample frame (a list) of the population. In leisure program evaluations, this is frequently possible because programmers often have a list of registered participants. Thus, programmers can use a list of registered participants as the sample frame.

Second, programmers determine how large of a sample to draw. This question does not have a simple answer and depends on the probability desired of obtaining a sample that truly represents the population. Consulting various resources, as discussed in Footnote 1 in the Random Sampling section, directs the reader to a reasonable solution to the sample size problem.

Programmers can redefine the program population to take advantage of the economies afforded by sampling. For example, if an agency's fall enrollment consists of 30 programs with 30 participants each, then the fall enrollment population is 30 classes times 30 participants per class, or 900 individuals. In this case, only 269 randomly selected individuals from the population of 900 need to complete the instrument. If the sampling was done randomly, the programmer could be confident with a specific percentage of probability that the information obtained would have been obtained with a census.

Randomly obtained sample data also require some cautions when being interpreted. For example, with data obtained under the circumstances outlined, the programmer can only generalize the findings to fall enrollments in the aggregate, but cannot generalize about individual programs. To generalize to a specific program, the programmer must define the individuals in the program as the population and obtain a sample appropriate to the population size.

Upon completion of a census, there are no issues of generalization unless not all individuals in the population responded. Then the programmer needs to be concerned of a biasing pattern for those who did not respond, for example, if the instrument was completed at the end of a program and five of the original 30 enrollees dropped out along the way. The programmer would be concerned about their views that have not been included in the data obtained. They may have dropped out of the program because of specific issues or concerns that have not been collected because of the timing of the data collection. As part of the evaluation process, some agencies attempt to follow up with those who drop out to ascertain why they discontinued the program.

After determining the size of the sample to obtain, programmers draw the sample. They accomplish this by using a random number generator, which can easily be found on the Web. For an example, go to https://stattrek.com/statistics/random-number-generator.aspx. Continuing with the example from above wherein the programmer needs to obtain a sample of 269 individuals of 900 individuals from fall enrollments, the programmer would have a list of individuals numbered from 001–900. The programmer would then enter in the random number generator that he or she wants to obtain 269 numbers from 001–900 and does not want duplicate numbers. Not duplicating numbers ensures that each person in the population has an equal and independent chance of being included in the sample. The program then randomly selects 269 numbers from 900. The numbers selected by the random number generator would be the individuals that the programmer would include in the sample.

The survey questionnaire is then distributed to the 269 individuals selected. If the programmer assumes that all information desired is distributed throughout the entire population, then a random sample best ensures random distribution of the data throughout the sample.

Measuring Park Usage[2]

In the NRPA 2018 Agency Performance Review, 95% of the agencies indicated that operating and maintaining park sites was one of their key responsibilities, followed by 92% of the agencies reporting that providing recreation programming and services was their second key responsibility. Indeed, this is a field of parks and recreation, and much supervised, as well as unsupervised, recreation activity occurs in parks. How much use open-access parks receive is often an unanswered question in many agencies, especially facilities that provide program opportunities but are not staffed, for example, a playground equipment area. A research group from the Rand Corporation has been developing techniques for answering this question for over a decade (McKenzie, Cohen, Sehgal, Williamson, & Golinelli, 2006). The result of their work is an instrument and process for using it called the Systematic Observation of Play and Recreation in Communities (SOPARC).

Results of their work have provided an observation schedule and a process for using it. Generally, they found that observing a park 16 times per week (i.e., four times per week at four times of the day) was sufficient and allows generalization of results to total park use (Cohen et al., 2011). In another study, this recommendation was implemented through observations of parks 12 times per week: "Tuesday, 8 AM, 11 AM, and 2 PM; Thursday, 12 PM, 3 PM, and 6 PM; Saturday, 9 AM, 12 PM, and 3 PM; and Sunday, 11 AM, 2 PM, and 5 PM" (Cohen et al., 2016, p. 410). The focus was on neighborhood parks averaging 8.8 acres, and observations were conducted for 1 week spanning the spring/summer season in 2014.

This body of work is too large to be reported fully here. But their method provides programmers with an opportunity to systematically document park usage, especially physical activity. Their techniques implement some of what this chapter has already covered including developing a good observation schedule, having a protocol for using it, and systematically sampling park usage to predict overall usage. For completing data analysis, we recommend observations on a seasonal basis with the use of time series comparisons of results, as well as comparisons by

---

[2]This work has been occurring since 2006 and has been pursued by a work group from the Rand Corporation mostly funded by federal health agencies. The key articles chronicling its development have been included in the references for this chapter. The body of work is too large to be included in this text, but an online version can be accessed at https://www.rand.org/health/surveys_tools/soparc/user-guide.html.

neighborhood and other variables relevant to the community. Providing open-access park usage consumed 45% of operational budgets in 2018 for many park and recreation agencies (NRPA, 2018). In many cases, the results of this effort have not been documented. Doing so is a sizable but important task. We recommend that to make the task accomplishable, agencies begin by studying one third of their parks each year and build on this effort as resources become available.

The effects of the most recent study from this research group were reported in *Parks & Recreation* (Cohen & Lueschner, 2017) and indicate that parks are a wonderful neighborhood resource for physical activity but that they are underutilized for this purpose. These researchers were most interested in documenting physical activity, whereas park and recreation professionals would also espouse social, relaxation, and other leisure pursuits occurring in parks. But parks are an important resource for physical activity and for improving public health. Many park and recreation agencies have embraced this outcome as one of their strategic goals. Some of the recommendations these researchers offered include offering more supervised activities in parks, implementing more focused marketing efforts that increase awareness of parks, and installing targeted facilities such as walking trails. Documenting what is occurring in parks and other open-access venues is an important agency evaluation activity that is not being systematically pursued. Doing so would provide excellent accountability.

Data Sources

When identifying data sources, programmers should obtain information from people who are in a position to have the information desired. Many may have an opinion about the quality of a program, and it is important for programmers to obtain a variety of viewpoints. However, some individuals are better situated than others to know what happened in a program. For example, the program participants, the program leader, and the program supervisor who made occasional visits while the program was in operation may have firsthand information about what occurred. The evaluator should therefore identify the sources from whom the most knowledge can be obtained and make certain that evidence is systematically collected from these sources. The evaluator can then use additional information collected from other sources to provide further insight and to validate the data obtained from the primary information sources.

> Some individuals are better situated than others to know what happened in a program.

Other Considerations in Data Collection

Programmers have many possibilities for timing data collection. The results will depend on when data are collected. Standard practice involves obtaining preprogram data at registration and postprogram data at the final program session. There is some question about this technique, because the evaluation does not include individuals who have dropped out of the program. They may have valuable insights into the program. However, a mail-out to all who originally registered for the program is a costly but more inclusive procedure. The availability and use of e-mail for this purpose reduces its cost.

Programmers must also be concerned with the intrusiveness of the evaluation procedure. Participants register for programs to participate in them, not to complete evaluation forms. This is another reason that the evaluation instrument must be well focused in the first place. Participants may not be willing to answer all of the questions the programmer can develop. A general guideline here is that if the instrument cannot be completed in less than 10 minutes, it is probably too long and needs to be further revised and focused. There is also an ethical problem: If programmers believe an individual's leisure is important, they will not want to intrude unnecessarily.

Analysis: How Can the Evidence Be Analyzed?

After collecting data, programmers analyze them to determine what the data indicate about the program. In this step, the programmer places the data into a meaningful pattern that gives insight into the worth of the program. The programmer can conduct an analysis in many ways. The method chosen should provide insight into the concerns of the evaluation audience and should be appropriate for the type of evidence collected. In addition, the audience should be able to understand the analytical technique. For example, it is not useful for the programmer to use statistical regression if the evaluation audience does not understand this statistical technique.

> If the instrument cannot be completed in less than 10 minutes, it is probably too long and needs to be further revised and focused.

Because the data to be analyzed will be either quantitative or qualitative, the analysis should be appropriate for the type of evidence gathered. Statistical analysis is one method of placing quantitative data into a meaningful pattern. It should include reporting the distribution of scores (score tallies or percentages of responses in each category), measures of central tendency (mean, mode, and median), measures of dispersion (variance and standard deviation), and measures of association (correlations). Evaluation data analysis is seldom used for making predictions about future programs, but focuses instead on reporting current program outcomes and on interpreting the meaning of the documented outcomes.

Quantitative data analysis is useful for analyzing evaluation data, but much of evaluation data is qualitative, naturalistic evidence that must be pieced together into a coherent whole with rhetorical comment. When writing up this material, the programmer should remember that its primary purpose is to share the participant's leisure experience with the evaluation audience (Howe, 1993). The meaningfulness of qualitative data can often be made apparent through a comparison of evaluation results with another known entity. A number of comparisons could make the data more meaningful:

- Time series data: Compare program results over time.
- Discrepancy comparisons: Compare intended versus actual program inputs, processes, products, outputs, and outcomes.
- Need reduction: Compare results obtained with the amount of need in the community. How much need was met (reduced) with the operation of this program?
- Standards: Compare program results with established standards, legal mandates, or administrative directives.
- Inter- or intra-agency comparisons: Compare program results with other programs in an agency, or compare the program with similar programs in other agencies.

Techniques for making these comparisons include critical review, journalistic accounts, historical review, and content analysis. In all data analysis, the primary objective is to develop information that provides meaningful insight about the results and effect of a program so the worth of the program is made apparent.

Reporting: How Can Evaluation Findings Be Reported?

Communicating the results of an evaluation can take many forms. During the early, formative stages of a program, oral reports and short written reports can be used effectively. Other reporting formats that have given the evaluation audience insights into programs include testimony from participants, movies, still photographs, videotapes, slideshows, and participation in the program by the evaluation audience. These formats can be used effectively in various situations.

Even with the many possible reporting formats, a written, summative report with the familiar spiral binding seems to be the most common. This practice will likely continue because of its universal understandability, its documentary value, and its ease of access. In preparing such a report, the practitioner faces many decisions about what to include and how to organize it. The following section provides a guide for organizing an evaluation report, along with an outline of the recommended content of sections for inclusion in the body of such a report.

Organizing the Evaluation Report

The typical evaluation report contains the following sections and is organized in the sequence outlined in the next section:
1. Title page
2. Author or authors and their affiliations
3. Evaluation audience—who will receive the report
4. Executive summary—a one-page summary of the procedures and results
5. Table of contents
6. Lists of tables, figures, and photographs
7. Body of the report

8. Appendices—all items not likely to be available elsewhere, such as survey instruments, data tables, letters of testimony, and newspaper articles
9. References

Contents for the Body of the Report

Item 7, the body of the evaluation report, can contain many sections. It is not recommended that all sections described in the following paragraphs be included in every report. The sections included should be determined by the purpose of the evaluation, the audience who will receive the report, and the process used for evaluation.

Purpose of the Evaluation

All reports should specify why the evaluation was conducted so that the programmer can conceptually outline the framework for the evaluation. Purposes include, for example, improving the program, documenting accountability, improving planning, aiding policy analysis, assessing program impact, aiding managerial monitoring, and justifying continued funding.

Evaluation Questions

This section is the next logical extension of the Purpose section. It tells the reader the major questions asked in the evaluation study and the criteria used in making evaluative judgments of worth. Content in this section establishes the content validity of the evaluation questions. This section makes apparent that the questions relate to the purpose of the evaluation.

Description of the Program

This section outlines the history of the program (if it has one) and the setting, including the location, the persons using the service, and the activities of the program. It portrays to the evaluation audience the five *W*s and the *H* of a journalistic story: the who, what, when, where, why, and how of the program.

Evaluator's Background

This section establishes the credibility of the program's evaluator. It includes information such as the evaluator's affiliation, the evaluator's academic and professional background, a bibliography of other evaluation work or academic work, and an exploration of the evaluator's values and biases. It exposes who the evaluator is and how he or she views the evaluation process.

> It is the responsibility of the evaluator to present the evaluation audience with a report that is comprehensible to them.

Summary of Regulations

This section includes a summary—and possibly an interpretation—of federal, state, local, professional, or administrative regulations and directives affecting or mandating the program evaluation. Many evaluations undertaken today are mandated because of participation in some externally funded program. A brief explanation of such an arrangement would be in order.

Data-Gathering and Analytical Methods

Regardless of the data-gathering technique used, an accurate and complete description of how the data were collected should be included. Procedures for analyzing the data should also be reported. If social science techniques have been used, the conventions normally applicable for reporting them should be observed. However, depending on the evaluation audience, additional interpretation beyond that normally required in the academic press may be in order. It is the responsibility of the evaluator to present the evaluation audience with a report that is comprehensible to them.

Findings

This section reports the summarized data and interprets their meaning. Helping the evaluation audience understand the findings should be paramount in reporting them. It is important that findings be conceptually integrated into the report. Organizing them around some of the key evaluation issues or questions identified earlier in the report is one useful method. Others that have been used include organizing results along geographic areas, age groups, or program areas. Again, the only principle to follow is to use the method that leads to the clearest understanding of the findings.

Use of the Report

One problem interfering with the use of evaluations has been the lack of action based on evaluation reports. Evaluators can attempt to remedy this situation by suggesting how the evaluation audience can use the results and the report. Some possible uses include (1) using the report as a beginning and collecting the same evaluation information over time so that time series data can be developed; (2) releasing the whole report or sections of it to the press for a public relations program; and (3) using the report as a catalyst for public action on an item of public concern that may have come out of the report. Evaluation takes scarce resources from agencies. The more potential payoffs from these expended resources, the more likely an agency will engage in evaluation.

Contract

Any evaluation done by an consultant from outside an agency should be conducted with an appropriate contract. The final report usually includes a copy of this document and a brief review of how the contract has been fulfilled through the final report.

Conclusions

This section answers value judgment questions. What was the worth of the program? Evaluation has not occurred until these judgments are made—the programmer has only gathered and reported data up to this point. No matter how scientific the data-gathering phase, evaluation does not occur until the information has been integrated with a value system and a judgment has been made about the worth of the program.

In developing this section, the programmer should stick to the original purpose of the evaluation and the data that have been generated. However, the unintended collateral outcomes sometimes have more effect than the intended ones. The programmer can cite additional findings beyond those mandated by some type of preordinate evaluation design. The report becomes stronger if additional audiences that concur with the conclusions can be cited. Letters from participant observers and comments from the staff, the press, and other parties of interest should be used.

Minority Reports

Evaluation is not value free. Although the programmer may start with objective data, during the process of evaluation those data are interpreted and a final judgment of worth made with subjective values. Often a significant divergence of opinion evolves from such studies—issues can be simultaneously good and bad from different perspectives. These differing views can come from a minority of the evaluation team, the program participants, project staff, special interest groups, and so forth. Significant dissent should be accommodated in the final report.

Any evaluation study should include the evaluation purpose, questions, methodology, results, findings, and rationale and logic of the conclusions. As does the scientist, the evaluator exposes the findings, as well as the logic used to reach conclusions, so the results can be challenged with alternate interpretations. Programs supported with public money in a free society should be open to this kind of scrutiny.

Recommendations

What kind of future action should be taken with the program? Usually only three alternatives exist: continue the program as is, continue the program with modifications (at either a higher or lower level than at present), or drop the program. During the investigation, if evaluators discover modifications they believe will strengthen a program, they should identify these in the report. A recommendation of termination or continuation of a program varies with each situation, and the evaluator has to make the best decision possible depending on prevailing circumstances. Either course of action should be accompanied by a rationale anchored in the purpose and findings of the evaluation.

Additional Considerations

By selecting appropriate sections from the above list, an evaluator can assemble a logical and thorough report. Other points that may help evaluators prepare evaluation reports include the following:

1. Know when decisions are to be made, and submit all reports on time.
2. Issue formal and informal reports as work progresses.
3. Make informal reporting sessions a time for problem solving.
4. Make the report descriptive so that those unfamiliar with the program can gain insights into its activities.
5. Prepare different reports for different evaluation audiences. Of course, different conclusions cannot be reported, but explanations of details may be different for different audiences.
6. Expand on your work by examining collected data to see if they could be reanalyzed and reinterpreted to answer other evaluation questions.

The evaluator, either in-house or out-of-house, must accept the responsibility for presenting the evaluation audience with a final report that is understandable in their terms and frame of reference. The foregoing discussion will give evaluation report writers a coherent framework to use when organizing an evaluation report.

The preceding outline for planning an evaluation is a useful guide for developing it. It is also useful for analyzing the suitability of an existing evaluation model for a specific evaluation project. Programmers must consider many things when planning an evaluation. The preceding discussion will help the programmer organize and focus the evaluation effort.

Communicating Evaluation Results

Reporting evaluation results and the managerial actions taken as a result of evaluation findings builds credibility with external publics. Through evaluation reports, the programmer provides evidence of the benefits that resulted from participation in programs and provides evidence that the programming staff has engaged in ongoing managerial review and action while operating program services. As a programmer, ultimately you are demonstrating that you are a good steward of the resources entrusted to you.

> Credibility is built when programmers share evaluation results of all types including successes, modifications, and cancellations.

Credibility is built when programmers share evaluation results of all types including successes, modifications, and cancellations. They should highlight evaluations of particularly noteworthy activities, modifications, and failures. In successful activities, programmers can stress documented program outcomes that are consistent with the benefits specified or the mission priorities. In programs that will be modified or cancelled, they can stress the managerial actions they are taking to improve or replace services.

The following sample evaluation passages can be used in the three outcome situations the programmer will likely encounter. When writing these passages, the programmer must keep in mind the communication axiom that asks, *who says what to whom with what effect?* You, the program manager, are communicating to the evaluation audience and external publics that you are a good manager who is constantly reviewing your services and improving them to ensure they are delivering the benefits promised. After reading these samples, complete Exercise 20.3.

Sample Evaluation Report Passages

Each samples was written with a different assumption about the agency preparing the report.

A Program That Will Be Modified—Military Recreation

(NAME), Morale, Welfare, and Recreation Director, announced the results of the evaluation of the Base _____ program. Participants in the event reported that they valued the program because of the opportunities it provided them for _____ (achievement, skill improvement, socialization, etc.).

Results of the evaluation also indicated a need to schedule the program at a more convenient _____ (time, place, etc.).

　　　　　　OR

Results of the evaluation also indicated a need for better trained _____ (officials, leadership, etc.).

As a result of this evaluation, (NAME) said, "The _____ program is being revised to better meet participants' expressed needs. Specifically we plan to _____. I believe next year's participants will be very pleased with our revisions to this program. This is part of our ongoing evaluation of services that enables us to modify our programs to better meet mission and participant needs."

A Program That Will Be Continued—Public Recreation

(NAME), Director of Recreation, announced the evaluation results of the After-School Latch-Key program today. Participants in the event reported they valued the program because of the opportunities it provided them to _____ (list opportunities).

Results of the evaluation indicate that significant benefits are being provided. Parents report that their children who participated had increased opportunities for personal development, to meet new friends, and to enjoy positive recreation activities after school with their classmates in a safe, supervised environment.

Because of the excellent evaluation report, the After-School Latch-Key program will be continued as it is currently being offered. This evaluation is part of our ongoing effort to evaluate services and enables us to document the benefits provided to our participants and the accomplishment of our mission in the community.

For a Program Cancellation—Private Golf Club

(NAME), Social Director, announced today the results of the annual evaluation of the Club's _____ program. Participants in the program reported they were not satisfied with this program because _____.

Club personnel reviewed and analyzed the program evaluation data for this program and have determined that the program is not meeting staff or customer expectations. (Give more specific reasons if you have them.)

As a result of this evaluation, the _____ program has been cancelled and a new service will be designed. (Name the new service if you already know it.) This action is part of the Club's ongoing evaluation and review of services. According to

(NAME), Social Director, "These evaluations enable us to eliminate programs that are no longer benefiting our customers and thereby enable us to introduce new, more beneficial programs."

Conclusion

Programmers conduct evaluations of program services to aid in program development, to better manage the programming organization, and to provide accountability for program services. This chapter outlined a nine-step procedure for planning an evaluation. Programmers can use these steps to plan an evaluation or analyze an existing evaluation model.

All evaluations can be improved through better research designs, randomized methods of obtaining a sample, and schedules for obtaining observation and interview data. This chapter discussed how programmers can improve these techniques. It also discussed an outline for developing evaluation reports, suggested content for these reports, and gave sample publicity releases for completed evaluations.

References

Campbell, D. T., & Stanley J. C. (1963). *Experimental and quasi-experimental designs for research.* Chicago, IL: Rand McNally.

Cohen, D. A., Bing, H., Nagel, C. J., Harnik, P., McKenzie, T. L., Evenson, K. R., . . . Katta, S. (2016). The first national study of neighborhood parks: Implications for physical activity. *American Journal of Preventive Medicine, 51,* 419–426.

Cohen, D. A., & Lueschner, K. (2017, July). How can neighborhood parks attract more users? *Parks and Recreation, 52*(7), 38–41.

Cohen, D. A., Setodji, C., Evenson, K. R., Ward, P., Lapham, S., Hillier, A., & McKenzie, T. L. (2011). How much observation is enough? Refining the administration of SOPARC. *Journal of Physical Activity and Health, 8,* 1117–1123.

Denzin, N. K. (1979). *The research act* (2nd ed.). New York, NY: McGraw-Hill.

Grotelueschen, A. D., Gooler, D. D., Knox, A. B., Kemmis, S., Dowdy, I., & Brophy, K. (1974). *An evaluation planner.* Urbana: University of Illinois at Urbana-Champaign, College of Education, Office for the Study of Continuing Professional Education.

Henderson, K. A., & Bialeschki, M. D. (1995). *Evaluating leisure services: Making enlightened decisions.* State College, PA: Venture.

House, E. R. (1977). *The logic of evaluative argument* (N.7) Los Angeles: University of California, Center for the Study of Evaluation.

Howard, D. R., & Crompton, J. L. (1980). *Financing, managing, and marketing recreation and park resources.* Dubuque, IA: Wm. C. Brown.

Howe, C. Z. (1980). Models for evaluating public recreation programs: What the literature shows. *Journal of Physical Education and Recreation, 51*(8), 36–38.

Howe, C. Z. (1993). The evaluation of leisure programs: Applying qualitative methods. *Journal of Physical Education, Recreation, and Dance, 64*(8), 43–47.

Krejcie, R. V., & Morgan, D. W. (1970). Determining sample size for research activities. *Educational and Psychological Measurement, 30,* 607–610.

McKenzie, T. L., Cohen, D. A., Sehgal, A., Williamson, S., & Golinelli, D. (2006). System for Observing Parks and Recreation in Communities (SOPARC): Reliability and feasibility measures. *Journal of Physical Activity and Health, 3*(Suppl. 1), S208–S222.

National Recreation and Park Association. (2018). *2018 NRPA agency performance review: Park and recreation agency benchmarks.* Retrieved from https://www.nrpa.org/siteassets/nrpa-agency-performance-review.pdf

Patton, M. Q. (1997). *Utilization-focused evaluation* (3rd ed.). Thousand Oaks, CA: Sage.

Stat Trek. (n.d.). [Online random number generator and table]. Retrieved November 20, 2018, from https://stattrek.com/statistics/random-number-generator.aspx#table

Suchman, E. A. (1967). *Evaluative research.* New York, NY: Russell Sage Foundation.

Weiss, C. H. (1973). *Evaluation research.* Englewood Cliffs, NJ: Prentice-Hall.

Worthen, B. R., & Sanders, J. R. (1973). *Educational evaluation: Theory and practice.* Belmont, CA: Wadsworth.

Additional Recommended Reading

McNamara, C. (n.d.). *A basic guide to program evaluation.* Retrieved on November 20, 2018, from http://managementhelp.org/evaluatn/fnl_eval.htm

Walking for Fun
Photo courtesy of Cincinnati Recreation Commission. Photo by Tiffany Stewart.

21 Developing a Comprehensive Evaluation System

KEY TERMS

Comprehensive Evaluation System, Importance-Performance Evaluation, NRPA Park Metrics, Satisfaction-Based Evaluation, Goal and Objective Evaluation, Discrepancy, Triangulated Evaluation, Formative Evaluation, Summative Evaluation

Step 8: Evaluation

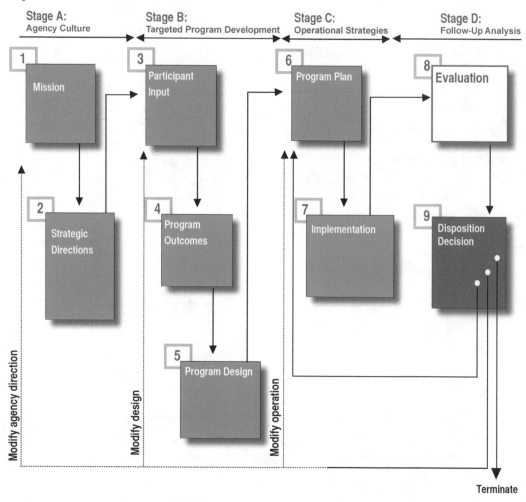

No single technique can adequately address all evaluation questions. Comprehensive evaluation in an agency requires the use of several techniques. For programmers to implement comprehensive evaluation in an agency, several management activities must happen. First, the agency allocates resources, including staff time, training, and the materials and other resources needed for conducting an evaluation.

> The agency allocates resources, including staff time, training, and the materials and other resources needed for conducting an evaluation.

Second, agency managers create an open evaluation atmosphere. While conducting evaluations, an agency might find program inadequacies. It is the responsibility of managers to create a sanction-free atmosphere for the agency to identify and deal with problem programs. Program managers who want only good evaluation reports can get them by severely sanctioning the first programmer to deliver a report about a problematic program. But if hoping to identify programs that are performing inadequately is a purpose of evaluation, the agency needs to create an atmosphere in which programmers can report these programs without adverse sanction.

Third, the agency assesses how it is currently evaluating. Every agency makes judgments of worth about program services and makes disposition decisions with this evidence. After identifying the current system, the agency should work to make it more formal and systematic. Incorporating ideas developed in this chapter and Chapter 20 into the system will help agencies achieve this end.

If program outcomes were not achieved, staff will need to discuss whether this failure was due to a faulty design of the daily activities and procedures (animation plan) or inadequacies in other situating elements.

Components of a Comprehensive Evaluation System

An agency needs to consciously develop a comprehensive evaluation system. To be comprehensive, the system should be made up of the components of formative evaluation, summative evaluation, ongoing in-depth evaluation, an evaluation database, and strategic evaluation processes. Each component fulfills a unique role in providing a comprehensive evaluation program for an agency.

Formative Evaluation

Formative evaluation occurs during program implementation; its enhances new programs. The data produced must be readily available for the agency to facilitate the adjustments needed during the trial-and-error period of program development.

Summative Evaluation

Summative evaluation occurs at the end of a program to provide the data needed for the agency to make a final, summative judgment about the worth of a program, and to assist with its future operation. Because a programmer may be responsible for evaluating many programs, summative evaluation procedures cannot be as cumbersome as the evaluation techniques used for in-depth analysis.

Ongoing In-Depth Analysis

Ongoing in-depth analysis of program services involves using evaluation techniques to thoroughly investigate and judge the worth of a program. In some cases, however, this component is so time consuming that only a portion of the agency's programs can be evaluated in this manner in any one year. In this case, it is recommended that all programs be evaluated on a rotating, scheduled basis, for example, every 3 years. The triangulated evaluation procedure, outlined in subsequent paragraphs, helps the programmer to accomplish this analysis. An appointed evaluation review committee can conduct an in-depth program evaluation by using evaluation techniques appropriate to the program. Evaluation committees can be made up of only staff, staff and board members, community advisory committee members, participants, or any combination of individuals who would be qualified to judge the worth of a program service. The use of committees helps achieve buy-in for the evaluation and can help programmers accept evaluation results, whether they are positive or negative.

Evaluation Database

An evaluation system also provides the agency with an evaluation database. This database contains a pool of systematically collected information about the worth of agency programs.

Strategic Evaluation

Finally, the agency uses this database to prepare strategic evaluation reports. It may be required to develop these reports to answer unanticipated questions from a board, the public, or other sources. Too often, agencies cannot answer unanticipated questions because they have no database to analyze.

This chapter outlines five models for conducting recreation program evaluations. The five models provide examples of a variety of approaches to leisure service evaluation, and each implements specific components of a comprehensive evaluation system. Many other evaluation models are in use, but these five provide the reader with a good background for approaching recreation program evaluation. With each model, we include the evaluation outline explicated in Chapter 20, to explain the logic and technique of each model. Exhibit 21.1 outlines how the evaluation techniques discussed in this chapter fulfill the five components of a comprehensive evaluation system.

Importance-Performance Evaluation

Martilla and James (1979) reported that importance-performance analysis is a useful technique for examining the desirability of product attributes. The technique is based on research findings demonstrating that participant satisfaction is a function of both participant expectations about attributes of a program they consider important and participant judgments about their experience with agency performance on these attributes. In importance-performance evaluation, participants take a test before participating in a program; this test determines which program attributes are most important to them. Participants also take a postprogram test with the same items as the preprogram test. The postprogram measurement determines how well the agency delivered the identified program attributes.

One of the most useful features of the technique is the method used for reporting results. Results of the pre- and post-measurements are plotted on a two-dimensional matrix, as illustrated in Figure 21.1 (page 416). Importance data are plotted on the vertical axis of the matrix. The resulting quadrants are named (in clockwise order from the upper left-hand quadrant) "concentrate here," "keep up the good work," "possible overkill," and "low priority."

Where each piece of data is plotted is a function of both its importance to the participants and their judgment about how well the agency delivered the attribute. Data reported in the "concentrate here" quadrant represent attributes that were important to participants but that the agency did not, in the participants' judgment, deliver well. Data reported in the "keep up the good work" quadrant were important to the participants, and in their judgment, the agency delivered them well. Similarly, the logic of the remainder of the matrix can be ascertained.

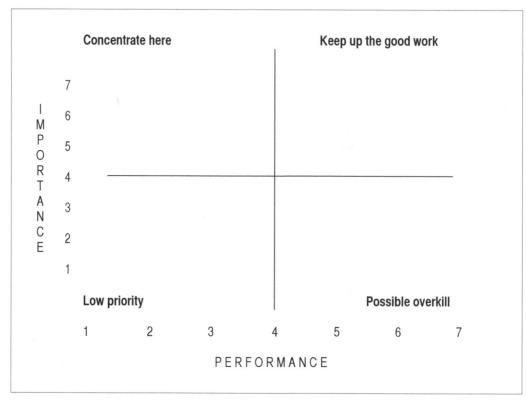

Figure 21.1. Importance-Performance Scoring Matrix

Importance-Performance Evaluation Plan

This section discusses the evaluation plan for importance-performance evaluation.

Purpose. The importance-performance evaluation judges the worth of agency performance in providing program services based on participant perceptions about the importance of program attributes and performance of the agency on selected attributes. This technique is particularly useful for formative evaluation of new, developing program services or for evaluation of existing services whose attendance may have dwindled.

Audience. Program supervisors and administrators are the most likely audience for this evaluation technique. Importance-performance evaluation is useful for program development and for monitoring how well the agency is meeting participant expectations. It is not especially useful for establishing agency accountability, nor does it produce a good comprehensive, summative evaluation.

Process. The first step involves developing a list of key program attributes for the agency to examine. The three recommended sources for obtaining these attributes include a literature review for the program being evaluated, knowledgeable staff, and focus group interviews with participants. Developing a list of pertinent program attributes for judging the worth of program services is an important step in this evaluation model and one that should be given sufficient attention. The second step involves developing an instrument that measures the importance of these attributes to potential participants and collects the importance data. The third step involves developing an instrument that collects performance data from participants and then collecting the data. The items included on the performance instrument are the same items included on the importance instrument, but with some modification for verb tense and other grammatical adjustments that make the instrument read properly. Exhibit 21.2 shows an example of importance-performance items. The final step involves plotting the data from the results obtained onto the matrix and interpreting them.

Exhibit 21.2. Importance-Performance Items

Importance

How important to you are the following features of our swimming pool program?

	Very Important			Important		Not Important	
1. Low admission for public swimming.	7	6	5	4	3	2	1
2. Opportunity to take swimming lessons to improve your swimming.	7	6	5	4	3	2	1
3. Cleanliness of pool.	7	6	5	4	3	2	1
4. Opportunity to meet new people.	7	6	5	4	3	2	1

Performance

How well were you satisfied with the agency's performance on the following items?

OR

Below are various features of our public swimming program. How well did the agency perform on these items?

	Very Satisfied			Satisfied		Not Satisfied	
1. Keeping the cost of admission for public swimming low.	7	6	5	4	3	2	1
2. Providing lessons for improving your swimming.	7	6	5	4	3	2	1
3. Providing a clean pool.	7	6	5	4	3	2	1
4. Providing opportunities to meet new people.	7	6	5	4	3	2	1

Issues. The issues examined in importance-performance evaluation concern participant judgments about the importance of key program attributes to their participation in and satisfaction with a program. The second issue deals with participants' judgments about how well the agency delivered the key program attributes.

One problem with importance-performance evaluation is the assumption that what is important to participants is static. Elsewhere, the text has established that a program is a dynamic, emergent production. Because of this, participants may initially be attracted to a program, based on a set of perceptions about what they consider important. Throughout a program, however, what is important to participants may change. Evaluators using this technique should remain cognizant of this possibility.

Evidence. The evidence collected reflects participant perceptions of importance and performance on key program attributes.

Data gathering. Data are gathered with the instruments developed before and after a program. Guadagnolo (1983) reported that the instruments can easily be administered on-site and need not be mailed to participants. He also indicated that a questionnaire seems to be easily understood and is therefore easy for participants to complete, which leads to high return rates.

Analysis. Data are analyzed on a matrix, with the vertical axis representing importance and the horizontal axis representing performance. See Figure 21.2 for an example of importance-performance analysis of the items included in Exhibit 21.1.

Resources. The resources needed for conducting this evaluation include instrument printing, time for instrument development, data collection, analysis, and reporting.

Reporting. From the analysis illustrated in Figure 21.2, the reader can interpret and report results of an importance-performance evaluation. In this case, it is evident that item 1 (a low admission price for swimming) is not an important issue to participants, but they believe the agency did a good job at keeping the price low. The agency may be doing an overkill on this item. Item 2 (providing lessons to help participants improve their swimming skills) was an important issue to participants, but they did not believe the agency did a good job in its instructional program. This is an item the agency needs to concentrate on. Item 3 (providing a clean pool) was important to participants, and they believed the agency did a good job. The agency needs to continue performing at its current level on this item. Item 4 (providing opportunities to meet new people) was not important to participants, and they did not believe the agency did a good job at helping them meet new people. Because this is not an important issue to the participants, the agency seems to be performing at an appropriate level, and no change in effort would be warranted.

Similarly, all items included in an importance-performance evaluation are analyzed and reported. The results are easy to interpret, and they provide the agency with clear managerial direction. Now complete Exercise 21.1.

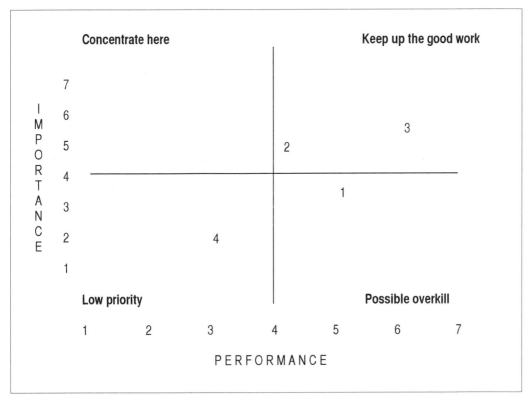

Figure 21.2. Analyzing Importance-Performance Items

The National Recreation and Park Association (NRPA) began its Park Metrics[1] evaluation system in 2009 to provide park and recreation agencies with a suite of tools for benchmarking their operations with peer departments across the USA. Participation is voluntary, and each year participating agencies enter their data into the national data bank maintained by the NRPA. Once data have been entered, local agencies can compare various features of their system and develop an annual performance review of their operations.

Each year, the NRPA publishes an Agency Performance Review that documents national statistics about agency performance. These are interesting and useful, but the reports that allow agencies to compare their performance to similar agencies are the most useful feature for ongoing management of local recreation and park operations. This is called *benchmarking* (i.e., comparing your agency's performance to a national standard or the median of your agencies' peers). The standard in this case changes every year because the performances of agencies across the country establish the standard. So the flexible real-time dimension to this evaluation process cannot be duplicated with static standards established by mutual agreement of stakeholders, which results in a single standard for all.

In 2018, 1,069 agencies across the USA participated in this research program. The system reports medians for most data, along with the performance of the lowest quartile and highest quartile. Medians are used for this type of data and are the recommended measure of central tendency to be used when there are large differences at the low and high end of a data set. For example, few communities in the USA have populations over 1 million people, and they could skew a mean to the high end if it were calculated, whereas they do not skew a median, which is the central most data point.

NRPA Park Metrics Evaluation Plan

Purpose: The purpose of NRPA Park Metrics is to provide "…a suite of tools…" (NRPA, 2018) that enable agencies to benchmark their operations and compare their operations with similar agencies across the country, which results in better ongoing agency management. This activity also results in the creation of a national database of park and recreation performance statistics that create a performance profile of the industry. Part of this profile can be seen in Exhibit 21.3 (page 422), which shows the dashboard for the 2018 park and recreation national performance data.

Audience: The primary targeted audience is local park and recreation managers. These data can help them better manage operations and capital investment decisions. If the manager uses these data to develop reports for board members and the local public, then the audience expands to stakeholders as well. Exhibit 21.4

---

[1]The NRPA Park Metrics program may be accessed by searching the Internet for NRPA Park Metrics or at https://www.nrpa.org/publications-research/ParkMetrics/

(page 423) shows the cover of the 2018 agency report from the Department of Park, Recreation, and Commercial Facilities in Mesa, Arizona. The reader can see how the system localizes the report for agencies.

Process: Agencies must enter their data into the database maintained by NRPA. They can complete these entries through the NRPA Park Metric webpage. Once all participants have entered their data and the data pool is complete, agencies have access to the data to prepare reports benchmarking their performance with the national data set or the median of agencies similar in size to their agency.

Issues: The quality of benchmarking rests with the quality of the benchmark available, as well as the accuracy of the agency's own reported data. NRPA Park Metrics is the only source of benchmarking data, so there is no basis for comparing it with other data. General practice is for agencies to accept it as valid and move forward with it as the valid benchmark to use for comparisons desired.

Resources: The agency must dedicate the time of an employee or employees to collect and enter data, as well as time to mine the database to develop local reports. For the uniqueness and usefulness of the data obtained, this is not an expensive undertaking.

Evidence: The evidence collected includes a variety of operational data including financial expenditures, revenue collected, program offerings, facilities operated, and others. The evidence reflects actual operations data, and this process is called *operations research*. Exhibit 21.5 (page 424) shows a table from the 2018 NRPA agency report on Outdoor Park and Recreation Facilities—Population Per Facility. The first column shows the percentage of agencies reporting that they have this type of facility, which gives the reader some idea about the prevalence of these facilities in community park and recreation agencies. Exhibit 21.6 (page 425) shows a bar chart from the 2018 NRPA agency report on Programming Offered by Park and Recreation Agencies. It shows the percentage of agencies reporting they offer this type of program. Now complete Exercise 21.2 (page 425).

Data Gathering: The agency will develop a method, if one does not already exist, for tracking and collecting the data needed for entry into the system. If the agency does not already have procedures for this, it will need to make an initial investment of resources to create the collection system. Once created, the system should operate efficiently and relatively inexpensively.

Analysis: Because of the framework used for collecting data, initial analysis is straightforward. The agency's entries can be downloaded and compared to national data and to data from their agency peer group (peer groups are determined by the size of community population). The data pool is robust, and many additional comparisons can be drawn from it depending on the questions local administrators want answered.

Reporting: The printout deliverable from the system includes tabled data about each item. The initial report is available in a deliverable format and may be distributed as received from the NRPA. Agencies may want to write additional local interpretation of these results for their local jurisdiction and audiences.

Exhibit 21.3. Key Findings Dashboard

2018 NRPA AGENCY PERFORMANCE REVIEW KEY FINDINGS

 OPERATING EXPENDITURE PER CAPITA: $78.26/YEAR

 REVENUE-TO-OPERATING EXPENDITURE: 28 PERCENT

 ACRES OF PARK LAND PER 1,000 RESIDENTS: 10.1

 FULL-TIME EQUIVALENT EMPLOYEES (FTES) PER 10,000 RESIDENTS: 7.9

 RESIDENTS PER PARK: 2114

AGENCIES OFFERING SUMMER CAMPS: 84%

 **AGENCIES OFFERING AFTER-SCHOOL CARE: 55%**

Exhibit 21.4. Local Government Report Title Page: Mesa, AZ

2018 NRPA AGENCY PERFORMANCE REPORT
PARK AND RECREATION AGENCY PERFORMANCE BENCHMARKS

Mesa Parks, Recreation and Commercial Facilities Department

NRPA National Recreation and Park Association

Because everyone deserves a great park

Exhibit 21.5. National Outdoor Park and Recreation Facilities Report, 2018

FIGURE 3: OUTDOOR PARK AND RECREATION FACILITIES—POPULATION PER FACILITY
(BY PREVALENCE AND POPULATION PER FACILITY)

| | | | Median Number of Residents per Facility | | | |
| | | | Residents per Square Mile | | | |
	% of Agencies	All Agencies	Less than 500	500 to 1,500	1,501 to 2,500	More than 2,500
Playgrounds	92%	3,600	6,132	3,558	3,000	3,572
Basketball courts	83	7,122	7,869	7,040	6,037	7,350
Tennis courts (outdoor only)	77	4,545	5,462	4,833	4,250	4,578
Diamond fields: baseball - youth	75	6,519	6,628	5,358	6,613	7,770
Diamond fields: softball fields - adult	66	12,000	10,957	9,491	12,083	14,725
Rectangular fields: multi-purpose	63	8,055	9,043	6,158	7,691	9,547
Diamond fields: softball fields – youth	59	9,900	10,495	8,181	9,255	12,121
Diamond fields: baseball - adult	55	18,880	15,000	13,367	18,140	25,179
Dog park	55	41,500	51,804	37,000	40,000	49,665
Swimming pools (outdoor only)	52	31,709	42,344	23,350	31,600	40,218
Totlots	47	12,104	19,766	10,625	14,850	11,301
Rectangular fields: soccer field – youth	47	6,039	5,584	5,082	5,900	8,773
Community gardens	46	27,587	37,571	30,346	28,605	27,042
Rectangular fields: soccer field - adult	42	11,383	10,250	9,833	11,692	15,746
Multiuse courts - basketball, volleyball	38	14,650	12,757	12,105	15,214	18,557
Diamond fields: tee-ball	38	14,511	11,270	12,763	13,045	18,557
Rectangular fields: football field	38	24,742	21,750	19,023	22,615	35,453
Ice rink (outdoor only)	16	17,310	11,168	13,669	17,072	25,500
Multipurpose synthetic field	15	41,719	35,238	20,888	28,728	54,161
Skate park	14	46,850	27,375	40,620	37,607	61,306
Rectangular fields: lacrosse field	11	24,060	12,522	17,500	22,119	29,924
Rectangular fields: cricket field	9	160,000	199,889	288,617	160,000	108,575
Overlay field	6	12,844	10,820	7,200	55,245	15,831
Rectangular fields: field hockey field	4	20,893	20,893	23,034	15,757	22,500

Implementation

The agency will need to join the NRPA system by completing an online application. At that time, various agency employees will receive passwords that allow them access for reporting their data, as well as for running reports from the database. To participate, the agency will need a data collection system and employees to operate it, in order to obtain the data required for entry in the NRPA system.

One output from the system is an annual report comparing the agency's performance to national performance data and data from peer agencies. The programmer can compare, for instance, how well the agency performed in any one year compared

Exhibit 21.6. Programming Offered by Park and Recreation Agencies, 2018

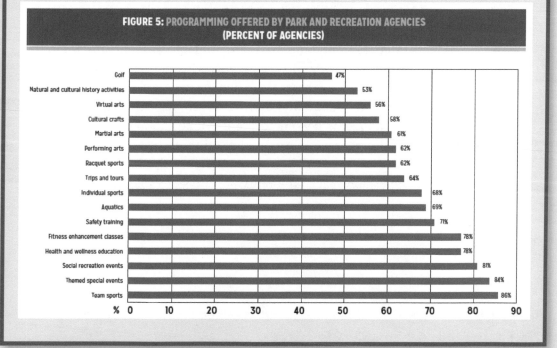

FIGURE 5: PROGRAMMING OFFERED BY PARK AND RECREATION AGENCIES (PERCENT OF AGENCIES)

Program	Percent
Golf	47%
Natural and cultural history activities	53%
Virtual arts	56%
Cultural crafts	58%
Martial arts	61%
Performing arts	62%
Racquet sports	62%
Trips and tours	64%
Individual sports	68%
Aquatics	69%
Safety training	71%
Fitness enhancement classes	78%
Health and wellness education	78%
Social recreation events	81%
Themed special events	84%
Team sports	86%

Exercise 21.2.
Applying Importance-Performance Evaluation

In class, review the data in Exhibit 21.6 and review the Activity Classification System displayed in Table 4.3 (page 66).

1. Now analyze the offerings of park and recreation systems in the USA during 2018. Are there any trends? Are there omissions? What are the dominant program offerings? What classifications of programs do not comparatively receive much attention? Why might this be?
2. Write a newspaper article for your local park and recreation department announcing national programming trends that are documented by these data.

to its chosen comparison groups. Exhibit 21.7 (page 426) shows a bar chart and table from the 2018 agency report for Mesa, Arizona, compared to national and peer group statistics (bar/column 1 is the Mesa data, bar/column 2 is the national data, and bar/column 3 is the peer group for Mesa (i.e., communities with a population density per square mile of over 2,500). This item compares Mesa's median (5.4) of "acres of parkland per 1,000 population" with the national (10.1) and peer group (8.2) medians. Although below both groups, Mesa lies closer to its selected comparison group than the national average.

Once agencies have some history in the system, they can track their own changes in performance with time series data reports. They can run other strategic reports about topics selected at any time. This robust system offers multiple options for preparing evaluation reports.

The NRPA Park Metrics evaluation system is valuable for benchmarking, that is, for comparing the performance of local agencies with national data and national peer group data. In some cases, deviation from these national standards may be intentional (e.g., an agency may have a larger than normal inventory of revenue-producing facilities, which would present as a deviation from national performance in reports). The programmer would need to account for this deviation and other deviations in local reports. Overall, the system helps local administrators track performance and establish accountability to local stakeholders.

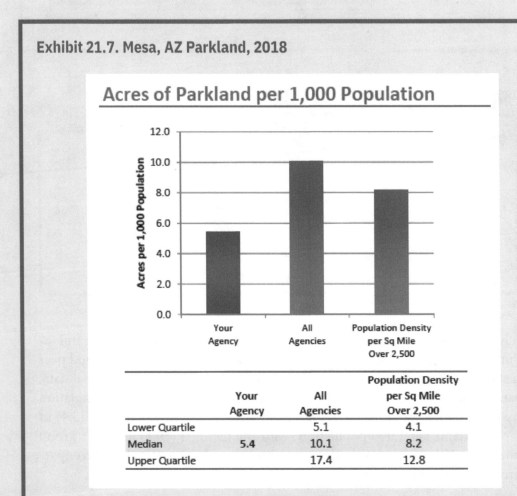

Exhibit 21.7. Mesa, AZ Parkland, 2018

Acres of Parkland per 1,000 Population

	Your Agency	All Agencies	Population Density per Sq Mile Over 2,500
Lower Quartile		5.1	4.1
Median	5.4	10.1	8.2
Upper Quartile		17.4	12.8

Satisfaction-Based Evaluation

Satisfaction-based program evaluation provides data about participant satisfaction with program services. Agencies can use these data to judge the worth of program services. The assumption of the technique is that agencies can best determine the worth of the programs by identifying the degree to which programs have provided leisure experiences for participants.

Mannell (1999) identified assessing satisfaction as one of the three social-psychological approaches to studying the subjective experience of leisure. He stated, "The satisfaction construct is an 'after-the-fact' assessment or experiential consequence of an earlier involvement or set of involvements" (p. 238). Participant-reported satisfaction with leisure engagement is a well-accepted measure of leisure outcomes (Beard & Ragheb, 1979; Christensen & Yoesting, 1977; Driver, 1977; Driver & Brown, 1975; Hawes, 1978; Tinsley, Barrett, & Kass, 1977; Tinsley & Kass, 1978). Thus, this evaluation technique uses participant-reported satisfaction with leisure programs as a theoretically valid evaluation criterion that agencies can use to judge the worth of leisure programs. The evaluation plan for satisfaction-based evaluation follows.

> The assumption of the technique is that agencies can best determine the worth of the programs by identifying the degree to which programs have provided leisure experiences for participants.

Purpose. Satisfaction-based evaluation provides theoretically valid measures of the outcome of leisure engagement. Agencies can use these data to develop program services and to account for the outcomes resulting from participation in program services.

Audience. This evaluation technique primarily serves program managers, program supervisors, and administrators.

Process. This evaluation technique requires the collection and analysis of participant-reported satisfactions with programs.

Issues. The major issue this technique investigates is whether programs are providing leisure experiences. Agencies determine this by investigating the amount and types of satisfaction a program provides.

Resources. The resources that agencies need to conduct the evaluation include a valid and reliable instrument for data collection, resources to collect the data, and the time to analyze the data collected.

Evidence. The evidence collected reflects participant-reported satisfaction with participation in a program.

Data gathering. Participants complete an instrument at the end of a program, thereby self-reporting their satisfaction with the program.

Analysis. Agencies calculate satisfaction domains and analyze the resulting data through time series or program-by-program comparisons.

Reporting. Agencies can report data on a program-by-program basis, in a summary report of a programming season, or in an annual report.

Satisfaction Domains and Items

There are 10 satisfaction domains with 25 items, as shown in Exhibit 21.8. Agencies can include some or all of the domains in an individual evaluation.

Exhibit 21.9 (page 430) shows the instrument for the satisfaction-based evaluation technique. Respondents score items on a 7-point Likert scale. The instrument also includes a "not applicable" choice. This choice allows respondents an alternative when they believe the satisfaction items are inappropriate or not applicable to a program. It includes an item investigating the importance of the program to the individual so that the agency can investigate this importance in relation to the participant's other leisure pursuits.

It is assumed that as a matter of public policy, it is preferable that agencies cancel programs that are less important rather than those that are very important to participants compared with their other leisure pursuits. The instrument also includes an overall satisfaction item that investigates participants' overall summative judgment about their satisfaction with a program. Previous use of this form has established that neither gender nor age biases responses to the items.

Scoring the Leisure Program Evaluation Form

Exhibit 21.8 shows a list of items and their domains. Domain scores are calculated by averaging the items scored in each domain for each respondent. For example, the scores for two subjects on the relaxation domain are illustrated in Exhibit 21.10 (page 431). In this case, Subject 1 responded to all three items in the domain. Therefore, the number 3 was used as the divisor in calculating the domain score for Subject 1. Subject 2 responded to only two items in the domain, so the number 2 was used as the divisor in calculating the domain score for Subject 2.

For a domain score across all participants in a single program, an average of all of the scores across all participants is calculated.

Programmers can use data from the satisfaction-based program evaluation in several ways. First, the data can document participant-reported program outcomes. With a postprogram administration of the instrument, programmers can gather data about what happened to participants in the program. They can use the data to document what is happening to participants in their programs and to establish accountability with their funding source. The technique provides systematically collected participant-reported outcome data resulting from participation in leisure services. With these data, programmers do not need to assert the value of a program based on hearsay. Instead, they can use data systematically collected from the participants themselves.

Second, programmers can analyze satisfaction data to determine achievement of programmatic goals. For example, in one administration of the instrument, the highest rated satisfactions on a Fall Foliage Tour were "fun," "environment," "social enjoyment," and "relaxation" (Rossman, 1983). Similar analyses of participant-reported satisfactions with different program services can aid the programmer in investigating whether program services provide appropriate satisfactions. This use of the technique aids in program development.

Third, programmers can compare satisfaction data from various programs to investigate the differences in satisfactions provided by different program services. For example, the reported satisfactions summarized for all athletic programs could be compared with similar data for all cultural arts programs. In this way, the programmer documents differences in the types of satisfactions provided by different types of services. This analysis will help the programmer in organizational management and determining appropriate program directions for the agency.

Programmers can use satisfaction-based program evaluation in several ways for various purposes. The data collected reflect participant-reported satisfactions with participation in agency program services. With this technique, programmers make judgments about the worth of program services by using data collected directly from program participants. Now complete Exercise 21.3 (page 431).

Exhibit 21.8. Satisfaction Domains and Items

Achievement

I learned more about the activity.
It was a new and different experience.
I became better at it.
My skills and ability developed.

Physical Fitness

I enjoyed the physical exercise.
It kept me physically fit.

Social Enjoyment

I enjoyed the companionship.
Enjoying it with my friends.

Family Escape

Escaping from my family for a while.
I was able to be away from family.

Environment

The area was physically attractive.
The freshness and cleanliness of the area.
I liked the open space.
The pleasing design of the facility.

Risk

I liked the high risk involved.
I liked the chance for danger.

Family Togetherness

Our family could do this together.
It brought our family together more.

Relaxation

It gave my mind a rest.
I experienced tranquility.
I got to relax physically.

Fun

I had fun.

Autonomy

I had control over things.
I was in control of what happened.
It gave me a chance to be on my own.

Exhibit 21.9. Leisure Program Evaluation Form

The statements listed below may reflect your satisfactions with this program. Please indicate by circling the appropriate number on each scale the degree to which each statement contributed to your satisfaction with this program. Statements that you believe do not apply to this program should be marked by circling the 0 in the Not Applicable (NA) column.

		Very Satisfying				Satisfying		Contributes No Satisfaction		NA
1.	I learned more about the activity	7	6	5	4	3	2	1	0
2.	I had control over things	7	6	5	4	3	2	1	0
3.	The cleanliness of the area	7	6	5	4	3	2	1	0
4.	I enjoyed the exercise	7	6	5	4	3	2	1	0
5.	I enjoyed companionship	7	6	5	4	3	2	1	0
6.	I liked the high risks involved	7	6	5	4	3	2	1	0
7.	I had fun	7	6	5	4	3	2	1	0
8.	It gave my mind a rest	7	6	5	4	3	2	1	0
9.	Our family could do this together	7	6	5	4	3	2	1	0
10.	Enjoying it with my friends	7	6	5	4	3	2	1	0
11.	I experienced tranquility	7	6	5	4	3	2	1	0
12.	Escaping from my family for a while	7	6	5	4	3	2	1	0
13.	It was a new/different experience	7	6	5	4	3	2	1	0
14.	I liked the open space	7	6	5	4	3	2	1	0
15.	I liked the chance for danger	7	6	5	4	3	2	1	0
16.	The area was physically attractive	7	6	5	4	3	2	1	0
17.	I became better at it	7	6	5	4	3	2	1	0
18.	It keeps me physically fit	7	6	5	4	3	2	1	0
19.	It brought our family together more	7	6	5	4	3	2	1	0
20.	I got to relax physically	7	6	5	4	3	2	1	0
21.	I was in control of what happened	7	6	5	4	3	2	1	0
22.	My skills and ability developed	7	6	5	4	3	2	1	0
23.	I was away from family awhile	7	6	5	4	3	2	1	NA
24.	It gave me a chance to be on my own	7	6	5	4	3	2	1	0
25.	The pleasing design of the facility	7	6	5	4	3	2	1	0

Exhibit 21.9. (continued)

Below are two statements about participating in this program. Please circle a number on each scale that best reflects your view.

1. Please compare this program with all of your other leisure pursuits. Compared with your other leisure, what priority would you assign this program?

   One I would least like to give up   One I would give up first

7	6	5	4	3	2	1

2. Which of the following statements reflects your overall satisfaction with this program?

Delighted	Pleased	Mostly satisfied	Mixed	Mostly dissatisfied	Unhappy	Terrible
7	6	5	4	3	2	1

Exhibit 21.10. Calculating Satisfaction Domain Scores

Relaxation Domain	Subject 1	Subject 2
8. It gave my mind a rest.	7	4
11. I experienced tranquility.	5	7
20. I got to relax physically.	6	No score
	18	11
	18 ÷ 3 = 6	11 ÷ 2 = 5.5

Exercise 21.3.
Using Satisfaction-Based Program Evaluation Data

In class, choose a program to evaluate using satisfaction-based program evaluation. Consider the following points:

- Is satisfaction-based program evaluation the most appropriate evaluation method for this program?
- How will the worth of a program be documented with satisfaction-based evaluation data?
- Which purpose of evaluation will be used to focus the evaluation?

Goal and Objective Evaluation

Using goals and objectives for program evaluations is a process model and a logical extension of using goals and objectives for strategic program development, program management, and design purposes, covered in Chapters 5, 6, 7, and 9. It has been used for years in education (Provus, 1971; Stake, 1967; Steinmetz, 2000) and applied to therapeutic recreation (Peterson & Gunn, 1984), where it is called discrepancy evaluation, which is the difference between intended and actual performance. Its assumes that the standards you developed are indeed standards you plan to accomplish (S). During and after a program, you observe or measure actual performance (P). Discrepancy (D), then, is the variation between standard and performance, that is, $S - P = D$ (Steinmetz, 2000). Performance could exceed the standard, in which case there is no discrepancy. Some organizations use a variation of this wherein they judge standards (program outcomes) to have been exceeded, met, partially met, or not met. Thus, programmers can implement this basic notion in many ways.

A desirable feature of the process is that agencies can judge not only terminal outcomes (standards) but also other program dimensions such as its implementation plan, staff performance, the suitability of the venue, and other situating elements. Thus, agencies can evaluate the performance of various program components, facilitating improvements as warranted. Because it is a process model, the content of the goals and objectives are not specified within the model but are provided through processes already discussed in the book. What follows, then, is a framework for implementing a goal and objective discrepancy evaluation process.

Three features to the model make it a distinct method:

1. Goals and objectives are developed hierarchically. They end with precisely specified expected outcome statements for participants, thus enabling a comparison of expected with actual outcomes (Peterson & Gunn, 1984; Steinmetz, 2000). Therefore, the programmer states exactly what is to be accomplished through the program. This was discussed in Chapter 9.
2. The actual operation of a program is compared with its design (Steinmetz, 2000; Stake, 1967). This feature requires the programmer to examine not only outcomes but also program inputs and processes. This expands the inquiry into possible causes of the discrepancies.
3. To the degree that specific program outcomes have been developed with input from participants and other stakeholders, the value system and sensibilities of these groups will have been incorporated into the evaluation process.

Thus, implementation of a discrepancy evaluation model requires well-written and valid program outcomes that the programmer uses to determine the worth of a program. Furthermore, the technique encourages an expansive view of a program, including its inputs, processes, and outcomes, rather than a focal, microscopic one focusing on a single program feature.

Goal and Objective Evaluation Plan

Purpose. The goal and objective evaluation plan judges the worth of program services by examining the discrepancies between the program's intended outcomes and actual performance.

Audience. This method is amenable to almost every stakeholder, provided that the terminal outcomes reflect their value perspective and interests. The process is adaptable but application sensitive; that is, it must be implemented correctly to provide valid results.

Process. The steps to the discrepancy evaluation method include (1) defining program standards (i.e., terminal outcomes as specified in Chapter 9); (2) determining whether a discrepancy exists between standard and performance (S – D = P) including terminal outcomes and other features of program operation; and (3) using discrepancy information either for changing performance or for changing program standards (Provus, 1971).

Issues. Goal and objective standards can be developed for measuring inputs, processes, and/or outcomes. Intended outcomes should always be developed. Whether the remaining metrics should be developed depends on the program under evaluation.

Evidence. The content of the confirming evidence depends on the evaluation metrics included in the statements. For example, previous examples often provided a completion date specified as the metric for determining accomplishment. Remember, SMART statements include performance metrics. Thus, the evidence for confirming its accomplishment should be evident to the staff and stakeholders associated with the program.

Data gathering. The techniques used for gathering data depend on the metrics included in the statements. Typical techniques include observations of participant behavior, evaluation surveys, attendance or other types of statistical data, interviews, and so on.

Analysis. The primary analytical framework involves comparing intentions with results and noting discrepancies. How well this can be accomplished depends on how SMART the standards statements were written and on the thoroughness of the observations and data collected.

Resources. Two principle resources needed include staff time and expertise in implementing the method.

Reporting. The typical report presents each outcome statement or standard as appropriate, along with the data gathered about it. This should include an analytical statement about whether the standard has been met, with a notation of discrepancies observed and how they can be reconciled. Or the programmer can use the evaluation monikers pointed out earlier: exceeded, met, partially met, or not met.

Implementation

The use of goals and objective evaluation is predicated on well-written SMART statements that the programmer uses to determine the congruence of performance with the outcomes stated and noting any discrepancies. Box D of Figure 9.1 (page 175) provides an example. Included are four program design outcomes for a bicycle maintenance and repair class that are the terminal performance outcomes that will be used to measure the accomplishment of Program 3. d. specified in Box C.

The procedure, then, is to conduct the class, determine the percentage of students who can demonstrate their ability to perform the four outcomes specified. For example, Outcome 3 requires that "after the second hour (of instruction) when requested, 90% of the students will be able to demonstrate how to repair a flat tire tube."

Determining congruence between intentions and performance and noting discrepancies is the basic method of goal and objective evaluation. However, to use the discrepancy approach thoroughly, the programmer needs to state not only behavioral outcomes, but also program inputs and process goals. Figure 21.3 outlines the basic analytical framework for discrepancy evaluation. The reader can observe in this figure the development of design goals with measurement objectives for program inputs, processes, and outcomes.

Furthermore, there is an assumed relationship between the inputs to a program, the animation plan, and the outcomes desired. To conduct an evaluation using goals and objectives, then, the programmer determines the congruence between intended versus actual observations of inputs, processes, and outcomes, and notes discrepancies for further analysis. In addition, the programmer examines the assumed relationships between inputs, processes, and outcomes to investigate their logic and validity. The programmer also notes discrepancies for further analysis.

The programmer can reconcile discrepancies to be more realistic by changing the metrics for judging worth. For example, in the current case, the programmer can modify the intended outcome so the desired result is that 80% rather than 90% of the students correctly demonstrate how to repair a flat tire tube. However, omissions in inputs or animation processes may also account for failures in outcomes. For example, one intended input may have been a videotape for each student to take home that explained and showed how to fix a flat tire tube. However, this feature may have been dropped due to budget constraints or to the late arrival of the tapes. Thus, the discrepancy in failing to reach the goal of 90% of the students being able to correctly demonstrate how to repair a flat tire tube may be explained by defects in staging the designed inputs of the program.

A similar analysis may also be demonstrated in the animation of a program. The amount of time spent demonstrating how to repair a flat tire tube may have been too brief or incomplete. Each of these could account for the failure of 90% or more of the students being able to correctly demonstrate the task.

Thus, the use of goals and objectives for evaluation is a flexible technique that the programmer can apply in many situations. It requires the development of SMART goals, objectives, and outcomes within a specific framework so that the programmer can make the analyses and judgments required to evaluate.

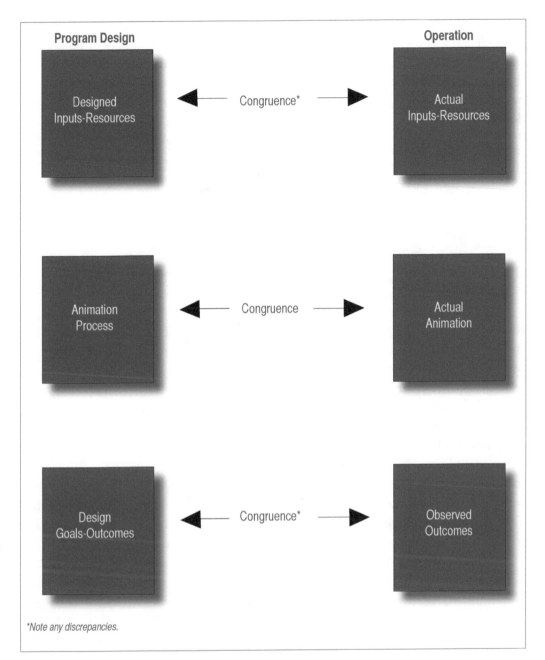

Program Design   **Operation**

Designed
Inputs-Resources   ◄— Congruence* —►   Actual
Inputs-Resources

Animation
Process   ◄— Congruence —►   Actual
Animation

Design
Goals-Outcomes   ◄— Congruence* —►   Observed
Outcomes

*Note any discrepancies.

Figure 21.3. Analytical Framework for Discrepancy Evaluation. Adapted from Stake (1967).

Triangulated Evaluation

Judging the worth of leisure services is a value-laden enterprise. A single program may be viewed as both good and bad at the same time from different perspectives. In addition, many evaluations use a single methodology to gather data to be reported for evaluation purposes. The technique used in social science for dealing with multiple perspectives and realities is triangulation (Bullock & Coffey, 1980; Denzin, 1978).

The triangulated approach to evaluation assumes the gathering of the data from multiple perspectives and with multiple methods. Fuszek (1987) adopted this strategy when conducting program evaluations in the parks and recreation department in Austin, Texas. Discussing the methodology used in Austin, he stated that "the primary emphasis [is] placed upon pragmatic or qualitative assessment—i.e., how do all the parts/players fit [or not fit] together to achieve program goals—as opposed to relying solely on quantitative measurement or efficiency studies" (Fuszek, 1987). He then outlined seven methods of obtaining data for judging the worth of program services. When undertaken, this multiple perspective, multiple method approach will more likely capture the true picture and worth of a program. The technique that follows is but one example of how programmers can apply the concept of triangulation to the evaluation of leisure services.

> The triangulated approach to evaluation assumes that the data need to be gathered from multiple perspectives and with multiple methods.

This example shows a triangulation of research methods and data sources. The research methods were developed from a series of consulting interviews that one of the authors conducted with programmers in five agencies. In these interviews, it was revealed that the two major methods programmers used to evaluate their programs were observation during on-site inspection of program services and interviews with participants. Both methods of data gathering are legitimate, but neither is usually implemented in an appropriate fashion.

Often, different programmers in the same agency looked for different items when making on-site visits. Therefore, there was no reliability of observations. The first step in improving this method of data gathering involves the program supervisors jointly developing a single observation schedule of what needs to be examined. Training program supervisors in observation data-gathering methods, as discussed in Chapter 20, is also necessary for improving this technique.

The second technique programmers used was talking to participants. Often these contacts involved informal public relations exercises rather than data-gathering sessions. Again, there were often as many different interview agendas as there were supervisors. In many cases, program supervisors simply chatted about whatever the participants wanted to discuss. This method of data gathering was improved through the development of an interview schedule. It can be somewhat intrusive having program supervisors with clipboards interviewing participants in program services. At the least, supervisors should have a few focused questions they want answered in these discussions. In addition to being viewed as public relations exercises, these discussions should be considered opportunities to gather data about the quality of program services from a primary data source—the participant.

Program supervisors should be prepared to validate unanticipated information they gather in these interviews. They can validate information by pursuing and verifying or refuting information from additional sources, usually other participants. In either case, they should validate and verify information through multiple sources.

The third method of gathering data is a questionnaire. Two instruments are recommended, one administered to participants and the other to face-to-face leaders. Gathering data with instruments either through a census or a survey is the third method of data collection in this example of a triangulated evaluation approach.

It is recommended that in addition to triangulating methods, programmers triangulate data sources. In selecting sources of information, the programmer identifies individuals who are the most knowledgeable about what occurred in a program. Some experienced programmers believe they can assess the worth of a program service by their own observation and analysis. A triangulated approach assumes that to obtain a more complete picture about the worth of a program, the programmer must obtain data from multiple perspectives. Furthermore, the approach assumes that some sources of information are better situated than others to have primary knowledge about what occurred in a program, so they are better sources of information. Part of triangulated evaluation, then, involves identifying primary data sources and designing instruments and techniques for aggressively and systematically gathering information from these sources.

In the current example, the three most knowledgeable sources include the face-to-face program leader, who has direct, first-line contact with a program; the program supervisor, who makes frequent supervisory contact with a program; and participants, who experience the service. They are therefore the three sources to be systematically pursued. Instruments and techniques for gathering data from these sources have been developed and are illustrated and discussed below.

Triangulated Evaluation Plan

This section outlines the plan for the triangulated evaluation procedure.

Purpose. The triangulated approach to evaluation helps program supervisors to make disposition decisions about program services. The data gathered in this approach provide the programmer with information for determining whether to drop, modify, or continue a program service. This technique helps with program development and organizational management.

Audience. Program supervisors and program administrators are the primary audiences for this evaluation technique.

Process. The process involves the collection of evaluation data from three sources with three data collection techniques and the summary analysis of this information.

Issues. This technique examines program leader, program supervisor, and participant views about program outcomes, inputs, and process.

Resources. Having instruments for data gathering, conducting training in using the instruments, and allowing time for data collection and analysis are necessary.

Evidence. This technique collects leader observations; supervisor observations and interview data; and participant-reported satisfactions with outcomes and arrangements, as selected by the program supervisor.

Data gathering. This technique includes three instruments, including the recreation leader or instructor evaluation form (Exhibit 21.11, page 440), the recreation program observation schedule (Exhibit 21.12, page 441), and the recreation participant evaluation form (Exhibit 21.13, page 442).

Analysis. The data are analyzed on the program evaluation summary format (Exhibit 21.14, page 442).

Reporting. The final report is written according to the format outlined in Exhibit 21.14 (page 442).

Instruments

The triangulated evaluation procedure includes three instruments. The first is the recreation leader or instructor evaluation form, presented in Exhibit 21.11. The agency employee with direct contact in a program completes this form. The items on the instrument are examples of what might be asked of this type of employee. Questions inquire about the adequacy of the program schedule, equipment and supplies, the facility, supervisory support, and program operation.

A second instrument is the recreation program observation schedule, presented in Exhibit 21.12. Supervisors use it to record observations of on-site visitations and inspections of program services. They can alter the items observed to meet the needs of their agency. Note the rating scale included on the instrument. Each rating number includes a definition, which improves reliability. Any item rated 1 should be taken care of immediately while the supervisor is on-site, and the supervisor will note the action taken in the section provided. Items rated 2 should be taken care of before the next session of the program, and the supervisor will note any action taken in the space provided. Items rated 3 should be taken care of as time permits and as alternative arrangements become available. Items rated 4 need no further action.

The instrument includes a designated area for recording additional data bits—unsolicited information gathered in the process of inspecting programs. In this section, program supervisors can add specific interview questions that they want participants to answer.

The third instrument used is the participant evaluation form, presented in Exhibit 21.13 (page 442). The exhibit presents a format for the instrument. To use this instrument, the programmer selects items from the item pool presented in the Addendum to this chapter after the Reference section.

It is recommended that to achieve some uniformity of evaluation data across all programs, the agency establish a list of five to eight questions to include on the evaluation instruments for all programs. Exhibit 21.12 includes an example of such a list. A program supervisor could then select from the item pool an additional eight to 10 questions that would specifically apply to the program under evaluation. In this way, some data are unique to a specific program. The reader will notice that the questions included in the item pool deal with program inputs, processes, and outputs. Any instrument should include an assortment of each type of question.

The final instrument used in the triangulated approach to program evaluation is the program evaluation summary format, presented in Exhibit 21.13. This instrument includes various pieces of information necessary for the programmer to evaluate a program comprehensively. The reader will notice that the outline includes a number of pieces of information derived from evaluation techniques explained in this chapter.

Section I, the statistical summary, reports five pieces of statistical data. These include data about participation impact, staffing requirements, program costs, program revenue, and a cost analysis of the program.

Section II assesses program goals. Specifically, the programmer answers why the agency is conducting the program and how it fits in with the overall mission of the agency. In this way, each program must be justified with data each time it is evaluated.

Section III, procedures, includes a brief explanation of operating the program. The programmer should not write the complete program plan in this section, but a much shorter explanation about what it takes to operate the program.

Section IV contains the summated evaluation data collected with the instruments recommended in the triangulated approach. In Section V, the evaluator analyzes the program by formulating responses to the questions using the evaluation data reported in Section III. By using this outline, the programmer analyzes the program on the basis of evaluation evidence rather than on hearsay or other less reliable information. The analysis must be supported by the data. In a similar fashion, after completing the analysis, the programmer makes a program disposition decision based on the results of the evaluation data to continue the program as currently operated, to drop it, or to modify it. When making either of the latter two decisions, the programmer provides the following information. For a program that is to be dropped, the programmer speculates about possible effects that dropping it might have on the agency. For a program that is to be modified, the programmer specifies the modifications to be made.

The organization of the summary format requires that the evaluation report be developed in a logical manner and that the decisions be based on logical conclusions drawn from systematically collected data. Evaluation is thereby based on an analysis of evidence systematically collected from agency participants and programs. Now complete Exercise 21.4 (page 444).

The triangulated approach to program evaluation suggests that multiple methods should be used for collecting data from multiple sources. An example of how this technique may be used was presented, along with a rationale for why each method and data source was selected for inclusion.

Conclusion

This chapter presented five models for use in leisure service evaluations. It outlined the theory behind each model and its assumptions. It explained how each model implements the nine-step evaluation plan. Before using the models presented or any other evaluation model, programmers must ensure that the model meets their evaluation needs.

Comprehensive evaluation in an agency should have five components. No single method can accomplish all five components. This chapter outlined contributions of each evaluation model to the components of a comprehensive evaluation.

Exhibit 21.11. Leader or Instructor Evaluation Form

Program   Date
Leader or Instructor
Season

Please help us evaluate and improve our services by answering the questions below. Your feedback is important to our operation. All information is confidential. Please place an X on each line to indicate your opinion about the quality of service.

	Rating				
	Poor				Excellent
	(1)	(2)	(3)	(4)	(5)
Program Schedule					
1. Length of individual program meetings	( )	( )	( )	( )	( )
2. Time program met	( )	( )	( )	( )	( )
3. Day of week program was held	( )	( )	( )	( )	( )
Equipment and Supplies					
4. Material provided for program operation	( )	( )	( )	( )	( )
5. Equipment provided for program operation	( )	( )	( )	( )	( )
Facility					
6. Appropriateness of facility for program	( )	( )	( )	( )	( )
7. Safety of facility and equipment	( )	( )	( )	( )	( )
8. Cleanliness of facility	( )	( )	( )	( )	( )
9. Facility access and preparedness— was facility open on time and ready to go?	( )	( )	( )	( )	( )
Supervisor Support					
10. Supervisor provided adequate orientation training	( )	( )	( )	( )	( )
11. Supervisor provided ongoing cooperation and direction	( )	( )	( )	( )	( )
12. In the absence of your immediate supervisor, were other Bureau personnel helpful in solving your problems?	( )	( )	( )	( )	( )
Program Operation					
13. For this program, was the number of people enrolled appropriate?	( )	( )	( )	( )	( )
14. How well were the Bureau's goals for this program achieved?	( )	( )	( )	( )	( )
15. My performance in this program was . . .	( )	( )	( )	( )	( )
16. Do you believe there is sufficient demand to offer this program again?	Yes	No			

Additional Feedback

Please give us additional suggestions or comments you believe will help improve our services or help you do a better job serving our constituents.

Exhibit 21.12. Program Observation Form

Program name
Date observed
Time observed from to

Location
Activities observed
Observer's name

Observation Checklist Rating Scale

4	3	2	1
Excellent	*Good*	*Poor*	*Inadequate*
No modification is warranted	Could be improved if alternatives were available	Alternative arrangements must be made before the next program offering	Immediate action must be taken to correct the situation

Observe the program and record your ratings for each item, based on the scale above.

	Excellent	Good	Poor	Inadequate
Facility				
1. The facility space is adequate for this program.	4	3	2	1
2. The equipment is adequate for this program.	4	3	2	1
Staff				
3. There is a sufficient number of staff on duty to handle this program.	4	3	2	1
4. Staff are available to participants.	4	3	2	1
5. Staff are courteous to participants.	4	3	2	1
6. Staff are in control of the program.	4	3	2	1
Program				
7. Adequate safety precautions are being practiced.	4	3	2	1
8. The program is consistent with the agency's advertised description.	4	3	2	1
9. The activities are appropriate to the program goals.	4	3	2	1

Action taken on problems noted
List all 1s and 2s recorded above and describe the action taken, including date.

Other observations
List positive or negative comments from participants (including name and phone if possible).

Exhibit 21.13. Participant Evaluation Form

The purpose of this evaluation form is to solicit your feedback on the recent program you attended so that improvements can be made for the future.

Using the 5-point Likert scale below, please indicate how strongly you agree or disagree with each statement by circling the response that most closely reflects your belief. All individual responses will remain anonymous and will be only used in a summarized form.

Strongly Disagree	Disagree	Neutral	Agree	Strongly Agree
1	2	3	4	5

It is recommended that the following eight items be included on all instruments. To complete the instrument, program supervisors will select other items from the Item Pool provided in the Addendum after the Reference section at the end of this chapter.

Item	Strongly Disagree	Disagree	Neutral	Agree	Strongly Agree
I had fun in this program.	1	2	3	4	5
My skills increased because of this program.	1	2	3	4	5
I enjoyed the physical activity in this program.	1	2	3	4	5
I made new friends in this program.	1	2	3	4	5
The program facility was adequate.	1	2	3	4	5
Overall, I was highly satisfied with this program.	1	2	3	4	5
My personal reasons for participating in this program were fulfilled.	1	2	3	4	5
In relation to all my other leisure activities, this program was very important to me.	1	2	3	4	5

Please comment further on this program in the space below. Return the form to the program leader or mail to the Recreation Agency. Thank you for your feedback!

Exhibit 21.14. Program Evaluation Summary Format

Program _____ Location _____
Dates of Operation _____

I. Statistical Summary

A. Participation Impact

Number of Sessions (NOS) _____ Number of Enrollments (NOE) _____
Potential Attendance (PA) = (NOS) × (NOE) _____
Actual Total Attendance (ATA) _____
Average Attendance (AVA) = (ATA) / (NOE) _____
Percentage of Attendance = (ATA) / (PA) _____

B. Staff

Number of Staff (NBS) _____ Number of Staff Hours _____
Staff–Participant Ratio = (AVA) / (NBS) _____

Exhibit 21.14. (continued)

C. Costs

Salaries _____

Equipment _____

Supplies _____

Facilities _____

Total (TOTC) _____

D. Revenue

Agency Funds or Appropriated Funds _____

User Fees or Nonappropriated Funds _____

Total (TOTR) _____

E. Cost Analysis

Net Cost (TOTC) _____

Average Cost per Participant (TOTC) / (NOE) _____

Average Cost per Participation (TOTC) / (ATA) _____

Percent Self-Supporting (User Fees) / (TOTC) _____

II. Goals: Why was this program conducted? How does it fit in with the overall goals of the [agency name]? What were the specific goals of this program?

III. Procedures: Briefly describe what is involved in operating this program.

IV. Evaluation Data:

A. Program Observations: Summarize reports from ongoing on-site supervision of the program. Number of visits and a general report of conditions found.

B. Leader or Instructor Report: Summarize the leader's or instructor's reports about program operations.

C. Participant Feedback: Report participant feedback about the program, including oral testimony, tabulated evaluation items, phone calls, and so on.

D. Other Data Bits: Information from other data sources.

V. Supervisor's Analysis of Evaluation:

What is this program accomplishing?

Who is the program serving?

Is this program the best allocation of these resources?

How does this program compare with other similar programs in the agency?

Does this program fit into the Bureau's mission?

VI. Program Disposition: This program should be:

A. Continued as currently operated.

B. Dropped (identify possible impacts below).

C. Modified as noted below.

Signature_____ Date _____

Examine the outline for the evaluation summary report, and discuss the following questions:

- What does each section of the outline add to judging the worth of a program service?
- What additional questions may be added?
- Which items may be eliminated? How would the usefulness of the report be altered if they were eliminated?

References

Beard, J. G., & Ragheb, M. G. (1979, October). *Measuring leisure satisfaction.* Paper presented at the Leisure Research Symposium, New Orleans, LA.

Bullock, C. C., & Coffey, F. (1980). Triangulation as applied to the evaluative process. *Journal of Physical Education and Recreation, 51*(8), 50–52.

Christensen, J. E., & Yoesting, D. R. (1977). The substitutability concept: A need for further development. *Journal of Leisure Research, 9,* 188–207.

Denzin, N. K. (1978). *The research act* (2nd ed.). New York, NY: McGraw-Hill.

Driver, B. L. (1977). *Item pool for scales designed to quantify the psychological outcomes desired and expected from recreation participation.* Fort Collins, CO: Rocky Mountain Forest and Range Experiment Station.

Driver, B. L., & Brown, P. J. (1975). A social-psychological definition of recreation demand, with implications for recreation resource planning. In National Academy of Sciences Committee on Assessment of Demand for Outdoor Recreation Resources, *Assessing the demand for outdoor recreation* (pp. 63–88). Washington, DC: U.S. Government Printing Office.

Fuszek, R. (1987, October). *Program evaluation in municipal parks and recreation.* Paper presented at the National Recreation and Park Association Annual Congress, New Orleans, LA.

Guadagnolo, F. B. (1983, October). *Application of the Importance-Performance Scale in program evaluation.* Paper presented at the Leisure Research Symposium, Kansas City, MO.

Hawes, D. K. (1978). Satisfactions derived from leisure-time pursuits: An exploratory nationwide survey. *Journal of Leisure Research, 10,* 247–264.

Mannell, R. C. (1999). In E. L. Jackson & T. L. Burton (Eds.), *Leisure studies: Projects for the twenty-first century* (pp. 235–251). State College, PA: Venture.

Martilla, J. A., & James, J. C. (1979). Importance-performance analysis. *Journal of Marketing, 41*(1), 77–79.

National Recreation and Park Association. (2018). *2018 NRPA agency performance review: Park and recreation agency performance benchmarks.* Retrieved from https://www.nrpa.org/publications-research/research-papers/agency-performance-review/

National Recreation and Park Association. (2018). *2018 NRPA agency performance review: Park and recreation agency performance benchmarks*—Mesa Parks, Recreation, and Commercial Facilities Department. Ashburn, VA: The National Recreation and Park Association.

Peterson, C. A., & Gunn, S. L. (1984). *Therapeutic recreation program design: Principles and procedures* (2nd ed.). Englewood Cliffs, NJ: Prentice-Hall.

Provus, M. (1971). *Discrepancy evaluation: For educational program improvement and assessment.* Berkeley, CA: McCutchen.

Rossman, J. R. (1983, August). Participant satisfaction with employee recreation. *Journal of Physical Education, Recreation, and Dance, 54*(8), 60–62.

Stake, R. E. (1967). The countenance of educational evaluation. *Teachers College Record, 68*, 523–540.

Steinmetz, A. (2000). The Discrepancy Evaluation Model. In D. L. Stufflebeam, G. F. Madaus, & T. Kellaghan (Eds.), *Evaluation models: Viewpoints on educational and human service evaluation* (2nd ed., pp. 127–143). Boston, MA: Kluwer Academic.

Tinsley, H. E. A., Barrett, T. C., & Kass, R. A. (1977). Leisure activities and need satisfaction. *Journal of Leisure Research, 9*, 110–120.

Tinsley, H. E. A., & Kass, R. A. (1978). Leisure activities and need satisfaction: A replication extension. *Journal of Leisure Research, 10*, 191–202.

Addendum: Leisure Program Evaluation Item Pool

The following items have been arranged by categories. Programmers should select items most pertinent to their operation or specific program.

Staffing
- The leader (instructor, coach, etc.) was on time for the program.
- The leader was well prepared.
- The leader was knowledgeable about the subject matter.
- The leader was excellent.
- The leader made the class interesting.
- The leader was dynamic.
- The leader motivated me to get better at the activity.
- The leader was boring.
- The leader attempted to cover too much.

Price
- This program was too expensive.
- The fee for this program was reasonable.
- I would have paid more for a program of this quality.

Scheduling
- The length of individual class meetings was too long.
- The length of class meetings was just right.
- Class meetings were too short.
- This program was scheduled at a bad time for me.
- This program was scheduled at a good time for me.
- The day of the week the program was scheduled was good (bad) for me.
- I would have preferred that the program be held on a different day of the week.
- The facility the program was held in was too small.
- I would have preferred that the program be held in a different venue (or facility).

- This facility was very enjoyable.
- This facility was inadequate.
- I had trouble getting to this facility.
- I would prefer a different location for this program.
- The facility was clean.
- The facility was dirty.

Program Structure
- The progression of this program was logical.
- This program was creatively planned.
- The level of this program was too difficult for me.
- Instructional materials for this class were excellent.
- This program went further into the activity than I desired.

Equipment
- There was not enough equipment available for this program.
- The equipment used in the program never worked properly.
- There was plenty of equipment to conduct this program.
- I had access to all of the supplies and equipment I needed for this program.

Club Organization
- I am an active member of this club.
- I seldom attend club functions.
- This club does not meet my needs.
- Club officers are doing an excellent job of running the club.
- The [agency] provides excellent support services to this club.
- This club's activities are one of my most important leisure pursuits.
- Club officers do not represent the desires of most club members.

League Organization
- This league involved too many games.
- League awards are overemphasized.
- League awards are important to me.
- League games were too long.
- The minimum number of players allowed on the roster was too small.
- The maximum number of players allowed on the roster was too large.
- Roster size for the league was adequate.
- The league entry fee was appropriate.
- Teams in the league were well matched according to ability.
- Game officials maintained good control of games.
- Game officials were knowledgeable about the rules.
- Game officials started play on time.
- Playing facilities were generally available at the scheduled starting time.
- Playing facilities were usually in excellent shape.

- This league was too competitive.
- Our team was not competitive in this league.
- [Agency] personnel were helpful.
- [Agency] personnel were available when needed.
- The league management system was adequate.

Social Media
- I follow this program on social media (check all that apply).
  - ☐ Agency e-mail list
  - ☐ Facebook
  - ☐ Twitter
  - ☐ [Add any applicable to the agency]

- I learned about this program from (check all that apply).
  - ☐ Social media
  - ☐ Agency's website
  - ☐ Former participant
  - ☐ Newspaper
  - ☐ Agency's brochure
  - ☐ Other

Future Intents
- I intend to continue in this program next session.
- I would attend a more advanced session of this program.

Program Outcomes—General
- This program was one of the best I've participated in.
- As a result of this program, I will participate in this activity more frequently.
- This program made me more aware of my own interests and talents.
- I looked forward to attending this program.
- I often remember my pleasant experience in this program.

Program Outcomes—Specific
- In this program, I developed skills and ability.
- This program introduced me to a new skill.
- Participation in this program increased my feelings of self-worth.
- This program gave me an opportunity to demonstrate my competence to others.

Physical Fitness
- This program kept me physically fit.
- I enjoyed the physical exercise I got in this program.

Social Enjoyment
- I enjoyed this program because it enabled me to be with others who have interests similar to mine.
- I enjoyed this program because I participated with my friends.
- I enjoyed the companionship of others in the program.
- I liked meeting new people in this program.

Exploration
- I enjoyed discovering new things in this program.
- I liked seeing new sights.

Autonomy
- I felt I had control over things in this program.
- This program gave me a chance to be on my own.
- This program helped me to get away from it all for a while.

Risks
- I liked the high risks involved.
- I liked the chance for danger in this program.

Family Orientation
- I liked participating in this program with my family.
- I enjoyed this program because it enabled me to be away from my family for a while.

Relaxation
- In this program, I enjoyed experiencing tranquility.
- The most satisfying aspect of this program was that it gave my mind a rest.
- This program pleased me because it relaxed me physically.

Junior Beach Runners
Photo Courtesy of City of Long Beach, Department of Parks, Recreation, and Marine.

22 *Making Decisions About Program Services*

KEY TERMS

Program Life Cycle, Introduction, Growth, Maturation, Saturation, Decline, Program, Modification, Life Cycle Audit, Marketing Mix, Program Elimination

Step 9: Disposition Decision

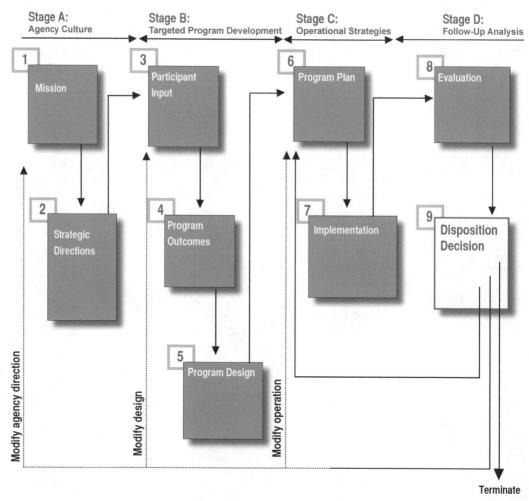

The final step in the Program Development Cycle involves deciding what will be done with a program—that is, its disposition. The final disposition of a program should be made on evidence gathered during the evaluation phase, thus using evidence-based decision making. The three choices include continue operating the program with no changes, modify the program, or terminate it. In actual operations, two of the choices are expansive. Modification includes a broad range of alternatives. In addition, programmers must consider many scenarios for dropping a program to avoid adverse publicity and pushback.

It is somewhat of a misnomer to include in the Program Development Cycle a single stage called the decision-making stage. Program development involves a series of decisions. Ronkainen (1985) agreed with this view: "Product development is a sequential process involving not one decision point, but rather a series of go/no decisions" (p. 97). The programmer faces a series of decisions when developing programs; at each step in the Program Development Cycle, the programmer makes a decision to proceed with the program concept or to abort it. Completing each step in the cycle also requires the programmer to make numerous decisions about the details of a program's design and staging.

Furthermore, program development involves strategic decision making. Ronkainen (1985) pointed out that the central element in strategic decision making is the "incomplete state of knowledge concerning the nature of the problem or the components which must be included in a successful solution" (p. 98). Decision making in program development is difficult partly because of the nonroutine nature of strategic decision making. They are wicked problems similar to those discussed earlier in the book.

Program Life Cycle

The ability of the programmer to determine the disposition of a program will be influenced by the current position of a program in the program life cycle. The program life cycle concept draws an analogy between a program and the biological life cycle of animals (Crompton & Lamb, 1986). It assumes that programs go through a transition analogous to birth, life, and death.

Figure 22.1 (page 452) presents a diagrammatic representation of the program life cycle, which includes five stages: design/development, introduction, growth, maturation, and decline. Every program in an agency's program inventory will be located at a different stage in the cycle. Each stage has unique characteristics.

Design/Development

This topic was covered in Chapters 7, 9, and 10. One more time, all marketing efforts depend on an excellent program design and staging. At this point, it is important for the programmer to be thorough in design and prototyping to ensure the program is ready to be introduced.

Introduction

> The introduction stage is characterized by the considerable amount of effort needed for a programmer to introduce and successfully launch a new program.

The introduction stage is characterized by the considerable amount of effort needed for a programmer to introduce and successfully launch a new program. Grgen-Ellson (1986) reported that three factors lead to the successful introduction of new services: thoroughly executed market research, a well-planned implementation, and continual monitoring and ongoing support of the new service. Even with thorough preparations, the agency's cost per participant will probably be high during this stage because of the relatively small number of program patrons and the relative high cost of promotion per participant.

During implementation, programmers monitor the new service closely to ensure it is being delivered as the program designer intended. They must deal with two marketing problems during the introduction stage: getting the target market to try

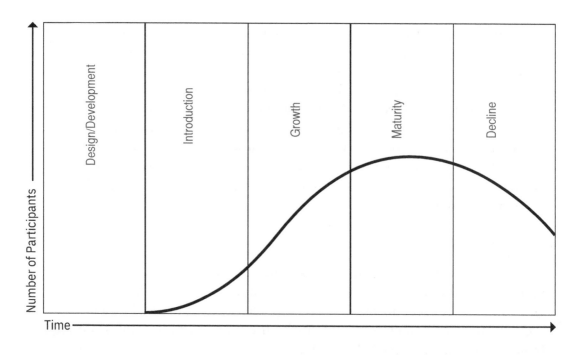

Issue	Design	Introduction	Growth	Maturity	Decline
Target Audience	Selected/ searched	Early adopters	Mainstream users	Late adopters	Laggard joiners and committed participants
Market Size (i.e., the number of participants)	As recruited for testing and development	Small	Growing	Largest number of users	Shrinking numbers
Competition	As identified and researched	Low	Moderate	High	Moderate
Management Focus	Developmental and experimental	Identify, welcome, and nurture new users	Scaling capacity for increase in number of users	Maintain unique program features to retain participants	Determine whether to push for rebirth, continue with core group, or discontinue program
Promotion	Build Anticipation	Inform	Persuade to use agency's service	Persuade and Sales Promotion	Remind continuing participants
Price	Forecast willingness to pay	Price based on costs and market's ability and willingness to pay	Price based on costs, competitors pricing, and what the market will support.	Established price may need to be discounted to attract new users or increase use by current participants.	Price increases will likely dissuade users. May need to use sales promotion strategies to lower price to participants.

Figure 22.1. Program Life Cycle

the program for the first time and getting the target market to continue using the service once they try it (Kotler & Andreasen, 1987).

Rogers (1971) identified a four-step process that individuals go through when adopting a new behavior pattern. The first step involves acquiring knowledge about the new service and becoming convinced it has value to them. In the second step, the prospective participant must be persuaded to participate, that is, to proceed from having an interest to being motivated to take action. In the third step, a person makes a decision either to accept the new program and participate in it or to reject participation. Often, the decision process is accompanied by either a vicarious experiencing of the program or by a trial of the service. The final step involves confirmation, during which an individual decides to become an ongoing participant or to stop participating in the service.

Growth

During the growth stage, the number of patrons in a program increases most rapidly. There is demand and growth. The major task programmers face during this stage is ensuring they can scale available service, that is, produce enough service to meet demand.

Dealing with excess demand for a program service is somewhat problematic. In a public agency, programmers face considerable political pressure to meet all the demand for a service. In a commercial agency, they also deal with considerable financial pressure to meet all current demand, because this ensures profitability. In any agency, an inability of programmers to meet demand has the potential for eroding the credibility of the agency in the eyes of its consumer public. The agency must therefore anticipate potential demand and be prepared to scale to meet it.

> During the growth stage, the number of patrons in a program increases most rapidly.

Profits likely grow during this stage. Since the initial and continuing promotion costs are now spread over more participants, advertising costs per unit will be lower. In this stage, agencies battles for market share and their degree of success at acquiring their targeted share will greatly influence the future of a program.

Maturation

During the maturation stage, program growth slows, as does the rate of increase in new patrons (Howard & Crompton, 1980). Usually, this is the longest stage for most programs. Thus, most programs sit in this stage and most marketing efforts deal with mature programs (Kotler & Armstrong, 1993). Programmers are cautioned that this is not the time to coast. It is important that they continue to manage mature programs by altering their marketing mix to meet the evolving needs and values of participants based on their feedback and

> During the maturation stage, program growth slows, as does the rate of increase in new patrons.

evaluation data. New markets for the program may be discovered through additional segmentation.

Decline

When a program's growth slows and the number of patrons enrolled levels off, the program reaches saturation and enrollments begin to decline. During this stage, enrollments are made up of mostly repeat participants. The management task in this stage involves serving an existing clientele.

> When a program's growth slows and the number of patrons enrolled levels off, the program reaches saturation and enrollments begin to decline.

The programmer can adopt the following four strategies during the saturation phase to help maintain program enrollment (Kotler & Andreasen, 1987):

Market leadership. Take leadership in program innovation. Try to maintain the agency's position as the best provider of this service through innovative program changes.

Market challenge. Take the offensive, and challenge the market leader through any number of strategies, including price discounting, program innovation, improved service, and better distribution.

Market follower. Try to maintain the current market share by duplicating the market leader. The market follower must know how to maintain its current customers by keeping its prices suitable and its quality high. It must also remain aware of market trends and be prepared to enter new markets as they open.

Market targeting. Try to identify a unique segment of the market that can be serviced without threatening the larger suppliers. By finding a unique, profitable market niche, the agency maintains a patron group for its service. Often this is accomplished in municipal operations whereby the municipal agency offers a bare bones, inexpensive service, while commercial operators cater to individuals desiring and willing to pay for a more high-end, prestigious service. Municipal versus commercial golf courses would be an example.

During the maturation stage programs may transition into declining enrollments. This may be rapid or slow and can occur for a variety of reasons. For example, specific types of craft activities can be popular in a given year, but the following year no one may be interested in them. Once a program begins to decline, the programmer decides whether to revitalize the program or allow it to die. Commercial operations usually have financial targets and once they are no longer meeting these, they eliminate the program. Weak programs in which participation has declined often take an inordinate amount of staff time and are economically inefficient. For these reasons, the programmer should consider eliminating programs that have seriously declined.

Life Cycle Audit

To manage a program, programmers should be able to estimate its current position in the life cycle. Exhibit 22.1 (page 456) illustrates a life cycle audit form that programmers can use to determine the current position of a program in the life cycle. The position of a program in the cycle should reveal typical program management problems.

Altering the Marketing Mix

Conventional marketing wisdom suggests that each stage of the program life cycle requires a unique marketing mix. At each stage, different components of the marketing mix (product, price, promotion, and place) will need to be changed so that they can help to continue the life of a program. Now complete Exercise 22.1 (page 457).

Program Modification

One of the most difficult programming decisions is knowing how and when to modify a program. Although a program may need to be modified at any time, the later part of the decline stage when enrollments begin to fall off is a critical time for considering altering the program.

An understanding of leisure theory provides the best guidance about modifying a program (Little, 1993). The leisure theory discussed earlier in the book suggests that to provide a leisure experience to constituents, a program must continue to be an immersive and engaging experience. Programmers must modify a program to keep it engaging. To monitor this, they closely watch for changes in patrons' reported satisfactions and outcomes. According to recent research conducted by the authors, they can also use visualization to experience a program vicariously, searching and experimenting with possible modifications. Remember that a service can be altered by changing any one of the six situating elements of a program. As outlined in Chapter 3, the entire program does not need altered, only one or more components of it.

Implementing Program Modifications

Almost all programs have a core group of participants who like things "just the way they are." Thus, programmers must understand such situations when recommending program modifications. The difficulty of successfully implementing a change in a program depends on the degree of change and the amount and type of information available about the advisability of change. The degree of change can range from small, incremental changes to large, major changes in the program. The information the programmer has about the advisability of change, or to justify the change, can range from a large amount of pertinent, detailed, quantitative information to a small amount of intuitive, qualitative, judgmental information derived from experience or casual observation. The quality and quantity of information will vary greatly and will affect how easily the programmer can implement change.

Exhibit 22.1. Program Life Cycle Audit

Program _____ Program Manager _____ Date _____

Program Impact Data

		Actual			Estimated	
	2017	2018	2019	2020	2021
Program Capacity	____	____	____	____	____
Program enrollment/attendance	____	____	____	____	____
% enrolled/attended	____	____	____	____	____
Staff–participant ratio	____	____	____	____	____
Average cost/participant	____	____	____	____	____
% of cost recovery	____	____	____	____	____

Life Cycle

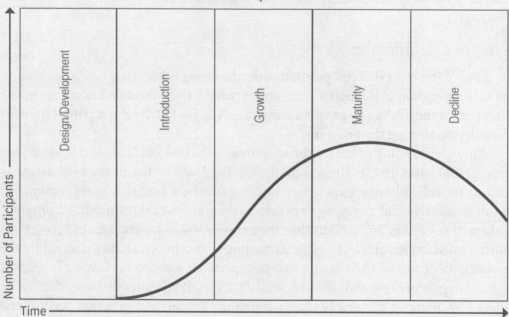

Place an X where you believe the program is currently located on the life cycle. Use the stage indicators below to help you place the program.

PROGAM LIFE CYCLE INDICATORS
(plus factors from table in Figure 22.1, page 452)

Introduction Stage
1. Percentage enrolled/attended is low.
2. Average cost/participant is high.
3. Promotion is information based to announce availability of program and to encourage enrollment.

Growth Stage
1. Percentage enrolled/attended is growing rapidly.
2. Percentage of cost recovery is increasing.
3. Average cost/participant is decreasing.
4. Program management activities are directed to scaling the capacity of the program.

Exhibit 22.1. (continued)

Maturation Stage
1. Enrollment increases level off.
2. Capacity is still at 75% of capacity.
3. Program management directed at sustaining the quality of the program to retain an established market.
4. Additional competitors are likely since this is a successful program.
5. Program should be at peak performance regarding staff/participant ratio and % of cost recovery.

Decline Stage
1. The number of new enrollments declines.
2. The percentage of capacity enrolled or attending declines to below 50% and if this drops to below 25% the program is in decline.
3. Staff–participant ratio declines and % of cost recovery declines. If program becomes non-profitable, a decision will need to be made about whether or not to subsidize it.
4. Management decision must be made to sustain, revise, or eliminate the program.

Exercise 22.1.
Altering the Marketing Mix

In class, select a program service and discuss how the marketing mix may need to be different at each stage of the program life cycle. Use the matrix below to guide your discussion.

Marketing Mix Components	Life Cycle Stages			
	Introduction	Growth	Maturation	Decline
Product				
Price				
Promotion				
Place				

After completing your discussion, consider the following questions:
- In which stage will the program manager likely need to scale service?
- In which stage do most programs operate for the longest period of time?
- Where is the promotion activity "to inform" most likely to be used?
- After introduction, altering the program itself would most likely be done in which stage?

Figure 22.2 is a graphic representation of four decision situations created by various combinations of information availability and the degree of change being recommended. Each quadrant of the matrix includes the mode of change to be recommended, which implies the degree of change that will result, and the basis or rationale for recommending change.

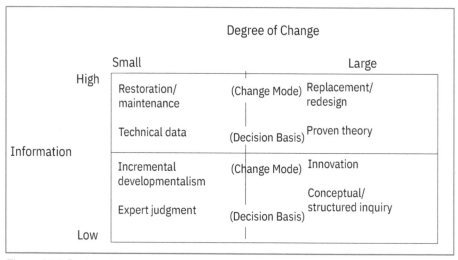

Figure 22.2. Decision Matrix

In the first decision quadrant, restoration/maintenance, a small degree of change is proposed. Technical information about the program is the basis for recommending this change. Restoration decisions are characterized by the use of technical information for implementing small, incremental changes that restore a program to its original design. Because the change is small and the information available is great, this change is usually easy for the agency to implement. An example of this would be a day care operation increasing the number of staff to comply with a new child care law. This change would continue the program as designed and keep it within the minimal requirements of the law.

In the second quadrant, a program is completely replaced with a new service or a completely redesigned service. The rationale for this is a proven theory or method. Although the change implemented is great, the information base for the change is also substantial; thus, the change is usually easy for the agency to implement. The only block may be a lack of understanding for the change by the patrons who will be affected. This situation requires the programmer to communicate the basis for the change to the patrons. An example of this would be replacing a traditional summer playground program with specialty camps, such as sports or arts camps, scheduled so that they may also serve as day care programs. The information base for such a change could be declining enrollments in the playground program, the success of similar camp programs in other communities, the expressed need in the community for summer day care, and an expressed desire for program services with a more defined focus.

The third quadrant is labeled incremental developmentalism, which involves small changes based on little information. The rationale for these changes is the experience and expert judgment of staff. Usually these changes are so small that the experienced practitioner is allowed the leeway to make them. Because the changes recommended are small, they are relatively easy for the agency to implement. This type of a decision is typical of the modifications made in many recreation programs developed through trial and error, with only small adjustments during each iteration.

Little (1993) provided several examples of modifying programs with this type of decision strategy. For example, in observing the operation of a summer day camp, she noted that varying levels of camper ability led to the need for the camp to alter certain activities so all of the children could feel competent. With a similar technique, she determined that a drama skit activity included in a weekend program operated for incarcerated mothers and their children could be retained if its implementation were changed. Mothers were not succeeding in creating skits but would act out prescripted skits. Both of these were small, incremental changes that could be made because of Little's understanding of leisure behavior and how it constrained participation in the current programs. Although the changes were small and the information used for justifying the changes seemed minimal, the knowledge base and analysis required for identifying them were not. Previous experience with programs and a knowledge of leisure behavior that was directly applicable to the current programs were necessary for successful modification of these programs. Changes of this type are easier for the programmer to implement if his or her credibility has built up over time with a record of successful changes.

The final decision quadrant is labeled innovation, which is characterized by a low level of information being used for recommending a substantial change. Creative thinking and innovative design techniques discussed in Chapters 10 and 12 are the typical methods used in developing the data needed for this type of recommended change. These techniques produce a low information level; these data are often considered "soft" since they are not derived from quantitative analysis. This is one of the most difficult changes for a programmer to have accepted. A successful track record of implementing innovative programs will help the programmer have this type of a change accepted. An example of this type of change would be the recommendation to begin a major new special event or program service never tried in a community.

Modifying programs is an essential part of program management. The programmer must develop the skills to analyze programs, to note their deficiencies, and to be able to recommend and have accepted the modifications that will keep them viable. Understanding the resistance in implementing modifications is important to the successful accomplishment of them.

The Balanced Scorecard

Current practice suggests that a balanced scorecard approach (Kaplan & Norton, 1992) may improve decision making about the future of program services. A balanced scorecard incorporates several performance measures into decision making rather than a single metric. For example, to be efficient, some organizations use only one metric to decide the future of a program. Examples could include its cost per participant, overall enrollment, or the leader–participant ratio. The balanced scorecard concept suggests multiple measures of success should be used and the metrics used should focus a manager's attention on what matters most with regard to implementing the mission and strategy of the organization.

Instead of a single metric, the agency uses multiple measures. The programmer can incorporate traditional measures but should add others to more broadly examine a program. The others include measures that reflect participant satisfaction with a program, financial performance, or efficiency of a program, and how well the program implements the strategy of the organization. Based on strategic directions developed earlier and displayed in Box B of Figure 9.1 (page 175), Figure 22.3 shows a balanced scorecard that would be useful for the Arlington County Department of Parks and Recreation.

Each metric is tied to an organizational strategy, and there are multiple indicators beyond financial performance. How many metrics are appropriate is an unanswered question. But, as discussed, usually three to five well-selected indicators about issues that matter to the strategic performance of the organization should be sufficient. Good management practice requires that top-level managers obtain consensus between board and staff about the metrics to be used.

The Birth and Death of Programs

An important implication of the life cycle concept is that in a healthy organization, some new programs will be introduced and some existing programs terminated each year. Introducing and terminating programs is a normal event in managing the program inventory of a leisure service organization. In addition, eliminating programs is an economic necessity in a recession situation. With static economic

Strategy addressed	Provide excellent programs, services, places, and spaces	Build community, promote wellness, and ensure equal access for all	Cultivate an effective, dynamic workforce.
Provide Excellent Programs	Participant reported satisfaction with programs, and services increased 5% from 2019–2020 in programs and services where measures were taken.		
Promote Wellness		MVPA documented with the SOPARC increased 7.5% from 2019–2020.	
Dynamic Workforce			80% or more of supervisory-level workforce possess the CPRP credential.

Figure 22.3. Balanced Scorecard Metrics

Notes: SOPARC is the System of Observing Park and Recreation Use in Communities (see Chapter 20). MVPA is Moderate to Vigorous Physical Activity observed occurring in parks when studied (moderate activity is walking and vigorous is running). This statistic is measured in person hours devoted to moderate to vigorous physical activity.

resources, the programmer can obtain the resources to introduce new programs only by eliminating some of the old ones.

It is therefore critical that a leisure service programming operation have a formal procedure for identifying new program services to launch and for eliminating program services that have outlived their usefulness to the organization and its stakeholders. The first two stages of the Program Development Cycle provide a formal procedure for developing and launching programs. The next section discusses a formal elimination strategy.

Program Elimination

Programmers tend to add programs, not eliminate them. Adding only new programs to an organization's inventory often leads to a deterioration of service quality. Eventually, the professional staff will simply be spread too thin to do a thorough job on each program. Even the best programmers have a limit on the number of programs they can successfully manage.

In most leisure service organizations, three primary forces work against eliminating programs: staff, patrons, and organizational political forces. Staff members too often develop an "ownership" of programs they have created. They are therefore reluctant to eliminate a program, because they consider its elimination a personal or professional failure. Programs have life cycles, and the useful life of almost all good programs eventually ends. Often, this termination has nothing to do with the competence of the professional staff—it is a predictable consequence of beginning a program. The only question is, when will it occur?

> Even the best programmers have a limit on the number of programs they can successfully manage.

Professional staff members need to realize that eliminating some programs each year is a normal and necessary part of program management. All viable organizations constantly search for new products and services to bring to the marketplace.

Not-for-profit organizations, municipal leisure service agencies, church recreation operations, and similar leisure service organizations with a third-party funder encounter two additional forces that make eliminating programs difficult. Patrons who make up a core group of participants will lobby against eliminating a program. These groups often show strong commitment to the continuation of a specific activity. Although usually very small, these groups show intense commitment, and they attempt to ensure continuation of "their" activity, regardless of its economic efficiency.

The second force is board members and higher ranking administrative personnel, who often respond to the efforts of groups lobbying for the continuation of a program that the professional staff has recommended for elimination. Because leisure services in these types of organizations are often subsidized, the agency may be able to continue economically inefficient services to preserve political harmony.

Programmers can best deal with the latter two cases by having program criteria established and accepted by the various parties before making disposition decisions. Making decisions from an economic profitability model is usually much more objective and easily determined. Because of this, commercial recreation operations have clearer decision criteria and require the elimination of unprofitable services.

After making the decision to eliminate a service, the programmer determines an elimination strategy. How will the service be eliminated? The rest of this section outlines three possible strategies for eliminating a program service.

Retrenchment

A program can be continued with reduced expenses. Often, because the retrenched service is not the same service originally provided with a higher level of funding, enrollments decline. The program literally dies of its own weight.

Staged

A reduction of a program service can be staged. Such a strategy can be phased in over time so that current participants can find alternate services to meet their needs.

Sudden

Sometimes a service is best simply eliminated immediately. This is often possible with services that have outlived their useful life and there is no advocate group left to resist.

Conclusion

The final step in the Program Development Cycle involves deciding the disposition of a program. It is important that decisions be justified through the evaluation data collected about the program. The current place of the program on the program life cycle partly determines the disposition of a program. The programmer decides whether to modify, eliminate, or continue a program. All healthy programming organizations add some new programs and eliminate some existing ones each year. Making data-based decisions with criteria agreed to in advance places the programmer in the optimal decision position and ensures success.

References

Crompton, J. L., & Lamb, C. W., Jr. (1986). *Marketing government and social services*. New York, NY: Wiley.

Grgen-Ellson, N. (1986). Increasing the probability of new product success. *Journal of Retail Banking, 8*, 25–28.

Howard, D. R., & Crompton, J. L. (1980). *Financing, managing, and marketing recreation and park resources*. Dubuque, IA: Wm. C. Brown.

Kaplan, R. S., & Norton, D. P. (1992, January–February). The balanced scorecard—Measures that drive performance. *Harvard Business Review 70*(1), 71–79.

Kotler, P., & Andreasen, A. R. (1987). *Strategic marketing for nonprofit organizations*. Englewood Cliffs, NJ: Prentice-Hall.

Kotler, P., & Armstrong, G. (1993). *Marketing: An introduction* (3rd ed.). Englewood Cliffs, NJ: Prentice-Hall.

Little, S. L. (1993). Leisure program design and evaluation. *Journal of Physical Education, Recreation, and Dance, 64*(8), 26–29, 33.

Rogers, E. M. (with Shoemaker, F. F.). (1971). *Communication of innovations*. New York, NY: Free Press.

Ronkainen, I. A. (1985). Using decision-systems analysis to formalize product development processes. *Journal of Business Research, 13*, 97–106.

Index

A

access to online material, 478
accountability for program inputs, outcomes, 382
accreditation, 101–102
ACTIVE Network registration software, 299
activities
    as leisure products, 65–68
    selling, 66
activity classifications (table), 66
Adirondack Extreme Adventure Course's mission statement, 113, 118
Adobe Spark, 276
adolescent characteristics, 41
adulthood characteristics, 41
advertising. *See* promotion
agency, allocating costs in the, 353–355
agency culture, determining (fig.), 92
animating program design, 194
animation, and situated activity system, 48–50
animation plan, 250, 253–258
annual schedules, 260
applied creativity, 221–223
appraisal, performance, 322–324
Arlington County Department of Parks & Recreation mission statement, 113, 114
Arts Council of New Orleans' mission statement, 118
arts organizations, 17
assessments
    assessing community needs, 105–106
    assessing individual needs, 96
    assessing leisure opportunities, 108–109
    assessing organizational needs, 99–105
    community needs assessment agenda (exhibit), 109
    marketing approach to organizational, 102–105
    needs. *See* needs assessments
    organizational assessment criteria (exhibit), 104
audit, program life cycle, 455–460
Authentic Happiness (Seligman), 1
autotelic activities, 8

B

background checks for job applicants, 319
balanced scorecard metrics (fig.), 461
balanced scorecard, program audit, 460–461
Banks, Russell, 197
benchmarking, 420
benefits-based programming (BBP), 210–212
Berners-Lee, Tim, 280
BFOQs (bona fide occupational qualifications), 319
black box of programming, 215–216
"blocking" in theater programming, 48
brainstorming, 228, 229
brainwriting, 229
break-even point, graphing, 368–369
Brinker International's mission statement, 114, 115–116
brochures
    distribution, 297
    writing, 271–272
budgets
    budget percentage method of (exhibit), 356
    percentage of, cost allocation, 356
    preparing line-item, 352
    in program plan, 247

C

cable TV public access programs, 283
cancellation plan in program plan, 248
candidate plans, evaluating, 195
CAPRA Assessment Criteria (exhibit), 102
Carl T. Johnson Hunt and Fish Center, Cadillac, Michigan, 361
Carnival Cruise Line's mission statement, 116
Cayuga Nature Center's mission statement, 113, 117
central location walk-in method of registration, 291–292
Chambers of Commerce, 283
Chase's Calendar of Events, 260
checklist for implementation of summer day camp program (exhibit), 251
Chickahominy Riverfront Park, Virginia, 57

children's Egg Hunt, 45

Chutes and Ladders game, 11

citizen advisory committees, 153–154

co-creation of experiences, 206

Commission for Accreditation of Park and Recreation Agencies (CAPRA)
    categories of standards using codified system, 131
    self-evaluation of public leisure service organizations, 101–102

commodities, 58–59

communication channels, 270–271

community needs, assessing, 105–106

community partnerships, 110–111

comparative needs, 152–153

comprehensive pricing, 338

Contract for Individual Services, 329, 331–332

contracting for personnel services, 328–330

Convention and Visitors Bureau, focus group example for (exhibit), 158

co-production, 59

corporate sponsors of events, 70

cost allocation methods, 355–358

cost objective, 353

cost recovery, 374

cost tracking systems, 357

cost vs. price, 353

costs
    See also program cost determination
    classifying into variable, fixed, 363–364
    presenting data, 364–371

cost-volume-profit analysis, 362

Covey, Dr. Stephen, 176

creative programming
    creative program design process, 224–225
    creativity in developing programs, 223–224
    four phases of creative process, 225–234
    generally, 220
    understanding applied creativity, 221–223

creativity
    described, 221
    in developing programs, 223–224

D

da Vinci, Leonardo, xiii

DaFont website, 277

Darbi, Kofi, 94, 113

data, presenting cost, 364–371

data gathering for program evaluation, 393–401

decision matrix (fig.), 458

decline, in program life cycle, 454

demographic and social trends, 97–98

design
    described, 188
    and development of programs, 451–453
    flyer, 276–277
    program. *See* program design

design tactics, 187, 190–192, 195

design thinking, 232

direct costs, 354

direct providers vs. facilitators, 52–53

disabled individuals, 246

discrepancy evaluation, 432, 433, 434, 435

Disney Imagineers, 197

Disneyland, 50

divergent thinking, 228–229

diversity, 97

drugs and "recreational drug use," 12

Dunn, Julia, 226

E

Easter Seals of Central Illinois's mission and program offerings, 135–136

Eau Claire Parks, Recreation, and Forestry Department, 131

economic trends, 99

economic value and activity, evolution of (table), 58

elimination of programs, 461–462

e-mail for program promotion, 282–283

employees
    See also staffing
    compensation, 327–328
    orientation, 320–321
    performance appraisal, 322–327
    training, 321–322

encounter block of Framed Experience Model, 189

engagement and leisure, 9–11

entrepreneurial, 60

equipment, 61–62, 64, 246–247

evaluation of goals, objectives, 432–435

evaluation reports, 401–403, 405, 406–408

Evening of American Folk Music (sample design), 200–205

event planner job description (exhibit), 315

events
    described, 16–17
    formats of (table), 69
    how organization's mission influences event development (exercise), 101
    as leisure products, 68–70
    off-road vehicle (table), 69
    relationships with definitions of leisure (fig.), 18

evidence for program evaluation, 389–393
exchanges and marketing, 163
exercises
  altering the marketing mix, 457
  animation plan, 258
  applying importance-performance
    evaluation, 419, 425
  co-creation of, 206
  communicating evaluation results, 406
  comparing purposes of evaluation, 383
  coordinating and collaborating strategy, 75
  cost-volume-profit analysis, 375
  creating revenue streams, 68
  develop program standards, 135
  developing needs assessment questions, 151
  developing program standards, 183
  developing recreation worker job
    description, 317
  ensuring stress-free, enjoyable queues, 305
  evaluation report, 444
  examining breadth, depth of activity
    program offerings, 67
  experimenting with programming formats,
    53
  explore your own black box of programming,
    216
  goal networking, 179
  how organization's mission influences event
    development, 101
  identifying issue and target goals, 211
  manipulating the six elements that situate
    programs, 51
  networking, 131
  panel discussion on registration, 301
  play cards to practice symbolic interaction
    theory, 30
  practicing the flow chart method, 253
  preparing news releases, 275
  programming as symbolic interaction, 34
  redefining problem statements, 230
  scheduling, 261
  specifying evaluation purpose, audience, 386
  symbolic interaction theory and you, 31
  systems approach to writing goals, objectives,
    137
  using all five senses, 192
  using employee appraisal instrument, 327
  using satisfaction-based program evaluation
    data, 431
  visual imaging from different
    perspectives, 193
  writing brochure copy, 273

  writing mission statements, 120
experience design, 187–188
Experience Design (Shedroff), 22
experience economy, developing leisure
  products in the, 57–70
Experience Economy, The (Pine & Gilmore), 6,
  22, 58
experience marketing, 70
experiences
  artistic and technical factors
    in design, 197–200
  designing interactive, 188
  designing leisure, 187–188
  implementing intentionally designed, 95,
    127, 143, 242, 269, 287, 311, 380
  as leisure products, 65–70
  marketing leisure, 162–168
experiencing leisure, 31–34
exploration, interpretation, and creative
  process, 231–232
expressed needs, 152

F

Facebook, 281
face-to-face interactions, 27
facilitators vs. direct providers, 52–53
facility scheduling, 261–264
fan experience, 14
fax-in method of registration, 294
felt needs, 152
Field Museum's mission statement, 119
fixed costs, 363–364
Flow Chart Method (FCM) for management
  plan, 250–251
flowchart for summer day camp program
  (exhibit), 252–253
flyers, preparing, 276–280
focus groups for needs assessments, 155–158
Ford Motor Company, 74
formative evaluation, 413
forms, registration, 294–299
forward-thinking, 76
framed experience design, 200–205
Framed Experience Model of program design,
  189–195
frames
  encounter (fig.), 196
  in Framed Experience Model, 195–197
  program (fig.), 194
freedom and leisure, 7–8
front desk attendant job description
  (exhibit), 316

G

games
  described, 11–12
  relationships with definitions of leisure
    (fig.), 18
Geneplore Model of creativity, 221–222
generation of approaches, and creative process,
  227–230
giveaways, and queues, 306
goals and objectives
  codification approach to networked, 131–137
  described, 78–80
  evaluation, 432–435
  hierarchical arrangement of mission
    statement with, 81–82
  how they differ, 82–83
  how to write, 80–81
  limits defined by (fig.), 83
  networked (example), 175
  networking in the organization, 129–130
  representative nature of, 83–84
  staff collaboration in developing, 84–85
  using to establish programming standards,
    130–131
Goffman, Erving, 38, 40
Gong Show, The, 49
goods as leisure products, 60–62
Google Images, 277
Gossamer Albatross airplane, 229
graphing cost data, break-even point, 367–369
growth, in program life cycle, 453

H

hashtags for needs assessments, 160
hierarchical arrangement of mission statement
  with goals, objectives, 81–82

I

Illustrator, 277
imagined interactions, 190–195
importance-performance evaluation, 414–419
inclusion plan in program plan, 246
indirect costs, 354
innovation, and creative process, 232–234
Instagram, 281
"Instagram effect," 97–98
integral planning, 233
intentionally designed experiences (IDEs)
  described, 213
  examples of, 213–214
  studies on, 214–215

intentions
  described, 147–148
  questions contrasting needs and intentions
    (exhibit), 149–152
interacting people, and situated activity system,
  40–43
interaction rituals, 27–30
interactionist approach, 24
interactions
  how produced in social occasions, 27
  occasions of, as emergent productions, 32
  occasions of, fragility of, 32
interdependent events and leisure programs, 39
interests and needs, 146–147
intervention goals (X statements), 180
interviews
  focus group interview problem statement,
    agenda (exhibit), 157
  for needs assessments, 154–158
  performance appraisal, 325
  for program evaluation, 394–395
  unscheduled interview agenda (exhibit), 155
intrinsic satisfaction and leisure, 8–9
intuitive and linear thinking, 228–230
iStock, 277

J

job
  analysis, 312–314
  description, 314–317

K

Kelly, David, 227
KSAs (knowledge, skills, and abilities), 312

L

leader or instructor evaluation form
  (exhibit), 440
leisure
  delivery systems, 108
  described, 4–5, 7–11
  experience, phases of, 25–26
  experiences, designing, 187–188
  experiences, marketing, 162–168
  experiencing, 31–34
  facilitators to, 25–26
  how individuals experience, 21–34
  of millennials vs. other groups, 97–98
  objects, nature of, 26
  occasions, deriving meaning from
    interaction in, 30–31

occasions, peoples' roles in, 33
occasions, structuring, 33–34
opportunities, assessing, 108–109
play. *See* play
program evaluation form (exhibit), 430–431
programming, symbolic interactionist approach, 25
sport. *See* sport
symbolic interactionist perspective, 23–24
leisure experiences, 59–60
leisure facilities, rentals, 65
leisure objects and situated activity system, 44–45
leisure products, developing in the experience economy, 57–70
liability release
  form, 296
  Santa Clara, California, Parks and Recreation Department's, 289–290
life cycle audit, 455–460
line and service units, 350–352
linear and intuitive thinking, 228–230
line-item budgets, 352
LinkedIn, 318
Local Government Officials' Perceptions of Parks and Recreation (NRPA), 340–341
losses, 370–371
Loyd Park, Joe Pool Lake, Texas, 21

M
MacCready, Paul, 229
macro environment, 108
macro segmentation, 42
mail-in method of registration, 292–293
management accounting, 337
management by objectives (MBO) statements, 74–75, 78–79, 127–128
management levels, 74–76
management plan, 250–253
management plan in program plan, 247
marketing
  and exchanges, 163
  leisure experiences, 162–168
  vs. programming, 168–169
  social, 105–106
  target, 166–167
  target, strategies, 167–168
marketing mix, 453, 455
markets
  described, 164
  segmenting, 164–165
maturation, in program life cycle, 451, 453–454

meaning, deriving from interaction in leisure occasions, 30–31
measurement studies, 357–358
measuring devices for mission statements, 80–81
Merage Jewish Community Center of Orange County's mission statement, Irvine, California, 117, 119
merit programs, and pricing, 343
merit services, and pricing, 374
Mesa, Arizona's local government report title page (exhibit), 423
Mesa, Arizona's parkland (exhibit), 426
metrics, 76
micro segmentation, 42
Microsoft Publisher, 276
minority reports, and program evaluation, 404
mission, the
  issues that must be analyzed to develop, 95–96
  relationship to individual, community, and organizational needs, 111–112
mission statements
  assessing individual needs, 96
  assessing organizational needs, 99–105
  demographic and social trends, 97–98
  described, 94–95
  examples (exhibits), 113–120
  framing, 77–78
  scanning, assessing the environment, 96–99
  technology, 98–99
  writing, 113–120
morality and recreation, 12–13

N
National Alliance for Youth Sport (NAYS), 15
National Outdoor Park and Recreation Facilities report (exhibit), 424
National Park Service's needs assessment definition, 153
National Recreation and Park Association (NRPA) park metrics, 420–426
Navy Morale, Welfare, and Recreation's mission statement, 116–117, 119
needs
  described, 146
  felt, expressed, comparative, 152–153
  from social justice viewpoint, 148, 152
needs assessments
  approaches to, 153–160
  conducting, 143–146
  developing questions (exercise), 151

integrating the approaches, 160–161
    need concepts, 146–148
    questions, 161
    using, 144–146
networking
    codification approach to networked goals,
      objectives, 131–137
    exercise, 131
    goal (exercise), 179
news releases, preparing, 272–276
normative needs, 148
NRPA park metrics, 420–426

O

obesity, 97
objectives and goals
    codification approach to networked, 131–137
    described, 78–80
    evaluation, 432–435
    hierarchical arrangement of mission
      statement with, 81–82
    how they differ, 82–83
    how to write, 80–81
    limits defined by (fig.), 83
    networked (example), 175
    networking goals and objectives, 129–130
    representative nature of, 83–84
    staff collaboration in developing, 84–85
    using to establish programming standards,
      130–131
objects, leisure, 26, 44–45
older adults
    characteristics, 41
    population growth of, 98
onboarding, 319–320
online material access, 478
online method of registration, 288
operational clarity, 129, 131
operational strategies, generally, 239
operations research, 421
optimal experience, 8–9
organizational assessment criteria (exhibit), 104
organizational hierarchy (fig.), 75
organizational management, 382–383
organizational needs, assessing, 100–105
organizations
    assessing needs, 99–105
    marketing approach to assessments, 102–105
    networking goals and objectives, 129–130
organizing rationale, and the mission, 100–101
outcome statements (Y statements), 176–178
outcome targets, outcome indicators, 212

outcome-based programming (OBP), 212–213
outcomes, individualized terminal
    performance, 179

P

park district service categories (exhibit), 345,
    346
park usage, measuring, 398–399
participant evaluation form (exhibit), 442
participant input, 142–144
performance appraisal, 322–327
performance review key findings dashboard
    (exhibit), 422
personal services, 62, 64
personnel service contracting, 328–330
persuasion, 269–270
phenomenology of experience, 25, 34, xiv
Photoshop, 277
physical exertion and sport, 14
physical objects, leisure, 26
physical setting, and situated activity system,
    43–44
physical skills and sport, 14
Picasso, Pablo, 226
Pinterest, 277
planning
    See also specific plan
    integral, 233
    program evaluations, 383–393
    programs, 40–50
play
    described, 13
    ongoing goals 4.0 (table), 137
    relationships with definitions of leisure (fig.),
      18
"play" in sport, 48
Play It, Measure It (Roark & Evans), 380
political climate of the community, 99
political science literature, 144
positive outcomes of good strategic directions,
    76–77
pricing
    considerations, 372
    cost allocation methods, 355–358
    cost-volume-profit analysis, 362
    developing comprehensive guide to, 338–339
    establishing a price, 371–376
    objectives of, 336–338
    policy implementation, 344–345
    price described, 353
    program cost pricing worksheet (exhibit),
      373

program services, 361–376
public recreation, 340–341
service category system philosophy, 341–344
privacy and marketing, 169
private programs, and pricing, 343
private services, and pricing, 374–376
problem definition, and creative process, 225–227
processing, questions to ask, 212
product development, 450–451
products, types of (table), 61–62
products described, 166
program cost determination
allocating costs in the agency, 353–355
establishing line, service units, 350–352
generally, 350
preparing line-item budgets, 352
program cost pricing worksheet (exhibit), 373
program design
animating, 194
artistic and technical factors, 197–200
building blocks of Framed Experience Model of, 189–195
in context (fig.), 186
creative programming. See creative programming
described, 187–188
designing interactive experiences, 188
designing leisure experiences, 187–188
discussion, 205–206
frame, 195–197
a framed experience design, 200–205
generally, 186–187
model (fig.), 187
program design standards, 181–183
program development
described, 6
and program evaluation, 382
targeted (fig.), 139
Program Development Cycle
disposition decision (fig.), 450
evaluation (fig.), 412
follow-up analysis (fig.), 380
implementation (fig.), 268, 286, 310, 336
mission (fig.), 92
operational strategies (fig.), 240
participant input (fig.), 140
program design (fig.), 186, 210, 220
program outcomes (fig.), 174
program plan (fig.), 242
strategic directions (fig.), 126

program evaluation
analytical framework for discrepancy evaluation (fig.), 435
communicating results, 405–408
comprehensive evaluation system, components of, 413–414
data gathering, 393–401
evaluation defined, 381
evaluation planner (exhibit), 384
five Ps of evaluation (exhibit), 389
follow-up analysis (fig.), 380
generally, 412–413
goal and objective evaluation, 432–435
importance-performance evaluation, 414–419
leader or instructor evaluation form (exhibit), 438, 440
leisure program evaluation form (exhibit), 430–431
leisure program evaluation item pool, 445–448
NRPA park metrics, 420–426
organizing evaluation report, 401–405
participant evaluation form (exhibit), 438, 442
planning, 383–393
program evaluation summary format (exhibit), 442–443
program observation evaluation form (exhibit), 438, 441
purpose of, 381–383
satisfaction-based evaluation, 427–431
triangulated evaluation, 435–439
program life cycle, 451–454
program location walk-in method of registration, 292
program management accounting system (PMAS), 337, 338, 350, 352, 353–355, 358, 362, 371
program modification, and program life cycle, 455
program observation evaluation form (exhibit), 441
program outcomes, 174, 176
program plan
animation plan, 253–258
described, 243–250
facility scheduling, 261–264
generally, 242–243
management plan, 250–253
risk management components in (exhibit), 249

sample (exhibit), 244
scheduling program cycles, 260–261
scheduling programs, 259–260
program promotion
    communication channels, 270–271
    generally, 268–269
    innovative promotional technologies,
      280–283
    persuasion, 269–270
    preparing flyers, 276–280
    preparing news releases, 272–276
    writing brochure copy, 271–272
program screening instrument (fig.), 235
program services, pricing, 361–376
programmers
    compensation, 327–328
    evaluating candidate plans, 195
    and situated activity systems, 39
    structuring leisure occasions, 33–34
    in tourism, 16
Programmer's Evaluation Cube, 228
programmer's evaluation cube (fig.), 110
programming
    benefits-based programming (BBP).
      See benefits-based programming (BBP)
    concepts defined, 4–17
    creative. *See* creative programming
    described, 5–6
    the focus of recreation and leisure services,
      xiv–xv
    implications, 17–19
    vs. marketing, 168–169
    offered by park and recreation agencies
      (exhibit), 425
    outcome-based. *See* outcome-based
      programming (OBP)
    plan of Eau Claire Parks, Recreation, and
      Forestry Department, 132–135
    a social science theory of, 23–24
    as symbolic interaction, 34
    targeted program development (fig.), 139
    unpacking the "black box" of, 215–216
programs
    animating, 48–50
    balanced scorecard, 460–461
    Caribbean Christmas theme (exhibit), 182
    cost structure of (exhibit), 354
    creating new, 223–224
    creativity in developing, 223–224
    described, 4–5
    design outcomes (exhibit), 177
    design standards, 181

designing. *See* program design
determining costs. *See* program cost
    determination
develop program standards (exercise), 135
developing. *See* program development
developing standards (exercise), 183
elimination, 461–462
evaluating. *See* program evaluation
fees, 297–298
guarantees, 299
interdependent events and leisure programs,
    39
merit, and pricing, 343
public, and pricing, 342
registration procedures. *See* registration
    procedures
scheduling, 259–260
services, making decisions about, 449–463
and situated activity systems, 40–50
"staging," 59
staging, 245–250
ten elements of a theme (exhibit), 181
promotion
    described, 268
    innovative promotional technologies,
      280–283
    and program plans, 247
    of programs. *See* program promotion
    sample promotional copy (exhibit), 273
promotional campaigns, 166
public interest, recreation and, 106–107
public meetings for needs assessments, 154
public programs, and pricing, 342
public services, and pricing, 372, 374

Q

queuing procedures, 302–307

R

random number generator, 397
rationality, 76
recreation
    described, 12–13
    pricing issues on public, 340–341
    and the public interest, 106–107
    relationships with definitions of leisure (fig.),
      18
    worker job analysis (exhibit), 313
*Recreation, Park, and Open Space Standards and
    Guidelines* (NRPA), 148
recreation and leisure services, the focus of,
    xiv–xv

Recreation in the Streets (case study), 121–122
recruitment of staff, 317–318
RecTrac registration software, 299
registration, and program plans, 247
registration procedures
    fees, credit cards, cancellations and refunds, 297–299
    generally, 286
    operating registration, 300
    queuing procedures, 301–307
    reasons for conducting registration, 287–288
    registration considerations, 300–301
    registration form, 295–299
    registration methods, 288–295
    registration software, 299–300
    technology in, 300
relationships and situated activity system, 47–48
rentals of equipment, venues, facilities, 64–65
reporting evaluation findings, 401
reports, organizing evaluation, 401–405
research design, 391–393
resistance to prices, 372
resource dependency, 100
resources for program evaluation, 388–389
retrenching programs, 462
revenue
    line, applying in program pricing, 369–371
    public leisure service agency's fees, charges, 145
    stream, 60, 62, 64–65, 66, 68, 69
Richard, Tudor, 221
risk management plan in program plan, 248–249
rituals, interaction, 27–30
Rossman, J. Robert, xi
rule of distributive justice applied to queuing, 303
rules and program structure, 45–47
rules in sports, 14

S
SAFE (Sequenced, Active, Focused, and Explicit) approach, 214
samples, selecting, 395
sampling, 395–398
sampling, random, 396–397
San Diego Park & Recreation Department's mission statement, 116
Santa Clara (California) Parks and Recreation Department's liability release, 288, 289–290
satisfaction domains and items, 428–429

satisfaction-based evaluation, 427–431
saturation, in program life cycle, 454
scheduling
    facilities, 261–264
    program cycles, 260–261
Schlatter, Barbara Elwood, xii
segmenting markets, 164–165
self-evaluation of public leisure service organizations (CAPRA), 101–102
self-reflexive behavior, individuals, 24, 27–28, 32, 40
Seligman, Martin E. P., 1, 29
seniors. See older adults
service and line units, 350–352
service category system philosophy, 341–344
service continuum, 50–52
service encounter, the, 63
services
    as leisure products, 62–65
    making decisions about program, 449–463
SERVQUAL model of customer service performance, 199
setup, in program plan, 248
Shutterstock, 277
situated activity system
    conclusion, 54
    overview, 38–40
    six key elements of, 40–50
SMART (Specific, Measurable, Assignable, Realistic, Time-based) format, 76, 78–80, 127–128, 136, 178, 180, 183, 433
social gatherings, 27
social interaction, 38, 132
social marketing
    assessing leisure opportunities, 108–110
    community partnerships, 110–111
    described, 105–106
    focusing on individuals, 111
social media
    for needs assessments, 160
    for program promotion, 281–282
social objects, leisure, 26
social occasions. See situated activity system
social policy literature, 143
softball product line, expanding (table), 68
software, registration, 299–300
space studies, 357
sport(s)
    described, 13–15
    "play" in, 48
    relationships with definitions of leisure (fig.), 18

sports management organizations, 17
staff
  collaboration in developing goals, objectives, 84–85
  plan in program plan, 247
staffing
  compensation, 327–328
  contracting for personnel services, 328–330
  generally, 310–312
  independent contractors, 329–330
  job analysis, 312–314
  job description, 313
  onboarding, 319–320
  orientation, 320–321
  performance appraisal, 322–327
  recruitment, 317–318
  See also employees
  selection, 319
  training of employees, 321–322
staging programs, 245–250
strategic directions, 78, 126–127
strategic evaluation reports, 414
strategies, target marketing, 167–168
strategy formation, 76–77
structure, and situated activity system, 45–47
summative evaluation, 413
Summit Metro Parks homepage, 280
supervising operations, 330–332
supervision
  See also employees, staffing
  generally, 310–312
  of operations, 330
  training outline for area supervisors (exhibit), 323
supplies, 61
surveys for needs assessments, 159–160
SWOT (Strengths, Weaknesses, Opportunities, Threats) analyses, 102
symbolic interaction
  implications for leisure programming, 25
  perspective, 23–24
  programming as, 34
  theory, 24–31
symbolic objects, leisure, 26
synchronized swim cost data (table), 365
synchronized swim program cost-volume-profit table, 366
Systematic Observation of Play and Recreation in Communities (SOPARC), 398
systems approach to writing goals, objectives, 137

T
tabling cost data, 364–366
target marketing, 166–167
technology trends, 98–99
telephone method of registration, 293–294
terminal performance outcomes, 179
thinking
  design, 232
  divergent, 228–229
  linear and intuitive, 228
time budget studies, 357
timing of programs, 259–260
tourism
  described, 15–16
  offices, 283
  relationships with definitions of leisure (fig.), 18
training of employees, 321–322
transitions
  in experiences, 200
  and frames, program (fig.), 194
triangulated evaluation, 435–439
Trivial Pursuit, 11
Tulane University Campus Recreation's mission statement, 118–119
Twitter, 281
2017 NRPA Agency Performance Review (NRPA), xiv

V
variable costs, 363
venue arrangements in program plan, 245–246
venue rentals, 64
visualization
  block of Framed Experience Model, 189–193
  using to solve problems, 458
  who uses, 190

W
walk-in method of registration, 291–292
Walmart, 59
wants
  described, 147
  questions contrasting needs and intentions (exhibit), 149–152
Warrior Games (U.S. Navy), 105, 122
WHALE WATCH, Kaikora, New Zealand, 206, 208

Who rock concert, December 3, 1979, 302
Woods Event Management, Inc.'s mission
 statement, 115–116
workshops for needs assessments, 154
World Wide Web, 280
writing
 brochure copy, 271–272
 flyer copy, 279
 mission statements, 113–120

X

X intervention goals, 180
X statements (intervention goals), 180

Y

Y outcome goals, 176–178
Y statements (outcome statements), 176–178
YMCA's corporate slogan, 107
YouTube, 281

Related Books

PASTIMES
The Context of Contemporary Leisure
6th Edition

Ruth V. Russell

LEADERSHIP in **LEISURE SERVICES**
Making a Difference
Fourth Edition

Debra J. Jordan
Ronald Ramsing

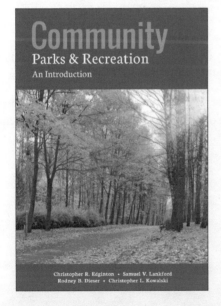

Community
Parks & Recreation
An Introduction

Christopher R. Edginton • Samuel V. Lankford
Rodney B. Dieser • Christopher L. Kowalski

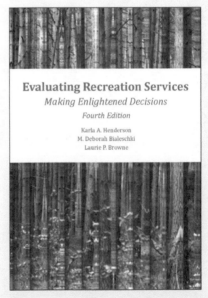

Evaluating Recreation Services
Making Enlightened Decisions
Fourth Edition

Karla A. Henderson
M. Deborah Bialeschki
Laurie P. Browne

Instructions for Bonus Student Resource Access

Bonus student materials are available for this title and can be accessed in the 'Ancillaries/ Resources' tab on the product page.

To view the materials:

1. Go to www.sagamorepub.com and log in to your account. You must be logged in for materials to be visible.

2. Search for *Recreation Programming*, 8th ed. in the search bar and click on the product page.

3. Scroll down on the product page and click the tab 'Ancillaries/Resources'.

4. Click on the link for student resources. Once open, you can download a PDF of the materials or you can continue to view the resources via the website.